Feelings and Moods

To my friend Matthieu Ricard,
inspiration, colleague, and tireless champion
of mind training

Feelings and Moods

Christophe André

Translated by Helen Morrison

polity

First published in French as *Les états d'âme* © Odile Jacob 2009

This English edition © Polity Press, 2012

Polity Press
65 Bridge Street
Cambridge CB2 1UR, UK

Polity Press
350 Main Street
Malden, MA 02148, USA

ISBN-13: 978–0–7456–5187–3
ISBN-13: 978–0–7456–5188–0 (pb)

A catalogue record for this book is available from the British Library.

Typeset in 10 on 11.5pt Palatino
by Servis Filmsetting Ltd, Stockport, Cheshire
Printed and bound in Great Britain by MPG Books Group Limited, Bodmin, Cornwall

The publisher has used its best endeavours to ensure that the URLs for external websites referred to in this book are correct and active at the time of going to press. However, the publisher has no responsibility for the websites and can make no guarantee that a site will remain live or that the content is or will remain appropriate.

Every effort has been made to trace all copyright holders, but if any have been inadvertently overlooked the publisher will be pleased to include any necessary credits in any subsequent reprint or edition.

For further information on Polity, visit our website: www.politybooks.com

Contents

Part Three Equilibrium

Part Four Awareness

Acknowledgements

My sincere thanks to all those who have been with me or in my thoughts during the writing of this book:

My parents. For the aptitude to moods and feelings and for everything else. The older I get, the more I discover how much I owe to them.

My patients, those close to me, the strangers I have listened to and observed. What they have confided, said or shown me is all that is human about this book.

My readers. Jacques Van Rillaer for the precision and the rigour of his comments (which I have not always followed – apologies Jacques!) and Nadine for her enthusiastic support. Séverine Strullu, for the pertinence of her philosophical viewpoint, and the example she embodies. Clémence Badault for the warmth and energy of his remarks. Jany and Valérie Siari, whose comments reassured me and made me smile and think.

My friends and bedside reading. André Comte-Sponville, for the rigour of his intelligence and his constant desire to be understood by everyone. Alexandre Jollien, for his sensitivity and his grace. David Servan-Schreiber, who taught me so much about the art of gentle healing. Zindel Segal, Lucio Bizzini and Pierre Philippot, who initiated me into psychotherapeutic meditation. Jon Kabat-Zin, who, through his writing, revealed mindfulness to me. And of course Matthieu Ricard, for everything he brings me each time we meet.

My editorial family. Odile Jacob and Bernard Gotlieb, for their confidence in me from the start. Jean-Luc Fidel for his opinions and judgement. Cécile Andrier for her commitment. Gaëlle Fontaine for her advice. Antonia Canioni, Jean-Jérôme Renucci, Carole de Fanti and Viviane Munoz for the kind and efficient work they do in distributing my work. Claudine Roth-Islert and Dominique Renoux for their help in transforming my writing into this beautiful paper book.

My own family. Pauline, Faustine, Louise and Céleste. For everything, of course.

Translator's note

I have translated the French expression *les états d'âme* as 'feelings and moods'. The expression presents a challenge to the translator given that âme can mean 'mind', 'soul' or 'spirit' depending on the context, and *les états d'âme* can therefore also mean 'state or frame of mind', or 'mental state'. In the context of this text it seemed to me that 'feelings and moods' is the most accurate rendering of the author's original intention.

I got up, drank a glass of water and prayed till daylight. It was like a great murmuring of the spirit. It made me think of all the rustling leaves which herald the dawn. What morning can be breaking in me?

Georges Bernanos, *Diary of a Country Priest*

The personal element . . . alone is what is eternally irrefutable.

Nietzsche, *Ecce Homo*

This book is about feelings and moods, their definition, their role. It describes how they affect us and how they enrich our lives: or cause us suffering.

It emphasizes how the foresight of poets preceded and illuminated the science of psychologists.

Above all, it shows how our feelings and moods can help us feel better and broaden our horizons: making us more lucid, wiser, and even happier.

A little girl falls over

Even as a little girl, you were always sensitive. The tiniest things could upset or thrill you: a gesture, a word, a sad face, a passing cloud or the sound of the wind.

For a long time you were troubled by these changing moods. You would have preferred to be less sensitive and more serene. You were trying to become an adult, and these childish reactions seemed to stand in the way of adult life. You did not know what to do about it. You tried simply closing your eyes and carrying on, in spite of these minuscule disruptions to your daily life. You sensed they could be deeply moving but, that was precisely the problem, you did not want to be moved.

Then, gradually, you learned to welcome those moments which both move and stimulate us. And to welcome too all the different feelings and moods, happy or painful, which arose from them and followed in their wake. Our feelings and moods are what is left in us once the bustle of life has died down. When we can pause to listen, watch, feel. You really enjoy those moments. In the end you came to understand and to accept that feelings and moods are the beating heart of our link with the world. Now you often get the feeling that your mind has really begun to exist, to breathe more deeply. You are not certain what that 'mind' is, but you sense that somehow it genuinely exists. And you know that your life can be both sensitive and serene. Gradually, you have changed. Thanks to these tiny, almost insignificant moments. These fragments of existence, feathers of life, drifting down from the sky. A silent metamorphosis: here is a description of what happened in one of those moments which thrill you and transform you.

You are waiting for a friend, or a bus. You have forgotten what it was you were waiting for, but you remember the wait. You can picture the exact spot where you were standing, the colour of the sky, the shop across the road. You see the father on his bike with his little girl – so cute in her plastic cycle helmet, perhaps 5 or 6 years old – sitting on the bike seat behind him, securely harnessed and strapped in.

The father gets off the bike and steadies it with one hand while he attaches the bike-lock to the railings. He leans forward: the bike wobbles and falls over, with the little girl trapped in her seat. He has not undone the straps yet. As she feels herself falling, you can see her face perfectly, your eyes meet. It is as though you are seeing everything that happens in her eyes: surprise, fear, incredulous despair. My father, the person I trust totally, forgot about me, abandoned me and made me fall over, *let* me fall over.

The father picks her up immediately. She is fine, completely unhurt. The solid bike seat into which she was so firmly pinioned has protected her perfectly. She does not even cry. Her father, upset and ashamed, lifts her gently up, muttering comforting words, unfastens her, gives her a kiss and takes her in his arms. Then the two of them go on their way. She is still not crying because of what has happened, but nor is she smiling. She looks puzzled, a little sad. At least that is your impression. You watch them go. They are holding hands. You stare at those two hands holding tightly on to each other. The sight is oddly comforting. Perhaps you were frightened too.

You feel in a strange state of mind. Not frightened, no. Not now, at least. Besides it all happened too quickly for you to feel frightened. And now you are filled with a gentle sadness, a peaceful yet intense sadness. And at the same time you are assailed by all kinds of different perceptions. Why all these disproportionate feelings? It is not as though you have just witnessed the collapse of the Twin Towers!

You pull yourself together and decide to call on your mobile phone to say you will be late. But your arm refuses to obey. Your body is not interested in the fact that you are going to be late. Nor is your brain. Everything in you is saying: leave it, it does not matter, why insist – as always – on moving on to something else? Stay here, with this. Your eyes still seek out the little girl and her father in the distance as they disappear around a street corner. You sigh. But what exactly did you see? Why did that little girl's expression of fear and distress – glimpsed for a split second – trigger all this tumult in you? This enormous tumult.

You think it over carefully and you begin to understand, or at least you think you begin to understand. In any case, it feels reassuring and helpful to go over what happened. You realize that this was no banal event. You witnessed a sudden flash of fear. A child who thought she was safe, and who suddenly realized she was not. Perhaps you identified with her? Or with her father? You think (it is strange): it is as though I and the entire human race fell off that bike with her. Mentally you shrug your shoulders: what is this outburst of compassion? Suddenly you hear this: 'What if she never trusts him again?' Not him or anyone else? And what if this tiny, trivial incident turned out to have done irreparable harm?

You shy away from this idea. You try to superimpose onto the image of the little girl falling that of her hand tightly holding on to her father's hand. That feels better. It is as though you cannot breathe properly. You focus on your breathing for a while. That feels better. That's it, you need to breathe deeply. It will do you good. You are just too sensitive. You feel better, but you still keep thinking, 'She's like me. She will never forget this moment. The fear. And what will she make of it later on? That's a mystery.'

Bah! All this thinking is beginning to get to you. You have decided not to keep waiting here for your bus, yes, that's it, you were waiting for a bus. You will walk instead. You set off, still full of what you have just been through. You keep walking, breathing deeply. Your mind turns to what awaits you today. You are back in the real world again. Or you have left it behind. Ah, yes – that phone call. Your mobile! Where is it? In your bag. You stumble on a stupid little bump in the middle of the pavement.

Lost in your thoughts, you almost fell over. You too. You smile. And off you go.

Part One

Existence

Our feelings and moods are the beating heart of our link with the world

Because something is intangible does not mean it does not exist.

Because something is subtle does not mean it is harmless.

Because something is complicated does not mean it is impossible to understand.

Because our feelings and moods are all of those things at once, and because they are elusive, does not mean we should give up trying to keep track of them.

Gods of living water
Let down their hair
And now you must follow
A craving for shadows.
Guillaume Apollinaire,
Clotilde

Chapter 1

Feelings and moods:
towards understanding

For I do nothing but go about persuading you all, young and old alike, not
to take thought for your persons and your properties, but first and chiefly to
care about the greatest improvement of the soul.

Plato, *Apology of Socrates*

What exactly are these feelings and moods of mine?

They are what I become conscious of when I detach myself from the
automatic reflexes of my daily life, when I stop 'doing' and allow myself
to observe what is happening inside me. This is no easy matter, since these
inner feelings are in constant movement. No wonder in English we speak
of a *stream of affects.*

My feelings are the internal echo of what I am currently experiencing or
what I have experienced in the past, or what I would have liked to experience, or what I hope to experience. They are also everything that keeps
going round in my head when I have said: That is enough. Stop. Do not
even think about it any more.

In short, our feelings and moods are a world in themselves.

Understanding feelings and moods

The notion of feelings and moods does not belong to the field of scientific
psychology but is rooted more in poetry and common sense. Nevertheless
it is a psychological reality: everyone knows what it means. As a psychiatrist, I see it as a concept which is functional and useful in my profession
even though poetic and vague; but after all, my profession as a psychiatrist is sometimes poetic and vague too! When we think about it closely,
our feelings are not part of a hazy reality but of a complex one.

One could define feelings and moods by describing them as the contents of our minds, conscious or unconscious, a mixture of physical
states, subtle emotions and automatic thoughts which affect most of our
attitudes. Generally speaking, we pay scant attention to them, nor do we

make much effort to understand them, or to think about them, or even to make them work in our favour. Fortunately they are quite capable of doing all that of their own accord: their role, and their influence on what we are and what we do, are immense.

Think of how you are affected when you feel down or upset. Think about your outbursts of anger, whether overtly expressed or not, but so often disproportionate to the immediate situation: are these often simply the result of ruminating over feelings of resentment, rancour, humiliation or simply of disappointment, of anxiety? Feelings which have been brooded over for some time, and which are all the more powerful because we were not even conscious we were doing so. Think too – feelings are not just about pain and torment – of the strength you can get from your bursts of excitement and enthusiasm, of how light your body feels when you are happy, of the uplifting effect of a good mood.

Our feelings and moods are more than just thoughts or emotions: they are both of these combined. No emotion is exempt from thought, no thought is free from memory, no memory exists without emotion, etc. Feelings are the expression of this great mixture of everything that is happening in and around us: a blending together of emotions and thoughts, of body and mind, of outside and inside, of present and past. A combination as rich as it is complex: mixed, unique, shifting, always beginning again, never exactly the same. Like the waves on the sea.

Feelings are not simply a jumble of ideas, emotions or sensations, but also a construction in their own right: the fusion, the synthesis which we carry out automatically, between the outside (physical state of the body and vision of the world) and the inside (reactivity to what is happening to us: we are *touched* by events). They are a cumulative psychological phenomenon: they bring together past, present and future, to create a sense of coherence and destiny. They are like the liquid in an electrical conductor: thanks to them everything is illuminated and made clear, we are inspired or threatened, our sufferings are gently eased or dramatically increased.

> I realise that I've been inadvertently thinking about my life. I hadn't noticed, but that's what I was doing. I thought I was no more in my leisurely stroll than a reflector of given images, a blank screen on which reality projects colours and light instead of shadows. But I was unwittingly more than that. I was also my self-denying soul, and even my abstract observing was a denial.[1]

In this short extract from his magnificent work *The Book of Disquiet*, Fernando Pessoa shows how feelings and moods have a permanent existence, without any deliberate intervention from us. We are more or less conscious of them and, in any case, they are always accessible to our attempts at introspection. Hence their importance in the notion of 'inner life', which acts as a kind of echo of 'external life' (even if things are evidently a little more complicated and confused). Our moods affect everything we do. You may think that when you are filling in an official form of some kind you are simply doing just that. But no, various feelings are vaguely taking shape as you do so: irritation at the time wasted on all this paperwork, anxiety about making a mistake, the desire to be somewhere else, even perhaps some childhood memories of grappling with homework at the dining table. Like a kind of psychological weather forecast, our feelings represent a mental climate, fine or gloomy, sometimes stable over a period of several days, sometimes changing several times in a single day.

What is left in us when the bustle of life has passed by

Another characteristic of feelings and moods is their remanence. Remanence is the partial persistence of a phenomenon once its cause has disappeared. Essentially, moods outlive the situations which justified or triggered them. They are also prone to resurgence: their reapparition, analysed in exquisite detail, days and years later, is one of the appeals of the work of Marcel Proust: 'A moment of the past, did I say? Was it not perhaps very much more: something that, common both to the past and to the present, is much more essential than either of them?'[2] Feelings and moods are the wake left by our actions and our gestures, all those chinks through which our past, or our expectations, invite themselves to the table of the present. They are everything left in us once the bustle of life has passed by.

We use a variety of expressions to refer to our feelings and moods: states of mind, humours, sentiments. In scientific literature, the term I prefer and which seems most appropriate is the one used by the neuroscientist Antonio Damasio, who refers to 'background feelings'[3], a term which nicely emphasizes their discreet nature.

There are numerous ways of getting in touch with our feelings. Often we simply need to stop. Stop what we are doing: working, running, raging against the world. Our feelings are constantly there, like a faint background noise. We stop and listen, just as we do in a forest when we stop walking and simply listen, when we hear the wind, the trees, the birds, all the murmur of the woods. Often simply stopping like this and paying attention to what is murmuring inside us is, initially at least, enough. Later we might want to go a step further and at that point we need to learn to listen to our feelings and observe them more intently, for example, through meditation, which we will be examining later, or through expressive writing, which we will also be looking at. There are numerous other methods and techniques which enable us to explore our feelings and moods, training us to observe them and to analyse them so we can surrender ourselves to them. Zen meditation uses the beautiful metaphor of a waterfall: each of us can observe our feelings at close quarters, like the walker who is able to slip behind the waterfall, sheltered temporarily between the rock and the tumbling torrent – a little damp, a little apprehensive, but protected and in a privileged position. One of the objectives of what is called 'mindfulness meditation' is to withdraw in a similar way, to watch feelings passing by, to analyse them and understand them. But without trying to stop the flow – after all, who would dream of damming a waterfall?

The subtlety and complexity of feelings

When I asked people around me to give me examples of some of their feelings and moods, their initial responses revolved round the idea of *positive* and *negative* examples. Positive moods included being in a good mood, feeling calm, relaxed, 'chilled out'. Negative ones included feeling down, being in a bad mood, feeling worried.

Yet more typically we experience a subtle mixture of both of these in which pleasant elements mingle with painful ones.[4]

In nostalgia, for example, this combination is clearly identifiable: this 'sentimental longing for or regretful memory of a period of the past, especially one in an individual's own lifetime'[5] contains both sweetness (pleasant memories) and pain (the fact that they are in the past). Remember, smile, but also feel pain because of the memory. Nostalgia is sufficiently enjoyable for us to want to indulge in it, and to go back to it nevertheless. That little touch of sadness acts like seasoning to food.

Disappointment is also a typical feeling. It stems from the memory of confiding in someone, an act which should be agreeable (confiding in someone is a good feeling: an indication that we have trustworthy relationships) but which has been contaminated by whatever caused the disappointment (being let down or betrayed). The initial bitterness is thus followed by a sense of shock: disappointment is not just an emotional suffering but also a re-evaluation of our vision of the world. We trusted and that is no longer possible. Strangely (to those not well versed in feelings) disappointment often ends up with a bitter-sweet taste: because in a sense it involves a painful satisfaction, a certainty (and certainties are more satisfying than doubts): 'I suspected as much, I should have suspected as much.' This is a feeling which causes violent pain at first, as emotions take over from thoughts, and then a more lasting pain later on, as the scars left by those emotions gives way to a sadder view of the world.

Guilt is another fascinating and complex feeling. Someone close to us asks us for help, we refuse because it is too complicated and because it does not seem especially important. Our refusal is accepted without comment. Yet we can see that we have caused offence, perhaps even pain. Still, the situation is by no means catastrophic – they can surely find some other solution. Except that . . . This brief exchange has provoked guilty feelings. We wonder if we should have refused after all. If in doing so we were acting in defiance of our values. It is an uncomfortable feeling. We feel sad too because we sense we have caused suffering, and because we have jeopardized a relationship which was important to us. We are disappointed in ourselves for not having been more available, more helpful. Then comes the feeling of irritation at not being able to be a little more selfish: why not after all! We feel annoyed with the person who came and asked us for this thing in the first place: everything was perfectly peaceful until then, we had never asked for anything ourselves! Then comes further remorse: the desire to go back in time and to say yes, to put a stop to these disagreeable feelings. Suddenly, an overwhelming sense of fatigue at having to make all these choices, reach all these decisions. A little flicker of anxiety too: what if one day I found myself in a position where I had to ask for help and everyone refused? Or if I was in a fix and nobody would help me? After a while, you start to weary of turning all these ideas over and over in your head. You decide it is time to try and move on. Not so fast! Do you really think your feelings can evaporate in a flash, simply because you decided they should?!

No, that is not how it works. Especially not with guilt, which plays such an important role in our psyche, forcing us to re-examine certain decisions which may turn out to have had a negative effect on other people. Guilt challenges our moral conscience and forces us to think again: was this suffering that I (perhaps) caused inevitable? In what way? Too little guilt makes us egocentric. Yet too much can make us unhealthily sensitive. Does it make us better people? I incline to think so, though not everyone would agree. This is the opinion of Theodore Dreiser, the American writer and militant anti-capitalist: 'Conscience never stops anyone committing a sin. It merely stops them enjoying it.' Well, there is that.

And what about all the feelings and moods nobody has even put a name to! I remember a friend telling me how, having been promised a promotion to a prestigious though demanding and difficult professional position, he found himself feeling simultaneously excited, flattered and anxious. What could such a combination be called? He then described how, when he subsequently discovered he had not got the job after all, he went on to experience a second 'baroque mixture of moods' (his words): is there a name for feeling simultaneously disappointed and relieved? Yet such feelings are commonplace! And what about the moods evoked by music: who could put a name to that strange feeling of intense and serious happiness, of muted tragedy, which the sound of the viola da gamba[6] can induce, so that we could share it more easily? Often no name can be found and perhaps it is just as well that, in this itemized and well-charted world, some feelings remain *unnamed*. Occasionally the finest writers manage it, and reading them is a revelation: what we had vaguely sensed is suddenly made clear to us. Proust, once again, with that famous account of the anxieties associated with his childhood bedtimes:

> My sole consolation when I went upstairs for the night was that Mamma would come in and kiss me after I was in bed. But this good night lasted for

so short a time: she went down again so soon that the moment in which I heard her climb the stairs, and then caught the sound of her garden dress of blue muslin, from which hung little tassels of plaited straw, rustling along the double-doored corridor, was for me a moment of the utmost pain. So much so I reached the point of hoping that this goodnight which I loved so much would come as late as possible, so as to prolong the time of respite during which Mamma would not yet have appeared.[7]

With his precise attention to the details of the present moment and his subtle awareness of the slightest shifts of his mind, Proust remains the unsurpassed explorer of feelings and moods. Writers had understood and described everything long before psychiatrists came along. As Freud said on the subject, 'Everywhere I go, I find a poet has been there before me.'[8]

The role of time: feelings and moods as the essence of our lives

Our feelings and moods are profoundly influenced by the link with time: the past (nostalgia, melancholy, shame, guilt), the present (pride, satisfaction, boredom), the future (anxiety, worry, confidence . . .).

In pride, for example, there is happiness linked to a sense of achievement, to the memory of obstacles encountered and overcome (including formerly negative moods re-examined in the light of the present), etc. I remember a friend of mine, lolling in a hammock in the garden of his new house and declaring: 'I've never felt as happy as I do right now, in *my* hammock, outside *my* house!' Some of his friends were horrified: 'What? Since when have you become so completely materialistic! Are you saying you are happier now than on your wedding day, or when your children were born?' Embarrassed reply from my friend: 'No, no, I just meant that everything is summed up in this instant, in my house, in my hammock. All of those past moments, with my wife, my children, all of you, and now this, only means something because all the people I love are here, with me. And I'm thinking about the pleasure my children will get from this house when they are older, and all that.' Relief all round. This was not merely happiness of the present moment but something connected to both the past and the future. Not just a selfish happiness, but an altruistic one too. These moods of proud happiness were indeed complex ones.

There are other examples too. Curiosity, a state of mind associated with the present, is a mixture of energy, confidence, the desire to know and to act, here and now.[9] Serenity is all about the tranquillity of the moment, but also the experience of being at peace with the past, and a feeling of confidence about the moments to come; which is why it produces a strong sense of coherence, of acceptance and of strength to face whatever may come.

There is also the awareness of passing time, and of ageing, itself a rich source of feelings and moods. Anxiety, for example: 'I'm getting old. What's going to happen to me? Or rather, how quickly or slowly is it going to happen? How am I going to end up?' Or surprise: 'Already? What an unpleasant shock to find it's happening to me! Yes, of course I *knew* all about it. But now, I *feel* it too.' Or sadness: 'What a pity to lose all those things: vigour, freshness, youth . . .' Or regret: 'I've wasted so many moments without fully appreciating them.' But also tenderness ('Everything is so much simpler now, so much clearer and calmer'), curiosity ('I wonder what will happen to me?'), calm ('I don't have to be constantly competing in that exhausting and stressful way in order to prove my value or my importance: I don't care about that any more'). All of that in the space of a moment, because we sensed the passage of time in our life.

Then there are also those feelings which can be grouped together under the heading of confidence: the ones based not only on a series of successes and certainties, but also on the memory of the suffering and distress associated with past defeats, of how we got over them, what we learned from them; and on the anticipation of difficulties to come and of our capacity to face them. Confidence can be anxious if there is somehow the idea that we *ought to* emerge victorious from these confrontations; it will be serene if we accept in advance the idea that this will not always be the case.

Not surprisingly, childhood is an inexhaustible reservoir of future moods, since at that period of our lives we are less inclined to filter everything that happens to us by a process of rationalization, less apt to analyse the experiences life brings. Children are curious and open and live very much in the present, storing up a bank of extremely intense memories. For many years they are not fully conscious of their feelings. Then suddenly, it all changes: all parents have witnessed the first signs of feelings and moods in their children. What is that little boy thinking about as he cuddles his favourite toy and gazes into space? Or this one, left out by the other children, watching them playing from the far end of the playground, without even crying? These moments of transition from fleeting, quickly soothed emotions to more enduring feelings and moods. Opinions are divided as to whether the onset of moods and the emergence from childhood should be viewed as a blessing or a curse. The writer Éric Chevillard wrote: 'For some people, childhood resembles a kind of unhealthy state in which they feel extremely vulnerable and from which they emerge into maturity happily cured; for others on the contrary, the end of childhood marks the beginning of their long agony.'[10] Yet we could also regard this ability not to forget and erase, this transition from light-heartedness to seriousness, from rapidly changing feelings to enduring ones, as an immense opportunity for us, and an enriching experience: it is our feelings which enable us to transform our scattered memories into a life path. Becoming an adult means being able to say: 'I used to have memories, now I have a life story.' In this way, our feelings are able to extend the present moment considerably with echoes of the past and the future. From creatures of the present we turn into creatures with a past and a future. Dreaming of eternal life . . .

Feelings and moods and identity

Through our feelings and moods we are reacting not only to the event which triggered them, but to what this event represents in our lives as a whole. In this way, events are put into perspective, they become part of our identity, our biography: my feelings remind me, sometimes dramatically, what this event means to me, in the context of my particular life.

This is why memory plays such an important role in feelings. The memory of everything we have been through and experienced, and of our reaction to it. Our past is marked with impressions ready to surface in their entirety: personal memories (this is what is called our *autobiographical* memory) are typically complex 'mental objects' stored in our brains in the form of feelings. The flashbacks (with apologies for the anachronism) immortalized by Proust are typical of these: we become aware of a confused feeling which gradually turns out to be a mix of extremely complex elements (sensory, emotional, psychological . . .). Our feelings ensure that we remember the kind of discrete moments which remain anonymous within our biographies, the ones which are sometimes overshadowed by the big memories, by the unforgettable moments, but which are deeply significant and an essential element in weaving the fabric of our past existence. The big memories are simply the decorations and the medals: our moods are the fabric, the garment itself. They are associated with all the things we willingly forget, but which matter, which carry weight, which make us who we are: and which sometimes abruptly resurface.

Certain periods in our lives are so rich in feelings and moods that they end up playing what could (if the importance of moods were not sufficiently recognized) almost be described as a disproportionate role in the construction of our identity. Less in terms of what we have done, but by the discrete and invisible intensity of what we have experienced: there are the best years of our life, and there are the most intense and profound ones. The two do not necessarily coincide.

For what gives an individual their identity is perhaps less the public acts than the secret habits, less the carefully mapped-out plans than the vague daydreams. Our feelings, that most secret part of ourselves, are also what reveal most about who we are. Those close to us recognize or sense it. The true essence of a person often lies in their feelings: which is why we object to other people reading our private diaries. A friend with whom I was discussing this one day told me she periodically threw all her diaries away, once she had 'got things off her chest', for fear that later, after her death, her children or other people might come across them. She felt they represented a shameful part of herself, that they contained too much darkness and too many *bad* thoughts, albeit sincere ones; bad in that they 'could cause suffering', but also in that they 'could modify the image others have of me, the love and esteem they feel for me'. I remember the ensuing discussion in which I explained to her that, on the contrary, these diaries perhaps revealed not the worst, but the best of her, that they represented what was most moving, most sincere, most fragile, uncertain and fluctuating: her changing feelings and moods. And that it was a good thing that this should be preserved. I remember another friend, horrified by the violence and pain expressed in her son's diary, which she had come across by chance. She knew he was sensitive and subject to bouts of depression. But by reading the diary, she had inadvertently stepped into the intimacy of his feelings and his state of mind had become palpable, and much more disturbing. The anguish of a parent confronted with their children's secret pain.

As a psychiatrist, I am inordinately fascinated by writers' personal diaries, even more so than by their novels. This is not mere voyeurism (in my opinion at least), but rather a taste for material which is genuinely alive, raw, unadorned, spontaneous. Moreover, I am by no means alone in this. Virginia Woolf wrote: 'I sometimes think only autobiography is literature; novels are what we peel off, and come at last to the core, which is only you or me.'[11]

Feelings and moods as a link to the world

'The streets of Vienna are full of absent Jews.'[12]

In a single phrase, a writer ignites our feelings – such is the power of literature. These words evoke the aftermath of the *Kristallnacht* ('crystal night' or 'night of broken glass'), in 1938, during which militant Nazis attacked their Jewish compatriots, burning their synagogues, looting their shops (after first smashing the shop windows – hence the name 'crystal night', a reference to the fragments of broken glass which littered the pavements). Terrified and traumatized, the Austrian Jews took refuge in their homes and deserted the public places: *an absent presence.*[13] And deeply moving for us who have just read that simple phrase which sums up all the feelings of horror, of shame, of anger, of sadness.

Being interested in your feelings and moods is not a purely egocentric thing. In the French expression *état d'âme* the word *âme* can refer both to the mind and to the soul (see translator's note on p. x). The soul is defined as that 'which animates sensitive beings', in other words, the living. It enables us to go beyond our intelligence, or at least to take it into another direction. For the philosopher André Comte-Sponville we possess 'the soul as our own particular way of living in the world (subjective) and the mind as a way of living in the truth by freeing us from ourselves (objective)'.[14] The mind liberates and the soul accomplishes.

In effect, our feelings enhance our understanding of life: they are the result of the way we *perceive the world*, even down to the micro-events (we shall see later that there is a whole science devoted to studying how our feelings are triggered by the minutest detail). Thus, small events in life do not generate powerful emotions, but they trigger a range of feelings.[15] Remember how witnessing little incidents in the street – a child crying, a beggar sleeping off his wine and his poverty, a couple arguing – all of these things, provided you pay attention to them, can suddenly plunge you into melancholy, even though none of these events has any true bearing on your day or on your life. From an outside point of view, such scenes can have had no tangible impact on us. Yet, inside us, they linger on. And who knows where they might take us?

The origin of our feelings and moods is complex. It is not, or at least not entirely, a matter of simply reacting to our immediate environment: sometimes our feelings may indeed reflect this – we will be cheerful when there is a cheerful atmosphere – but this is not always the case – in spite of the prevailing cheerfulness, of the party going on around us, we will sometimes feel gloomy. When that happens, the contrast will inevitably make us much more conscious of our own feelings. And more conscious too of our difference, our singularity, of the gap that separates us from others, at this particular moment, or perhaps more permanently. In this way, our feelings can help us understand that something is not right in us, or around us, or conversely – let us not forget the happy moods too – that things are going especially and astonishingly well: like emotions, they are a sign that something has interrupted the constant, tranquil, predictable interactions which we have with our environment.[16] A little detail, a minuscule thing: suddenly, everything has changed.

Admittedly, these feelings are slight enough and can be improved by the smallest thing: a vague attack of the blues can be banished by a telephone call from a friend, or a walk in the country. But is that telephone call or that country walk really such a small thing? Or is it rather that our feelings make us more aware of the fundamental nature of these 'small things' in life, opening our eyes to their profound essence of grace and of chance, of which the fluctuations of our minds are both a reflection and a warning? And are our feelings not also capable of telling us, gently and discreetly, what is wrong? Can they not express our sensitivity to the smallest details, the ones our intellect or our reason urge us to forget: a tone of voice, a phrase almost drowned in a conversation, a gesture or a smile which are absent or which strike a false note.

So is this constant and unpredictable movement of our feelings, like breathing which never stops, uncomfortable? The answer is yes. Their existence rules out any form of 'mental air conditioning', of psychological asepsis, of any kind of steadiness in our inner equilibrium. For better and worse. Hypersensitive and hyperemotional people would sometimes give an awful lot to experience fewer feelings, or at least, less invasive ones. Yet, on the other hand, our need for them is so great, if our lives are to be genuine ones, that we often seek out a 'fix' of them in order to feel more alive: in the form of art – music, paintings, literature, cinema. Or we indulge in certain 'unnecessary' but important rituals (anything which is both unnecessary but important in our lives conceals inner feelings). I once had a neighbour who used to go into his daughter's bedroom every single day to open the windows and the shutters, even though she had left home many years ago. Perhaps he pretended to his wife that it was in order to air the room but I suspect, or at least I prefer to imagine, that behind this practical ritual lurked the joy tinged with sadness of breathing the air of his much-loved daughter's room, looking at the objects she had left behind, the palpable traces of her past, the walls between which she had dreamed and worked.

A life is not shaped purely by actions. Our feelings too bring density to our lives. And if the gap between our lives and our feelings became too great, we would no longer be sensitive individuals. Our lives would be empty, their inner spring would run dry, we would become the 'dead souls' of Nicolas Gogol's powerfully titled novel.[17]

Feelings and physical responses

A debate between philosophers. For Nietzsche: 'Body am I entirely, and nothing else; and soul is only a word for a part of the body.' To which Alain replies: 'The soul is what the body refuses. For example, that which refuses to run when the body trembles, to strike when the body is angry, to drink when the body is thirsty, what refuses to give up when the body recoils in horror.' And Gustave Thibon goes one step further, referring to both effort and fate: 'Today your body is more real than your soul: tomorrow your soul will be more real than your body.'[18]

In any case, our feelings are reflected in our physical states: we feel heavy-hearted when we are sad and light and energetic when we are in a good mood! There is also the feeling of heaviness and sluggishness associated with melancholy or the impossibility of keeping still when we are impatient.

Feelings and moods affect the body, but they are in turn influenced by it: we shall see how any form of physical activity – the same applies to light – tends (to a small extent) to favour positive moods. In women, menstrual cycles also affect these changes: this is the premenstrual syndrome where, during the few days preceding the menstrual period, women can experience a range of psychological modifications such as irritability, anxiety and mood swings.[19]

All of this is why, in our everyday lives, understanding our feelings and moods also means understanding our bodies: listening to them, meeting their needs, taking care of them, all without excess or obsession.

Feelings and ways of thinking

'There is nothing in the mind that was not first in the senses.' This empiricist maxim (empiricism is the philosophical movement which claims that all our ideas come from experience) reminds us that, if are we not pure souls, detached from their physical bodies, neither are we pure minds.

Our sensibility, which is inherent in our feelings, will shape the way we think. And this in turn will provoke certain feelings.

As in the body, the influence exerted between feelings and thoughts is reciprocal. Indeed, they are two aspects of the same phenomenon, like the two sides of a playing card. A feeling is an inextricable mixture of definable and identifiable thoughts, and of subjective impressions more difficult to put into exact words. But it is also an original creation: just because we think this or that does not mean it will be associated automatically with this or that subjective impression.[20] A personal sense of success or failure will not necessarily lead to pleasant or unpleasant feelings. Everything is rapidly restructured according to all manner of other elements of our personality, our past: this is why there are bitter successes and contented failures.

Often, when we are in a certain mood, our thoughts are initially vague and incomplete, like clouds blown by the wind, fragmenting, breaking up and forming again, eluding our grasp. Left to their own devices, these thoughts now firmly attached to feelings live their own lives, like children whom adults have forgotten to supervise and look after. Our feelings are a natural thought process, untamed, archaic. But by no means useless. This explains why we are often more efficient at doing things under a slight emotional influence (we are referring to feelings and moods rather than full-blown emotions). Laboratory rats too learn their tasks better under the influence of some kind of moderate and appropriate emotion; and their performance deteriorates if they are prevented from feeling these emotions by the severing of the vagus nerve, which transmits information about what is happening in their bodies.[21]

We know too that in what we call intuition, we are informed by a subliminal perception, which activates unconscious thoughts and subtle emotions. Each time we sense that someone is not telling us the truth or is hiding something from us, our intuition is in fact acting on the subconscious perception of facial asymmetries and other tiny incoherencies in the other person.[22] It is this perception which triggers the feeling of doubt often associated with such moments: we feel physically ill at ease, slightly oppressed and intellectually perplexed, lacking proof against the other person but with the absolute conviction that something is not right. This kind of doubt is not purely intellectual: our doubt also, and primarily, expresses itself in that sense of being physically ill at ease.

In summary: feelings and moods are subtle emotions linked to thoughts

Emotions are always at the heart of feelings and moods, but more often than not without the evidence in terms of *a tendency to action* which we associate with straightforward emotional experiences: for example, when we are angry (strong emotion), we shout, we draw nearer to the other person (without necessarily being aware that we are doing so; this is what the term 'tendency to action' means). But when we are simply irritated (a mood), we are more inclined to distance ourselves from the source of the irritation (because we sense that is the best way to avoid aggravating the conflict). Anger makes us feel 'beside ourselves' whereas we are perfectly able to control and to conceal our irritation.

Feelings are associated with 'internalized emotions', without the physical and behavioural visibility of powerful emotions: a deep sorrow plunges us into prostration and immobility whereas melancholy does not necessarily stop us from functioning normally, to the extent that others may not even be aware of what is going on inside us.

In this way, our feelings and moods are rather like the enlightened and civilized cousins of our more ancient and less sophisticated emotions. They could be said to be subtle emotions, as opposed to the big-scale emotions, what are known as the 'primary' or elementary ones.

Amongst the differences between feelings and primary emotions is the fact that feelings are longer lasting and less intense; but more influential: their feeble and discreet nature and the fact that they are easily forgotten means that their power is underestimated (how a slight feeling of guilt can poison the entire day). And most significantly, their impact is more comprehensive, since they owe their existence not simply to a given situation (the 'starter' event that triggers powerful emotions) but to our relationship with the world in general.

Unlike emotions, feelings do not necessarily have a specific objective: they do, however, have origins, even if these are not always clear. Emotions are usually a 'response' to something that 'happens' to us; feelings, on the other hand, can come from within us; they can be *auto-generated*.[23]

Emotions radicalize and simplify our perception of events. Feelings complicate it, but in return render it more subtle.

Emotions are 'social agents', which affect our relationship with others and with the world,[24] and feelings are more 'internal agents', affecting our relationship with ourselves and our view of the world (which can also result in us changing many things, though at a slower pace). Emotions tend to push us to external action, feelings initially trigger inner reflection.

Feelings and moods can persist in the wake of strong emotions, lingering on after these have passed (for example, in the aftermath of a great joy or a major disappointment). And they can also prepare the ground for these: moroseness leading to bouts of depression and sadness. Resentment fuelling outbursts of anger. Panic erupting against a backdrop of anxiety. Clouds before the storm, then lingering overcast skies.

All the research shows that our emotional lives often run their course on an emotional level which is discreet rather than intense: in the form of feelings and moods rather than strong emotions. Research on how we perceive our inner states similarly suggests – good news – that positive

Relative infrequency of powerful emotions as opposed to feelings recorded in a study based on 10,169 random sample observations, from 226 people

Emotional states	Intensity recorded (%)		
	Very little or none	**A little**	**A lot**
Negative			
Fear	73.8	22.6	3.6
Sadness	66.5	28.7	4.9
Anger	74.8	20.0	5.2
Disgust	67.1	27.5	5.4
Guilt	77.2	19.0	3.8
Contempt	74.7	21.0	4.3
Average	72.4	23.1	4.5
Positive			
Joy	33.4	47.9	18.7
Interest	30.5	54.5	15.0
Excitement	38.4	43.3	18.3
Average	34.1	49.5	17.3

Source: Watson, D., *Mood and Temperament*, New York, Guilford Press, 2000, p. 9

feelings are more frequent than negative ones (in spite of the fact that the range of negative emotions is greater): approximately 75 per cent generally positive and 25 per cent generally negative (from a total of 17,000 on-the-spot 'samplings' of feelings[25]). We shall of course examine this in more detail later.

According to these studies conducted with people in 'real-life' contexts (volunteers carry on with their normal daily activities, simply noting down their moods every time a small pocket alarm goes off), our daily lives are conducted in a relatively calm emotional climate which tends to be both complex and varied.

In the end, we spend relatively little time in the grip of powerful anger and more time preoccupied by our irritations. More time with a feeling of melancholy than one of genuine despair. More time preoccupied by minor worries than by major anxiety crises.

Feelings and humanity

Being human means having the capacity to reflect on ourselves, on our coherence, our motivation. Who am I? Why am I here? Why do I get up in the morning? This is what is known as reflexive self-consciousness: in other words, the exceptional ability to reflect upon oneself, the capacity to self-analyse. Even more significant than opposable thumbs (considered to be what characterizes the human species, giving them the major edge over apes) are our feelings and moods: opposable to our animal nature and our reflexes!

Animals have emotions, humans have feelings as well: an awareness of their emotions, thoughts about these emotions. Although . . .

It appears that certain animals, such as elephants for example, also experience feelings. A female elephant is reported to have been seen 'turning the body of her dead calf over and over again with her trunk and feet during a period of several days'. We can of course simply put this behaviour down to a reflex of attachment or conditioning. But this would show little respect or compassion for the poor mother elephant, particularly as even more disturbing examples exist: on another occasion, again with elephants, a family group were observed for a whole night watching over the body of one of their own, killed by poachers; and on yet another, a young elephant was seen attentively examining and smelling its mother's bones.[26] Such examples would indeed suggest that our animal cousins can also have feelings.

Perhaps what we should be saying is that, amongst those animals capable of self-awareness, humans have by far the most complex feelings and moods, along with an unlimited capacity to reflect on and express them, to the extent that their feelings can lead to them changing the course of their lives.

Which is why *not having feelings* is tantamount to ignoring one's humanity. Beware of anyone who claims 'not to have feelings'. Apart from anything else, it is impossible *not* to have them. People can only suppress, hide or deny them. In so doing they are denying their humanity and depriving themselves of what is perhaps the best aspect of it: introspection. This argument of 'feeling' as opposed to 'understanding', of knowing through experience as opposed to knowing through knowledge, should encourage us to accept, observe and love our feelings and moods. We should take every opportunity to increase our understanding and our access to this very complex world.

The richness of feelings

I am fascinated by feelings and moods. I marvel at the complexity that lies behind this everyday and often unspoken experience, at these feelings which represent so many unique and intimate moments and convey so much about our identity and our place within the world.

This is why, in my work as a psychiatrist, I have never been bored with a patient. Never once! Sometimes, the more sensitive of them worry about whether they are 'good' patients, with an apologetic: 'I'm afraid I'm boring you with all my silly little stories.' But that is never the case. Their stories are interesting and surprising and they touch me personally.

There are days when I am tired, or not at my best, when my own moods interfere with my ability to listen. When that happens I may indeed stifle a yawn or look heavy-eyed, but that is only because I am preoccupied and distracted by my own problems and not because I am bored by their story. I love hearing about people's feelings – like the sound of the sea inside a sea-shell – making me aware of an even more distant murmur.

Chapter 2

Feelings and moods: the pain and the pleasure

In summing up, I wish I had some kind of affirmative message to leave you with. I don't. Would you take two negative messages?

Woody Allen, *Monologue*

'How are you, Faustine? Are you in a good mood this morning?'
'I hate that question. It puts me in a bad mood!'

It was said as a joke, but the father gets the message that he should give up trying to investigate the moods of his adolescent daughter: trivial as it seemed, the question was too intrusive. And it failed to respect the reticence about psychological intimacy – and the difficulty of putting it into words – so common in this age group. But the anecdote also illustrates the proximity of our two great families of feelings: positive and negative . . .

Positive and negative feelings

Our brains and nervous systems are organized in such a way that we naturally tend to classify everything we feel, and everything that happens to us, into two, and only two, registers: is this experience an enjoyable one (positive register) or an unpleasant one (negative register)?

This categorization of our 'basic' experiences is based on an evolutionary system: at the very bottom of the scale of living and animate creatures (paramecium, insects), sensations are grouped in the same way, inciting the creatures to gravitate towards anything which is favourable to survival, and to run away from anything which threatens it. Our feelings start out in the same way!

And research in neuroscience proves that it is in this simplified way that our brains comprehend the world:[1] as 'good/not good', or 'agreeable/disagreeable'. Before progressing, as our cerebral capacities mature, to a more detailed analysis along the lines of 'desirable/undesirable' (development of a capacity to anticipate), 'good memory/bad memory' (capacity to remember), etc.

This means that we are programmed, as animals, to experience positive and negative feelings. However, as humans, we will also introduce a little more subtlety and complexity into the story.

More negative than positive feelings?

'What is sad, at least for the ordinary man, is that we are going to die, that we are not happy, or so little or so badly, and that we are constantly going round in circles, without ever finding the way out.'[2] In his long philosophical poem *On the Nature of Things* (*De rerum natura*), the Latin writer Lucretius (who is believed moreover to have committed suicide) presents a sombre and tormented version of his Epicurean vision of the world. Yes, Epicurean, for Lucretius is an Epicurean philosopher whose work reminds us that Epicureanism is not the simplified hedonism it is seen as today. It too has a darker and more solemn side to it. But Lucretius is by no means alone. Many others have thought along similar lines. Pessoa, for example: 'Life for most people is a pain in the neck that they hardly notice, a sad affair with some happy respites, as when the watchers of a dead body tell anecdotes to get through the long, still night.'[3]

As human beings are we therefore condemned to struggle against our neurasthenic tendencies and against sadness or the emptiness of existence? Or are these theorists of suffering, these 'addicts of melancholy',[4] simply the victims of their own depressive tendencies, individuals who have failed to construct their happiness? And who, like all of us, tend to confuse their own feelings with a universal vision.

There are, however, a number of arguments to support their view. For example, in all languages, there are more words to describe negative feelings than positive ones.[5] What does this predominance, in our words if not in our brains, mean? Is it a question of necessity (this is the evolutionary theory)? Is it the result of errors of perception and perspective in our relationship with the world (this is, for example, the famous 'Zeigarnik effect')? Or is it the reflection of a reality (life is hard)? Let us attempt to get a clearer picture.

More negative feelings than positive ones? The survival instinct

So called 'evolutionary' theories emphasize that everything which exists in humans, whether physical or mental, plays, or has played, a role in the survival of the species as a whole (and incidentally in that of the individual as well).

So, for example, if we are placed in front of a computer screen: (1) when asked to spot a word, we are quicker at detecting a negative word than a positive one, where both are presented to us in a subliminal manner (too rapidly for us to be able to 'see' them consciously); (2) in response to the question 'Was this word positive or negative?', we are more accurate in identifying negative words (whereas for positive words, responses are the same as those we would have given randomly); (3) if, on the other hand, we are asked the meaning of the negative word we thought we saw, we are unable to do so (not surprisingly; after all it was extremely rapid and this primitive brain of ours which is programmed to detect dangers is less efficient when it comes to learning to read![6]). In other words, it seems as though our brain were made to detect dangers even before understanding and analysing them.

Numerous studies have come up with comparable results, such as our ability to pick out hostile faces in a crowd more rapidly than we do friendly ones.[7]

Our capacity to detect the negative is therefore more rapid, but it also involves a more intense reaction (thus having a greater impact on our responses): if the brains of volunteers are stimulated by being presented with what are known as 'emotional' images (such as smiling or hostile faces, naked people or violent scenes) or with 'neutral' images (expressionless faces or household objects), automatic cerebral responses (registered as electric potential visible on the electroencephalogram and clearly involuntary) will be stronger after seeing the emotional images than after the neutral ones. Stronger reactions then, if emotion and feelings are involved, but also longer-lasting reactions to negative emotional stimuli rather than to positive ones: it is clear that our brains were fashioned so as to make us focus on the sources of any potential problems.[8]

Thus it would appear that, in the interests of survival, we are cerebrally 'wired' so our attention is drawn more rapidly, more forcibly and for a longer time to situations likely to provoke negative emotions and reactions. Does that mean that the way our cerebral machinery is constituted condemns us to depression and anxiety? Perhaps so, and this is an advantage when we are faced with dangerous or even uncertain situations.

But then, once the danger has passed and the situation is more or less understood or resolved, we need to get to work on bringing back pleasanter moods, on restoring our well-being! And, fortunately for us, various studies show that our brains also have the capacity to analyse (not *detect*, but analyse in order to understand) positive information more rapidly than negative information. No doubt because, since positive information is less threatening, it requires a lesser degree of vigilance, and therefore allows us more time for reflection than for action (obligatory when danger threatens). But also, according to some studies, because 'positive' concepts are simpler: for example, to describe moods we say *happy and unhappy* but not *sad and un-sad*. The positive mood therefore often comes *first*, with the negative one in second place, defined in contrast to the positive one. Similarly, it requires fewer words to say 'Mary is here' than to say 'Mary is not here.'

Positive ideas and images should logically, therefore, be simpler to memorize. This explains why our memories (in most cases at least) store more positive memories than negative ones.[9] However, these studies are based on volunteers who have no psychological problems, and things are a little different in the case of people suffering from anxiety or depression. And of course, a store of positive memories, especially subconscious ones, is not enough on its own to ensure happiness.

If belonging to the human race implies being primed to be over-attentive to the negative (and the moods associated with it), we have nevertheless been given a second chance. A bit as in the story of the Sleeping Beauty when, after the wicked fairy's curse ('You will prick your finger on a spindle and fall asleep for a hundred years'), there is still one more fairy to come. She cannot undo the evil spell (just as our efforts cannot undo our natural tendencies) but she can cast a counter-spell ('Yes indeed, but a Prince Charming will come to your rescue'). And in our own story, the mood fairy, bent over our cradle, had this to say: 'All right, little human, your emotions will indeed naturally lead you to feel fear and sadness, but you will be saved by your feelings (provided you work hard on them)!'

The animal aptitude for negative emotions facilitates reaction. The human aptitude for feelings facilitates reflection.

More negative feelings than positive ones? The 'Zeigarnik effect'

Our automatic leaning towards the negative may also have another origin: that of a bias in memory, as in the famous 'Zeigarnik effect', a classic in experimental psychology.[10] This concerns our tendency to remember more clearly (but also, alas, to ruminate over) an action or a task that was interrupted. The original experiment by the Russian psychologist Bluma Zeigarnik consisted in asking children to carry out about twenty small tasks (using modelling clay, beads and other puzzles) over the course of a day. She allowed them to finish half the activities, but organized things in such a way that the rest remained unfinished. Shortly afterwards, the children were asked to remember everything they had done. The unfinished tasks were cited twice as often as the others. Zeigarnik's hypothesis was that the small amount of tension triggered by the sense of having 'things to do' was satisfied by finishing tasks, and this meant they could more easily be consciously forgotten (though not unconsciously: for example, we use our successes to construct a network of positive subconscious memories which we can draw on at a later stage). Not being able to complete a task that had been started, on the other hand, made it more memorable, probably because the tension of having 'things to do' remained: this associated the memory with a negative emotion which then made it more memorable.

We shall be re-examining this in the context of feelings associated with worry and anxiety. After all, for the majority of people, this could easily be a slogan or a motto: 'Finishing things is good for us!'

In the context of our modern lives, we might indeed wonder if the endless multiplication of interruptions, demands, distractions and the excessive fragmentation of our professional lives and activities do not in fact amount to a gigantic succession of interruptions and frustrations, which we are scarcely even aware of. But which nevertheless unleash an oppressive wave of negative moods . . .

More negative feelings than positive ones? Because life is hard

One final hypothesis: we are more inclined to experience painful feelings simply because life is hard! We know, for example, that there is a clear link between the number of adverse life events and the risk of depression.[11]

But the following is also true: we groan and suffer when life is hard, but we omit to sing, or at least not loudly enough, when life is good! Unfavourable life events or situations tend to trigger more negative feelings than their favourable equivalents produce positive ones: we rage against the broken-down boiler, but we fail to rejoice at our daily supply of hot water. We should do more of that, as an exercise in lucidity and happiness! Here too, a substantial amount of research confirms the existence of this phenomenon.[12]

There is moreover an even more astonishing phenomenon which regularly emerges from research on feelings and moods: negative feelings generally stem from stressful life events. Positive feelings, on the other hand, are more likely to be rooted either in a physical sense of well-being (for example, after some kind of physical activity or a good night's sleep), or in enjoyable social interaction (enjoying time spent with other people) than in positive or memorable life events.[13] Of course, pleasant events can also help trigger agreeable moods, but the events are not strictly necessary. In the long term, the decisive factor seems to be more a matter of having access to regular physical and social pleasures.

General tendencies associated with positive or negative feelings: welcoming or mistrustful, open- or closed-minded, expansive or withdrawn

Just as positive feelings are linked to attitudes associated with openness and accessibility, negative ones tend to favour withdrawal and avoidance. This is further evidence of the link between feelings and emotions, one of the functions of which is to dictate our initial reaction to situations which threaten to be upsetting or unexpected. Thus we experience feelings associated with openness: interest, curiosity, enthusiasm; and those associated with avoidance: irritation, contempt, disgust, anxiety.

These responses, as well as preceding contact with people or situations, can also result from such contacts. If the outcome is gratifying or is judged to be successful, we are likely to feel joy, pleasure, good humour, all of which will encourage further contacts. But if it ends in failure or is disagreeable, we are filled instead with sadness, disappointment, resentment, aversion, which will compromise or limit further contacts.

Positive moods contribute to the expansion of our view of the world: when we are happy, we feel secure, we enjoy things, we are ready to observe and admire what surrounds us. Negative moods, on the other hand, are more inclined to make us focus on what seems dangerous or difficult; and when (for example in the case of anxiety or fear) we look carefully around us, it is not with an open mind, ready to embrace beauty and novelty, but with a mind which is closed in on itself and intent on one objective, one single question: is there danger, yes or no? Nothing else interests us. We focus on keeping a close watch on the world instead of observing it in all its beauty.[14]

Finally, negative feelings lead us to 'process information' slowly, carefully, attentively, meticulously, in a way that might be described in scientific jargon as 'procedural': step by step and cautiously, as though crossing a minefield! They give us the sense that time is passing more slowly.[15] Positive moods, on the other hand, tend to make us respond to our surroundings in a way which is rapid, comprehensive and intuitive, what could be called 'heuristic': psychologically we are jumping for joy![16]

All these psychological and scientific observations have, inevitably, already been explored by poets and philosophers. In his book *La joie spacieuse*, the philosopher Jean-Louis Chrétien emphasizes that 'joy makes us more alive in a wider world'. He reminds us that 'as soon as joy is present, everything expands', and uses the beautiful image of 'joy in spate'. He also points out that this question of joy, and of all the states of mind and feelings which go with it, also has the capacity to make us stronger and more lucid: 'It is only when the space becomes deeper that the heart grows stronger, and it is only when the heart grows stronger that we are able to see and experience this deepening of space.'[17]

What purpose do positive feelings serve?

Acceleration, openness and expansion of our relationship with the world are thus the principal consequences of positive moods: they are therefore adapted to secure and peaceful environments. We are now going to look in more detail at some of their qualities in order to find out what they can teach us in terms of our everyday lives.

In general, positive moods enable us to have better self-control: that is to say that they help us engage in behaviour patterns which require some kind of immediate constraint (in the present) for deferred gains, for example by taking steps today (diet, exercise) in order to stay healthy in the future.[18] This is partly why depressive tendencies are so often associated with failed attempts at healthy 'behaviour patterns' (increased alcohol consumption, smoking, lack of exercise). And it also explains why people on a diet or trying to give up alcohol or tobacco are so vulnerable to fluctuations in their feelings and moods: many lapses can be blamed on a fit of the blues.

These benefits of positive moods are evident at an early stage: children who are in a good mood are capable of exercising better self-control, like being able to wait longer for a larger reward (when someone says, for example: 'I can give you one sweet now or two in five minutes' time. What do you prefer?'[19]).

Positive moods also result in greater discernment about which goals to aim for: if someone feels good about themselves, they are more likely to succeed because (unconsciously) they are careful to choose goals which they have a reasonable chance of achieving.[20] Whereas people who are trapped in more painful moods are more likely, where they do not simply give up too soon, to make choices which exceed their strength or their abilities, and, in the latter case, since they also tend to have less mental flexibility, they persist with them for too long.

Moreover, being in a good mood does not render us deaf and blind to what is wrong or to what could be improved in our lives, nor does it prevent us from changing things. It has been shown, for example, that people in a positive mood are more receptive to criticism directed at them.[21] And to think that so many bosses favour a bad atmosphere in the belief that too much enjoyment might encourage slack performance! (Photocopy this page for them, but, if you want to be sure they take notice, get them in a good mood first by cracking a joke or two.)

Positive moods also make us more persuasive,[22] and they help us to memorize useful information more accurately.[23] In 'real life' (research is carried out in a laboratory), this explains why it is important to create a positive atmosphere in the workplace, or in education, if we want to ensure what we have to say is listened to and retained.

We prefer positive moods, yet we should be aware that, with their tendency to rapid generalization, they can also be misleading. So, for example, we often take our feelings to be a source of information: this is obvious in the case of sadness, but it equally applies when we are in a good mood. This is why most people are more satisfied with their lives when the sun is shining.[24] The sun may indeed boost our morale, but does it make our lives better too? (Though perhaps, on reflection, that is not such an absurd idea.) In general, research confirms our tendency to judge our existence more positively from the perspective of a good mood.[25] Yet negative moods have the same effect, the same power to have a generalizing influence on our judgements. Take insomnia, for example: if you ask someone about their state of happiness after a sleepless night, the reply will not generally be very encouraging.[26] Similarly, when volunteers are presented with an existential issue, they tend to perceive it to be more serious and preoccupying in the afternoon (when they are beginning to feel tired) than in the morning.[27]

It is perhaps reassuring to know that, once we are aware of all this, we are less likely to fall into the 'trap': if we are told that the fine weather or our personal satisfaction over some small successes is influencing our existential satisfaction, our reaction is to start judging in a more detached manner (did I hear someone say 'More's the pity!'?).

But no, all of this is reassuring: we have, now and always, the choice to influence our feelings by using discernment.

What purpose do our negative feelings serve?

Let us now examine the impact of negative moods, of these 'sad passions', as the philosopher Spinoza called them.

We have seen how negative feelings can make people focus on the tiniest details, making mountains out of molehills and splitting hairs. As a result these feelings often go hand in hand with behaviour patterns associated with excessive checking, notably in people already prone to be over-meticulous or obsessive.[28] They also lead to a tendency to slow down: one of my patients told me that in his bad moments, he often felt *'ralentriste'* ('slowed-down-sad' – a play on words indicating the feeling of being slowed down by sadness). Negative moods, contrary to what is often assumed, lead to people taking less care of themselves and of their health.[29] They spend more time ruminating over their fear of illness, but in the end, are less inclined to pay attention to keeping themselves healthy than more cheerful people.

The onset of sad moods can cause people to give in to tempting stimuli should they be confronted with them; buying goods they do not need, consuming products or substances which promise instant improvement such as sweet foods, alcohol, coffee, tobacco.[30] But how then can we explain what happens in depression, where traditionally the person has no desire for anything at all? As in the famous line in Mallarmé's poem: 'The flesh is sad, alas! and I have read all the books.' In fact, this is not always true: for a start, the depressive state can also involve giving in to a range of unhealthy or destabilizing pleasures, like eating too much, smoking or drinking (all of which incidentally end up undermining self-esteem and aggravating the depression). These are in fact sad moods, pre-depression rather than the illness itself: the balance has yet to tip towards disgust with everything, and such sources of easy, undemanding pleasure can still be tempting, precisely because we are suffering. But, beware of the self-punishment that follows afterwards! Because we know these things are 'bad', we feel guilt at having drunk, smoked, eaten, thrown money down the drain. Those close to us sometimes reproach us for these excesses too. And we know that the onset of guilt, at a conscious or unconscious level, makes us harder on ourselves and more inclined to punish our own transgressions.[31] This is the danger of negative moods: whereas the capacity to self-repair is an inherent part of our inner equilibrium, they tend to push us to self-punishment or to making things worse for ourselves when we feel things are going badly. They end up locking us in a vicious circle from which, conversely, positive moods can help us to escape.[32] Consequently, it is extremely important not to neglect the little pleasures in life (going for a walk or meeting up with friends) when we are feeling down. And to have a sound understanding of the overall dynamics of *all* our feelings.

The arithmetic of feelings and moods: positive and negative do not cancel each other out

Contrary to what is sometimes thought, an increase in negative feelings does not necessarily prevent us from feeling any positive ones. And, inversely, an increase in positive feelings does not always eliminate negative ones. We have seen that certain moods, such as nostalgia or sadness, can be mixed. Thus the link between positive and negative moods is not a one-dimensional one where an increase in positive feelings corresponds to a decrease in negative ones and vice versa. The diagram below represents this mistaken view of our feelings by showing them as a rope which can be pulled from one end or the other, with a neutral state in the middle.

In reality, however, our feelings and moods operate on a more two-dimensional register (as shown in the second diagram). This means it is common to find oneself in a state combining both positive and negative dimensions of our feelings. For example, the tension associated with stress can be both stimulating and exhausting: it is therefore associated with high levels of both positive and negative feelings. The suffering associated with depression is based on high levels of negative moods and low levels of positive ones. Feelings of well-being are associated with a high level of positive moods and a low level of negative moods. Finally, the emptiness of apathy results in a low level of both positive and negative moods.

Still on the subject of this two-dimensionality, the absence of negative feelings does not necessarily indicate the presence of positive ones. When everything around me is going well, I feel neither stressed nor happy, but at peace (though clearly, depending on the circumstances in which we find ourselves, being at peace could be considered as a distinctly positive mood!). Curbing your negative feelings when someone says 'Don't cry' does not signal the return of positive moods, nor does it make you smile

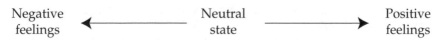

Negative feelings ← Neutral state → Positive feelings

One-dimensional model of feelings

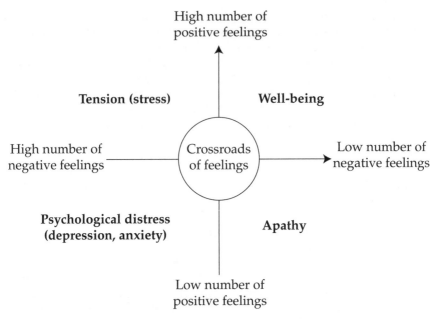

Two-dimensional model of feelings

again. In the same way, when we say 'Things aren't too bad' or 'I can't complain', our discourse indicates that although we are not overwhelmed with negative feelings, we are not exactly basking in positive ones: it is a question of peace, not felicity.

This theory of the relative independence of positive and negative feelings also enables us to have a clearer understanding of the role played by money in happiness: it has more impact on negative feelings (by limiting them) than on positive ones. In the long term, money can significantly reduce the impact of negative life events. In particular it helps to reduce the likelihood of feelings of stress and material uncertainty: when our car or our central heating boiler breaks down, we do not need to worry about being able to afford to pay for the repairs. But, on the other hand, money does not lead to more positive feelings – or at least not in the long term – perhaps because rich people do not generally begin each day by whispering 'How lucky I am to be rich and to have lots of money!' Money does not bring happiness directly (which is only right) but it does offer protection from stress (which is not such a bad thing). And I am referring to stress here (by which I mean feelings associated with real and current worries) but not necessarily anxiety (which does not always need to be based on real worries).

Positive and negative feelings and moods are therefore relatively independent. However, in zones of extreme activity (in the context of emotions rather than feelings) the two poles of positive and negative are relatively incompatible: so, for example, too much stress, over too long a period, gradually blunts the capacity to feel pleasure. And exacerbates all the negative feelings.[33] Similarly, whereas sadness (a mood) does not stop us experiencing joy, depression (severe emotional disturbance) generally blocks out the capacity to feel pleasure of any sort.

Yet in our everyday lives we experience more feelings and moods than powerful emotions. This is just as well: feelings and moods are more relaxing, and enable us to experience other more subtle sensations and perceptions. Which is why it is better (for those who care about their inner lives) to embrace our feelings without necessarily, or immediately, always seeking to 'correct' them towards the positive. Their coexistence within us brings texture, flavour and contradiction to our lives: in other words, humanity.

Creativity and feelings

'When we poets are sad, instead of getting rid of our sadness, we try to give it a name.' This may indeed be San Antonio[34] rather than Baudelaire, but it is still well put. Sometimes negative feelings are seen as desirable because they are associated with increased levels of creativity. Indeed, when I teach students or give lectures on positive psychology or happiness, I am often asked about creativity and suffering. We still cling to the notion that happiness makes us sleepy and a full stomach leads to apathy. But is it as simple as that?

In support of this view, a number of studies have shown that the experience of suffering from depression can sometimes lead to an increase in creativity;[35] though with the one – significant – condition of having got over the depression! Otherwise creativity is non-existent. It is worth pointing out that these studies focus on normal people rather than those already recognized for their genius or creativity, for whom it is a different story, probably precisely because of their extraordinary abilities. For such people, there seems to be a clear link between their mental condition (often bipolar illness, a great exaggerator of moods) and their creativity. Sadly, their extraordinary creativity also leads to extraordinary instability; as one of my patients, a talented painter, observed: 'Mad geniuses are even madder than ordinary madmen.' However, having treated or encountered some of these, my feeling is that their genius is not entirely the result of their suffering, but rather that it has successfully resisted it. Often, it is not a case of 'brilliant *due to* misfortune and instability', but rather 'brilliant *in spite of* misfortune and instability'.[36]

To summarize: if someone has been depressed they can be more creative once they are cured of the depression. If someone is a genius, they will automatically be more creative whatever their state. But what about those of us who are neither ex-depressives nor blessed with genius?

Well, that is precisely where positive moods gain the upper hand!

This was demonstrated in an amusing and elegant study.[37] Volunteers were asked to take part in a video game which involved helping an appealing little mouse find its way out of a maze. The game was very simple and the way out could be found in a matter of minutes. Those involved were divided randomly into two groups. One group was told that the mouse needed to get out of the maze to escape from an owl that was chasing her in order to eat her. The other group was told that the mouse needed their help to get to a tasty morsel of cheese. The volunteers who managed to rescue the mouse from the clutches of the owl subsequently (in another test) showed significantly less creativity (about 50 per cent) than those whose goal was to reach the cheese! So, the fact of being put into a slightly negative mood (having to escape and be vigilant), even in such a minimal and relatively trivial context, subsequently affected their capacity to find solutions and be creative. Whereas the presence of mildly positive moods (helping a nice mouse reach a tasty bit of cheese) had the opposite effect.

Another lesson that can be drawn from this experiment is that doing the same thing, but in two different states of mind, brings about different results. The feelings that accompany all our everyday actions are much more important than we realize. When we talk about 'giving meaning' to what we are doing, especially with reference to our ordinary activities (gardening, washing up, reading a story to our children, doing our job, giving up our seat on the bus to an elderly person), this is what it is all about: what we say and what we feel as we are doing something can enhance or invalidate the beneficial dimension of our actions. We will look at this in more detail at a later stage.

To conclude on the subject of those of us who are not geniuses (which is after all, most of us), many studies on moods and creativity show that while positive feelings tend to make us more flexible,[38] negative ones make us persevere more.[39] And both of these are equally necessary to creativity: perseverance without overdoing it.

Light and shadow

An ability to accept and to cultivate all our feelings is a considerable asset. There is much to be said for developing a certain degree of psychological diversity in ourselves. According to a classic metaphor in humanist psychotherapy,[40] it is about being the chess board rather than the pieces, about not trying to play black against white, positive against negative, but instead, understanding that both are useful. And that, without them both, there can be no game, and nothing to play for.

Buddhist philosophy for its part says that there are two kinds of emotions: those which increase peace of mind and those which reduce it. Similarly feelings become problematic if they detract from our equilibrium and our inner richness instead of adding to these.

Clearly all this is not simply a question of positivity or negativity: there are unwholesome joys, toxic pleasures and delights, which impoverish us in the long term. Take the pleasure of revenge, or of domination, for example: or that of *schadenfreude*, the pleasure of seeing others fail, that mixture of joy and guilt;[41] and perhaps quite simply all the feelings associated with pride, so easily contaminable by the instinct for dominance and the need for superiority.

Conversely, some suffering can be a good thing, opening our eyes to certain aspects of reality, like those associated with compassion. The kind of suffering which can be the antechamber to a form of liberation from all suffering. Buddhism refers to renunciation, or to the *spirit of* emergence: 'to understand perfectly the extent to which we are vulnerable to suffering, the Dalai Lama explains, and once we have recognized this absolute vulnerability . . . we can glimpse the possibility that our minds will be able to free themselves from it'.[42] This mood of disillusionment, sad and painful as it is at first, is what enables us, according to Buddhist thinkers, to understand the futility of placing too much emphasis on the *Samsâra*, or in other words, the world of material illusions, that 'theatre in which the human being undergoes the experience of suffering through the false attachment to things'.[43]

The ideal of permanently positive feelings, understandable as it may be, is not therefore either realistic or desirable: we need darkness to give depth to the light. Shadows add to the beauty of the day and that is why the evening or morning light is often more beautiful or more subtle than that of midday. Is the night not beautiful too? Yes, but only because we know that daybreak will follow.

Each of us has our work cut out, then: life, as we have seen, will inevitably bring us our share of adverse events and the negative feelings which go with them. And it is up to us to take care of our inner states and to illuminate our days.

Chapter 3

Rumination and losing control

Only man, snatching his full share of bread and air, dabbles with unsuitable concepts, gets distracted by dreams, gorges himself with thoughts.

Joseph Delteil, *La Fayette*

'It's snowing. The town is completely buried in white ... It must be snowing in Rasinari too, on my mother's tomb. Last night I saw, what we call seeing, that tomb and my mother, lying young in her coffin.'[1]

When Cioran, that melancholy thinker, observes the falling snow, his feelings make him drift slowly through a sequence of images and of thoughts which merge with what he is feeling at that moment.

In this way, if we allow them the space to do so, our feelings too are capable of modifying each instant of our lives, enhancing them with a constant movement towards the past, or the future. Or enriching them with other presents: like Cioran, watching the snow falling and thinking of it falling at the same time on his mother's tomb.

Feelings create a parallel world, a virtual world: a treasure or a trap?

Our feelings create in us an echo of the external world which can continue to develop indefinitely, carrying us along with it. This undoubtedly means that we are often better able to analyse, understand and feel this external world. This enrichment, brought about by our feelings, thus enhances our capacity to think and reflect.

But the existence of these feelings as a permanent echo of our experiences in life can also be problematic. If, for example, they distort our perception of reality, or replace it with something else. Remember Plato's allegory of the cave. In his famous dialogue *The Republic*, the philosopher describes a number of men imprisoned in an underground cave. These men have never seen the light of day and their only perception of reality is obtained from the shadows projected on the walls of their narrow and confined world by the small amount of light that penetrates the cave. In spite of what they believe – they genuinely see what they see and it really exists, but it is not the *full* reality of the world – they live in error and unfulfilment. Our feelings can mislead us in a similar way, locking us in a virtual world which is in fact simply a withdrawal from the world, a reconstruction of it, admittedly more or less under our control, but false, deformed, cut off.

All the more so because our feelings and moods feed on themselves: sadness makes us sensitive to sad things, making us feel even sadder. Our feelings make us behave in a way that reflects them: resentment sparks off conflicts and misunderstandings which validate and rekindle the initial feeling of resentment. Gradually, as they develop, our feelings can turn us away from reality and draw us into their world. In doing so they offer us 'escapes from reality', like turnings off a main road. This does not only apply to negative moods: euphoria, for example, that mixture of joy and heightened self-esteem, can also be a dangerous loss of contact with reality. Elation, from the Latin *elatus*, describes this exaltation based on the unregulated inflation of the ego (one of my Latin teachers would often repeat to us, in order to remind us of humility, this saying: 'Elation? Alas!').

There is also the phenomenon of remanence, which we have already referred to, where feelings and moods are capable of outlasting the situations which justified or provoked them. With the risk, unless we are vigilant, of their perpetually recurring: our feelings plough their furrow in us, in a very real sense, by activating 'synaptic motorways' for processing information in our brains, always skewed in the same direction. After a while, we tend to rely excessively on our internal sensations, taking our feelings as a permanently valid source of information: this is the scientific model of *mood-as-input*,[2] where what is felt subjectively becomes a valid signal on which to judge reality and act accordingly. We could also call this *emotional reasoning*: if I feel sad, it means the situation is a sad one; if I feel tense, it is because danger exists: if I feel angry, it is because there is an offence or an injustice. Evidently this is not always the case, and we can sometimes make mistakes which can have serious and long-lasting consequences.

A painful mental climate: the example of dysphoria

In psychiatry, the term *dysphoria* is used to describe a cocktail of painful, distressing and generally long-lasting feelings. Dysphoria comes from the Greek *dys* ('difficult') and *phorein* ('to bear, put up with'): that which is difficult to bear. Dysphoria is when someone can no longer bear *anything*; whereas euphoria means being able to bear *everything* (which in itself leads to other problems . . .).

Dysphoria is situated between normal sadness (of which it is a 'pepped up' version thanks to the presence of other negative feelings) and clinical depression (which it can precede or follow). It represents a dangerous *flirtation* with depression itself. It is not an illness but usually a temporary state. However, it can be either a harbinger of the arrival of more severe psychological difficulties, or the aftermath of these, the scar.

Dysphoria is a mixture of all the unpleasant feelings which can affect us: sadness, irritability, tension, anxiety. It is also associated with a lability between feelings: we can move between them abruptly and quickly, with the result that our reactions to the events of everyday life are amplified during episodes of dysphoria. For women, the premenstrual period often triggers dysphoria. Insomnia, fatigue and failure can do so for all of us.

Dysphoria not only affects us internally but can also disrupt the way we react to events in our lives. Generally, it makes us react more when things are going badly, and less when they are going well.[3] As a result, dysphoria restricts what is called the 'capitalization of positive moments': all human beings need to be able to rejoice about the good things that happen to them, first of all, because it is enjoyable to do so, and also because taking the time to savour or 'chew over' good moments strengthens our memory of them, thereby providing us with a 'positive memory reservoir' to help us face adversity.

Amongst my close acquaintances there are a few with a special gift for happiness, of whom I have already spoken in one of my books on that subject.[4] One of these, a retired engineer, once described how he had gained the maximum enjoyment from an invitation to a reunion party with his former colleagues:

> As soon as I received the list of those attending, I sat myself down in my favourite armchair, and, taking each name in turn, I allowed myself to think in detail and at length about all the good moments we had shared. During the little ceremony, I made sure I found time to speak to all the people I liked, conscious all the time of how lucky I was to be seeing all of them together, one last time, in such a lovely atmosphere. And then afterwards, I remembered all the little gestures, the friendly words that had passed between us, that whole atmosphere of human warmth. So much happiness all from that one little moment!

The negative effects of dysphoria

People suffering from dysphoria, as opposed to those who are not, pay more attention to the negative words they are presented with (in tests where the time spent on different types of words is measured to the hundredth of a second). Those unaffected by dysphoria, on the other hand, move quickly on from them, and spend significantly more time on positive words.[5] In a similar way, research has also studied in detail the eye movements of people with dysphoria when shown positive, negative or neutral images. Although they do not necessarily spot the negative images more easily than the others, their eyes 'fix' on them for a longer period of time.[6]

All this results in a kind of negative psychological glue: faced with all the little moments where we see, read or hear something negative in our day, some of us (sometimes for reasons other than sadness: dysphoria can also be triggered by anger or by anxiety) will 'dwell' on what is not going well, on what is not working, and gradually immerse themselves in negative thoughts. It is like a herbal tea, an infusion of negative affects. As a result, on any given day, these vestiges of sadness will make the difference: because of being bogged down in our dysphoric moods, we will feel we have encountered more problems than other people, whereas in fact we have simply given them more attention.

Dysphoria also makes people experience what are called 'biases in anticipation': their minds generate less positive anticipation, or, where anticipation occurs, it is less enjoyable.[7] In a sense, dysphoria puts us off getting involved in enjoyable projects or stops us enjoying them. Whereas looking forward positively to good moments (thinking about the evening ahead, the weekend, holidays, etc.) and taking comfort from these thoughts are part of what makes our lives agreeable.

When moods become chronic: why we sometimes get bogged down in suffering

Many psychological processes lock us into unpleasant or pathological moods from which we are unable to emerge.

More often than not, this happens unintentionally and unconsciously: few of us are very lucid about the moment we begin to lose control and to ruminate excessively on our negative moods.

Yet sometimes we are consciously aware that we are causing ourselves harm. Why then do we continue to do so? And why, so often, do we even take a sinister pleasure in it? Once again, this is a 'classic' example of mixed moods: the satisfaction (however limited) of making oneself suffer (a little).

This can – and almost always does – result from a habit, either our own or one we observed in our parents as a child: the father spending the whole Sunday brooding over work worries, while the mother says 'Children, run along and leave your father in peace – he's got things on his mind.'

It can also, bizarrely, come from the feeling of control obtained as a result of giving in to our gloomy moods: at least there, we know what is going on; we are in control, on familiar territory. As one of my patients said: 'Ruminating – yes, that's something I'm good at!' Whereas the rest of our lives, on the contrary, are dominated by the feeling of uncertainty, the impression that we are not holding the reins. Finally, submerging ourselves in negative moods can also procure us the dismal pleasure, a kind of sub-pleasure, of satisfied misery ('I always knew I would only end up suffering'). We prefer to be right, even miserably so, and to ponder our misfortunes, rather than pull up our socks and say to ourselves: 'Instead of doing everything possible to make yourself feel awful, go out for an hour's walk. If it doesn't help, at least it won't be any worse than staying at home ruminating over things.'

There is one particular book in the Bible that I often find myself returning to, and which still, after thousands of years, has a similarly profound effect both on new readers and on biblical scholars.[8] It is Ecclesiastes, or 'The Preacher', with those memorable lines: 'Vanity of vanities. All is vanity and the pursuit of the wind.' It consists of a series of ruminations and lamentations, of gloomy reflections on existence, of negative and nihilistic visions: 'He that diggeth a pit shall fall into it; and whoso breaketh an hedge, a serpent shall bite him. Whoso removeth stones shall be hurt therewith; and he that cleaveth wood shall be endangered thereby.'[9] We can practically hear the sighs of the author (these reflections are traditionally imputed to Solomon, though this hypothesis is rejected by modern researchers). One of my colleagues once entertained himself by counting the positive and negative valencies in Ecclesiastes.[10] His diagnosis: with 75 per cent negative monologues against only 25 per cent positive ones, the author, be it King Solomon or not, is clearly suffering from an anxio-depressive disorder!

Rumination: negative feelings perpetually recycled and unfinished

'Somewhere near Cape Horn, on the Chilean side, there is an island called the island of Desolation. I am haunted by this place.' This little note in Cioran's *Cahiers* haunts me too.[11] It strikes me as the height of absurdity and humanity at the same time.

Ruminating is 'a repetitive focus on the causes, meanings, and consequences of one's depressed mood'.[12] We also use the term *brooding*. Indeed, ruminating involves being inactive, sitting on problems and keeping them nice and warm, underneath you, allowing them to grow.

One can moreover wonder about the risks inherent in certain psychotherapies centred on rumination, in which the patient is encouraged to go over and over whatever it is that is tormenting or bothering them instead of actively seeking to resolve or accept the problem. But that is another story.

It has been demonstrated that rumination makes people focus on the problem and its consequences, rather than on possible solutions which could be envisaged or put in place. Wrong target, wrong direction. A huge amount of time is wasted ruminating over the possible causes of an illness rather than seeking a cure.[13] Which leads to the aggravation of potential problems (one can always say to oneself later 'I knew I was right to be worried'). So, for example, in a study based on women who had had breast cancer, the 'ruminators' went to the doctor on average two months later than the 'non-ruminators'.[14] Their thoughts were constantly focused on the lump in their breast, yet they did not make an appointment, and instead simply continued to worry.

Rumination involves a significant element of avoidance of the problem and of the need to take action: since taking action could end up forcing us to face up to a real problem – just as it could equally reveal that no problem existed, or that a solution was available – we prefer to continue to ruminate rather than find out! Rumination is also associated with moroseness and with a sense of helplessness. Back to our fascinating Ecclesiastes: 'All the rivers run into the sea; yet the sea is not full; unto the place from whence the rivers come, thither they return again. All things are full of labour.'

There is also in these constantly repeated and sombre arguments the belief that, in order to solve a problem, a long period of reflection is necessary, and that the longer that reflection goes on, the more chance there is of finding a suitable solution. Which is not always the case.

And finally, there is an element, an obsession almost, of judgement in rumination (again, we find this too in Ecclesiastes): this initial reflex, this tendency to pass judgement on things (good or bad) and to identify who is guilty or responsible (oneself or others), to see problems as mistakes or failures (who is in the wrong?).

It is all very well to judge. But what purpose does it really serve? Sometimes it is best not to judge. And it is always best not to do so too quickly.

Rumination: the vague and endless 'whys'

The feelings associated with rumination are nothing but long chains of half-thoughts, of half-finished snatches of thought, which never come to anything or reach a conclusion, since they always stop on the threshold of any possible decision: definitely a case of *'cogitatus interruptus'*! Ultimately they have no other purpose, and perhaps no other conscious goal, than to maintain a state of dysphoria. Rumination has no clear objective, which is why it cannot have any clear goal. Feelings and moods are perpetually recycled, yet remain frozen, unable to move forward and always returning to the same point. Rumination is the helpless submission of our minds to a circular and closed thought process: we are going round in circles. And we know it. Yet we are incapable of regaining control. We can only wait until something comes along: sleep, a powerful or prolonged distraction, an encounter, a task which is either sufficiently absorbing or which is capable of triggering other equally powerful feelings.

One reason why it is so difficult to stop rumination is that, in the

absence of a conscious and precise goal ('finding a solution and not allowing this problem to wear me out or to do me harm') the process tends
to function along the lines of *emotional reasoning*, as mentioned earlier:
where the emotional state is taken as a reliable indication of the existence
of a problem ('if I'm afraid, it's because there is some kind of danger; if
I'm sad, it's because something awful has happened; if I'm anxious, it's
because there's going to be trouble of some sort'). But rumination means
that negative moods and their emotional dimensions become chronic and
linger long after any potential problems have disappeared (if indeed any
existed in the first place). If we are not careful, we can easily find ourselves trapped, remaining prisoners of our ruminations until exhaustion,
an intrusive event or simply the passage of time come to our rescue.

The central question asked in rumination is: 'why?'

'Why didn't I make that decision, why did I do or say that, why did
it happen to me?' Thus rumination associated with sadness (rumination
can also be associated with anxiety in the form of worry, which we shall
look at later) focuses on asking: (1) why am I so sad? (ruminations on
the *reasons* for my sadness); (2) what does my sadness mean? (ruminations on the *significance* of my sadness); and (3) why can't I shake off
my sadness? (rumination on the sense of *helplessness* in the face of my
sadness).[15]

Then begins an endless cycle: whether answers are found or not (and
often there is no satisfactory one), these questions keep on being repeated:
how? why? how? why? how? why? how? why? how? etc.

When we are down, the slightest thing can trigger this cycle: a question
with no possible clear answer ('Will that work out?', 'Will I get what I
want?', 'Have I done the right thing?') or a minor vexation ('Why did she
say that to me?', 'Why did they do that to me?', 'Why didn't that work?'),
and the mechanism is set in motion.

Asking oneself 'Why?' is dangerous unless we are then capable of
saying 'Stop!' If not, our whys turn into an endless cycle and we go into
detail upon detail, why upon why. Not surprisingly a constant flow of
'yes, but why?' questions is one of those metaphysical games favoured
by children determined to drive their parents mad. Our rumination can
sometimes resemble those interminable conjugal rows where instead of
asking 'What do we need to do to make up with each other and make sure
it doesn't happen again?', we ask 'Why did you do or say that to me?'
Rumination is an interminable biblical quarrel with existence: 'Oh life,
why are you treating me like this?'

Essentially, rumination drags out worries and unfortunate events,
making them last even longer, as if they were not already bad enough!
It causes them to expand, allowing them to spill over into the rest of our
lives, into the past ('it's because I didn't do such and such that all this has
happened') and the future ('now that means this will happen'), eventually
completely clouding our assessment of what we should be doing about
the problem in the present.

To the tune of 'I should have . . .', rumination facilitates a *presence of the past*: the past reinvents itself and masquerades as the present, and in so doing, effectively takes its place. And suddenly we are no longer living. Instead it is as though we are listening to an old scratched record, endlessly playing over the same fragment, but which we can no longer remove from the turntable, any more than we can switch off the sound, or leave the room.

Beware of rumination: rumination is not the same as reflection

Rumination tends to be self-centred. And that is another of its problems since it encourages us to close in on ourselves, and therefore prevents us benefiting from, or listening to, the advice and the experience of others who might be able to help us. The more we try to approach a problem by focusing on ourselves ('it always happens to me, what's going to become of me, nobody understands, nobody can help me . . .'), the more damage we will incur in terms of the onset of negative moods.[16] Reflecting through the eyes and the experience of other people, however, asking them for help and advice, all help to lighten the emotional weight of reflecting on our problems. That is the true nature of reflection!

In effect, our ruminations often go unnoticed by us simply because we *think* we are genuinely reflecting on things.[17] But rumination is not genuine reflection: it is sterile, as we have seen. It often takes place on a broad and general level: it is more about wanting to know what something means and why than about wondering what the different elements of the problem are, and what exactly should be done.[18] Often rumination is a painful process so we try to get away from it by attempting to think about something else, or by doing something, but the negative feelings are still there, acting as a backdrop. As a result, we end up not doing anything properly: neither the activity we are engaged in, nor the process of reflecting on the problem. The lucid and efficient solution would be to decide exactly what it is we want to do and then do it whole-heartedly. But that is no easy matter and, as we shall see, requires a certain amount of training. In spite of appearances then, rumination bears not the slightest resemblance to reflection; we would be better off going for a walk, or doing some gardening or some odd jobs. At least that would do us more good than continuing to ruminate and might even trigger some slightly more positive moods, perhaps even bringing us closer to a solution.

Another problem is our tendency to attach too much importance to rumination: in a survey amongst the general population, in response to the question 'What do you do when you feel depressed?' a third of people replied 'I try to work out why I am feeling down.' Which, although perfectly acceptable, is in fact often not the best approach, or only if they genuinely do try to work it out and then go on to try out some solutions,[19]

Differences between rumination and reflection

Rumination	Reflection
Looks for faults, mistakes, blame: 'Who should be criticized or punished?'	Looks for solutions: 'What should I do now?'
In general, tends to magnify the problem	Tends to relativize, to understand the importance of the problem, but without exaggerating it.
Tends to judge	Tends to understand
Over-simplifies: for example, 'This is all because of one thing.'	Takes account of the complexity (without drowning in it): most problems generally have more than one cause
Focuses on what has happened, the 'why?'	More inclined to look to the future, to focus on 'what to do next'
No precise goal (therefore easily bogged down)	Aims to resolve the problem or to extricate oneself from it
Tends to approach situations from broad, general perspective: 'Help, help! A massive problem!'	Tends to approach situations in a precise and step-by-step way: 'How can I break my big problem down into a number of smaller ones?'
Focuses on the problem: 'What a catastrophe, what a disaster, what a mistake, what a mess.'	Focuses on the solution, on putting things right and prevention: 'What do I need to do and how can I put things right?'

instead of simply continuing to ruminate on the reasons why they feel low. In reality, the best approach, if we want a clearer view of things, is to focus on the *hows* rather than the whys: how am I functioning at the moment? How do I feel about the object of my distress? How should I set about – or not – trying to feel better? It is only when the dysphoric moods have lifted that we can really tackle the question of *why*, which otherwise, nourished by our gloomy mood, will simply see us slip back into rumination mode.

Rumination could be likened to inflammation, our body's natural mechanism for defence and healing, but which has gone beyond its initial purpose and become a pathology in its own right: what should have been simply a process of reflection aimed at solving a problem turns into a never-ending series of painful and unhelpful feelings. In severe cases of depressive or anxious rumination, medication (tranquilizers or anti-depressants), which can be prescribed in such circumstances, will act like the analgesics and anti-inflammatories used in cases of chronic back pain: they will not cure the cause of the pain but will ensure that it does not become paralysing. Even so, they should not be a substitute for reflection – of a practical nature! – on the longer term: what do I need to do to make sure the problem does not recur?

Nowadays cognitive psychotherapies targeting rumination are based on a number of protocols.[20] Patients are offered a specific treatment: dissociation (using techniques to distance themselves from their thoughts), observation (learning meditation techniques), limitation of time spent in worrying (establishment of a specific amount of *worry time* each day – not to be exceeded!). The idea is that rumination prevents the natural psychological healing of mental suffering. If something is bothering us, it is better to confront it head on rather than ruminating over it ('why has this happened to me?') or running away from it ('just don't even think about it'). For we have at our disposal all we need to recover from our suffering: we know, for example, that following a trauma, the vast majority of people (more than 80 per cent) show no pathological symptoms of psychological shock. But only if no attempts are made to interfere with the healing process (by rumination; by insisting on suppressing any disagreeable thoughts because of their association with the trauma; by avoiding situations which activate the memory . . .). And even in those less dramatic everyday situations capable of inducing – or awakening – our tendencies to ruminate, we should still look for inspiration in the same methods: remaining vigilant about slipping into 'rumination mode', and confronting anything that is bothering us (and not in the oblique way we use when we keep turning things over in our minds).

From showers to storms: how feelings can spiral into psychological pathologies

Feelings are not just a matter of inner well-being; they also play an important role in many psychological conditions, ranging from bulimia to anxiety and including depression and addictions. They can be implicated before, during or after these problems.

Before, by increasing vulnerability: experiencing, and dwelling on, painful feelings, without being fully aware that this can expose us to the onset of various psychological illnesses, if we are already predisposed to them.

During, by aggravating the situation: feeling agitated, overwhelmed and threatened by our feelings and ruminating over them does not facilitate healing.

Afterwards, in the invisible scars and the various factors responsible for relapses: the instability of feelings and moods in the period following illness is a significant factor in its recurrence. And, sadly, most psychiatric illnesses are recurrent ones: that does not mean relapses are inevitable, but only that we will inevitably be faced with the possibility of them occurring at different points along our way. And that we will need to resist such opportunities actively when they occur.

We will return later in greater detail to the notion of the scars resulting from depression. But painful feelings also play an important part, for example, in our relationship with food and the potential problems associated with eating. We know that bulimia is often triggered by inner experiences of sadness, anxiety, loneliness or simply a sense of tedium and emptiness.[21] An incapacity to identify and adjust our feelings in response to life events is clearly one of the principal mechanisms in this inability to resist the desire to eat (which, of course, has nothing to do with hunger).[22] Personal efforts and therapies targeting these feelings are effective in the prevention of bulimic behaviour within at-risk populations, such as adolescents.[23]

Even without being affected by bulimia (the condition in which victims indulge in bouts of excessive over-eating), however, our moods affect our tendencies to graze (eating between meals) or to binge eat (over-eating at mealtimes). Similarly, people who are overweight are inclined to eat too much when they feel anxious or upset. And the introduction of stress to people on diets can often undermine their resolutions.[24] Our painful or difficult feelings, if left unidentified, can unconsciously push us to over-eat. And this can subsequently trigger other disagreeable feelings linked to low self-esteem: resentment, shame and self-loathing. Which will certainly not help matters, either in terms of our feelings or in the tendency to take refuge in food.

Generally speaking, the tendency to take refuge in a variety of substances such as tobacco, alcohol or cannabis is – initially at least, before it becomes so much a reflex that the link is no longer perceptible – an attempt to escape from painful or simply unpleasant feelings.[25] An unfortunate attempt, sadly: they will return even more forcibly, and in the meantime we will have become addicted to the substance in question, and therefore less able to face the feelings except through new forms of escape. Generally speaking, negative moods are the most significant elements of the desire to smoke or drink. Either as a way of coping with the feelings of tension and helplessness; or because those feelings have already been suppressed, leaving an uncomfortable void and the sudden 'out of the blue' desire to consume the substance our bodies have become addicted to.[26] And, as with depression, relapses and other lapses in abstinence result from the onset of moods which are misinterpreted, denied or unsuccessfully regulated. Which is why, in all these pathologies of dependence, a focus on feelings and moods (awareness and self-observation) is of such prime importance in the long term.

Finally, we should remember that all this applies not just to established pathologies; the moods associated with adolescence, for example, even though generally accepted as normal, should not be allowed to get out of hand: there is some evidence to suggest that in certain cases this can lead to an increased risk of episodes of depression in adult life.[27]

Our feelings make us vulnerable because of our failure to understand, accept and regulate them

Why does all this happen? Why can we not simply block those negative feelings which seem anodyne at first, but which, little by little, end up causing us genuine harm? We are victims, at such sensitive moments, of an 'emotional cascade'.[28] In this tumult of sadness, anxiety, resentment, all our ruminations end up spiralling out of control and unleashing a tide of confusion and distress. One of my patients once compared this experience to what happens when you are trying to find something on a high shelf without bothering to use a stepladder and everything suddenly tumbles out on top of you. These cascades of painful feelings, abruptly spiralling out of control, are the origin of the attacks of despair in the depressed, of panic in the anxious, of resentment in the inhibited; and of all our outbursts of distress.

Such crises arise as a result of our *lack of awareness* of the importance (or even the existence) of our feelings. And also, often, of our *lack of expertise* in dealing with them.

Research shows that the majority of us do not have a clear awareness of what improves or aggravates our feelings, or of what affects our emotional stability.[29] Knowing and understanding the effects our feelings can have on us is often a key element in enabling us to cope when we need to.

In one particular study, volunteers were asked to read a dramatic story in which the driver of a car killed a child because he was in a hurry and was driving too fast, and to imagine that they *were* that driver. They were asked to think about how they would feel in such circumstances and instructed to put those feelings down in writing. They were then told that before the second test on the story in 15 minutes' time (to give them time to recover), there was to be another experiment, this time on taste. For this, they were asked to test various biscuits. The aim was to observe whether the number of biscuits eaten was affected by their emotional state. At this point in the experiment, half of the volunteers were given a brief warning speech: 'Contrary to popular belief, eating does not bring emotional relief.' Not surprisingly, the volunteers whose attention had been drawn to the possible influence their feelings and moods might exercise ate on average noticeably fewer biscuits than those to whom nothing had been said.[30] The fact that they had been alerted to the process meant they were less likely to be victims of it. Most of them of course already knew that we tend to eat more when we are upset. Yet this knowledge, stored somewhere in the depths of their memory, lay dormant, unattainable and useless. By telling them about it, the researcher had *woken up* this knowledge, linking it to the current situation and making it operational. We ought to be able to do this of our own accord: but that involves not bypassing the first stage, which consists in saying to ourselves 'That story about the child who was run over has somehow upset me – I know it's only a story and that it's just part of a psychology experiment, but it has genuinely affected me. I can feel it in my head, in my body, in my whole mood.' Just having that kind of humility and that awareness could help us so much.

But for that we need a certain amount of expertise, both to be clear about the subtle movements of our minds, and in order to know what to do next. An aspiration to be able to manage our feelings and moods is undoubtedly one reason for the fascination Buddhism has exercised on the West. Although there is clearly much more to Buddhism than this,[31] its emphasis on what the monk Matthieu Ricard called *mind training* seems to many of us to offer a promise of enhanced inner well-being for which there is really no equivalent in our materialistic daily lives.[32] For some time now psychotherapy has been looking at ways of preventing relapses by helping vulnerable patients develop additional capacities to cope with the fluctuations in their feelings and moods. As we shall see later, this does not only consist (far from it, in fact) in 'controlling' them or in preventing them from developing or existing. On the contrary, it is about accepting their existence, learning to live with them, and knowing how to tame them: sometimes listening to them, and sometimes refusing to follow their lead.

Our feelings: not so trivial after all

The endless return of our painful feelings may indeed be a reality, but what makes them more painful still is our reluctance, our inability, to embrace them and make space for them within us. In his famous *Letters to a Young Poet*, Rainer Maria Rilke magnificently explores the precious, and in his view, vital role that feelings can play in our lives. In the 'Eighth letter', he speaks to his young correspondent about sadness:

> If it were possible for us to see further than our knowledge reaches, and a little beyond the outworks of our intuitions, perhaps we should then bear our sadnesses with greater assurance than our joys . . . But I ask you to consider whether these great unhappinesses did not pass through you. Whether much within you has not changed, whether somewhere, in some part of your being, you were not transformed while you were unhappy.

With such words, Rilke encourages his correspondent to pay the closest attention and to show the greatest respect to his feelings and moods: for him this is the best – the only – way to live and to resist what he calls 'these illnesses which accumulate in our being', as a result of our lack of attention and our ignorance.[33]

Chapter 4

Introspection

I know what you are going to say to me. You have to get inside yourself. . . .
I did go inside myself on a number of occasions. But the problem was, you
see, there was nobody there. So, after a while, I felt frightened and I came
back out and made some noise to reassure myself.

Jean Anouilh, *The Waltz of the Toreadors*

'As I walk I observe the movements of my consciousness. Some days it
is like looking into a stream where the water is crystal clear and you can
see the stream-bed itself and all the movements of the water-plants and
the fish. That is how it is today. Everything that is happening in my consciousness seems clear: the sound of the wind, the colour of the trees and
the sky, the scent of the forest, distant memories (of childhood autumns)
and more recent ones (this summer's walks in the Pyrenees), thoughts
about the death and the resurrection of nature, agreeable thoughts about
the present (the imminent birthday of one of my daughters, something
a patient said to me at the hospital this week, the stone in my shoe
that I have decided not to remove and am accepting as a harmless but
undesirable little presence: "It can serve as an exercise in acceptance").
Everything is clear. It is as though I am discreetly observing my feelings
through the keyhole. No, not even that: I am one with them. This tranquil
tumult, this unending mixture of sensation, of thoughts, of fragments of
emotion, all passing by in a constant flux; or rather, this perpetual movement embodies all the different aspects of one single mood of serenity.
This serenity stems no doubt from the fact that, at the moment, I am
not troubled by any misplaced judgements on the desirability, or not,
of certain of these thoughts or sensations: I accept them all. But this
is easy: there is nothing particularly painful in my life at the moment.
But perhaps it is also a sign that my long years of practising meditation
bear fruit – at least occasionally. On another occasion, I was waiting one
morning to watch migrating birds in a hide in the woods: silence, stillness, almost nothing to see, no trace of the "entertainment" we have come
to expect constantly in our modern world, just as we do in the cinema.

Then, after a while, in all this stillness and quietness, a sense of oneness begins to take shape, in which everything that is happening is somehow synchronized; the sounds, the colours, the beating of my own heart and the flow of my thoughts: slowly a single mood of serenity rises within me. It will not last, I know. But in the meantime it is as wonderful as it is strange.'

Feelings and self-reflection: a pointless obsession or the building blocks of freedom?

'Feelings? But they just drive you crazy, don't they?'

Yes, indeed they can. But we can also occasionally use our brains for other things than for work or for leisure. In this age when nobody lifts the bonnet of a car (leave it to the specialists), it would be a pity if the same were true of our minds, if self-reflection were confined to the psychiatrist's couch (I get the impression that, for some of our patients, their meetings with us psychotherapists represent the only time they stop to question or think about themselves).

If we are not careful, we will end up only using our brains for *doing* things, and we will forget to feel ourselves *being*, to watch ourselves simply living. As a result, we will end up missing out on half of our lives. No great loss, some might say, that still leaves the other half: our actions, our reactions to the demands of our environment. But if we dismiss our feelings, if we pay no attention to them, we will end up being no more than simply 'machines for living', as Paul Valéry puts it. And a troubling or depressing sense of emptiness will sometimes overwhelm us, the moment we stop acting or reacting.

We need introspection; we need to look inside ourselves. Of course if we look too far into ourselves, we can end up losing our balance and drowning. Nor is introspection enough on its own: we need to live too, and action and social interaction teach us and show us a great deal about ourselves. It may even be that they tell us more than introspection does about *what* we are. But certainly less about *how* we come to be like that and *what it means* to be what we are.

And after all, practising introspection is a bit like taking time to tune a musical instrument, ensuring that it will sound better next time it is played. How many of us go to the trouble of regularly retuning our minds?

Take what happens when we have just had an argument with someone. We immediately get on the phone and pour out our feelings into the sympathetic ear of someone who, not having witnessed the scene, takes our side completely. Then we go back to whatever it was we were doing, ruminating on the whole thing.

Or look at what happens when we get stuck on something we are working on. First we feel irritated, then we get up from our chair in search of a change of scene. Or we check our e-mails, go out for a coffee or, worst of all, smoke a cigarette.

By acting in this way, we are simply running away from our feelings instead of embracing and examining them.

Paradoxically, it is in the aftermath of this kind of behaviour that the risk of rumination, which we have just been looking at, is at its greatest. Since that little wound provoked by our feelings has not been properly cleaned and examined, the problem will come quietly back, lingering somewhere in the background of our activities, like the ghosts of the situation: ruminations.

Why, at such moments, do we not take the time to breathe deeply, to stretch and ask ourselves 'What's going on in me? What is wrong? What is this uncomfortable feeling? What should I accept and what can I change?' And then get on with something else and see what happens: if the unpleasant feelings come back, perhaps the task of introspection and pacification still needs doing. In that case we need to take time to reflect on things, now, later, this evening, with a clear mind.

Why not get into the habit several times a day of asking questions like 'How's everything going in there?' Why not sound out our feelings as regularly as possible?

Without this gentle gymnastics, we will find ourselves constantly between a rock and a hard place: either drowning in our feelings (rumination) or refusing to pay them attention (running away, and in this case running away from ourselves).

Whereas, as always, the best way forward is to find a happy medium: a quiet introspection but one conscious of its limits.

Feelings and self-awareness

Feelings are the expression and the seat of self-awareness.

The role of sensibility in our quest for interiority has of course been explored at length by many philosophers. After the 'I think therefore I am' of Descartes came the empiricism of the Scottish philosopher Hume, who emphasized the central role of 'sensory experiences' rather than a purely abstract and rational knowledge.[1] Later still, Rousseau brilliantly re-examined and developed this idea of an emotional and sensitive basis for the self, which could be summed up as 'I feel therefore I am.'

If we do not feel, we cannot understand or learn effectively: out of two stories we have listened to, we will remember more distinctly the one which affected us emotionally.[2] That is why the existential experiences which have most impact on us are based on feelings and moods: we never remember anything insipid or impersonal, anything that does not involve the emotions. These *existential* experiences, these moments when we are aware of *existing*, correspond, if we think carefully about it, to a particular equilibrium: we feel both separate from what is around us (enough to be able to step back and observe) and at the same time part of it. Feelings of identity and belonging are mixed together, interior and exterior, as in our feelings.

What the neuroscientist Antonio Damasio calls *'the feeling of what happens'* is based completely on what he calls 'background feelings'.[3] 'These feelings are not in the foreground of our minds [. . .] In one way or another, however, background feelings help define our mental state and color our lives.'

Damasio quotes Malebranche on this subject: 'It is through light and through a clear idea that the mind sees the essence of things, numbers and extensions. It is through a vague idea or through feeling that the mind judges the existence of creatures and that it knows its own existence.'[4] In summary, he emphasizes how the consciousness we have of, and bring to, our inner states considerably enriches our thinking and gives us a sense of identity.[5]

Can we observe ourselves?

As soon as we start to look closely at something, we modify it. In the same way, the consciousness we have, or strive to have, of our feelings modifies them: it can make them last longer, disappear or change. Like an estuary, our consciousness is a place where the internal and the external, the intentional and the unintentional, flow into each other. A space of infinite richness and infinite complexity. And then, as soon as we try to observe one of our feelings, we realize that in fact, instead of observing it, we are watching ourselves in the process of observing it. It is rather like trying to stalk wild animals: at first we only succeed in making them run away. Then, gradually, we understand the situation better and learn the trick of approaching very slowly, downwind. Any attempt to become acquainted with our feelings requires the same patience: developing self-awareness is a skill that needs to be learned.

This leads us to the realization that there are different levels of self-awareness.

It can be *rudimentary* or embryonic. This is the case at those times in our lives when we are overwhelmed with *'things to do'*, suffocating under the demands of our circumstances and only really capable of two basic states: doing and sleeping. We are constantly in the midst either of doing something or of recuperating from it, and consequently introspection and self-reflection are non-existent: no time, no energy, no desire.

It can be *clear*. Thanks to certain moments when we have time to feel ourselves existing without being in the grip of overwhelming emotions or pressing external pressures. But also as a result of regular training and patient and attentive work (meditation, keeping a diary).

It can be *superior*. As in the case of those people who have set aside a significant part of their lives for reflection and meditation. Or for any of us when we experience what I shall be discussing later in this book under the name of *moments of awareness*.

Becoming an expert on your own feelings

The tradition of self-knowledge and self-awareness is an ancient one. The modern notion of interiority is often attributed to St Augustine in his *Confessions*.[6] For the first time, someone was talking about their inner life, about their feelings and moods and about their personal journey. It was, of course, a piece of propaganda for the Christian faith, but one which followed, in a moving and convincing manner, the inner journey. Prior to Augustine, people thought in terms of 'we' rather than 'I'. And when Socrates said 'Know yourself', he was not urging us to discover the joys of introspection but rather to the awareness that each of us needs to have of their own limits if they are to hold to their rightful place, since he went on to add 'Know that you are not a god, and act accordingly.'[7]

Much later, in his *Essays*, Montaigne put the 'game of I' onto a more spontaneous and less militant level, offering his readers a self-portrait made up of his reading, reflections and life experiences. Nor did he attempt to conceal any of the difficulties of what he was trying to do: 'We go forward with the current, but to turn back towards ourselves is a painful motion.'[8] It is true that introspection is also – or should be – an act of lucidity, a lucidity which can be defined as 'the love of truth, even if the truth is distasteful'.[9] Knowing oneself certainly often involves some element of disappointment. But that is no reason to denigrate yourself or to flee from yourself.

For our modern sensibilities, it is of course *Rousseau* who introduced the art of introspection in the modern era with his *Confessions*. Here is what he says in his *Discourse on the Arts and Sciences*:[10] 'O Virtue! Sublime science of simple souls, are so many troubles and trappings necessary to know you? Are your principles not engraved in all hearts, and is it not enough in order to learn your laws *to commune with oneself and listen to the voice of one's conscience* in the silence of the passions?' (The italics are mine.) For the highly sensitive Jean-Jacques, self-knowledge, once the tumult of our immediate reactions has abated, is in addition the antechamber of virtue.

Returning to introspection: in what circumstances ought we to break off regularly from our actions and our judgements in order to examine what is going on within us?

In moments of *suffering*, of course, which bring us so forcibly back to ourselves. Take, for example, the unhappy love affairs of the poet Guillaume Apollinaire, 'conscious of his suffering, giving himself up to it willingly, the better to describe it'.[11]

In moments of *fulfilment*: when we are aware of a harmony between our feelings and moods and the circumstances in which we find ourselves. For example, when we feel joyful in joyful surroundings. At such

moments, we become conscious of our feelings because they are in tune
and in harmony with our surroundings; and this awareness brings us an
acute sense of belonging.

In moments of *disharmony*: when our feelings are incompatible or clash
with our surroundings. For example, when we feel in a sad mood in joyful
surroundings. The awareness of this discrepancy is always painful: 'Why
can't I manage to feel happy at this party, in this life, in this relationship,
this job?' Once again it is the failure of the famous 'every reason to be
happy'. A useful and almost comforting failure, reminding us each time
that happiness does not inevitably result simply from the accumulation of
fortuitous circumstances. This realization can sometimes also come from
feelings which are not painful but which leave us with a troubling sense of
being out of step with other people: 'I am odd, not like other people, and
not like I normally am.'

Finally, in moments of *autonomy*: when in spite of negative surroundings we somehow feel uplifted. Such moods leave us with a curious
sensation of strength and amazement, as though acting like some kind of
internal umbrella against adversity.

Many of us have also experienced intense and enjoyable feelings and
moods under the influence of alcohol or other drugs, which, contrary to
what is sometimes thought, can also help us open up to ourselves and
to the world. Not surprisingly, psychiatrists tend to focus more on those
people who have been enslaved and ravaged by alcohol; but perhaps they
should look more closely at all those others who manage, through the use
of alcohol, to experience (albeit fleetingly) moods of tranquillity, kindness
and confidence. Can lessons be learned from our occasions of mild drunk-
enness? Why do we not say to ourselves more often 'If I feel like this after
drinking, if I feel better even though nothing else has changed, it means
the solution lies in me, if I could only reproduce these light-hearted, confident moods without resorting to alcohol'? Or should some people avoid,
as in a board game, 'landing on the alcohol square' and instead go directly
to the 'introspection' square?

Getting in touch with our feelings: introspection

Reflecting on yourself is no easy matter: remember what Jean Anouilh's
character has to say on the subject in the epigraph to this chapter. In fact,
it is simply a matter of taking the time to do it. Our society encourages us
to be constantly either entertaining ourselves or responding to some kind
of stimulus, consuming things or obeying social, professional or family
demands. In short, we are encouraged to distance ourselves from who we
really are.

Yet introspection needs time and leisure: sadly these are two qualities
which have become rare and precious in an era where every moment
has to be filled and accounted for, in this age of constant *distraction*.

Etymologically, 'distract' (from the Latin *distractus*) means drawn apart: by 'distracting' ourselves, we spend our time never being ourselves.

It is true that it is no easy matter to focus on our inner selves. Try it now. Put this book down, and try to observe your feelings and moods for a few minutes, five for example. Observe what is happening inside you. Well? Your mind is going in all directions. You find yourself thinking about all manner of little things, you notice a slight buzzing in your ears, a bit of an ache in your back. You feel as though you are 'incapable of concentrating', or at any rate not enough to be able to observe your feelings. In the end the whole process begins to irritate or depress you, and you long to return to the security of *doing* (quickly, do something) rather than linger with the uncertainty of *being* (simply being there and seeing what happens, without expectations). That is perfectly normal.

Most of us are similarly incapable of spontaneously praying, meditating, even of genuinely observing a minute's silence in honour of someone who is absent or no longer with us. Too many distractions and, above all, a lack of training. And yet our need to work on getting back in touch with ourselves is greater than ever, living as we do in an era which is constantly stealing our time and attention. We need time to reflect on our lives instead of rushing from one activity to the next. We need to inhabit our lives fully instead of simply filling them.

It is a task which is both attainable and fruitful. Research has shown that the careful and calm scrutiny (without ruminating!) of our negative moods can mitigate their potential damage.[12] Practising introspection also enables us to become aware of all the self-polluting and stressful little thoughts we inflict on ourselves when we are in a negative frame of mind. This reminds me of my patients' surprise during group therapy sessions when I catch them staring into space for a moment and ask 'What kind of thoughts are going through your mind right now?' (I do not say 'What are you thinking of?' because they are not *thinking* about anything at all, they are simply *inhabited* by thoughts.) Surprised by the question, they immediately make the effort to become aware of their feelings and moods and often discover that they are in the process of ruminating; they may not have been aware of it, but they were ruminating; and usually on negative thoughts.

As I write this, I remember Sylvie, a patient of mine who was extremely kind but who had major problems of self-esteem and was suffering from depression and social phobia. In the course of a group meditation session to help prevent relapses into depression, we were working on gratitude:[13] each person in the group had been asked to think every evening of a moment in the course of the day when he or she had felt gratitude towards another human being. She made us all smile when she told us that one day she had felt gratitude 'towards the person who had invented diet Coke', her favourite drink (she would enjoy one every evening, when she got home). We moved on to other things but I could tell from her faraway look that she was no longer concentrating. Guessing what might be happening, I asked her what was wrong: she admitted that she was ruminating over what she had said, that she thought she must have sounded silly with her diet Coke example, and that the examples of gratitude that the others had come up with seemed much more intelligent. Whereas, for the therapists and for the other patients, her example was, on the contrary, evidence of genuine reflection and sincere originality. But, in the meantime, she was in the process of becoming bogged down in painful feelings and moods without even being fully aware of it herself. We had only recently begun the therapy . . .

Getting in touch with our feelings: moments of illumination

By *illumination* I mean here all those experiences which are outside our control, those feelings that suddenly surge into our consciousness, out of the blue. These are moments when we are suddenly acutely aware of life, of its inner worlds, through the feelings and moods which come over us unexpectedly. Such moments of illumination, of heightened awareness, require complete acceptance of the experience of the present moment. These experiences can also be retrospective: we understand at a later stage why a particular moment changed our view of the world and moved us so profoundly.

Moments of illumination can occur at any time: a child crying, a single star shining in the winter sky, the sound of our footsteps in a deserted street, an old poster hanging torn and forgotten on a wall . . .

When people talk about such moments, they describe a range of sensations: like a tear in the veil which was preventing us from seeing, a door opening into an adjacent room and suddenly allowing us to see beauty and harmony or the unsuspected suffering and vulnerability of those close to us or of any human being.

When people talk about these experiences, they often refer to the simplest of things: an object, a sound, a light, a memory which suddenly stops us in our tracks. We pause inwardly, aware that something is happening, even though nothing appears to have changed.

When people analyse such moments, they realize that these simple things, these simple moments, are in fact linked to something important, something very important: the absence of someone we love which opens our eyes to the importance of that love (parents going into the bedroom of a child who is away on holiday), or a falling leaf which awakens in us an awareness of death and of eternity. These are not hallucinatory or ecstatic experiences: the world remains the same, but is simply seen through different eyes, through the eyes of the whole being and not only from an intellectual or utilitarian perspective. It is as though everything is clear and transparent.

Sometimes we simply continue on our way without being enriched by the experience. But, at other times, it remains with us forever.

These experiences of sudden awareness can be subtle or overwhelming. They are always moments of opening up to the world, and in the end should be seen with that sense of wonder described by Michel Edwards, poet and professor at the Collège de France:[14] 'Being filled with wonder gives us a sense of beginning. [. . .] The experience of wonder is also the presentiment of something else, the conviction of some potential yet to be fulfilled in ourselves and in everything we see. Do we not suddenly see [. . .] that there is another way to live?' For him, the sense of wonder serves to 'reveal to us what the world could be like if we experienced it on a deeper level'. Our moments of illumination are like so many wonders bursting in upon our lives.

At a later stage in this book we will look in more detail at how we can cultivate such moments: by connecting with nature, regularly seeking moments of quiet contemplation (stepping into a church or a place of worship in an overcrowded and noisy town, sitting down, focusing on our breathing and observing what comes to us; and doing it as often as possible), learning to meditate.

If we seek such moments of intense awareness, it is important to free ourselves from permanent and invisible social influences, like that of advertising, which has insidiously accustomed us to function along the lines of 'look here, look there'. Our lives should not be a guided visit led by people who want to make us buy their useless junk or to sell us their activities to fill up our time. Like those coach tours where the bus stops in front of the souvenir stalls and the holiday-makers end up spending more time in these than in the places they are supposed to be visiting and admiring. We shall be looking in detail at these moments of awareness and at the battles against the pollution of our minds.

Getting in touch with our feelings: keeping a diary

I have a confession to make: I keep a diary. Well, the word 'diary' is somewhat ambitious; let us say that I always have a little black notebook with me in which I write as much as possible – and as quickly as possible, before the memory of my feelings and moods fades with time – about anything I find touching or interesting. These jottings are not *thoughts* – there is nothing finished or polished about them – they are feelings, impressions, 'things seen and experienced', which are the foundations and the breeding ground from which all my subsequent reflections and 'thoughts' (when are any!) spring. They are my encounters with people, with the world, with nature. Ordinary lives contain so many interesting things. All the anecdotes in this book originate in these notebooks. I have a very bad memory and am incapable of making things up, of creating things. I could never have been a novelist: I can only write about what I have seen, heard or experienced.

Naturally, I love re-reading what I have written. It is like living it all over again. Indeed, if I did not enjoy going back to them, if it was not for the pleasure of rediscovering the emotion behind these encounters with life, I would very soon tire of keeping these notebooks. For it is tiring and time-consuming work. And no easy task: putting things down in writing brings them into sharp focus. It gets rid of any illusions we might harbour too: once on paper, many of the ideas that seemed so brilliant in our heads suddenly start to look rather banal; many of the brainwaves which seemed so promising turn out to be rather vague. A diary is often an excellent antidote to intellectual laziness and over-inflated egos: it forces us to work hard and to think carefully. And to be selective too, for not everything in the vast tumult of our feelings and moods is worthy of attention. This is what the New Zealand writer Katherine Mansfield wrote in one of her novels:[15] 'I don't believe in the human soul. I never have. I believe that people are like portmanteaux – packed with certain things, started going, thrown about, tossed away, dumped down, lost and found, [. . .] until finally the Ultimate Porter swings them on to the Ultimate Train and away they rattle.'

Well, if we remain convinced that our feelings and moods have meaning, a little meaning at least, then the diary is the perfect observation post. The American writer Thoreau referred to his journal as 'a calendar of the ebbs and flows of the soul'. And Jules Renard pointed out that the vocation of a diary is that of a place where we can work on ourselves: 'Our diaries must not simply be idle gossip as is too often the case with Goncourt. They must help us to form our character, to correct it constantly, to restore it to equanimity.'[16]

Diary writing as self-therapy?

But diaries are not only of interest to writers. In addition to the pleasure of introspection, what also interests psychiatrists and psychologists is that a considerable number of studies have shown that keeping a diary is good for our health, that it can exert a calming effect on our emotions in difficult times in our lives.

One of the pioneers of the scientific approach to the benefits of 'expressive writing' was the American psychologist James Pennebaker.[17] One of his first studies was based on a very simple protocol: it involved asking volunteers who were not suffering from any particular psychological difficulties to write about the most traumatic experience of their lives, every day for four days, for an uninterrupted period of 15 minutes (this instruction about the duration of the activity was given particular emphasis, and indeed meant that there was sufficient time for the subject to be addressed properly without distraction and in sufficient detail). The participants were divided into two groups: one group was encouraged to describe their feelings in detail, the other was instructed to 'relativize' and to write in a 'dispassionate' way.

At the end of the experiment, the group who had written 'in detail' about their feelings – as opposed to the 'dispassionate' group – were found to have benefited substantially in terms of their subjective well-being in the medium term (over the next fortnight) and also objectively in terms of their long-term health (on average they needed fewer medical appointments over the following year). The immediate psychological effects, on the other hand, were not very comfortable: many of the participants in the group writing 'in detail about their feelings' said they had found this experiment in 'expressive writing' disturbing, though they still considered it to be interesting and enriching on a personal level.

Incidentally, and this probably explains the above, the authors of the experiment were surprised at the high number of painful and often traumatic life events (rapes, suicides, mental illness, drug addiction) which featured in these accounts – and in the lives – of these upper middle-class American students. A comment on the universal nature of our suffering and our hurt.

Pennebaker subsequently carried out a number of additional studies which further confirmed the power of writing not only to clarify and soothe our painful feelings and moods, but also to have a similar effect on our biological variables (improvements in immune reactions or blood pressure, for example). Other studies followed, led by other researchers and other teams, confirming the benefits of writing about what is on our minds. Many studies have pointed to the reduction in the number and intensity of depressive symptoms in a wide variety of people, ranging from students[18] to women who had suffered severe trauma,[19] and including patients undergoing psychotherapy, when writing was found to enhance the benefits of the therapy.[20] It should be emphasized that we are not talking about *curing* the illnesses in question, but about making what are nevertheless substantial improvements in the condition of people suffering from them. The writing cure needs to be used in combination with other efforts but its role is nevertheless extremely interesting. Expressive writing has also been recommended with considerable success to people who have suffered from an episode of depression in the past, and who are therefore at risk from further episodes.[21]

Writing a diary: a users' guide

On the basis of this data which initially focused on painful and even severely traumatic experiences, we can formulate a number of rules to guide us in writing a diary.

First, the efficacy of the *writing cure* hinges on an obvious fact: in order to come to terms with a painful experience, we must first acknowledge and accept it, if we are then to go on to talk or write about it. Which is why denial and 'emotional retention' have such serious consequences in terms of damage to physical and moral health. Next, putting something into words and a narrative brings increased coherence to events and moods which might otherwise feel somewhat unfinished. And 'unfinished' is psychologically toxic: few of us are capable of feeling at ease with emotional issues which have been closed without being properly 'dealt with' (cf. the Zeigarnik effect already referred to). Moreover, studies comparing the effect of talking about, writing down or simply reflecting on painful life experiences clearly demonstrate that writing and discussion are far more beneficial than solitary reflection.[22] Why is 'simple' reflection often of such little use? Because it quickly degenerates into rumination! Whereas it is much more difficult to ruminate in writing:[23] the process which seemed perfectly acceptable when it was going on in our minds suddenly seems absurd and toxic.

In fact, one of the healing mechanisms of writing lies in the reorganization of the painful experience which otherwise often continues to generate chaotic and confused feelings and moods. The act of making ourselves transcribe these feelings into a coherent written account has a beneficial effect. One could point out that a discussion with a close and sympathetic person could produce the same effect. Except that, in the case of a verbal exchange, we are more aware of the other person, we (usually) feel more concerned about not boring or upsetting them. In addition, the person we are talking to will respond, which may either complicate our task (if they fail to understand or disapprove) or simplify it (if they anticipate us and are able to help us bring out our feelings). Also, in the context of a verbal exchange, the more support we receive, the less space there is for our own words and thoughts to keep flowing. Which sometimes exonerates us from searching thoroughly inside ourselves and uncovering certain deeply hidden feelings. Which is why solitary writing is so important, since it forces us to explore our thoughts to the limits. On the same subject, it is worth noting that the progressive decline in letter writing in favour of phone calls, e-mails and texts is in the process of provoking considerable psychological shifts as immediate and rapid interaction replaces more prolonged attention. These changes may indeed be beneficial to the social animal in us. But they are definitely less good for the mental animal we also are, and for the understanding of our feelings and moods.

Let us return to the diary. Giving coherence to our feelings and moods by writing about them has an undeniable therapeutic effect. This restoration of coherence to life experiences people have been confronted with is beneficial in depression, for example, where studies have shown that the more the writing started to include links of causality or temporality (like *that's why, thus, so, and then*) and words linked to introspection (like *I understood that, I realized that*), the more progress was likely to follow.[24] In a way, these expressions are indicative of a restored sense of coherence and self-understanding. Similar results have also been demonstrated by analysing the spontaneous verbal utterances of patients suffering from depression and undergoing psychotherapy at different stages of their recovery.[25]

Similarly, an interesting study was carried out to look at how expressive writing could subtly affect social discourse: volunteer writers had agreed to wear a small microphone which recorded their conversations, in 30-second 'snatches' every 12 minutes, over a period of several days. The idea was to find out not so much *what* they were saying as *how* they were saying it. The findings showed that, in comparison with the 'prediary' period, the fact of having made the effort to put their feelings down in writing resulted in an increased frequency of positive words and of verbs in the future tense.[26] Happiness is possible once we have accepted our pain, and focusing our attention (provisionally) on ourselves enables us to look towards the future.

What also seems to be beneficial is the way feelings and moods gradually evolve as the writing process continues, rather than being a cut-and-dried matter obvious from the very outset. In the studies, people whose stories were already coherent and well-constructed benefited less from the writing process than those whose initial understanding of their feelings and moods was of a more limited nature. What matters is the process of construction and comprehension. If everything is clear from the start, and yet the symptoms of suffering still persist, there may be grounds to suspect that the account produced by the individual is more about protective 'off-the-shelf' thoughts than genuine introspection. Therapists are all too familiar with such patients with their well-rehearsed discourse who give the impression they are telling their story for the hundredth time. If improvement is to take place, there must be introspection and not simply a recital of facts.

Another important piece of advice: write down your feelings without necessarily and frantically seeking to resolve them instantly ('Why do I have these feelings? How am I going to get rid of them?'). The opposite of rumination is not rushing immediately to take action but instead engaging in clear and calm reflection. First write things down, take a close look at them, understand what has happened, what impact it has had on us, be precise and honest, without disguising or hiding the truth of our feelings.[27]

Following on from this, attention needs to be given to the choice of style. This was demonstrated in another study in which volunteers were invited to write a short piece after experiencing some kind of failure. They were instructed to use one of two writing styles: either 'experiential' (a blow-by-blow description of *how* they felt during and after the situation), or 'evaluative' (describing *why* they felt like that). The use of the second style aggravated the situation for everyone, with a greater number of intrusive thoughts in the ensuing hours.[28]

So, in your diary, describe in detail what has happened, before (and sometimes *instead of*) examining the causes; the *why* can wait until later when emotional activity has calmed down.

Studies have also sought to identify which people benefit most from expressive writing: as so often in psychotherapy, it turns out to be those who are starting from the lowest point. This is the 'floor' effect: the worse a person is at the beginning of a treatment, the higher the percentage of improvement will be. Very often these are people who in normal circumstances do not express their feelings and do not want either to admit to them or to focus on them in detail. In other words, they are more often men (rather than women). More often individuals who frequently experience hostile feelings: those with anger problems or suppressed anger, rather than genuinely peaceful people, who are more inclined to challenge the legitimacy of their feelings of annoyance. More often people with alexithymia; in other words, those individuals who find it difficult to identify or name their emotions. And more often 'big ruminators', rather than 'small-scale' ones (given that everyone indulges in rumination to some extent.) For the last of these, writing forces them to confront the problem genuinely instead of going through the motions of thinking about it and ending up feeling even worse. The effort of writing clearly unblocks the *'cogitatus interruptus'* typical of rumination. Indeed, research on written accounts of feelings and moods by people prone to rumination shows a further benefit in terms of social behaviour (on top of internal well-being): the individuals involved sought out opportunities for genuine exchanges of communication rather than simply looking for an ear to pour their woes into.[29]

Finally, as is often the case in attempts at self-help, positive expectations are extremely important and diary writing should not be undertaken without convictions. When it comes to our feelings and moods, there is no point in pretending: sincerity alone matters and has benefits for our well-being.[30] Let words and feelings flow freely from the pen. Remembering that 'words are older and more powerful than the men who speak them'.[31]

Introspection: above all a way of opening up to the world

Should we rely on our feelings and moods to open us up to the world? Indeed we must.

In his *Conseils spirituels* Maître Eckhart, a Dominican monk and medieval Rhenish mystic who died or disappeared in mysterious circumstances in 1327 on the way to Avignon, where he was going to defend his ideas in front of the papal Curia, wrote:

> Should you wish to plunge deep into yourself with all your internal and external faculties, you would then reach a state without images or constraints, where interior or exterior activity were absent. [. . .] That does not mean that we should run away from our interiority, detach ourselves from it or deny it, indeed the opposite is true: we must learn to act in it, with it and by it. In such a way that interiority turns into effective action and effective action leads back to interiority once more, and we accustom ourselves then to acting without compulsion.[32]

Eckhart was not urging us to abandon the world in order to approach a state of Grace, but rather to frequent it. For him, spiritual awakening meant going through two stages: 'being amongst things and close to people', then 'making a blessing out of everything'. Our work on feelings and moods seeks to do exactly that.

Part Two

Suffering

Crossings and rebirths

Living: suffering

Anxious minds, heavy hearts, prisons and the erosion of resentment. Despair.

No more struggling, tirelessly learning to let the wave pass over us, like a swimmer who has not yet drowned. Accept suffering, welcome it, yes welcome it and observe it: there is always a way out somewhere. Hold on, hold on, breathe inwardly, and, above all, keep your eyes open.

There it is, the way out . . .

You are walking in Paris alone inside a crowd
Herds of buses bellow and come too close
Love's anguish clutches your throat
You must never again be loved.
Guillaume Apollinaire, Zone

Chapter 5

Painful feelings and moods

It's not just that the spirit, when the flesh ails, falls ill too,
But often it's tormented by what hasn't happened yet,
Sick with dread, worn out with fretting; or gnawed at with regret
For sins that were committed sometime in the past. And add
Ailments that are only of the mind, like going mad,
Or losing the memory of things. And add that it sinks down
Whelmed beneath the pitchy waters of Oblivion.

Lucretius, *On the Nature of Things*

'A short time after your father's death, you came to spend a few days in the family home to help your mother sort out his things, because it was too hard for her to do on her own.

You came across piles of papers he had hoarded in his desk, tiny fragments of his existence: letters from friends, postcards from places he had loved, correspondence from the latter years of his working life, when he had been unable to find a job and was in great distress. At the time (you were a schoolboy) you had not fully realized the sheer intensity of that distress, but it was unmistakable in these copies of the cover letters for job applications, letters in which he had tried to convince hypothetical employers who no longer wanted him because he was too old and unqualified. A distress you also felt as you went through the files where he painstakingly stored both the letters and their replies, all of them negative. What must he have felt, as the files grew ever fatter, month after month? Gradually his own letters dried up, until eventually, he stopped writing altogether. After that he took to treating his despair with alcohol, that old friend who never lets you down and slowly but surely kills you in the end.

This was a pre-psychological man if ever there was one. And there were many of them in his day: *Never complain, never explain.* Never share the feelings which, in any case, you are trying desperately not to feel.

All alone in this quiet and gloomy study where he used to hide himself away, right at the back of the house, you began to understand the distress and solitude which had engulfed him at that time. You thought again about the sufferings you have come across in your own life: the friends on the point of divorce, a girl friend who is dying, your children crying at their grandfather's funeral, the youngest daughter, sitting on your lap during the mass and whose hiccups and sobs you felt in your own body, as her tears soaked your hands. A simple and banal moment of vertigo, a sudden awareness of human suffering. Then slowly came a gradual stirring of your feelings, memories of sufferings, moments from your childhood, memories of your sadness on the beach where you and your family went every summer, you saw again the poor carpet sellers making their way along in the blazing heat, bent double under their wares, desperately hoping to sell one of their miserable rugs. You never saw anyone buying one and that haunted you.

Outside, in the garden, a blackbird was singing.'

Pain and suffering

Is there a difference between pain and suffering? By pain, we mean the starting point, an unpleasant sensation or feeling. The word 'suffering', on the other hand, is used more to describe the subjective impact of the pain. To suffer therefore means enduring, putting up with pain.

There is physical pain (such as everyone has experienced, at least to a minimal degree, such as toothache, or back pain) and mental pain (like bereavement or unhappy love affairs).

You can see what I am getting at: whereas pain originates from anatomical lesions and is unambiguous, suffering always has a psychological element (an element only): feelings and moods have their part to play. Notably in the vicious circle of suffering and pain in which pain forces us spontaneously to cut ourselves off from the world and focus on ourselves, thereby creating even more space in our minds for suffering. And suffering gradually becomes a rumination on the pain, incessantly returning to it.

Pain is always unwelcome. And everything must be done to avoid it, whenever possible: removing a stone from a shoe, taking a painkiller for toothache, prescribing morphine for metastases in cancer patients.

Pain should not have to be tolerated where a solution can be found either to alleviate it, or better still, to remove it altogether.

Pain does not make us grow, it diminishes us. It does not enrich us, it shrinks and weakens us. It is an alienation from the world around us, imprisoning us in ourselves. Fighting pain is exhausting and uses all our energy. We could be doing other things. Pain is destructive, making us vulnerable rather than strengthening us. Alphonse Daudet (author of 'Mr Seguin's goat' and 'Little good-for-nothing' in *Letters from My Mill*) devoted an autobiographical work to his experience of the neuropathic pain associated with the tertiary syphilis which would eventually carry him off. He called it *La Doulou* (Provençal for 'pain') and painted a far from rosy picture: 'My pain fills the horizon and colours everything in sight. Gone is the phase where pain can make a better person and deepen understanding; gone too the one where it embitters, where the voice and the whole physical mechanism are little more than a groan. Now it is a hard, stagnant, painful torpor. An indifference to everything.'

Ötzi, Buddha and Jesus

Modern medicine means pain can be substantially reduced and in our daily lives we suffer far less than people did in the past.

We have largely forgotten today the extent to which our ancestors experienced physical suffering. How for them, pain was always present, at the heart of the human experience. The history of medicine shows us that the humans who came before us suffered a great deal: analysis of their bones reveals, for example, that many of them developed premature arthritis and tuberculosis of the bones, both extremely painful conditions. There were large-scale sufferings (for example, the high mortality rate of children and women in childbirth) and smaller-scale ones (head-lice, fleas, cold, lack of comfort). Studies of the body of Ötzi, the prehistoric man found in perfect condition in the Alps in 1991,[1] revealed that he was riddled with arthritis and infested with parasites. He was about forty years old.

Pain was so omnipresent that for a long time the predominant Western approach was to see the battle against suffering as a sign of inner strength: 'Man is an apprentice, pain is his master, / And no one can know himself, who has not suffered.'[2]

One of my friends, a talented psychiatrist but subject to depression, once said, when I asked how he was getting on, 'Well! I'm suffering as usual, but as long as I'm suffering I know I'm still alive, so . . .' A fine motto, this: 'I suffer therefore I am.' And the recognition that suffering is an inevitable part of our lives is no doubt an important stage. But it should never be more than just a stage: the more important thing is what we are going to do once it is over.

This relationship with suffering has been a central question in major religions and philosophical movements. In the past, Christianity gave it a disproportionate emphasis: Adam and Eve chased out of Paradise and condemned to suffer (this is the point in Genesis where we find the expressions 'In the sweat of thy face shalt thou eat bread', 'in sorrow thou shalt bring forth children'), Jesus taking on our sins and suffering for us to the point of agony, the martyrs of the early church, the redemptive dimension of suffering . . .

I recall from my childhood the big pictures of those martyrs thrown to the lions that our teachers showed us in history lessons: I found myself thinking, somewhat ashamedly, that I would have far preferred to kiss the feet of the Roman gods, whom I thought generally rather picturesque, than to endure such suffering. Later, in my secondary school, our Greek teacher told us the story of Epictetus, the Stoic philosopher who was subjected to various tortures by his cruel master. As this brutish master was about to crush his leg, Epictetus said calmly to him 'You're going to break it.' And then 'You've broken it, I said you would.' And the story too of the young Spartan who had rescued a fox cub and hidden it in his tunic. Reprimanded by his tutors for fidgeting, he said nothing and remained impassive, even though the fox cub was in the process of devouring his stomach. Brr! I still tremble at the thought of it. No wonder I wanted to become a doctor! Later still, I discovered to my amazement that in Buddhism, the role of suffering is just as central as it is in Western culture, but with some differences regarding how to respond to it.

The legendary story of the young prince Siddhartha Gautama tells us that, escaping the gilded existence he had led in his father's palace, he discovered, over the course of four famous journeys, the reality of the human condition, meeting first with an old man (we are going to grow old), then with a sick person (we are going to suffer), then a dead man (we are going to die), then a monk (we can take action). After a whole lifetime of adventures and reflection, the person who had in the meantime become a *Buddha* (a Sanskrit word meaning 'enlightened') set out his famous 'Four Noble Truths': (1) suffering exists; (2) suffering can come at any time; (3) suffering can cease; (4) there is a path which leads to the cessation of suffering.[3]

Jesus and Buddha both sought to ease human suffering. Jesus did so in the guise of a miracle worker, an extraordinary healer and therapist, while Buddha took on the role more of the master and teacher (which his long life – about eighty years – made possible). Even though I love the figure of Jesus passionately, it seems to me as a doctor that when it comes to suffering, Buddha's teaching has more to offer us in our daily lives. Buddhism has after all been referred to as a 'healing doctrine'.[4] This is what is currently happening in psychotherapeutic practice: an integration of certain elements of the Buddhist tradition into the treatment of physical and mental suffering. We will return to this subject later.

Working on the avoidable element of our suffering?

Clearly there are two essential elements in our suffering: (1) the cause, which is not always accessible or modifiable; (2) our attitude to it, which is partially in our control.

It is important that each individual understands how to cope with the sufferings life brings. Whenever I see a new patient for the first time, I spend a long time discussing what has worked, or not worked, in any previous attempts to relieve their suffering. Medication? Personal efforts? How do they cope with pain? By seeking distraction? Throwing themselves into frantic activity? Gritting their teeth? Sometimes I also ask how much suffering they are prepared to accept in their lives. To show, or suggest, that it is perhaps this we should be aiming for, rather than the total and triumphant suppression of all pain. But, and this is important, I make it very clear that we are going to take action in response to the suffering. I do not really believe in suffering as an opportunity for growth, or at least I have no lessons to offer on that subject. I have more often encountered suffering which stunted people, hardening and diminishing them. My attitude is not therefore 'Endure!' but rather 'Pain is an inevitable part of our existence. That means some degree of suffering is also inevitable. Let us accept that. Then let's look at what we can do about the causes of the pain. And limit the element of suffering.' I call this 'working on the avoidable aspects of our suffering'. These may be limited (if I have toothache) but are often significant (particularly in mental suffering). All our experiences of suffering contain an element which we can learn from and an element which destroys us. Let us not forget the former by categorically refusing to suffer, but let us not ignore the latter either.

Montaigne and Nietzsche

With regard to suffering, philosophers have often expressed the conviction that we should not insist on eliminating it altogether. Montaigne wrote: 'Neither is pain always to be shunned, nor pleasure always to be pursued.'[5] And Nietzsche added: 'The worst disease of mankind has arisen from the struggle against diseases.'

The fight against the suffering caused by mental pain is not simply a matter of a few sporadic efforts but instead a radical rethink of our relationship with the world. It requires self-awareness, a relentless and thorough 'mental training' based on appropriate exercises. We need to bring an ecological approach to our feelings about suffering: like a gardener or a farmer avoiding weed-killers and chemical fertilizers which will poison the earth and make things worse in the long term, we should opt for long-term solutions and avoid artificial ones (alcohol, drugs and sometimes sedatives even when these are not needed). When confronted with suffering, we need to consider how long it might go on for: a whole lifetime! And we need to consider what is at stake: our well-being, our lucidity, our freedom.

It all starts, as we shall see, with acceptance. Just as we cannot leave a place we have never accepted arriving in, so we cannot escape from suffering unless we have acknowledged its existence. We need to keep returning to the starting point of what *is* rather than what *should be*. Not 'I shouldn't have to suffer so much, why, why?' but rather 'This suffering is here. I have to accept it. And then, take action in order to limit it, to dilute it, to absorb it into my life. But for that to happen I have to start living again instead of only focusing on the suffering.' We need to be able to look around us, to begin to move on.

Chapter 6

Anxieties

Nobody punishes themselves as much as I do, and for everything. For the slightest thing is a pretext for torment. And I can do nothing about it.

Cioran, *Cahiers 1957–1972*

'During a long period of my life, I would wake up early in the morning, at about 5 or 6 o'clock, already tormented with anxiety about what lay ahead: a whole day to be faced. Mondays were the worst (after the melancholy of Sunday evenings): a *whole week* to get through! I would get up quickly, and get myself going, anything to reduce the anxiety, to bury the sense of unease in activity. By Monday evening, things already started to feel better. The countdown to Friday had, unconsciously no doubt, already begun in my mind.

This agonizing solitude on first waking up did not stop when I got married, even with a partner at my side: I was hardly going to wake her up at 5 o'clock every morning to tell her about my anxieties and to hear myself saying there was nothing to worry about! I felt so vulnerable in those waking moments when you are not yet connected to other people, to projects, to things that need doing, to the world! At those times we are alone, naked in our condition as fragile human beings. It is like the moment when a computer is first switched on and yet still seems frozen, that instant before it connects to the internet and locates its software, word processing, spreadsheets, etc.

In these awful wakening moments which await 'life's worriers', as my children call them – unaware of the extent to which I am one – our psychological defences are not fully in place: all those projects, plans, 'things to do' that enslave yet comfort us, until our anxieties come back to haunt us again.

I was like Sisyphus, condemned by the gods to everlastingly pushing his rock up to the top of the mountain and seeing it roll back down again each time. This struggle with anxiety had to be begun all over again in my head each morning. My worries, when it came down to it, were worries about living.

And yet my life was a perfectly ordinary one with only the normal worries, the harmless upheavals. As Cioran observes: 'We are all jokers: we survive our problems.' So I survived. But what a struggle. With occasional pangs of guilt, and new anxieties: there are those worse off than you, think about people who *really* have problems, *genuine* problems, think about people who are ill, for example. And, incidentally, if I wake up like that when I am in perfect health, what would it be like if I was really ill? I often thought about that: what must it be like to wake up and then suddenly remember you have cancer?

How can we live with both physical and mental anxiety? How can we deal with that?'

Yes, how indeed?

Worries and anxieties

In order to understand anxiety and anguish we need to understand worry. Worry is this 'state of being anxious or troubled over actual or potential problems'.

The object of our worries is every possible aspect of daily life: the health or wealth we would like to have, or have but are afraid of losing; the love, affection, esteem others have or do not have for us; things that need doing, bills to pay, absences, delays, unexpected events. We shall see later that the tendency to worry, especially in its pathological forms, is based on a major intolerance of uncertainty. The question 'What is going to happen?' immediately throws opens the floodgates for all kinds of anxious rumination.

These worries gives us little respite or rest. Which is why they lead to anxiety: to feel anxious is to be in a state of unease, of disquiet. This mood is described in detail by Portuguese writer Fernando Pessoa in *The Book of Disquiet*.

It is interesting that in English (and in French) the term *worry* is used indifferently to describe the source (a worry) and the phenomenon (to worry). This overlap speaks for itself: when we worry, part of the boundary between what is happening and what we think about it breaks down, and we can confuse our worrying (internal state, personal vision of things, intimate feelings of insecurity) with the worries that life puts in our way. When we are worried, we frequently lose the capacity to step back from things as well as the ability to distinguish between 'What is happening?' and 'What do I think about it?'

Worry, as a feeling, is therefore often an amplification of *worries*, in the sense of annoying or upsetting events. But these are no figment of the imagination, no *ex nihilo* creation: the worry events generally really do exist. They take many forms . . .

There are macro-worries, such as worries about the future of the world. One of my patients, who was suffering from a minor form of schizophrenia, referred to what he called his 'metaphysical anxieties'. He would sometimes telephone for an urgent appointment: 'My meta-physical anxieties are back!' He would worry desperately about the end of the world, about the risk of the sun exploding, about atomic war or widespread terrorist attacks. As a child, in addition to the usual anxieties about death and what lies beyond it, he was already tormenting himself with anguished thoughts about heaven, normally a comforting notion. Unfortunately his childish anxiety transformed this potential solution into a new source of torment: 'But how is God going to find room in heaven for all these people?' For hell to be crowded, fair enough! But heaven . . .

And then there are the micro-worries, mainly centred on our own little universe. In fact our macro-worries about the state of the world are often merely the extension of these: if we are afraid of a global catastrophe, it is because we ourselves and the people we love would obviously be caught up in it.[1] Micro-worries are inevitable: there is always something to torment ourselves over or something capable of going wrong in our lives. Yet it would be a mistake to smile at them or to dismiss them as negligible in the balance sheet of our troubles.

As Montaigne observed: 'The rout of little ills more offend than one how great soever.' And psychotherapists know only too well that the repetition or the constant presence of these little worries can be extremely wearing. It is what I refer to with my patients as 'the vice of things that need doing': the sensation of being caught between all the things that need doing (the ones we can see in front of us) and all the things not yet done (the ones that are at our backs, that we sense crowding oppressively in on us). We shall see that the solution does not lie – or not only at least – in getting all these things done!

Nietzsche describes what it feels like to 'perish under a burden one can neither bear nor throw off'.[2] This is exactly how we can feel about those 'things to be done': we cannot reject them (we have to live after all) but nor can we free ourselves from their grip. And, in his *Cahiers*, Cioran concludes, on the same subject: 'Trifles promoted to the level of cosmic reality. [. . .] I am manipulated by them [. . .] like an insect. A sense of intolerable humiliation.'[3]

But, in the end, it is not the size of the worry that matters, but its legiti-macy in the view of others or ourselves. In any case, our mind flits from worry to worry like a bird flying from branch to branch: it cannot do otherwise. What gives weight to a worry is not its objective nature but the feelings and moods it triggers. For, even if worry can be improved by the absence of events, obligations, responsibilities, commitments, even if it generally diminishes in the more peaceful interludes in our lives, it dwells first and foremost in ourselves: in our tendency to decode and understand the world around us as a vast machine endlessly generating obligations ('you absolutely must do this before this evening') and threats ('If I don't do it, then . . .'). And in our exaggerated sense of our responsibilities in this petty world of ours.

Anxieties and worries as feelings and moods

Anxiety and worry both belong to the same family of feelings and moods. As well as a feeling, anxiety can also be the equivalent 'powerful emotion' – sometimes so powerful that it can become pathological. As a feeling, anxiety is lighter, subtler, more changeable and omnipresent than the emotion.

There are numerous terms in all languages to describe the thousand and one facets of anxiety: we can feel harassed, tormented, concerned, worried, stressed, preoccupied. I like the word 'preoccupied'. Being *pre-occupied* means having your mind already cluttered up in advance, occupied by worries. As a result, there is little space left for other aspects of life, no place for other feelings like, for example, the little moments of happiness each day can bring. Or only a limited or contaminated one, as Pessoa observed: 'In my heart there's a peaceful anguish.'[4]

On the face of things, anxiety is perhaps the most discreet of all moods. The one which shows least on our faces or in our behaviour. Which hardly ever prevents us living a normal life, or smiling and laughing. Even when we are tormented as only those close to us know we can be. There is a whole universe of anxieties slumbering inside each of us, ready to be awoken at the slightest opportunity or the slightest gap in our vigilance at keeping ourselves constantly busy, our minds always absorbed in a task. As in this extract from Cioran's *Cahiers*, where the contemplation of a humble clock acts as a kind of dynamite:

> Gare du Nord. A clock shows the time in minutes: 16.43 – I found myself thinking that this particular minute will never come back, that it has gone for good, swallowed up in the anonymous mass of the irrevocable. That the theory of eternal recurrence seemed futile and groundless. Everything disappears for ever. I shall never see this moment again. Everything is unique and without importance.[5]

When we refer to anxiety we usually distinguish between various levels ranging from minor worry to a more intense level of anxiety we could also call anguish.

In general, acute anxiety describes violent emotional states, where there is an intense physical experience and a sense of impending catastrophe. The anxiety attacks described by our patients in psychiatry are usually associated with a sense of impending death (which explains their propensity to rush to emergency services, since their heart rate at such times makes them feel at risk), or of depersonalization or insanity, the feeling that they are going mad. We are a long way from the classic definition of acute anxiety as 'groundless fear': without immediate external threat perhaps, but certainly not without grounds!

In its less intense form, anxiety or worry can also be a lighter state, more psychological than physical, more to do with our everyday existence ('What will become of me? Will I be able to do what is expected of me as a human?') than with life and death ('Will I cease to exist?'). This is why we often say that severe anxiety expresses the fear of death whereas worry refers to the fear of living.

Like all feelings, anxiety is a physical presence in our bodies: a tightening in the throat, a dry mouth, a feeling of suffocation and shallow breathing, the muscles tense almost to the extent of being painful in the back of the neck or in the back. Taking care of ourselves physically could help towards partially alleviating the suffering caused by anxiety. And developing a closer awareness of our physical sensations could also enable us to detect all those times when we are on the brink of starting to worry even before our minds have realized what is happening.

The physical markers of worry can indeed help us recognize its progression through various degrees of intensity: (1) first we feel a sense of unease or disquiet; there is not necessarily any particular problem we are aware of, but we do not *feel* right, in the sense that we are not relaxed, not confident about the future, not safe; there is no specific *presence* of a problem, just an *absence* of peace of mind; (2) next, we start to feel concerned, worried; something in our mind is preoccupying us, the presence of an identified problem which we are beginning to ruminate on, in the mistaken belief, as always, that we are reflecting on it; (3) at this stage, we start to feel anxious; the body gets in on the act and we begin to feel more and more tense, as though we may be about to run out of road; this is the first indication of catastrophic scenarios appearing in the far distance of our feelings, like big black clouds on the horizon; (4) we feel acutely anxious; as though we can no longer control either our bodies or our minds, our feelings become increasingly painful and uncontrollable; we want to call for help . . .

Why are we so anxious?

Is it because of our long history of being hunted? It is not so very long since we took over the planet as an animal species. When it was not we who ate the other animals, but they (or some of them) who fed on us, our capacity for worry was a guarantee of survival: being careful meant living longer, and therefore having more children, who incidentally we taught to be careful too. And the 'not-worried-enough' disappeared; though at least they did so joyously. That is why, according to evolutionary psychologists, humans have such an aptitude for anxiety:[6] we are all descendants of ancestors who survived thanks to worry.

In addition to our genes, however, we have our brains and our intelligence. We are capable of looking ahead, a capacity which has certainly proved to be a considerable advantage to our species (thinking about establishing stocks of provisions, anticipating where enemies might attack from, etc.). Yet this capacity for anticipation, which arose from the need to predict where problems might come from, inherently implies the potential to veer into over-anticipation: anxiety. This phenomenon can moreover be observed in neuro-imaging:[7] different cerebral zones are involved when we move from straightforward anticipation (feeling without excessive emotive power and with the potential to control the situation) into worry and anxiety.

Animals also anticipate, but in the shorter term with reference to their immediate future; they remain in the 'future of the present'. Humans are capable of much more virtual temporal extensions in that they can project forward to the distant future. This is the 'and what if?', which is so characteristic of moods of anxiety.[8] What if this was the end of the world? What if nobody loved me? What if I lost my job? What if I missed my train? What if the film has already started when I get to the cinema?

And there are our metaphysical capacities too. This is what certain thinkers call the 'universality of the sense of ontological distress': all humans have dramatic feelings about their identity as living creatures, as mortals, as tiny insects lost in the vast universe. We should remember that ontology is the study of the being simply as a being, as opposed to the study of its appearance or attributes. In other words, 'Who am I?' (or 'What am I?') rather than 'Where am I running to and what sort of state am I in?'

Another philosophical hypothesis suggests that we are worried because we are all orphans in this world. Because 'taken as it stands, as it appears in the intuition of the moment, the world is mute. The silence of the world is probably the principal source of anguish.'[9] Try as we might tirelessly to construct beliefs and seek for meaning, our anxiety still remains, for, in reality, there is nothing, and we know it.

Then there is our condition as mortal animals (like the others) but with the knowledge of our mortality (which other animals generally do not have). As Woody Allen said, 'As long as a man will consider himself mortal, he will never really feel relaxed.' For our intellectual capacities feature our introspective consciousness: we are capable of observing ourselves, and of reflecting and ruminating about ourselves. And because of that, we know that we are going to die long before we are actually dead. Hardly surprising then that we feel ill at ease.

Finally, and as if all that was not enough, there are social changes which exacerbate our worries. Our modern world has gradually distanced us from the notion of destiny, making us less fatalistic ('What happens to me is the result of phenomena, either divine or natural, which are beyond my control') and with a greater sense of responsibility ('I am responsible for what happens to me'). Of course such changes are not without their benefits: broadly speaking we are more active as citizens than at any time in the past. But they also have their dangers, as the balance tips from personal responsibility towards guilt ('If I fail, it's my own fault').

A number of studies have highlighted a narrow correlation between a sense of personal responsibility and anxious moods:[10] feeling responsible for a particular problem in our lives tends to make us unable to 'drop' the problem, and as a result we quickly slip into excessive worry and rumination.[11] If so many things trouble us in our lives it is because we think we have to do something about them: it is the 'I've got to do it' mantra of worried people. And when they fail to do it, they say: 'I should have done it.' Tormented first by worries, then by regrets.

It is undoubtedly this shift towards more and more responsibility which explains why adults generally worry more than children. And it also means that people who tend to be anxious are often extremely useful to others: since they think about everybody else's problems as well as their own, their entourage can relax and switch off their own worry systems. After all, someone else is ready to take on the responsibility to do whatever it takes to avoid potential problems: finding the route, keeping an eye on the time, etc.

Be that as it may, some researchers have been struck by the rise in average levels of anxiety in the Western world, amongst North Americans for example:[12] on the basis of large samples of people, it is clear that levels of anxiety continued to rise between 1950 and 1980. In terms of anxiety, it seems likely that the social and cultural context will turn out to be the third significant factor, alongside genetics and the emotional and educational influences of childhood. It is therefore not only because we are anxious that the modern world frightens us, but our anxiety also stems from the fact that this world is threatening – and even more importantly, uncertain. That does not mean we should give up attempting to keep our anxieties within the limits of what is reasonable and useful. We must remember that it is not them that will help us change the world, but rather the lucidity and the actions they could have inspired us to.

All of this explains why it would be hard for us not to feel anxious and insecure at times. This is what makes us 'creatures of fear'. And why it is so crucial for us to understand our feelings of anxiety if we do not want to be overwhelmed by them.

The dynamics of worry and anxiety

'My mind is constantly scanning the future! It's like a radar that is always on, attempting to spot problems before they even arrive!' a patient once said to me. Worry is indeed rumination about the future.[13] It consists of a succession of negative and painful feelings about what *might* happen (but when we are anxious we are more likely to use the future tense and say 'what *will* happen') in the more or less distant future.[14] In our anxious anticipation we are guilty of what is effectively an error of grammatical mood, confusing what *might* (conditional) with what *will* (indicative) happen.

This explains why we are not content merely to make predictions, but insist on sticking to them subsequently.[15] The process has been closely studied by cognitive psychotherapists: (1) we are permanently generating hypotheses about the potential dangers ahead, (2) we mistake the hypotheses for certainties, (3) we react as though they were realities. In the bodies and brains of anxious people, there is no clear difference between thinking about a problem and experiencing it. If I start thinking about my own death, gradually my body and my mind will begin to react as if I am indeed about to die.

Eventually however, this complete tension of our whole being becomes too much to bear: at that point we try to escape from it, by attempting, unsuccessfully,[16] to get rid of our worries, by thinking about something else, or by throwing ourselves into some kind of activity. But, since this distancing process involves a less thorough 'surveillance' of the problem, we end up coming back to it. And we keep coming back to it, again and again.

This constant movement of confrontation and avoidance, the relentless rhythm of anxiety, is vividly described in this quotation from Woody Allen:[17] 'I believe my consumption has grown worse. Also my asthma. The wheezing comes and goes, and I get dizzy more and more frequently. I have taken to violent choking and fainting. My room is damp and I have perpetual chills and palpitations of the heart. I noticed, too, that I am out of napkins. Will it never stop?' Or else: 'Still obsessed by thoughts of death, I brood constantly. I keep wondering if there is an afterlife, and if there is will they be able to break a twenty?'

A good example of one of the ways humour can function in response to anxiety: as soon as we get a little too close to what we are afraid of, quickly change the subject and lower the tension with a flash of wit.

And our anxious rumination is triggered in this way: we feel we can only control our worries by running away from them (refusing to think about them or thinking about other things). But, at the same time, after a while, we start to feel subconsciously unhappy about leaving unresolved problems in our wake. So, we go back to them, but it is all too complicated and we end up running away again, etc. And in the end, these comings and goings keep us busy and distract us, but also tire us out and wear us down. These are the 'gratuitous anxieties' our patients refer to, exhausting and pointless.

How we lock ourselves into anxious feelings: the fanaticism of the worst

For goodness' sake! Why do we carry on like this? Why do these endless worries keep coming back all the time? Why can't we simply learn some life lessons from them? We have all seen and felt on numerous occasions how pointless it is to worry: either because there was no danger, or because it was not as bad as we thought and we survived, or because in any case our worrying did not have any impact on the scenario. There are many answers to these whys.

Anxiety is like belonging to a particular faith. To some extent this applies to all our feelings and moods since they all tend to make us subscribe to a particular view of the world, but it seems to be even more acute in the context of our moods of anxiety, mainly because we do not pay sufficient attention to them: we are much more wary, for example, of our angry moods, which we know can end up making us overstep the line; and we are quicker to recognize our sad moods since these make us feel physically weary and slow to act. But anxiety is extremely good at whispering in our ear: 'I am your friend I am the epitome of prudence, lucidity and vigilance. Trust me! Together we can move forward!'

In order to understand anxiety, we need to know its creed. Here then is the Holy Trinity of the anxious: (1) the world is full of dangers and threats; (2) I am vulnerable, and those I love are vulnerable too; (3) we can survive, or increase our chance of survival, but only if we take all adequate precautions – not to do so would be foolish.

This perception of a dangerous world logically implies an extreme desire to avoid the slightest risk (it is like working in a bacteriology lab: hygiene is not to be taken lightly[18]).

Clearly the foundations of this creed are not completely absurd and contain some – but only some – element of truth. And while they may indeed aid survival, they do little to enhance quality of life. We need therefore to modify them: (1) yes, the world is dangerous, but particularly at certain times and in certain places; away from these we can feel quite safe; (2) it is true that we are vulnerable, and it is worth taking some precautions; but not to the extent of taking *all* precautions possible and wrapping ourselves in cotton wool; (3) it is true that being careful increases our chances of survival; however, there is no point in transforming that into an obsession which affects our quality of life, by enabling us to survive longer, but only because we are locked in a hyper-protective cage.

Our anxiety also persists because we brood on it, because we nourish it by shutting ourselves up in our convictions. *We become intolerant to other views of the world.*[19] When we are trapped in anxious feelings, we tend to react with astonishment or anger towards those who are happy, carefree or otherwise optimistic: we see them simply as people who *lack* something, for example intelligence or lucidity, and not as people who have something *more* than we do, for example an aptitude for happiness. We take pleasure in the thought that they have never encountered anxiety, either by luck ('Life has been kind to them'), or by denial ('They are burying their heads in the sand'), or by stupidity ('They've never understood the way the world works'). We do not enjoy life and we fail to understand why others should do so: 'I've got better things to do than to go around rejoicing: worrying is much more important, much more useful!' This superiority complex which comes over us when we are in the grip of our anxieties is a strange phenomenon. At such times, someone who sees things in a calmer light than we do is happy-go-lucky, reckless even! A poor heathen who has failed to understand our beloved Holy Trinity.

Cioran wrote: 'Anxiety – or the fanaticism of the worst'.[20] As is often the case with his aphorisms, each word is significant: the *worst* evokes the catastrophic scenarios to which we subscribe in the grip of anxiety (any situation which is not 100 per cent controlled *must* end in catastrophe). And fanaticism refers to that intolerance of contradiction or of sound argument which we display at such times; as though we are blindly *willing* the worst to come, if only to confirm our convictions, like religious fanatics. I recall a woman explaining to me why she had given up trying to calm her husband, who was suffering from pathological anxiety (and who did not want to 'come and see the psychologist').

> Everyone stood back to allow him to calm down on his own, or rather to wait for him to calm down with the passage of time. All our arguments only served to fuel his anxious rage and his *end of the world* rhetoric. Our attempts to open his eyes simply added fuel to the flames. So then we just allowed his anxiety to die out of its own accord, smothered under the weight of its own absurdity.

This rigidity that engulfs us in our anxious moods, these negative convictions that we possess at such moments, can help to explain certain unexplained bursts of anger if we are contradicted or crossed.

Our deep-seated conviction that *worry is a good thing* is another reason behind the persistence and the recurrence of our anxieties. Thus, in response to the question 'Why worry?', those prone to anxiety will have no shortage of answers: to motivate yourself ('By worrying about things, I feel it helps me cope better'), to solve problems ('I only work well under pressure'), to prepare for the worst ('I prefer to start out by envisaging the worst in order to be better prepared'), to avoid the worst happening ('It enables me to prepare myself in advance'), to ward off the worst ('If I think in terms of success, it might bring me bad luck').[21]

This last group of responses reminds us that anxious moods also contain an element of 'magical thinking', of superstitions based on the principle of 'you never know'. I once heard an example of magical thinking from the lips of the writer Camille Laurens: 'Misfortune only strikes when we stop thinking about it. Thinking about it all the time is a way of neutralizing it.' In other words: by worrying, I am taming the evil eye, holding its gaze, tricking it into not striking elsewhere.

And what is more, it works! Or at least, it appears to. With magical thinking, we win every time. If the problem does indeed turn out to be a genuine one, if the prophecy comes true, we can say 'I told you so!' If it does not: 'That doesn't mean anything, it could easily have happened, and there will be plenty of other occasions!' And quietly, or subconsciously, we whisper to ourselves 'If I hadn't worried about it, the catastrophe could easily have happened!' Like, for example, the anxious mother who, during a consultation, described how she had not allowed herself to go to sleep until her son had come home from the night-club: from the way she recounted her sleepless night, I was sure she was perfectly convinced that her anxious vigil had protected her son! And that she thought 'Allowing myself to go to sleep is like abandoning my son to face danger on his own. By staying awake, I can help him.' I asked her about this. You can guess her reply!

From anxious moods to constant anxiety

There is no clear limit between 'normal' and pathological anxieties. At the two extremes, these are of course as different as day and night. But the boundary between the two poses the same problem as the dawn: at what precise moment does the day begin and the night end?

There is a form of anxiety, which doctors call reactive anxiety, in which we react to existing, concrete events (being unable to pay debts, knowing someone who is seriously ill). We fear the *consequences* of a *real* event, one which has already occurred. Once this event in our lives is behind us, *resolved*, our anxious feelings disappear, leaving us in peace.

A notch above this takes us to more pronounced predispositions to anxiety: we dread the *arrival* of certain *impending* events (we have to take an important exam or go for a job interview, we are going away on holiday, moving house). All of these are going to happen, but we do not know if they will *go well*. Which means we can ruminate at length beforehand. And then, there is also the anxiety about what has not yet happened, what may never happen, but *could* happen (losing your job, falling ill). And, since for anxious people, 'anything and everything may happen at any moment', life itself is an anxious matter. The severity of our anxiety is based to some extent on this *crescendo* of anticipation: worries about what is already there, about what is going to happen, about what might happen.

In the top position on the podium, our entire personality, our whole view of the world is inhabited by anxiety.[22] 'Anxiety has taken me over completely', a patient once told me. For example, automatic reflexes exist even outside the painful presence of anxiety: the tendency to anticipate, to think about what is coming next, even on holiday; the tendency to be unable to relax either physically or mentally. A constant preoccupation with the future: 'What is going to happen next?' Not living in the present moment, but in the one to come. This way of thinking is bearable as long as our lives are well ordered, calm, predictable, steady, under control. But if they accelerate and become more complicated, we start to feel powerful surges of anxiety. At certain moments, the feelings of anxiety become so dominant that they begin to affect other feelings and moods (for example, we can feel only nervous happiness: 'It won't last', only anxious joy: 'It's wonderful, but alas, tomorrow the worries will be back again'), and to disrupt them too (leading to sudden and inexplicable outbursts of anger or fits of depression). At this stage, the feelings of anxiety are no longer perceived as excessive or undesirable but as the simple truth.

As anxieties can be resolved by action, there is the danger of falling into a certain addiction to action: quick – get moving, do something. Work, for example! Worriers are often highly productive,[23] which is why bosses like anxious colleagues. Yet their professional success does not always correspond to a personal sense of fulfilment (as we see from talking to the partners or families of worriers). For anxiety makes people prioritize survival over quality of life. Moreover, financial and social success is often motivated solely by the objective of guaranteeing security: putting aside enough money 'for a rainy day' (a typical phrase used by worriers), and securing a professional status high enough to prevent the need to worry about the future (or, in the language of worriers, the setbacks that lie in wait).

Sometimes worriers need to recruit partners to share their anxieties, and can even end up exaggerating the situation so as to persuade someone else to worry along with them. This is illustrated in a joke I am fond of. An anxious banker telephones his associate: 'Hello? OK, here's the news on our business: it's all perfectly straightforward – it's a catastrophe! I haven't got time to tell you anything more at the moment. Just start worrying, and I'll be there as soon as I can.'

Worry as an illness: chronic anxiety

'Fear is so much a part of me that I cannot imagine living without constantly asking myself: "Am I afraid right now? And now, am I not afraid?" There are some people in my life who seem not to live like that. I am very fond of them, they do me good, but in some way, they seem like aliens to me. And probably they think exactly the same about me – unfortunately.'

Generalized anxiety is the illness of excessive and uncontrollable worrying. Why an illness? Because worry is constantly present, because people are unable to contain it and as a result they suffer from numerous complications: physical pain, insomnia, difficulties in concentrating or remembering things. Their quality of life is significantly affected, in more or less the same way as it is for those suffering from depression.[24] These people suffer from an excessive emotional reaction to all sorts of situations, and from a global dysregulation of their feelings and moods in general.[25]

Generalized anxiety involves a view of the world which is extremely marked by the omnipresence of potential dangers. A mother suffering from this condition will find it very hard to allow her children to go to school on their own, since in her view the street is a place entirely peopled with paedophiles and drunken drivers. A patient once described the behaviour of his mother, who suffered from the condition:

> She would kiss me at each little separation as though it was for the very last time. She used to measure my legs every week to make sure I hadn't contracted my Breton grandmother's hip problem. Because she was so afraid I would hurt myself, I never ran, so as not to upset her, because I could see what a state she would be in if I did. As she was really anxious about my future, I made sure I always got good marks at school. Sometimes I was scared I might make her die of sorrow if I let her down: I had once heard that expression and I thought my mother was genuinely capable of *dying of sorrow*.

Generalized anxiety is capable of triggering catastrophic scenarios extremely quickly. When someone is very anxious, their assessment of situations becomes more radical and they lose any sense of nuance. For them the universe is split into two categories: what is dangerous and what is not. Faced with uncertainty or potential problems, they head straight for the catastrophic scenario, the worst possible outcome. For example, a car breakdown instantly triggers a spiral of thoughts – often subconscious – along these lines: 'It won't be repairable; it's certainly going to be very complicated, very expensive, it will have to be replaced, I can't afford it, I can't manage without a car at the moment, it's a disaster.' Or like this account from one of my patients:

> It happened one morning. I didn't feel too bad, my worries were more or less at a normal level for me and then, suddenly, as I was having breakfast with my wife, she made some comment about something that needed repairing, like the washing machine or the cellar light, and bang, a wave of anxiety and a voice shouting in my head: 'You're not going to manage, you've got too many things to do, you won't get it done . . .' And that was it, the anxiety attacks were back, my breathing was faster, I felt I needed to do something, to get started on something in order to reduce the mountain of things that needed doing, and even more importantly, so as not to be hanging around doing nothing; I don't know if throwing myself into doing things really helps, but one thing is sure, if I didn't do it, it would be worse. Once it's passed, I can see that it's all do-able, that I will get there, that my wife was right when she tried to calm me down, but I just turn into an *alien* at those times. Like the superhero in the Hulk films who turns into a monster when he gets angry: only in my case it's when I'm anxious.

For these patients, in addition to the permanent anxieties, there are also the regular attacks of over-anxiety: waking up in the night, increased tendency to rumination, anxieties spiralling out of the tiniest worry. Major crises of anguish or mini-crises, upsetting moments of panic. At such times, patients see all potential problems as possible or quasi-possible, and they react emotionally as though all of them were real and present.

One of my patients, a mother, had for example anxieties about food when she was most afflicted: 'What if we can't manage to use up everything I've bought and have to throw it away?', or, conversely: 'I haven't bought enough!', which kept her awake at night. She also had an extremely anxious relationship with her freezer: 'What if it stops working and I have to throw everything away?' and worse still: 'What if it stops working, and everything defrosts and is contaminated by bacteria, and then starts working again without us realizing what's happened, and we eat the contaminated food and are all seriously ill?' etc.

Night-time anxiety attacks are often the most acute, since we start ruminating without any possibility of being able to take action in order to distract ourselves, and since we are incapable of curbing our anxieties, things rapidly spiral out of control. It is a kind of 'anxious madness', even if anxiety normally of course bears no resemblance to madness: worrying does not mean we are out of our minds, the problems envisaged are genuine, it is simply our assessment of them that is out of proportion. In these violent outbursts of anxiety, all problems are potentially endless and insoluble (they will last forever, will keep coming back and will never be resolved in a satisfactory manner . . .). Of course, the problems end up being resolved and we do not go mad. But what an exhausting process!

Initially, people suffering from generalized anxiety tend to consult their doctor because they are troubled by the physical symptoms (colitis, neck pain, back ache). They gallantly put up with anxiety, the psychological suffering, because it is something they are accustomed to, and they are not always capable of recognizing that it has become excessive and toxic and is spoiling their lives. Often it is someone in their entourage who finds it harder to put up with and who persuades them to seek help. Or else they come to us when they are depressed, exhausted and worn down by their incessant and disproportionate anxieties. Many of these big-scale worriers end up experiencing depression at some point in their lives.[26]

The fear of not being able to cope

There is a continuity between stress, anxiety and depression, a progression of these feelings and moods according to our perception (right or wrong) of whether or not we are capable of adapting to a given situation.

Stress is a form of anxious reaction to real worries and pressures. It produces feelings based on worry and a desire to act and to perform, sometimes accompanied by a small amount of excitement in certain people (those who frequently use the word 'challenge'): 'I must succeed!'

Anxiety in the face of a problem corresponds more closely to the question 'And what if I don't succeed?'

And *depression* corresponds to 'I won't succeed!' Depression is often considered to be a sort of terminal illness, the result of the anxious wear and tear caused by exhausting confrontations with the world, or with our view of the world.

It could be said that when we are anxious, we are in reality half-way between the state of 'pure' anxiety, which would allow us to go no further than the question 'And what if I don't succeed?' (but that is impossible, the strong current of anxious anticipation forces us to continue the monologue, and it is not reassuring), and that of pre-depression ('I won't be able to do it'), which we try to fend off by doing everything possible within the given situation, or going back to ruminating over the source of our anxiety.

Patients suffering from generalized anxiety often experience waves of despair, moods dominated by the tension between anxiety and the desire to stay in control on the one hand, and despair and the desire to give up on the other. With in addition always the shame and bewilderment at finding themselves in this state.

I remember one of my patients, a financial manager, who once found himself in some administrative difficulties. His car had been stolen and the thieves were regularly using it to commit further offences. As a result, over a period of weeks he found himself first with a series of fines and penalty points on his driving licence, then with administrative threats, due partly to errors in the police and judicial systems and partly to the fact that he was late in getting the various forms and declarations filled in. After numerous phone calls, letters and other attempts, he ended up spending a whole day going from one police headquarters to another (in the Paris region), including his own local headquarters and the ones where the offences had been committed, etc. At one point, when he was in a queue at the Bobigny police headquarters, he found himself thinking suicidal thoughts, an experience which terrified him. Why this close encounter with depression? My patient was bemused:

> It was all completely absurd! On the one hand I was probably scared – stupidly but subconsciously – that the whole thing would degenerate, and that I would end up being thrown into prison. But, and this is what really scares me most in the end, I wonder if it wasn't linked to the very violent and oppressive feeling I had of wasting my time. But in what sense? In the context of all the things I needed to do: mow the lawn, get on with my job, be with my children, repair the shutters, read all the magazines and books piled up on my bedside table ... It's completely crazy and absurd to have suicidal tendencies just because you feel you are wasting your time!

Treating pathological anxieties

It goes without saying that generalized anxiety requires treatment. Not necessarily involving medication: I recall a hyper-anxious patient who came to see me at Sainte-Anne in order to get my opinion on her case, and who began the session by saying: 'I've come to see you because all the doctors I've seen have wanted to put me on medication!' (After an hour of discussion, I told her I agreed with them.) Our temptation to prescribe is strong because medication is indeed highly effective in the treatment of anxiety. Tranquillizers, taken over a limited and specific time, are used to avoid the peaks of anxiety, which can be very distressing. The anti-depressants known as 'serotonergic' (from the same family as the famous Prozac) are prescribed as a basic treatment, to be taken every day for several months, and bring clear and lasting relief to the majority of patients.

But, in both cases, stopping the treatment can prove difficult, unless patients have in the meantime learned to deal with their anxieties other than by swallowing pills. And also, the feeling that a significant proportion of our problems stem from the way we react to life means that, very often, people seek something more than just medication.

This is why we almost always recommend our very anxious patients to undergo a psychotherapy treatment: either as an alternative to medication, or as a substitute, or to be used in combination with it as a way of reducing the dose. Existing research tends to indicate that in the long term the most effective therapies are generally the interactive ones (discussions and advice with a view to modifying the patient's psychological and behavioural habits), such as cognitive and behavioural therapies.[27]

The aim of these psychotherapies is to help the patient to apply the kind of advice we shall be referring to at the end of this chapter in the context of their daily lives. These psychotherapies are all based on an attitude which could be described as 'ecological' in that it is not a question of 'pulling out' the bad ideas and inadequate feelings as we might pull out weeds (or worse still, resorting each time to 'weed-killers' for worries in the form of medication or alcohol). Instead it is about learning how to listen to and understand our anxieties calmly and then seeing what can be done about them, as in the little example below.

A patient of mine had just found out she was pregnant. Naturally she lost no time in starting to worry about this new event: 'And what if I don't love this child as much as my first daughter?' Those close to her did their best to reassure her ('That won't happen, you'll see, everything will be fine'), which of course did not work. There is nothing unusual in this: if we deny the problem that is oppressing the anxious person (by saying 'That won't happen'), or if we counter their convictions ('it will all go wrong') with an alternative one ('it will all turn out fine'), it is hardly surprising that they remain unconvinced. They are locked into their faith in their anxieties.

In the discussion we then had together, my aim was not to do the same thing (since it had clearly not worked) but instead to teach her to respect and listen to this anxiety and then see what could be done about it. 'It is possible, after all, that you might love this baby less. But tell me why you think that might happen?' The result was that the patient began really to think about the matter, rather than simply seeing it as horrible or undesirable. I tried again: 'Let's try and put it in a clearer way: do you think you would love the baby *less*, or *differently*?' The discussion continued on the subject of the different ways of loving your various children. 'And even if it does happen, even if you do love this child less, what do you think will happen? Would it mean that you would hate it? That the child would suffer horribly as a result? That she would feel abandoned and rejected?' Which enabled us to discuss the role of the baby's father (their relationship was extremely complicated at the time) and the fact that she would, of course, still love this child, that she already loved it in fact. Adopting a concerned and respectful attitude to our patients' anxieties enables them also to adopt the same attitude, without awkwardness.

The anxious feelings expressed by my patient were by no means absurd: in fact we do indeed often spend less time with younger children than with older ones. And it is also true that younger siblings have to share their parents' time from the moment they are born. So does that mean that less time = less love? Why not, after all; at any rate it is interesting to ask the question rather than simply ruling it out at any price. But to do so, we need to take *everything* into account: remembering that sometimes it can be an advantage to arrive in second place, precisely because you are less likely to be so smothered by love! Remember to see the bigger picture too and to think that even if the second child – perhaps – gets a little less love from the mother, they will get it from their big sister, who is looking forward to the baby's arrival impatiently, or from their father, who will suddenly find he has a little more space. And so on.

The last I heard was that all was well for this second little girl, and that there was no shortage of love for her.

How to control feelings of anxiety

One of my patients told me, on a day when she was feeling low, that 'anxiety always wins'. I do not believe we are condemned to accept that it will always win, but we do indeed need to accept that feelings of anxiety are always ready to enter our lives, like undesirable guests. That we should nevertheless make an effort to welcome them and to listen to them, making the best of a bad situation. But we will do all that even better if we adopt some of the following approaches.

Not identifying with your worries

It is all a question of distance, the famous distance we so often lack once feelings of anxiety start to take hold. The fundamental issue here is to see the worry as a symptom, to see yourself ruminating. It is essential to recognize worries in their very earliest stages, in the same way that firemen watch out for the first signs of fire: it is much easier to put out the flames when they have only just taken hold. But to do that you need to have learned to recognize the worry as a sterile rumination rather than a useful process of reflection. When we tip into 'anxiety' mode, we make the mistake of concentrating too intently on the worries and problems, and not enough on our capacity to exaggerate and brood over them. We are simply focusing on the wrong thing.

Questioning your anxieties

For example, by asking 'What category of problem am I fretting over?' It is worth getting into the habit of grading one's worries, giving them a score between 0 and 100 where, for the majority of us, the worst (100) would be to lose a child or a partner. Once we begin doing this, we realize that most of our worries are situated between 0 and 20. We will still have to deal with them, of course, but in a more relaxed way. Without feeling we are dealing with some very serious matter.

We can also keep a diary of 'invalidated worries': a record of all the times when we said 'I'm going to miss my plane, fail my exam' and when it did not happen. Actually writing them down, in a little notebook, on our newspaper. One of my patients got into such a state of furious anxiety on one occasion when he thought he had missed his plane (which he ended up catching) that he had his boarding card framed and hung in his office with the caption 'never again'; he was the only person to understand its significance, but he wanted to make sure he would never forget the lesson.

Stepping back into the real world and getting rid of a certain number of delusions . . .

Delusion 1: With a bit of effort, it is possible to control everything.
Reality: No, we cannot control everything.
Delusion 2: If we are careful, we can manage to avoid problems.
Reality: No, problems are part of life.
Delusion 3: Uncertainty can only lead to danger.
Reality: No, many things that are uncertain resolve themselves of their own accord.

Resist the temptation always to control everything

We often wear ourselves out by wanting to have control over our lives, to an absurd extent. In our anxious moods, we are often under the illusion that control is an effective solution, a response to the vagaries of life.[28] But the desire to get everything under control leaves us with an exhausting sensation of never getting to the end of all we need to do. We are condemned to be constantly overwhelmed. As a patient once described:

> One day I realized that I would never see the end of it. That I couldn't continue to do everything. At that point, I made the only possible decision, which was – precisely – to stop trying to do everything! I decided I would have to learn to live with lots of things left undone, and to accept that I would never do them. At first, it was hard: to be sitting on the sofa, listening to music, and to see all those little things that needed doing in the room, or to think, by association, of all the things that needed doing round the house, or to feel I hadn't helped my children to understand their maths properly, all of that made me want to get up, to tell myself I had no right to be sitting there as long as all those things had not been finished. Which will never happen . . . But I forced myself: I told myself I had the right to relax a bit. And I made myself stay on that sofa, listening to music. Gradually I began to relax. And I carried on like that with all sorts of little things. And contrary to what I had previously thought, by just letting things go occasionally, I hadn't turned into a tramp or a slob. I was just a bit more cool.

Ah! All those interminable 'to do lists' of our anxious thoughts! When we are anxious, the world is composed solely of 'missions to accomplish'. As a result, simply living becomes a worry, and relaxing or doing nothing, a sin.

Accept that we cannot keep up with the world

Work at it tirelessly. That does not mean that we have to resign ourselves to chaos: often when you make suggestions to anxious people they take your advice to its extreme, as a way of proving to you that it is not only misplaced, but also dangerous: 'Let go? You mean not bother about anything? You want me to let myself be exploited by everyone? All right, you'll see what happens.' But no, it is not about going from one extreme to the other: we just need to find a half-way point, somewhere between doing too much and doing too little! To accept that we are not all-powerful. That disorder and uncertainty are an inherent part of the living, changing world in which we live. That if we do not learn to tolerate them, our lives will be extremely exhausting.

We also have to accept the fact that there will be many things we will never be able to do in our lives. Both big and small things. Ranging from the items we will not be able to repair to the countries we will never visit. The little disappointments of our omnipotence, of our appetite for life. Sad? Yes. But this sadness will perhaps be less painful and more productive than the strain of the illusions ('Do everything!') which we desperately adhere to. In therapy, I often joke with my patients on this subject: 'I've got some good news: that world without worries that you dream about does exist. And some bad news: it's called heaven and it's not for right now. In the meantime, we're going to try and get along with the world we've got, the one called Life.'

Understand your allergy to uncertainty

In fact, we are worried by the unknown. 'What is going to happen now? Tomorrow? In a year's time?' All these questions can provoke feelings of anxiety as well as of curiosity. Worry is often seen as a way of rejecting uncertainty.[29] An example from our old friend, Woody Allen: 'What is it about death that worries me so much? The timing, probably.' It is a philosophical truth that the most distressing thing about death is not death itself (which is a certainty), but knowing when it will occur (which is, generally, uncertain). We prefer to fill the troubling emptiness of uncertainty by taking action (escape through action) or by anticipation (escape through rumination). Research in this field shows that the more anxious we are, the less tolerant we are of ambiguity and uncertainty.[30] With the behavioural consequences associated with this intolerance of uncertainty: perfectionism, excessive checking, reluctance to trust others or to delegate, an excessive need for reassurance and for information. All of which may indeed reduce the amount of uncertainty in our lives. But which also increases the amount of stress and fatigue.

Faced with an intolerance of uncertainty, ask ourselves the question: what can I do?

Reduce the uncertainty or increase the tolerance? It is of course possible to reduce the amount of uncertainty in my life: I can always take my holidays in the same place (to avoid the uncertainty of disastrous holidays), go to the same restaurant (to avoid disappointment), only go away for the weekend if every detail is minutely planned and organized (to avoid unpleasant surprises), etc. But (1) how boring it will be!, (2) I will still keep encountering these damned unexpected things, and that will only make me ruminate even more (perhaps not out of anxiety, but anger, disappointment, etc.). Trying to control uncertainty and all possible catastrophic scenarios is exhausting. And sometimes entertaining for other people. I was once greatly amused by a couple of anxious friends who had invited us round and who told us about their concept, a classic of anxious thinking, previously unknown to me, of the 'spare meal'. If you have a lot of guests, or really important ones, always make sure you have a spare meal ready, in case: (1) the first one gets burnt or doesn't turn out as it should, (2) one of the guests does not like or is allergic to what you are serving, (3) you drop the dish on the floor as you are carrying it to the table . . .

A better solution is to boost your tolerance of uncertainty! How can we train ourselves to do this? By no longer over-protecting ourselves and over-planning, for example. You can go away for a weekend with your partner without having planned exactly where you will stay. Or organize an evening with friends without having prepared the meal in advance. Or let your partner do the shopping (if it is normally you who does it). Of course, it will not necessarily be as good as if everything had been all completely organized in advance in the usual way. But so what? Does it really matter? Are we not after all training ourselves to put up with uncertainty and imperfection? How can we succeed if we never encounter them?

Learn to accept problems

When we are in the grip of anxiety, we almost begin to feel problems should not exist at all! To take them as proof of some kind of incompetence (our own or that of others) or anomaly. Which leads to a negative attitude and an anxious perfectionism: the more negative feelings I experience, the more likely I am to perceive any problem as a threat rather than simply a demand, a more or less normal difficulty, in any case something to be solved.[31] The very existence of the problem is seen as abnormal.[32] No doubt as a result of a certain pessimism and doubts about our capacity to resolve it (low self-esteem is clearly a cause of anxious feelings). But the problem with this is that the anxiety is then focused on the problem (since we see this as something abnormal, something unacceptable) rather than the solution (since in order to look for a solution, you must first accept the existence of the problem). This is acknowledged by those patients who have made progress in this area: 'Rumination is not a solution', 'I was always anxious, but not always productive', 'I thought about my problems constantly, but not in the right way.'

Fully acknowledge the existence of adversity

And make space in our lives for it. Accept that problems exist and take them for what they are: problems to sort out, not impossible and threatening dramas. A flat tyre, an unsuccessful holiday, a child having to repeat a school year: these are problems associated with being alive and active, not dramas. I remember one occasion when I was travelling, hearing the pilot give his passengers a little philosophy lesson after a delay of one hour: 'Good morning ladies and gentlemen. This is your captain speaking. The delay is due to our having had to change planes as there were some problems with the previous aircraft. We apologize for this delay of one hour. But better to be an hour late in this world than an hour early in the next.' Accepting problems, adversity, that means accepting – and preferring – life.

Take time to face up to your fears

If I find myself dreading what I think is going to be a catastrophe, I sometimes find it helpful, instead of trying to reassure myself ('No, it's not going to happen'), to accept the possibility ('All right, it could happen'), and then examine the consequences. It can be useful to ask yourself what impact the issue you are worrying over today will have in a few months, or years. All that is part of the same approach: sometimes (not all the time!) stop trying to reason with yourself or reassure yourself, and say: 'OK, and if that happens, what then, and what will you do?' And force yourself to focus on this question, instead of running away from it (by thinking of other things) or denying it (by saying 'But no . . .'). This exercise is clearly more difficult in the face of major adversity: death or illness. But the approach remains the same: confront and face up to the issue. Even to the point of being able to accept, sincerely and profoundly, the following ideas (sentences used by my patients concerning themselves): 'Death is part of life', 'Life is a terminal illness', 'I may die', 'People I love may die', 'And that's exactly why I am determined to be happy!'

Since we will die (a certainty) and suffer (a probability), perhaps we should follow the advice of the humorist Pierre Desproges: 'Live happily while waiting for death'? But to do that, we must first learn to stop being obsessive and over-anxious about death.

For that reason, in cognitive[33] and existential[34] psychotherapy, we work on avoiding painful images. When something is too upsetting to look at (think of an animal that fills you with disgust or a scene in a horror film), we look away. The same happens in our minds: if an image is too awful, we push it aside. But something needs to take its place and that is where worry steps in. It has been demonstrated that worry is a form of avoidance, less painful to put up with than distressing images which tend to become associated rapidly with feelings of anxiety. This too has been measured using variables such as heartbeat or electroencephalograms: worry provokes a less intense level of activity in our bodies than the images of catastrophe our mind produces when in a state of anxiety.[35] In a sense, it is a way of 'diluting' our violent fears in an attempt to come to terms with them. But, alas, it does not always work: worry is an imperfect protection and in reality stops us from becoming habituated to virtual catastrophic scenarios. Which is why we recommend bypassing it in favour of a direct confrontation with the latter (with the aid of a therapist if the scenarios are too painful).

Ultimately these therapies are simply modernized versions of those advocated by the ancient Stoic philosophers who recommended meditation exercises designed to get us used to the idea of old age, ruin, death and other catastrophes. We have to accept the possibility of drama, the proximity of tragedy in our lives. And living in spite of that is wisdom. As opposed to no longer living because of it: that is anxiety.

Can we live a life of disquiet?

Can we live a life of disquiet, as Fernando Pessoa puts it? Yes, what else can we do but accept a share of adversity and uncertainty in our lives? And constantly bring our minds back to the present, as this maxim of La Rochefoucauld reminds us: 'We make better use of our abilities by endeavouring to bear our misfortunes, than in seeking to forestall possible catastrophes.' We need to live and act in the present, then. To be in life with all its adverse currents, 'like a fish in water. In permanent fear of the frying pan.'[36] No, I am joking . . .

Chapter 7

Resentment

How much more grievous are the consequences of anger than the causes of it.

Marcus Aurelius, *Meditations*

And my own affairs were as bad, as dismal, as the day I had been born. The only difference was that now I could drink now and then, though never often enough. Drink was the only thing that kept a man from feeling forever stunned and useless. Everything else just kept picking and picking, hacking away. And nothing was interesting, nothing ... And I've got to live with these fuckers for the rest of my life, I thought. God, they all had assholes and sexual organs and their mouths and their armpits. They shit and they chattered and they were dull as horse dung. The girls looked good from a distance, the sun shining through their dresses, their hair. But get up close and listen to their minds running out of their mouths, you felt like digging in under a hill and hiding out with a tommy-gun.[1]

Apologies for the unrestrained tone of the extract, but these lines from the American writer Charles Bukowski, taken from his book *Ham on Rye*, seemed an appropriately graphic introduction to our examination of the feelings and moods associated with anger and resentment. And to the suffering and damage which so often accompanies them.

The universe of resentment

In focusing on resentment, we are not only interested in anger as a crisis and a powerful emotion, but also in the feelings and moods associated with it: those which precede and facilitate anger (bad moods, hostility) and those which follow it (rancour, hatred), those which explain it (envy, misfortune) and those which replace it (sulking, scorn). There is evidence that, in most cases, anger and resentment are attempts – with only mediocre success – to regulate our other painful moods.[2]

Resentment is thus a way of ruminating on our anger and misfortune like an extended reproach to the world and to those around us. An attenuated form of this is to be found in negativity, that mood in which we see almost everything around us as stupid, ugly, naive, pointless. Just as resentment is anger which avoids exploding, negativity is resentment which avoids aiming at too-specific targets; we feel resentment towards certain people as a result of certain kinds of behaviour, but we feel negativity towards life and any form of human initiative, enthusiasm or movement. Let nothing move, because everything is a target for criticism!

Resentment is a permanent recycling of our hostile feelings, like a long-suppressed anger, constantly smouldering, endlessly rising from its ashes like a sinister phoenix.

It can manifest itself from time to time in any one of us, in response to some specific event in our lives. It is sometimes frequent, for example in timid people, who never dare to say what bothers or hurts them, and who therefore keep brooding over things. As in these lines from Cioran: 'Almost every day I have outbursts in which I attack someone or other, in words or in my imagination. Soliloquy of a polemicist. We express our fury as best we can.'[3] And it can sometimes be so regular that it becomes a way of life, as in the case of those very angry people who realize perfectly well that they cannot spend the entire day raging and shouting. So, when they are not raging and shouting, when they are not complaining, they ruminate on their resentment. And lock themselves in pathetic lives dominated by anger, bitterness and rage.

As is often the case, the feeling is perhaps more dangerous and destructive than the powerful emotion: resentment is sometimes worse than anger, in that it is longer-lasting (chronic in some cases) and less likely to be perceived by the person feeling it as problematic. Which is a mistake, since though those around us may sometimes protest against our (for the most part sporadic) outbursts of anger, they end up avoiding our resentments, if these are ongoing. And that means avoiding us too.

Resentment is a way of diluting anger, of spreading it over time. But that also means that it ends up spreading through our whole lives, since the natural movement of feelings is to expand and take up all the available space in us. Moreover, resentment means losing out on one of the rare benefits of anger, which generally incites us to action. Resentment, on the other hand, is often an aborted anger in which internal eructations and gesticulations take the place of discussions and explanations with the people involved.

Resentment shares the same sources as anger. Either frustrations, hindrances, obstacles, attacks on your personal interest or the results of being inconvenienced, put out (by the *stupid so and so* who is badly parked, the *woman driver* who isn't going fast enough and who slows down at the amber light instead of accelerating, the *idiots* who contradict me or interrupt me when I am saying something). Or violations of rules, a failure to respect public interest: the louts who allow their dogs to piss on walls or to shit in front of people's doors, the petty cheats who fiddle and swindle. Or attacks on one's self-esteem, perceptions of social rejection: someone criticized me, said something bad about me, forgot about me.

In all these cases, things did not go as we were expecting. And we are not prepared to accept that. It is always, when it comes to negative feelings and moods, the same problem of non-acceptance: we focus on what should have been rather than what is. But what causes events to make us hostile rather than sad is the fact that we attribute responsibility for them to others.[4] If we perceive our problems to be the result of bad luck or fate, we are more likely to feel sad; if we see them as coming from ourselves, we will have feelings associated with lowered self-esteem; but if we think they are caused by others, then resentment will erupt.

Feelings of resentment are generally linked to an experience of failure and helplessness. Even if what irritates us is not directed against us or does not immediately concern us. There is evidence that a previous experience of failure subsequently makes us more critical of other people. Whether we have experienced failure on a specific occasion, or see our whole life in terms of a failure, we will still be vulnerable to feelings of resentment. Sometimes a sense of personal disappointment is the cause. Often our resentment is partially directed at ourselves, a feeling of regret at not having coped better with minor irritations and major transgressions. As Jules Renard observed, for example: 'Why are you bad? – Because I lack the strength to be good.'[5] Or, as Cioran put it, more bitterly: 'Pessimism is the coming together of an ineffective kindness and an unsatisfied nastiness.'[6]

Resentment and sadness are very close. Often, as we have said, what causes resentment could just as easily have caused sadness. Indeed, sadness is almost always present, underneath the anger. So, why do we get angry instead of getting sad? Perhaps because it is less painful? And more efficient? Perhaps also, we get angry instead of sad when the events provoking resentment seem unacceptable because avoidable: 'They could have been more careful', 'They could do things differently, but they don't, out of neglect: they couldn't care less, or out of ill intent: they've got it in for me.'

There is also the question of its effectiveness and of the social image it is associated with: resentment may seem a more promising way of putting right the wrongs we have suffered (many people allow themselves to be governed by anger and fighting moods, seeing this as a means to potential victory), whereas sadness is seen more as the mood of the submissive victim, the loser.

Sadly, this often turns out to be the case! In competitive environments where power issues play an important role, anger works better than sadness as a way of impressing other people.[7] But, be careful, this only applies if you already have a certain amount of power;[8] otherwise, the outbursts of subordinates are seen simply as a sign of lack of self-control. So, if our ambition in life is to exercise power over others, let us continue to cultivate our feelings of resentment, punctuated from time to time with healthy outbursts of anger. That works reasonably well in certain contexts. But it will be sad and stressful. If, on the other hand, our aim is simply to be a human being, it would be a pity to rule out playing the 'sadness' card, which would make us more intelligent, more sensitive, more lucid. And probably more efficient too, as we shall see later.

We are wrong to prize anger, both in psychological and in medical terms. In the face of something which fills us with outrage, expressing our anger may indeed appease our feelings in the short term, because it is preferable to the frustration of not doing or saying anything when we feel annoyed.[9] But in the long term, anger becomes toxic: we have known for a long time that it increases the likelihood of sudden death, both from heart attacks and from more general causes.[10] And that hostility towards others, anger felt but not expressed, in short all feelings of resentment, are bad for the heart.[11] And then there is all the damage caused to relationships: negativity which leads to isolation, outbursts which end up provoking conflicts, rancour which prevents forgiveness and ends up pointlessly severing relationships. Not to mention the complications, the onset of secondary infection arising sooner or later through feelings of guilt at having made another human being suffer, at having added to the world's unhappiness.

Resentment as rumination

Being in a 'bad mood' or 'out of sorts' involves ruminating on our hostile feelings. The French word for resentment, *ressentiment*, is particularly apt – 're-sentiment' suggests the constant reviving of feelings of anger which is a fundamental element of resentment. Anger itself (like most powerful emotions) is too costly in terms of inner energy for us to allow it to erupt too often or last too long. It is like running: it is certainly quicker than walking but after a short time, we find we are out of breath, and we have to stop. In the same way, our anger *must* stop at some point because we are exhausted by it (and so are our coronary arteries). Resentment in all its forms can, on the other hand, stay with us for much longer, slowly eating us up.

Pema Chödrön, a Buddhist nun, wrote:

> If you aren't feeding the fire of anger or the fire of craving by talking to yourself then the fire doesn't have anything to feed on. It peaks and passes on. It is said that everything has a beginning, middle and end, but when we start blaming and talking to ourselves, things seem to have a beginning, a middle and no end.[12]

Various research has shown that ruminating on one's anger by focusing on the 'why?' – 'Why did they do that to me?', 'Why so much hatred?', etc.

– can result in resentment becoming chronic, with thoughts and memories connected to the original event resurfacing with increasing frequency. It seems highly preferable, as always when seeking to avoid rumination, to begin by focusing on the 'what?' and the 'how?': 'What exactly happened?', 'How did it all start?', 'What was my feeling and understanding of the situation?', etc.[13]

As with all negative feelings and moods, resentment tends to make us get bogged down in the details (he did this to me, she said that . . .) and withdraw into ourselves and into our own point of view. Research has shown that making the effort to reflect on what has happened from the point of view of other people (how would an outsider have interpreted and described the situation? And how did the person, or people, I was in conflict with experience the situation themselves?) can diminish feelings of resentment, with a reduced frequency of intrusive thoughts and memories associated with the problem and a lower level of physical stress (notably numerous variables linked to respiratory and cardiac rhythms).[14]

Working on our hostile ruminations in this way is essential if we are to avoid the behavioural consequences which might otherwise result. By retreating into resentment, we are locking ourselves into a punitive perception of the problem: in order to put an end to our suffering, we dream of being able to punish those responsible, or for fate to do it for us. We feed on the bitter jubilation of various punishment fantasies. With these in mind, we wait patiently, convinced of the truth of the proverb 'Revenge is a dish best eaten cold.' We convince ourselves that our present incapacity to punish is merely a temporary setback, and *await* the opportunity to take our revenge. But, in the course of such a wait, in a climate so dominated by hostile feelings, our resentment gnaws away at us and blocks out any possibility of moving on or of forgiveness. Because *we are looking for punishment rather than resolution*, we see people not as someone to discuss things with, but simply as guilty parties. And the deeper our resentment, the more firmly we close the door on any prospect of progress either through reconciliation or through forgetting (or rather, not forgetting, but allowing calm to be restored).

For example, if we feel resentment against someone close to us, we reassess that person and the relationship we have previously had with them, focusing exclusively on negative elements. There must indeed be good reasons to hate that person if we are to cast ourselves in the role of victim and/or sheriff rather than that of wrong-doer! We do not want to forgive, at best we expect apologies. There is always the ultimate possibility of a punitive reunion, but without necessarily the accompanying desire to break the ties completely. We want to force the other person to acknowledge somehow we are in the right, as among wolves, where the defeated animal symbolically offers his throat, the most vulnerable part of his anatomy, to the victorious animal.

In the psychological absurdity of these processes, the most astonishing phenomenon is pre-emptive resentment: we imagine in advance that the person in front of us will stand up to us, refuse whatever it is we consider we have a right to, that they may even perhaps be aggressive towards us. So we get angry with them *in advance*. We prepare ourselves, or rather condition ourselves, for a conflict. Which of course we risk provoking by working ourselves into a fury before we even approach the situation. Timid people are often the victims of this anticipated agitation: in preparing themselves to ask for something or to make some kind of complaint, they are so afraid of getting 'no' for an answer that they mistake their anticipation for reality and find themselves already detesting the person who – in their anxious fantasies – will surely pronounce this 'no'. As a result, they either give up (for fear of their anger) or approach the situation already 'worked up' and make their demand in a shaking and aggressive tone, much to the amazement of the other person!

Feelings and moods associated with anger

A considerable number of feelings are associated with anger: acrimony, bitterness, condemnation, animosity, pique, hostility, rancour, wrath, irritation, annoyance, exasperation, spite, irascibility, dissatisfaction, irritability, indignation . . . The list is a long one, which says a lot about our lives, or at least about the way we live them. At some future time, if philologists turn their attention to our dictionaries, they will come to the conclusion that our lives were not easy. Or that we were terrible complainers! Here are a few of these different cocktails, all based on resentment.

Bitterness, that feeling where we keep going back over our conviction that we have been disappointed, betrayed, underestimated, misunderstood. In spite of having made efforts and trusted people and allowed ourselves to hope that this would bear fruit. A mixture of disappointment, sadness, resentment and sometimes shame. And always a deep sense of disillusion about life and humanity. Here too, this shift to a more diffuse mood results from our tendency to see our disappointment in terms of our entire lives, summoning up the ghosts of our past disappointments. Otherwise, it is not bitterness that we would feel, but disappointment, a much more straightforward feeling to deal with.

Cioran, who liked to compare the feelings and moods of different European countries, noted in his *Cahiers*: 'Calle de la Amargura – it was in Valdemosa. Can you imagine Bitterness Street in France? And what about Paseo de los Tristes (Sadness Way) in Grenada.'[15] Let us shoulder our bitterness, transform it into disappointment, into sadness. Let us walk, chatting with Cioran as we go, along Bitterness Road, then into Disappointment Square, and on to the garden of Sadness. There, things will be better: we will be able to start really understanding what is happening to us, and to move on to other things: turning into Acceptance Alley and strolling along Action Avenue.

Sulking: on close inspection, how strange this is! It is an attitude which can only exist in relation to people who love and value us. And who we think, or hope, might change as a result of our sulkiness. In the presence of people who are indifferent or ill-intentioned, sulking would be absurd and pointless. Which is why sulking is by nature childish: only the child who is sure of being loved resorts to sulking; not the neglected or ill-treated one. The same is true within the couple, or the family, or within social groups. We only sulk because there is, or has been, love or affection or esteem.

Like bitterness, sulking often involves sadness and anger; and perhaps more frustration than disappointment. But the dominant feature is the desire to punish the other person by depriving them of ourselves! To make them suffer because of our ostensible withdrawal from the relationship: we refuse to speak to them, to look at them and of course to make any positive gesture towards them.

In common with so many negative feeling, sulking is often associated with the morose delight obtained from suffering by inflicting suffering on ourselves. The feelings and attitudes associated with sulking are most often to be found in people with low self-esteem, who feel they have no other means of modifying the situation or the relationship, or who are afraid that open conflict or argument would be too great a risk. If we are to stop sulking, we need to learn to value ourselves more and to communicate better!

Contempt manifests itself more often amongst people who have high self-esteem, or who are seeking to boost it. As in sulking (the two are closely linked – contempt is a form of sulking, but from a position of power), we punish the other person by depriving them of ourselves. But with the clear intention of destroying the relationship and a desire for exclusion rather than aggression, for a lasting rejection rather than a transient punishment. And also a need to demonstrate superiority.[16] There is pride and disgust in contempt: a dangerous mixture indeed!

Negativity, already touched on briefly, is the propensity to disparage things in advance: everything is pointless, absurd, futile, pathetic, stupid. This mood contains a strong dose of sadness, along with a little touch of resentment directed at the energy and confidence of other people, offensive to us because it is a violent reminder of our own painful passivity. Any form of negativity also contains an element of sabotage, a desire to stifle initiatives, a sense of irritation directed at enthusiasm and spontaneity. In a provocative epigram addressed to one of his enemies, Piron (himself the intellectual adversary of Voltaire in eighteenth-century Paris) described this attitude in these words: 'What is the goat doing in this pretty crib? / Does he look pleasing there? Does he want to please? / No! He is the eunuch in the middle of the harem. / He does nothing and harms those who want to act.'[17]

When we give in to negativity, it is because we secretly seek, by means of our words and our warnings, to bring other people into our pre-depressive state, to drag them down with us. Naturally we do not put it in quite those terms ourselves but certain militant negativities (obstructing plans, systematically opposing other people's arguments) are none other than the desire not to find ourselves alone at the bottom of the pit.

It is interesting not to see negativity only in other people but also to observe it in ourselves. A few years ago, thinking about my own negative tendencies, I noticed that in discussions with other people I would often start my contributions with a little verbal tic: 'No, but' or 'Yes, but'. I realized of course that these little 'buts' were evidence of inner feelings based on impatience, irritation, a desire to rectify what the other person was saying. Even in really small doses, and without meaning any harm, that is what it was: I was probably saying 'no' too often in my head. So, I decided to be more attentive and to eliminate all those pointless 'yes, but' and 'no but' phrases. Since then, whenever I catch myself using one of them, I take a closer look at my feelings: 'Watch out, my friend, you are only listening in order to correct: listen properly first; then you will know if you should continue with a "yes" or a "no", but please, no more "buts". No more of those subliminal little pollutions which subtly alter the relationship between you and the person you are talking to!' So if you should ever find yourself talking to me one day, let me know how I am getting on.

Irony is defined as an indirect way of making a fool of someone or of attacking or criticizing, by feigning naivety or ignorance. 'Irony' comes from the Greek *eironeia*: 'the act of questioning by feigning ignorance', a process Socrates often used in his discussions with others. It is a head-on form of attack (as opposed to spreading gossip, for example), but sufficiently polite and polished to place the other person in an awkward position: if he gets angry, he loses; if he submits, he still loses. He can only respond by placing himself on the same footing of polished spitefulness. Which not everyone is capable of doing, a fact ironists use to their advantage. For the use of irony in a conflict reveals its true nature: it is a powerful 'trigger' of anger and resentment in the target. In fact, irony both sparks off anger and renders the expression of it ridiculous in advance.

Irony is a weapon. Like contempt, it originates in feelings in which there is simultaneously a sense of superiority and of condescending irritation towards the other. Based on the desire to disparage rather than improve, it has a toxic effect on relationships between people, in that it increases tensions and resentments without attempting to find any solutions. Its only advantage, from the spectator's point of view, is that it is sometimes funny. But as Jules Renard observed: 'Irony is essentially a game of wits. Humour would be more a game of emotions, of feelings.' That is why humour brings people together whereas irony separates them. And is proof of a hardened mind set, and of negative feelings, as Stendhal emphasized in criticizing 'French society, made up of dry beings for whom the pleasure of demonstrating irony stifles the happiness of having enthusiasm'.

Rancour ('bitterness or resentfulness, especially when long-standing') is based on the desire for retaliation and for punishment: the individual concerned has decided to freeze the memory of the offence by preventing the natural healing of the injuries inflicted on their self-respect normally brought about by forgetting or by distancing. Getting on with their lives again would allow other experiences gradually to wipe out the pain of the offence. But in rancour, especially when it reaches the stage of hatred,[18] the individual has, in a sense, halted their life so as not to forget. And at the same time has decided to carve the statue of a monster slowly in the shape of the offender: as time goes on, details confirming his dark side are collected and added. The period preceding a divorce (and of course divorce itself) are, for example, often times when these slow and sinister mechanisms come into play, where we actively increase our resentment and rancour towards the partner. A process which at least appears to have the advantage of making us feel less sad about separating. But which also causes considerable suffering, as well as complicating any future reconciliation (if there are children, for example).

Resentment and the couple

'Can it be possible, over a period of almost half a century, to observe only one side of the creature with whom we share our life? Do we, through force of habit, select from their words and gestures, retaining only those which nourish our grievances and uphold our rancour?' asks François Mauriac in his novel *The Knot of Vipers*. Alas, yes.

Living as a couple (and as a family) is a state in which numerous resentments can take root. There are so many possibilities for frustrations and misunderstandings, unless these can be cleared up on a regular basis through dialogue or through enjoyable shared experiences. When we live with someone, we frequently find ourselves at 'crossroads of divorce', where it is all too easy, blown along by the winds of resentment, to take the wrong turning.

In a relationship, conflicts are normal. The difference between successful and unsuccessful couples is less to do with the frequency of conflict than with their intensity (how far do they go?) and their impact (do they leave behind them feelings of resentment which will poison what happens next and hinder reconciliation?). In such pathological conflicts, punishment is preferred over resolution, dominance over collaboration (who is right? who should be punished? who should apologize to the other?).

Successful couples have the capacity to 'let storms blow over', even if they have not fully resolved their problems. Because sometimes there are problems which simply cannot be resolved (relationships with in-laws are a classic example). Such problems must be tolerated, and overlaid with love, affection and the passage of time. The partners take care not to discuss them too soon. And in the meanwhile, the positive feelings experienced and shared together have softened the resentment, stopped the partners from brooding over it, and paved the way for friendly discussion.

For unstable couples, on the other hand, the slightest conflict makes things worse, and any attempt to discuss matters automatically turns into a source of conflict in which we are irritated by the attitude our partner adopts in the exchange. The writer Éric Chevillard observes: 'A delicate operation: taking the heat out of a quarrel can be like trying to gut a fish without piercing the bile duct.'[19] But often the bile duct ends up getting pierced, and we ruminate on the conflict, which then causes a 'crystallization' of all the various memories of other conflicts. Our memory gives them a coherence they do not necessarily possess, using them to elaborate a story of failure, of misunderstanding, a sense of having been cheated ('this is no longer the person I loved'). The more we think about it, the more we activate the cerebral circuits which, in every future argument, will recall this story of fraught relations which now sums up our couple. And, after a while, we end up seeing the other person purely as an aggressor, as someone we are constantly at odds with, we see only the bad side of them and associate them solely with negative feelings.

Since this is – a fact often neglected – a source of considerable suffering for us, and because suffering tends to make us withdraw into ourselves, we then become completely oblivious to the suffering of the other person. Hence the importance of couple therapy sessions[20] where one person is asked to talk about his or her feelings, and about nothing else, without judging their partner's behaviour and without blaming them. While the other partner, some distance away and sometimes with their back turned (to ensure greater concentration on what they hear), listens in silence. These therapies also seek to introduce couples to non-violent communication,[21] to help them understand the need to listen and reassure the other person before seeking to be listened to in turn. The basic principles of this non-violent communication involve emphasizing the 'I' rather than the 'you' (instead of 'what you did or said to me', saying 'what I felt when you did or said it'), expressing your own feelings rather than interpreting the other person's intentions ('I felt as though . . .' instead of 'you're always trying to . . .'), discussing behaviour rather than passing judgement ('you did this' instead of 'you are a . . .'), trying always to refer to precise and specific facts rather than to generalize ('this is what happened' instead of 'it's always the same, ever since I've known you, you always . . .').

Self-resentment

Feelings of anger directed at oneself are a particular but fascinating case.
It is estimated that at least 10 per cent of the anger we feel is directed

at ourselves:[22] in my opinion this figure could be considerably higher for certain people. When we analyse self-directed anger across a wide range of people (not necessarily patients with psychological problems), we discover that it is something they find easy to remember and talk about.[23] We also find that much of what is judged 'unreasonable' anger often turns out to be self-directed anger.[24] Since the problem with this kind of anger is that there is nobody else involved, such outbursts frequently end up with people hitting out at inanimate objects. An angry patient once told me that whilst on holiday in a rented cottage in Brittany he ended up hitting his head several times a day on a low door frame; one day, after the fiftieth bump on the head as he went from one room to the next, he let fly a powerful kick at the door in question, fracturing his big toe. 'In the space of a second, I had ruined my summer. After that spectacular outburst of anger, I had to watch my temper more carefully. As my wife said: "You've already spoiled the holidays with this, so don't go poisoning the atmosphere any further! You'd better not do any more moaning and complaining, we know what you're like."' For anger directed at oneself of course triggers feelings of self-resentment. Which is why all of this is often associated with problems of self-esteem, in which feelings of enduring self-resentment are very much in evidence: we wish ourselves harm, we hope to be harmed, and sometimes we end up doing ourselves harm, and we might even go so far as to say, after having done so: 'It serves you right!'

In his epic poem, *The Divine Comedy*, Dante travels through the different circles of Hell, where those who have sinned are eternally punished. In the fifth circle, as he is crossing the Styx, the river of Hell, he notices angry people in the mud who are beating each other and sometimes tearing at their own flesh – 'tearing each other piecemeal with their teeth'.[25] And not far away from these are the melancholy, who continue to groan just as they did on Earth. Dante situated anger not far from sadness, and touches on self-resentment: further proof of his genius.

Illnesses of anger and feelings of anger

Many pathologies are based on feelings and moods of resentment and poorly controlled anger.

The best known and most closely studied over the last few years are those cases of pathological anger, notably in the form of 'road rage', because of the danger to public safety which they pose, by increasing offences against the law, accidents, altercations and even murders.[26] Driving is indeed a high-risk situation, where the sense of freedom and omnipotence is activated (by the power of the car, and sometimes by the stimulating effect of playing aggressive music at top volume) but where the drivers find themselves confronted with errors, or simply with the *existence* of others (drivers who are not going fast enough, pedestrians trying to cross the road, etc.). Not to mention all the frustrations that have to be endured because of the Highway Code, speed limits, traffic jams or the difficulty of finding somewhere to park.[27]

We also know that resentment frequently affects weak and vulnerable people, such as those with social anxiety disorders, and to a lesser degree people who suffer from shyness.[28] With fragile individuals, it is extremely important to tackle this distress-related resentment during psychotherapy sessions. It is often the cause of much additional suffering. And can sometimes even lead them to adopting misguided attitudes: in the face of what they take to be hostility or contempt or abuse, they try to harden themselves, to give as good as they get, but they are inevitably fighting a losing battle. We should always ask ourselves what feeling of fragility lies behind our outbreaks of bad temper.

It is worth pointing out that suppressed anger and resentment can also be associated with bulimic behaviour, resulting in crises of eating frenzies.[29] There is nothing surprising about this: oscillations in moods often lie behind the impulse to eat, as we have seen earlier.

Finally, there are also cases of 'hostile depression', in which the dominant emotional expression is resentment rather than sadness:[30] the symptom of misanthropy replaces the depressive complaint, but always against a backdrop of mental suffering. In bereavement too, there can sometimes be an element of resentment, towards the living (people who still have their children) or towards the deceased (who failed to do what was needed to stay alive). Here is the account of a patient describing a lunch with his father, who was depressed following the death of his wife:

> It was really sad. Without being aware of it, he was full of hatred towards his neighbours, because they were still living happily together; towards the doctors who had not (according to him) given my mother the appropriate care: towards all those anonymous people who drove badly or made him waste time in the checkout queues at the local supermarket. As he recounted his daily routine, interspersed with these surges of hatred, obviously linked to his own suffering, I began to feel sadder and sadder. In the end I told him that all this resentment was bad for him. He seemed to be listening, but then said that no, in fact these little outbursts of hatred did him good and that he felt better as a result. That wasn't how it seemed to me. It's odd how people manage to blind themselves about the benefits of anger.

Resentment in all its forms is closely linked to an inaptitude for happiness.

Anger and pain

On one single occasion, I was insulted by one of my daughters: the youngest of them had just had to have a lumbar puncture as a result of a health problem. Lumbar punctures are already extremely painful procedures (a huge needle is inserted between two vertebrae in order to drain off some cerebrospinal fluid), but the after-effects can be even worse because unless you remain completely horizontal you can experience violent pain or severe headaches. I was carrying her in my arms so as to move her gently from the living room to her bedroom when I must have somehow jolted her, causing excruciating pain. I was submerged under a flood of insults such as I had never encountered before. The episode has become part of our family mythology, especially the particularly choice utterance: 'You useless clumsy idiot.' Too much pain . . .

A good deal of research has focused on the very close links between anger and pain.[31] Not surprisingly, results show that emotions and feelings of anger magnify the perception of pain and that, conversely, any form of pain is likely to trigger feelings of resentment. This is evident in the expression 'flayed alive', which reminds us of the existence of the suffering behind the aggressivity.

The children's cartoon *Kirikou* features a wicked witch who, we discover, owes her wickedness to a huge thorn stuck in her back which has been there for so long even she has forgotten about it: everything changes when the hero, young Kirikou, pulls it out.[32]

We know too that any attempts to suppress the feeling or the expression of resentment make us subsequently even more sensitive to pain.[33] If we suppress our feelings, our tolerance of physical pain is lowered. This is true of all feelings, but applies to a greater extent in the case of resentment than in other negative feelings, such as anxiety. But for all that, it is not advisable to give free rein to our resentment: the more we do so, the more likely we are to experience anger and the more prone we will be to future recurrences. We need simply to try and accept the experience of feeling anger in order to turn it into something useful and interesting rather than acting in an extreme way under its influence. The best way of avoiding suppressed anger (the worst kind) is not to resort to expressing your anger, but to use dialogue and discussion instead. With first a decompression period, a *time out* as Americans call it, time to go out, get some fresh air, perhaps go for a run. But certainly not a session of punchball, or any other methods supposedly designed to get rid of anger: they will only aggravate resentment and prepare the way for further outbursts of anger.[34] *Emotional draining* and catharsis do not work.

The madness of anger, the wisdom of gentleness: a few useful tips

Suppress anger and resentment? Hmm. Better instead to: (1) accept that they are inevitable in any normal life, unless we are extremely skilful or live in seclusion from the world, (2) realize that it is possible to learn to control them rather than simply hoping not to feel them, (3) understand that the first step in the process is to recognize that behind every one of our resentments there is suffering, and (4) genuinely desire to suffer less.

Begin by accepting and understanding the world as it is

Before we can change the world we need to change our expectations: it is as absurd for those most susceptible to resentment and anger to wish for a world where nothing would annoy them as it is for anxious people to wish for a world without risks or problems. We have no alternative but to accept psychodiversity (people who do not think as we do), the absurd, the pointless, the regrettable and the deplorable. In the same way that we accept storms, stinging nettles and hornets: on encountering these, we do whatever is needed rather than get angry. But, all the same, if I give up my anger, am I not simply admitting defeat, giving up on any hope of changing the world with all its injustices and its absurdities? In his work *On Anger*, the Stoic philosopher Seneca provides an answer to the objection: '"But against the enemy", it is said "anger is necessary". Nowhere is it less so; for there the attack ought not to be disorderly, but regulated and under control [. . .] So, too, in the case of gladiators, skill is their protection, anger their undoing.' We always act better if we are calm rather than angry.

Be conscious of the first signs of resentment

When we study the psychological processes in people experiencing some form of resentment, we see that they possess a sort of psychological alarm which is triggered whenever hostile thoughts seek to gain entrance to their minds. It is not therefore the external situation or people who are seen as problematic but the aggressive ideas. These people are aware that resentment is trying to get a hold in them, and are able to stop it before it begins its task of distorting reality.[35]

Accept anger and resentment in ourselves

Paradoxically, this is the best way of avoiding being overwhelmed by hostile feelings. Remember all those times when, if someone said to us 'Don't get angry like that', or 'Don't get in such a state', we tended to reply 'I am NOT angry' (the psychological defence mechanism known as *denial*) or 'YOU'RE the one who's making me angry' (another mechanism, known as *projection*). This anger must indeed be a painful or costly experience, if we are so anxious to avoid it! And yet, as with all emotions and feelings, acceptance is the first step to distancing ourselves from it. That means saying: 'Yes, you're right, I do feel angry. This is why . . .'

Resolve to be slow to get angry and not to hate anyone

As a result of exploring the meanderings of our unconscious motives, modern psychology has ended up considerably underestimating the importance of our conscious decisions in the processes of change.[36] Yet it is indeed possible to make the decision to allow less and less place for anger and resentment in our lives. At least, it is possible to decide to work towards that goal. With the understanding that, as in any struggle with our habits, there will be numerous relapses and resurgences of resentment: we have to accept that *it* will come back regularly without taking that as proof that what we are attempting is impossible, but simply accepting that these setbacks are part of the process of change. In France, and more generally in Latin countries, efforts to deal with anger are not given much priority, and there are more books devoted more or less directly to praising anger or the right to be angry[37] than there are manuals suggesting how it can be controlled.[38] In some other countries, anger is taken much more seriously: in the United States, for example, and in many other places, there are specialized treatment centres and internet sites dedicated to helping angry people become less angry.[39]

Bear in mind that there is no such thing as useful resentment

Gradually, learn not to tolerate resentment in yourself any longer. For example, getting angry because you have got lost when you were out for a walk during your holiday or on your way to friends for dinner. The first step is to force yourself to smile instead of getting annoyed. To do that, you need to think ahead and anticipate where irritation might occur. By telling yourself 'This is exactly the kind of situation where, at the slightest little incident, I quickly start to lose my temper. I'm going to calm myself down in anticipation. And assess immediately if it is worth getting annoyed or not. I'll start by accepting that getting lost is part of normal life.' It is true that now, with GPS systems, we can no longer use these little incidents to test our patience and restraint. And yet, as a consequence, the day our GPS breaks down, we will be even more helpless.

Getting rid of the myths: there is no such thing as 'righteous anger', and resentment is never justified

Beware of myths about anger: anger is never a good thing. In any case, if we aspire to inner equilibrium, it can only be tolerated as the alarm signal for a potential problem. And it must then be kept on a tight rein before any action is taken. Aristotle said 'It must serve us not as a leader, but as a soldier.' Action is good; action inspired by anger can be; but action under the influence of anger rarely is. Staying calm and refusing to get angry is not a sign of weakness. The great champions of non-violence, Gandhi, Martin Luther King, the Dalai Lama, were not – nor are not – weak people. We must be careful not to attach too much importance to 'righteous anger' – anger is hugely destructive in terms of social bonds. We are much more inclined to celebrate the benefits of anger rather than focusing on the enormous damage it does. Such celebration means that the strong and powerful allow themselves to get angry far too often, instead of trying to stifle their anger, or making an effort to communicate by some other means. And the weak reproach themselves for not being capable of acting like the strong. True, anger generates a certain energy, but it is a toxic, polluting and costly energy. It almost always overflows and gets out of control. It inflicts injuries that lead to fresh resentments, the seeds of anger and conflicts to come.

Never underestimate anger and resentment

After a conflict or a surge of anger, even muted and silent, even unexpressed, we should not immediately move on to other things: that is the surest way of allowing hostile feelings to survive and endure, and to ensure their return. If anger has been felt, it is because of something significant or serious, whether objective or subjective. Or because I am not myself at the moment. All of that deserves a little thought. So I pause, I make sure I am physically calm, and I reflect on what is going on. I ask myself what happened to get me into this state. And if I could have reacted differently. Simply asking the question and really trying to answer it. I ask how I can get in touch with what is important to me (being listened to, being respected . . .) without having to harbour all this resentment.

Do not ignore the sadness and fear that lie behind our feelings of anger

We need to listen carefully to the little voice of our original feelings lying beneath our resentment. Anger is often what is known as a secondary emotion, concealing a fear or a sadness which were the original cause of our suffering. The mother who watched her child cross the road without looking and who scolds the child before hugging them in relief experienced anger, even though fear was her first reaction. The same is true of our rancour when someone points out our inconsistencies and our mistakes: at first we experience the disappointment – sadness and disillusion – of being wrong. And then, of course, in addition to sadness and fear as sources of anger, there are all the anxieties that we now call stress. In stressful situations men are quicker to switch to hostile moods than women.[40] We know they are not as good at interpreting them.

Being able to talk about what is wrong is a good way of heading off resentment

Asserting oneself, expressing things calmly: these are things that can be learned, and it is clear that self-assertion therapies can have an 'all-purpose' effect, with the capacity to improve a wide range of anxious or depressive states.[41] The ability to communicate calmly and efficiently in effect exerts a key regulatory role over the whole of our emotional lives. It is not a question of giving up being kind, but nor is it about not saying what we have to say. Most importantly of all we need to think about non-violent communication as a means of expressing what we want: from an aggressive message, the other person retains only the aggression, not the message itself. After we receive a message we deem aggressive, we judge the other person ('Why did he do that to me?') rather than ourselves ('Did I really do what I am accused of doing?' or 'How could I have given that impression?'). We focus our thoughts on the other person and not on ourselves: we look for ways of making that person change, instead of changing ourselves.

Beware of adding to our resentment by sharing it with those close to us

Often, when we are annoyed about something, we confide in those close to us: this consists in telling them our version of the facts. Because they love us, they often accept our story at face value and therefore endorse it. And this support can indeed calm us down, and then help us to distance ourselves from the situation: that little dose of affection and esteem cheers us up and, soothing our sadness, soothes our resentment. Yet this biased ear can also reinforce it. On the basis of our abbreviated version of events, those close to us are too inclined to 'believe' us and risk making us take a step further towards a distorted vision of things: 'I am right and the other person is wrong. And I'm not the only one who says so: my friends think so too.' A sure recipe for ongoing resentment. Research has confirmed the phenomenon of what we now call 'co-rumination': we keep going over things with our friends. When this happens, our friendships may indeed benefit, but our lucidity does not; women seem to be particularly prone to this co-rumination, or at least, they admit to it more easily.[42]

Do not forget about your own happiness and inner equilibrium

At some point or other in my resentment, I need to ask myself sincerely: 'Do I really want to carry on like this? Does this mood feel right?' Feelings of anger and feelings of happiness are completely incompatible. Indeed this is the most radical incompatibility of all the subtle alliances of feelings: we can be happy in spite of sadness or anxiety. But we cannot be happy and angry. Anger systematically interferes with any sense of harmony and with our relationship with the world. In order to live happily (or more or less so) it is indispensable to develop an aversion to anger and resentment. Indispensable to begin to see anger as painful: not easy, but progress nevertheless.

Understand that resentment is both poison and prison

We need to become aware that resentment alienates and imprisons us: in its grip we lose out on happy and light-hearted life, by devoting too much of our energy and our thoughts to mulling over ideas of revenge and punishment. Steven Hayes, an American psychologist who has worked in this field, suggests that resentment should be seen as a hook on which there are two squirming, wriggling maggots.[43] The first maggot on the hook is us; the second is the person who has offended us. As long as we harbour hatred, we are condemning ourselves to remain on the hook. But the only means of escaping is by first unhooking the other person, in other words by forgiving him, so that we can then free ourselves (because the other one is blocking our exit from the hook – fishermen will understand).

The very, very complex issue of forgiveness

I remember giving a lecture on the psychology of forgiveness at a psychotherapy conference:[44] it sparked off heated discussions with several colleagues who were extremely reticent about the idea of addressing the issue of forgiveness in psychotherapy, especially when treating patients who had been victims of aggression. Many others (myself included) felt that, on the contrary, the more severe the harm, the more forgiveness could be a useful factor in helping victims recover their freedom and psychological well-being. Anyway, it is worth pointing out that in psychotherapy, there is no consensus with regard to the use of forgiveness.

Forgiving means regarding an insult, an offence, as something null and void, no longer feeling resentment because of it, abandoning any notion of revenge. Forgiveness is a fundamental issue in any society made up of social creatures such as we humans: given that suffering, offences and violence are omnipresent, whether intentional or not, the processes of forgiveness are indispensable to the survival of the species, which would otherwise constantly tear itself apart. We see early indications of this in monkeys in the form of reconciliation rituals following conflicts. The aptitude for forgiveness, so crucial in avoiding interminable and costly retaliation, is probably more than thirty million years old. It is part of a heritage shared with primates, common to large apes and to humans.[45] But the roots of forgiveness are also, and above all, religious and societal:[46] humans invented war, and the role played by resentment in history is greater than we imagine.[47] But humans were also capable of understanding the importance of making peace, and the necessity of renewing links once a war was over. On this subject it is worth pointing out that justice needs to exist (social regulation) in order for forgiveness (intra- and inter-personal regulation) to exist alongside it. Without justice, forgiveness would sometimes be imprudent.

Forgiveness is not only a ritual of social appeasement but also (and this is particularly so in the context of feelings, which is our focus here) a *process of psychological appeasement*: without which resentment and the incapacity to forgive will add further suffering to the initial injury. In psychology, forgiveness is defined as an 'inter-individual process through which an individual who has been injured by another (injustice) chooses to abandon any feeling of resentment towards the other person rather than seeking revenge'.[48]

Of course there are also cases of *pseudo-forgiveness*. The kind of forgiveness that comes after revenge: 'There is no injury that cannot be forgiven once vengeance has been exacted', Vauvenargues declared. Or the forgiveness that is socially imposed by the strong on the weak: 'I order you to forgive me.'

Once we have understood the importance and the significance of feelings, we have also understood the huge cost of conflicts, and the even greater one of those conflicts which become chronic as a result of rumination. And we are then ready to understand the importance of forgiveness and the liberating effect it can have on these feelings of resentment. This is no easy matter, for there are as many misunderstandings about forgiveness as there are about anger: 'Forgiving is neither forgetting nor effacing; it means, depending on each individual case, abandoning the desire to punish or hate, and even, sometimes, to judge', said André Comte-Sponville. In fact, forgiving does not mean apologizing, granting amnesty or absolving: when we forgive we are not denying the mistake or the offense, but simply deciding not to seek revenge for it. It does not mean relativizing the aggression in order to be able to forgive it. Nor does it entail reconciliation: forgiveness can be a private decision, not communicated to the offender, who we may, after all, have decided never to see again. And it is not about seeking apologies: even if the latter are sometimes helpful, we can and should decide to forgive primarily for our own sake, in order to free ourselves from hatred. Finally, forgiveness is not about amnesia or forgetting: we do not forget whatever it is that has happened.

There are sequences of therapies which are based on forgiveness, and these are used in particular by professionals treating people who have been victims of serious assaults (rape, hostage taking, physical violence). Of course the patient is always completely free to choose whether to forgive or not, and those who choose not to, or are unable to do so, are never judged: the greater the suffering, the more severe the level of violence, the more difficult it is. For some people, resentment seems to provide them with a crutch and a motivation: in such cases it is better not to insist but simply to wait. At some point however, the subject must be broached. Therapists using these approaches identify two phases: one called 'decisional forgiveness', the moment when the patient realizes that they are locked into resentment and the desire for revenge, and are therefore doubly victim of the initial violence they experienced; then a phase of 'emotional forgiveness', in which the patient is able to integrate fully the process of forgiveness, not simply on a conceptual level or in principle.[49] Just as resentment transforms the person who does not forgive in a negative and painful manner, 'forgiveness is an internal process which transforms the person who forgives'.[50] Forgiveness is therefore considered an extremely powerful tool for regulating emotional equilibrium.

Studies have identified certain factors which facilitate forgiveness: the fact that the offences are minor ones;[51] the existence of empathetic or close links with the offender;[52] the possibility of identifying with the offender: 'I could have acted in the same way.'[53] Generally speaking, it seems that the sense of well-being, once forgiveness has been given, is linked to proximity with the offender:[54] in other words, the closer we are, the more forgiveness is important and, above all, the more beneficial, it is.

Amongst the factors which hinder forgiveness are a tendency to ruminate;[55] the characteristic traits of negative emotionality – hostile, angry, neurotic, depressive;[56] the notion that forgiveness equals submission – for example, in a professional context, people find it easier to forgive their colleagues than their superiors;[57] wanting the offender to repent, or wanting to sever all links with him or her,[58] which clearly undermines the motivation needed to embark on the difficult process of forgiveness.

'I forgive easily, for the simple reason that I do not know how to hate. It seems to me that hate is painful', said Montesquieu. An awareness of the cost of resentment and a habit of forgiving regularly are a sound combination against the corrosion of everyday life. If one is fortunate enough not to have been given serious offence, it is important to view the practice of what I call *micro-forgiveness* as part of a healthy lifestyle, on a day-to-day basis and throughout our lives: acquiring the habit of not bearing grudges unnecessarily, of not judging too hastily acts which have hurt us. Defend yourself if necessary, but only with words and actions which have been stripped of resentment in advance. Try instead (since the offences are minor ones) to show compassion, as the philosopher Gustave Thibon notes: 'Seen from the outside, evil calls for punishment. From the inside, for pity.'[59] We shall explore the extent to which that can help us manage our feelings and moods.

Changing our view of the world

Resentment contains something resembling a false trail: the wish or the desire to punish, to restore order through punishment. If we must punish, then we need to be able to do so without resentment: that is the role of justice. The wish for justice is perhaps a sublimation, an acceptable version of the desire for revenge, its civilized side. In that case, long live sublimation!

For the rest, the better we can become at distancing ourselves from resentment, or rather, the more lucid we can become at identifying the source of our resentment – very often fear or sadness – the better it will be both for us and for society in general. In the words of Thomas Aquinas: 'Anger, which desires evil in the name of good, is a sin.'

Moreover, even more interesting than getting rid of resentment is the creation in ourselves of a psychological atmosphere in which it becomes a rarity. For example, by imposing on ourselves a discipline of empathy, of compassion even, by always seeking to understand other people's point of view. Showing ourselves to be *a priori* a kind person, and always taking care never to forget or lose sight of the potential good in people and things. Not simply as a *one-off* but as a guiding principle.

It is not merely tolerance that we are aiming for, but kindliness, benevolence.

What a task!

Chapter 8

Sadness

I thought I would die
From grief and weariness
I had stopped laughing,
It was still night.
Félix Leclerc,
Le petit bonheur

When my daughters were little, they sometimes played 'shopkeepers', which consisted in them setting up little 'shops' in the apartment we were living in. They would set up stalls in front of their bedroom door. Then they would wait for customers. That is to say their mother or myself, and, if they were lucky a grandparent or guest. We would go and 'buy' something from them every now and again and they were delighted. All of this took a considerable amount of time: selecting the objects, making the price tags, setting up the stalls, buying a few things from each other's stalls, squabbling with each other. It was incredibly sweet and yet, curiously, this game always made me feel profoundly sad. I would watch their little faces as they waited for customers to come, feeling a mixture of tenderness and sorrow. Such moments made me think of all the disappointments they would have to face in their lives, the fruitless projects they would get involved in, like so many other people. Without knowing that, in certain situations, even from the very start, there is no hope, no way out. Just as, right from the start, there were never enough customers for their shop. My sad feelings made me project their present situation into the future, a characteristic response to sad feelings, when a heavy foreboding replaces the light sadness of the moment. I was transposing their fragility as it appeared at the time, whereas in fact they might end up being bankers with flourishing business interests. But no, when we are unable to distance ourselves from our feelings, we take the present and project it on to the future. I have often tried to transform these wistful feelings into positive ones: 'They are having fun. For them, these are happy times; all they want is for you to pretend to be interested in what they are selling, and buy one or two items.'

But to no avail: the image of them sitting behind those little shops will forever be associated in my mind with a sweet sadness.

Understanding sadness

Sadness can be defined as 'an invasion of consciousness by a pain or a feeling of uneasiness which prevents any feeling of delight'. There are three significant words in this definition: 'invasion' (a vague general sensation, contaminating everything), 'pain' (unpleasant tone of feeble strength, to begin with at least), and 'prevent' (from feeling delight).

But only the first word – invasion – always applies; the other two are subject to variations.

Sadness is an *invasive* feeling which fills our minds completely. When we feel sad, everything about us becomes sad: the way we see things, the way we move, our tone of voice. However, feeling sad is not always *painful*, since it also has that particular quality of sweetness. In this respect it stands out from other feelings: think of anxiety, or hostility. There is no sweetness in feeling anxious. Nor in resentment either. But when it comes to sadness, it is sometimes there. Finally, sadness does not necessarily preclude happiness. On the contrary, there is, as we shall see, such a thing as sad happiness.

So, is sadness not such a serious matter after all?

Yes and no . . .

Feelings and moods of sadness

There are many different sorts of sadness, an infinity of them: gentle sadness in which you feel as though anaesthetized, even slightly drugged; heavy, suffocating sadness; the sadness of defeat, but also the sadness of certain victories (because someone had to lose); guilty sadness, when we have harmed someone we love, and indifferent sadness, when we no longer love someone. Using the word 'sadness' is like using the word 'flowers' or 'trees': there is so much that needs to be made clear and understood! Sadness is undoubtedly one of the most fertile resources of our inner lives; such is its power to bring depth, sweetness and weight to all our other feelings and moods.

In his *Cahiers*, Cioran, a specialist in dark moods, observes: 'Depression at every level, from tango to apocalypse. That is my usual mood.'[1] Not surprisingly there are a great number of words to describe the feelings associated with sadness: nostalgia, melancholy, heavy-heartedness, depression, the blues, despondency, gloom, sorrow. Some of these are associated with a particular culture or civilization and have become universal: the smog-filled melancholy of the English, the oceanic *saudade* of the Portuguese.

Sadness fuels various complex feelings and moods: all those sentiments of unfulfilment, inferiority, inaptitude, deception, solitude, despondency. Sometimes of relief: after the breakup of a relationship for example, when everything had become so complicated, it is possible to feel both sad and relieved, as in Léo Ferré's famous song, *Avec le temps* ('With time'): 'And you feel all alone perhaps, but at peace.' At such times sadness becomes a refuge: 'He took refuge in his sadness.'[2]

Sadness is closely linked to the passing of time. Present time: mournful, gloomy, morose moods. The past: nostalgia, regret, remorse, guilt. Future: despondency, loss of hope. And between the past and the future: feelings of disillusionment (the sadness of disappointed hopes and broken trust) and pessimism (the sadness of the futility of future efforts), which lead to the 'sadness of not being able to make action match our dreams'.[3]

And then there is of course *ennui* – the deep-seated, world-weary sadness, this 'pain of time', this sadness which slowly emerges in our lives precisely when life is lacking, when stimulation, chance encounters, changes, surprises are all missing. Ennui like a premonition of sadness, a sadness as yet unclear and undefined, but like a sadness yet to come, which will soon step out to take the air on the balcony of our souls. On the subject of these drifting, hazy sensations of sadness, André Comte-Sponville gives this excellent definition of melancholy, which he refers to as a 'light and diffuse sadness, which has no precise object and is therefore virtually inconsolable'.[4]

Then there is also a physical sensation which we suddenly become aware of: 'Sadness – fatigue that invades the soul. Fatigue: sadness that invades the body.'[5] For sadness is not only felt in the mind, it is also a physical state. It begins sometimes without words, without thought, without reason, in the body itself: we are heavy-hearted, we sigh, we are inclined to inactivity, slowing down, withdrawal. Sometimes intense sadness produces feelings of suffocation, of drowning. When we speak of feeling low, of being weighed down, we are indeed describing a body which feels crushed under the weight of bad news and the ensuing mental suffering. We are weary of desires, physical or intellectual, as in Mallarmé's famous lines: 'The flesh is sad, alas! And I've read all the books.'

Doctors are well aware that certain kinds of fatigue are physical manifestations of sadness, or depressions in which the body speaks: 'The opposite of depression is not happiness or joy: it is vitality.'[6]

Why do our minds stumble in this way?

Sadness because the world is a sad place?

Sadness would then be caused by the loss of our positive illusions, described by Cioran as our 'comforting errors'.[7] We do indeed deceive ourselves into thinking things are better than they are, but doing so is good for us and makes life easier. Such errors certainly exist and a good deal of research has shown that psychological well-being is nourished by a certain number of positive distortions of reality: there is a relative 'depressive lucidity' – in reality, a lucidity of sadness, for as we shall see, depression darkens people's judgement – often resulting in a clearer understanding of how things really are.[8] As Paul Valéry observes: 'To see clearly, is to see the dark side of things.'

Yet these errors protect us from the sadness and despair that could otherwise result from a thorough contemplation of the world as it really is. They allow us to believe that life is good, that the world is a welcoming place, and that happiness is easy. And so much the better, for this gives us the courage to act and paradoxically helps us towards achieving our desire for a good and beautiful world, ensuring that these optimistic prophesies are fulfilled. Believing makes it possible to change the world. But we must keep up our efforts, the illusion must be maintained. If it is not, the veil will be torn.

Sadness because humans are sad?

Is sadness a fundamental human state? Is it our basic psychological state, which only a certain amount of effort, distraction or illusion can prevent us from feeling? This vast issue of sadness and how it relates to the human condition, to our status as rational beings, is one which generations of thinkers have addressed.

Listen to the sombre voice of Pascal: 'Nothing is so unbearable to man as to be completely at rest, without passion, without business, without distraction, without occupation. It is then he feels his nothingness, his forsakenness, his insufficiency, his dependence, his impotence, his emptiness. Then from the depths of his soul comes ennui, blackness, sorrow, vexation, despair.' The German philosopher Schelling refers to a 'steadfast and profound melancholy', indissociable from thought. And George Steiner, a contemporary thinker we rarely associate with light-heartedness, speaks of the *sadness of thought* and writes: 'The existence of man, the life of the mind means an experience of this melancholy and the vital capacity to overcome it. [. . .] We are as it were created "saddened".'[9]

Sadness would therefore mean reverting to our true nature: we go from being a thinking reed (according to Pascal's description) to a leaning reed, and we tend to lean towards what is sad. According to Spinoza, it is 'man's passage from a greater to a less perfection [. . .] whereby the active power of man is diminished or hindered'. Where anxiety distorts our lives without completely preventing us from acting and from experiencing delight, sadness can be an amputation of our capacity to live. Few other feelings dissuade us from taking action to the same extent: resentment and anxiety, on the contrary, even drive us to do so.

Only sadness paralyses us. In reference to sadness, psychiatrists speak of a 'loss of life force'. And according to evolutionary psychologists, this is its natural function: immobilizing and slowing us down when we have been hurt or plunged into grief, as a way of helping us heal and restore ourselves. But this natural mechanism often malfunctions. This is why some forms of sadness are more dangerous than others. Sadness can enrich us or diminish us. Strangely, sadness can widen our horizons or shrink them, depending on its intensity. In its lightest form, it connects us to the world, but in a painful way, by rendering us hyper-empathetic and hypersensitive, extremely receptive to other people's misfortunes. But beyond that, in its more severe form, closer to depressive sadness, it is withdrawal that lies in wait: first with a sense of helplessness, then indifference, then desperation.

Sadness because we are constantly in mourning for something?

Sadness is of course triggered by the experience of mourning in its many forms: deaths (mourning someone we love), separations (mourning the end of a relationship), failures (mourning for our lost self-image and ideals), getting old (mourning our lost youth), illness (mourning the loss of health). It would be relatively easy to view life only from this perspective as an uninterrupted succession of losses and mourning.

This is what Scott Fitzgerald refers to in the opening phrase of his famous short story 'The Crack-Up': 'Of course all life is a process of breaking down'. The author, himself no stranger to depression, enlightens us further as he continues: 'but the blows that do the dramatic side of the work – the big sudden blows that come, or seem to come, from outside – the ones you remember and blame things on and, in moments of weakness, tell your friends about, don't show their effect all at once. There is another sort of blow that comes from within.'

For amongst the many wounds that provoke sadness, there is not only our mourning for what we have loved and what life has taken away from us. There is also the sadness of absence, the pain of things we have never had, never known and yet which we nevertheless expect: love, happiness, pleasure, beauty, adventure, harmony . . . The absence of these things in our lives overwhelms us suddenly and painfully: it is the sadness of single people, or of those who find themselves alone on a winter evening when everybody else is going back to a warm house and the company of their partner and children.

On close reflection, we may well wonder if any sadness is ever insignificant. At any rate, we need to listen to sadness, never dismissing it lightly: it almost always teaches us something interesting about our lives. Yet we should not always trust and obey it, feeling distress at its command: sometimes it can be short-sighted, even malevolent. Sometimes it is both right (the world is a sad place) and wrong (just because the world is a sad place does not mean we have to be sad too).

Beware of sadness

'Beware of sadness. It is a vice', wrote Flaubert in one of his letters to Guy de Maupassant. An even stronger warning comes in these lines from the Bible: 'As the worm doth eat the cloth and the rot enter the wood, so doth the sadness of man eat his heart.'[10] I remember one of my patients telling me, in response to my inquiries about her possible tendency to sad ruminations: 'No, no, never. I am *anti-depression*! I am far too fragile to allow myself to indulge in sadness.'

Could the sadness that we sometimes give way to be simply the luxury of those who are well? Like the wine we drink with an easy conscience because we are not (or not yet) alcoholics, but which is a dangerous drug for so many people. Could we, in adversity, become addicted to sadness?

I am fascinated by and deeply interested in sadness. As a psychiatrist, I am afraid of it, having seen too many patients relapse as a result of its influence. As a human being, I know that it is a risk which threatens me. My anxiety overwhelms me at times, but I do not feel (wrongly perhaps) that I could ever become phobic, or that anxiety would affect my health in any long-term sense. I do, however, intuitively feel that depression could at some stage strike me, if I do not take care to protect myself against it, to immunize myself, to barricade myself behind the protective barriers of happiness and a healthy lifestyle. As a result, I am a careful observer of its presence in myself and in others: those like my patients, the ebbs and flows of whose minds I know so well; and those close to me, whose fluctuating moods I observe.

Short-lived sadness teaches us a lot about ourselves, but when it is long-lasting, sadness represents a serious threat: 'Sadness is not so much a state as a transition: misfortune, less a transition than a state. [. . .] Misfortune is a sadness which takes hold. Sadness, a misfortune which passes.'[11]

When sadness gets out of control: do pre-depressive states exist?

Can a simple sadness, a 'normal' sadness, gradually lead to depression, or at least precede it, predict it? We are referring here to what are called the 'risk factors' of depression: without necessarily indicating that the illness is inevitable, their presence increases the risk of it occurring.

We have already discussed dysphoric rumination, which is unquestionably one of the risk factors. When individuals with a tendency to this kind of rumination were monitored over a period of several years, they were found to have a higher risk of depression.[12] Rumination focused on the self is of course one of the repetitive thought processes likely to trigger the onset of severe depression: a negative and obsessive self-image is a major risk factor.[13] Psychotherapists are all too familiar with this problem: amongst people with low self-esteem, rumination on their supposed inadequacies, their difficulties, their failures, triggers disproportionate feelings of sadness, often bringing them dangerously close to depression. The same is true of social comparisons, one of the scourges of our time, which instigates and encourages them.[14] We know that when we are emotionally fragile, during periods of dysphoria, we are more inclined to compare ourselves to other people, in whichever areas matter most to us, often unfavourably and in a way which has a pronounced impact on our sadness.[15] There is also dysthymia: this chronic and low-level 'near-depression', in which despite the permanent presence of symptoms of depression, the threshold of true depression is never crossed, manifests itself by numerous painful feelings on the register of sadness and fatigue. Psychiatrists tend to regard it as a form of 'mood disorder' and it clearly represents another risk factor for the onset of more intense episodes which are then referred to as 'double depressions': an even more marked depressive episode is superimposed on foundations already undermined by dysthymia.[16]

A word of warning: all this does not just depend on our subjectivity and our feelings. Adversity also plays an important role: in people who are pathologically depressed, a greater number of adverse life events are often a cause of their low morale.[17] These may be specific events (bereavement, unemployment, divorce) or ongoing day-to-day worries (difficult or unstable situations, problems relating to family life or to work). The latter appear even more likely, in the long term, to push us into depression than the former.[18] Which is logical enough: in 'major' adversity, we mobilize our resources and are supported by those around us; faced with 'minor' adversity, we are less conscious at the time of what we are going through, and those around us are also less inclined to offer support. Given the exponential rise of cases of depression on a global scale,[19] as the entire planet is gradually Westernized, we also suspect a link between depression and the 'modern' world: the more competition there is, the weaker solidarity is, the more emphasis is laid on individual performance and the more individual failures are likely to result in depression.[20] Certain studies suggest that the biggest risk factor for depression in our contemporary societies is linked not to losses and bereavement but to feelings associated with failure, humiliation and helplessness in the face of situations for which no solution seems possible.[21] Researchers were also interested in finding out which symptoms manifested themselves as a result of different life events. They found that that after an experience of failure, we tend to succumb to rumination, fatigue, pessimism and guilt: in other words, symptoms likely to provoke doubt and soul-searching. And that, after bereavements or major losses (in terms of relationships or status), we are more likely to display sadness and tears: symptoms which facilitate communication and consolation, the restoration of relationships.[22] Nature is well conceived, to some extent at least.

Whatever the circumstances, there comes a point when the repetition and frequency of feelings of sadness end up provoking a phenomenon of coagulation, of solidification: *these feelings converge*; their union gives a sense of continuity, of rationality, of sinister coherence to our everyday experience. The muffled beats of sadness gradually get louder, synchronize with each other and end up resonating. All the past, the present, the future now pulse with the same painful experience of life, with the same weariness of existence: sadness has extended its domain over our whole lives, over the whole world. Then fatigue sets in, followed by world-weariness. This is depressive sadness, which begins to distance us from life. This simple phrase by Anatole France, 'The sadness of night penetrated her heart',[23] expresses it powerfully and simply. The mind begins to grow gradually darker . . .

At this moment when dysphoria, anxieties and demoralization turn into *mental suffering*, we move into the phase of pre-depression, of 'the threat of depression'. These periods of general emotional disturbance are often accompanied by anxiety, worry, sometimes even storms of brutal anguish or despair, like those described by the American writer William Styron, with reference to his own experience of depression:

> It was not really alarming at first, since the change was more subtle, but I did notice that my surroundings took on a different tone at certain times: the shadows of nightfall seemed more sombre, my mornings were less buoyant, walks in the woods became less restful, and there was a moment during my working hours in the late afternoon when a kind of panic and anxiety overtook me just for a few minutes.[24]

Gradually, our vision of the world, and of ourselves in it, begins to change in a more enduring manner. What are we doing here? What can we really achieve? Our capacity to face daily life without difficulty begins to seize up. Now hardly anything, not even happiness, is capable of holding off the contaminating power of sadness: 'My joys are latent sorrows.'[25] Then the past is contaminated too, as we re-examine it in the sombre light of present sadness. We see it through a glass darkly. We recall past happiness now lost or derisory. We dig up forgotten suffering and mistakes: 'It is thanks to our depression that we remember those far off incidents of uncouth behaviour which we had buried in the furthest, deepest regions of our memory. Such fits of depression are the archaeologists of our shame.'[26] Or else, in Léo Ferré's hauntingly sad song *Avec le temps* ('With time'), our awareness of time passing and taking everything as it goes, becomes more oppressive and present: 'With time . . . With time, everything goes away. Even the dearest memories have an ugly face.'

So it is with the feelings associated with sadness.

Then comes the temptation to give up, to stop struggling. In psychopharmacology there is a cruel laboratory experiment: in order to test the anti-depressant potential of a new molecule, mice are placed in a bowl filled with water. The bowl has smooth sides so there is nothing for the mice to hold on to and they are therefore forced to keep swimming in order to escape drowning. This is called the 'forced swimming test'. A molecule is deemed of interest if it enables the treated mouse to swim for longer than the untreated mice: after a certain time, the latter, worn out and discouraged, stop swimming. The anti-depressants, on the other hand, significantly prolong the swimming time, or in other words the time spent struggling against despair and discouragement. We shall see later that when we feel too exhausted to struggle, allowing ourselves to sink into depression can be a kind of refuge.

At some point, it becomes very difficult to pull yourself out of this pre-depression state. It is what one of my patients called 'the cancer of sadness':

> It's just like cancer: our bodies produce cancerous cells all the time, but our immune system is on the look-out for them and destroys them as they appear; then one day one successfully gets through the barrier and starts reproducing. When you are depressed, the same thing happens: we constantly produce sad thoughts but normally our mind intercepts them, challenges them, forces them back or destroys them; but sometimes, sadly, it fails to do so, and an invasion occurs leaving us overwhelmed, riddled with the cancer of sadness.

At that point, we start to absorb all the sadness around us: 'My heart is like a sponge absorbing sadness', said Gide.[27] We begin to suffocate. Describing his mental suffering, Styron said: 'In my case, this suffering very much resembles drowning or suffocation.'

It may be that depression is simply an exacerbation of sadness. It is possible that many of these slow, suffocating climbs towards the summits of sadness do not end up turning into severe depression (because we are fortunate enough to have good genes or a good past, or at least not to have had the worst sort). It is possible that they simply continue to be extreme and painful forms of sadness, never quite tipping into the depression we shall now be discussing. But the one certainty in all this is that understanding and controlling these feelings of sadness are essential if we are either to live better lives or to avoid falling into depression.

The disease of sadness? Depression as a living hell

'Every act of life from the morning toothbrush to the friends at dinner had become an effort. I saw that for a long time I had not liked people and things, but only followed the rickety old pretence of liking. I saw that even my love for those closest to me had become only an attempt at love.'[28]

Depression . . . So much has been written about this affliction that it almost seems there is nothing left to say! For psychiatrists, depression is an illness and diagnosis is made on the basis of a certain number of symptoms which need to be present, almost all day, every day: a sad mood, lack of interest in things which we previously enjoyed, and which we actively sought out (activities, relationships with family and friends); feelings of low self-esteem; physical problems: fatigue, loss of appetite, insomnia; sometimes thoughts of death. If only some of these symptoms are present, and with an element of inconsistency, it is probably not a depressive illness. We need to respond to the suffering, but not necessarily in a medical context, not necessarily with medication. If, however, the symptoms are all there, if they represent a divergence from how that person usually feels, and if they persist over a period of several weeks, it may be that the patient has indeed reached the stage of depressive illness.

Depression is a very serious disturbance: it is no longer the domain of feelings and moods, no longer just about feeling sad, but an illness which must be treated quickly and thoroughly. For the longer it is left untreated, the sooner and more often it will return, for longer periods. We shall see that the current obsession of psychiatrists is not just about treating the depressive episode but also about avoiding future relapses. What kind of treatment is appropriate? Medication, therapy, personal efforts on the part of the patient. A combination of all three is often ideal, though not necessarily at the same time.[29] In the treatment of depressive illness, medication is more or less indispensable (psychotherapy is almost impossible at this stage because the brain has slowed down to such an extent). But psychotherapy should be involved at the earliest possible stage, because it offers the most effective protection against relapses. As for any personal efforts, these are what will remain in place once the therapy has ended.

Once depression has taken hold, it tends to create the conditions of its duration and strength by means of a number of what are called 'self-sustaining' mechanisms. At this stage the depression no longer relies on external causes: even if these have ceased to exist, the illness is now self-sufficient and feeds on itself.

For example, it has been demonstrated that, unconsciously and unintentionally, people suffering from depression pay more attention to sad faces, noticing them more quickly and looking at them for a longer time than they would happy faces.[30] In the same way, depression makes us pay prolonged attention to angry faces (in contrast to people not suffering from depression, who tend to look away from disagreeable expressions more quickly: avoid focusing on miserable people if you want to keep your spirits up![31]).This research is not just anecdotal: it sheds light on what it is that makes a depressed person's day even more depressing! Although this research was conducted in a laboratory, with faces coming and going on computer screens, we can assume that the same also applies to real-life situations: for example, when walking in a crowded place, people suffering from depression are attracted more strongly to sad or sullen faces than to smiling ones. Which reinforces their belief that the world is a sad and dark place, and inevitably does little to improve their mood.

People with depression need to see stronger and more intense expressions of joy in order to recognize positive emotions in people's faces.[32]

That means, following on from the previous research, that for a depressed person to notice them, smiles need to be much broader and much more obvious. Because, in comparison with someone who is not depressed, people with depression will be less inclined to notice them and may even miss them completely.

Another extremely interesting finding, and one we shall be looking at in detail, comes from research showing that these unconscious distortions can be corrected by anti-depressant medication:[33] under these treatments, we are once again capable of noticing other people smile! These studies on the micro-mechanisms of anti-depressants are fascinating, throwing light on exactly how these molecules bring our patients back to well-being. But they may also provide inspiration for certain strategies to be used in psychotherapy and in everyday life: paying closer attention to the faces of people we pass in the street and making an effort to pay more attention to happy faces could be part of the thousand and one mini-strategies to restore or maintain morale. Which explains the widespread practice of carrying about or displaying the smiling photos of people we love: the little surges of positive feelings these provoke inevitably have a positive effect on our mental well-being.

What is true for faces also applies to words. Whereas people who are not depressed tend not to notice sad words and react more quickly to positive words, depressed people tend to do the opposite: they react more quickly and intensely to sad words.[34] Depending on our mental state, the same reading matter, especially if it is a sad story, will have a different effect on us! Reading a newspaper can be extremely disturbing for people with severe depression, in that the majority of news stories concern tragic or worrying events, rather than cheerful ones. And the same applies to the images: they will focus longer and more attentively on any painful ones.[35]

Bogged down in sadness

A good deal of research confirms what we have already discussed at length: it is rumination which lies behind this tendency to become 'bogged down by negativity'. Depressed people are 'glued' to what is wrong, to what causes suffering, to what makes them sad. Against their will perhaps, but glued nevertheless. They cannot stop brooding on these things. In the case of sad faces to which they have become over-sensitive, for example, the ruminations are along the lines of: 'The world is a sad place, people are sad. And it's all very sad!'[36] Then there is evidence that after a short time, the depressive state itself becomes the object of gloomy ruminations: 'It's obvious I'm never going to get out of this.'[37] The stronger the tendency for rumination (even before the onset of depression) the greater risk there is that the depressive episode will be prolonged and severe: logical enough.[38] Given the significance of these phenomena in terms of the persistence and recurrence of depressive symptoms, cognitive therapists are currently seeking to develop specific techniques based on the problem of these unhealthy ruminations. This is one of the explanations for the current, and at first sight surprising, surge of interest in meditation in the world of scientific psychotherapies. We shall be discussing this at a later stage.

Another unconscious mechanism is also involved in sustaining depressive sadness: it has been shown – in a cruel experiment – that when watching a comic film people suffering from depression 'stop themselves' smiling.[39] When their faces are filmed, the first trace of a smile can be seen, but is then suppressed. The same inhibition reflex also exists, though to a lesser extent, in people who have suffered from depression in the past, but are no longer affected. We do not have any very convincing explanation of this censoring of emotionally positive facial expressions, except the suggestion that such expressions somehow disturb the established 'depressive equilibrium'. However, suppressing smiles in this way is one of the micro-factors contributing to another consistent piece of evidence emerging from the study of severe depression: people who are depressed gradually find themselves cut off from other people, since contact with them is less agreeable and more oppressive than with those not affected by depression. And this is a further aggravating factor ('I get on everyone's nerves, everybody wants to get away from me, I'm going to end up left completely on my own'). Broadly speaking, it is as though people suffering from depression unconsciously seek to make sure other people also see them in a negative light. This explains why, paradoxically, people with severe depression unconsciously choose to frequent people who reject them because that reinforces their own negative self-image. This has been demonstrated in couples, for example: they pay more attention to their partner's reproaches than they do to any compliments they receive. But the same applies to all social interaction. People close to victims of depression need to be careful not to fall into the trap.[40]

Memory is also modified by depression. We have known for some time that after reading a list of words, people with depression remember more negative words than positive ones. This is due to a number of mechanisms. First there is a kind of 'magnetization' effect: when someone is in a particular mood (like sadness), it is the memories associated with that mood that are more easily recalled.[41] There is also an effect linked to rumination: events which have been the subject of extensive rumination produce memories which are more easily brought to mind.[42] And there is also the fact that depressed people, in contrast with those in good health, make less effort to eliminate negative feelings from the flow of their consciousness.[43] Specific training has been tried out to help depressive people control such self-aggravating micro-mechanisms more effectively, and the results are encouraging.[44]

These memory disturbances are long-lasting. Even when they are cured and in remission from depression, on average nine months after the episode, depressed subjects have a deficit in the specificity of their positive memories: they think about these in a more abstract, more distant way.[45] The beneficial effects of such memories are therefore less tangible in terms of these people's mental well-being. Similarly, people suffering from depression have more generalized and less precise memories: when asked to recall some good memories, they respond with vague phrases like 'my last holiday on the coast' or 'going to the cinema with friends'. In fact the more precise and specific we are, the more successful we are in activating positive feelings and the better we end up feeling![46] On that basis, we can always try and help them by getting them to talk – in detail – about good things, even if they would not do so spontaneously.

In depressed patients, we find a greater frequency of painful images and intrusive memories (ones that intrude onto consciousness involuntarily). And these intrusions cause suffering, impede reflection and maintain the depression.[47] Depression is also associated with numerous sleep disturbances, and with sudden dreamlike episodes which are strange and painful.[48] In his autobiographical work *Route de nuit*, the philosopher Clément Rosset describes the disruptions to his sleep pattern during a period of depression:

> On the strangeness of certain dreams and nightmares, the sensation that they do not belong to me, that they are nothing to do with me whatsoever. It felt as though the dream-maker had made a mistake; in other words, and this is obviously very disturbing, it was as though I had just dreamt *someone else's* dreams. [. . .] The common theme of these dreams, most of which I've forgotten now, seems to have been this: we were in the process of finalizing something, something that was of no possible interest and in any case could not possibly work.[49]

The consciousness of people suffering from depression is not only full of gloomy ruminations but also chaotic, with the eruption, whenever they try to concentrate or to reflect, of negative thoughts which are as undesirable as they are painful. This explains why depressed people experience concentration difficulties. But there are other problems too. For example, their capacity to be distracted: when they need to work, people with depression are more easily distracted by external stimuli (noises, interruptions, physical sensations), paying excessive attention to these, and remembering them, to no purpose whatsoever, and as a result they are less able to concentrate on their principal task.[50] It has also been demonstrated that they put more effort into simple intellectual tasks than is required:[51] they are capable, as the saying goes, of making a mountain out of a molehill. As for that 'depressive lucidity' which we referred to with reference to sadness, it no longer applies once depression is truly established. Not only do depressed people fail to detect errors any more effectively than other people, but once errors have been detected and a reaction is required, they cope less well, victims at such times of their own slowness and of their inability to make decisions.[52]

There are many other studies too, but the overall picture is clear enough already, is it not? Depression is like drowning and action must be taken to save the victim. First by throwing a lifebelt: in the form of anti-depressant medication. Then, by teaching the person to swim; this is the psychotherapy. And by making sure afterwards that they will keep going to the swimming pool and swimming their lengths regularly so as to keep on the right track: these are the 'anti-depressant efforts' which need to be introduced into daily routines. But we have not yet come to the end of our examination of the inner workings of depressive illness.

Depression as a dissociation and a retreat from the world

'When you surrender, you do not suffer. When you surrender, even to sadness, your suffering ceases', said Saint-Exupéry. When you are tired of life, giving up can seem, initially at least and from the outside, like a kind of refuge.

But not suffering any more means giving up living. It means resigning yourself to a dreary and insipid life which can be lived without suffering. Alas, it does not work, and the suffering persists. Sure, when we stop fighting, we feel a sense of relief, at least temporarily. But all too quickly back come the ruminations on the theme of 'I've fallen so low.' Gradually, other sufferings set in. No longer associated with failure, bereavement or loss, the new suffering comes from the realization of your own inadequacy, from the breakup of social relationships, for depression is solitary and misunderstood; even the most understanding or better-informed people close to us will still tend to expect more of us, to say: 'He (or she) should pull themselves together a bit.' And then comes the other risk, that of our gradual dissociation from the world.

Whereas sadness and the feelings associated with it manifest themselves initially as a kind of hypersensitivity to the more sombre aspects of the world around us, severe depression, once it gets beyond a certain phase, distorts emotional reactivity. For a long time it was thought that depression increased the capacity to experience negative feelings and diminished that for positive ones. In reality, that first suggestion needs to be corrected and refined, and probably only applies to the early stages or minor forms of depression. Once the depression has become more intense, the overall capacity to feel *all* forms of feelings, positive or negative, is blunted. Which is logical enough in that acute depression is a form of retreat destined to spare and protect the sufferer from the things in life which he or she can no longer face. Its only virtue, initially at least, is in providing an analgesic effect, freeing us from the pain of having to face up to things.[53]

It is when we are still on the crest, at the frontier, that the reactivity to negative things still exists. An indication that we are still in the realm of the living. When the illness of depression takes hold, for real, we slip into another universe, inhabited by the living dead. Research on this desensitizing effect of depression also shows that any remaining reactivity sufferers still possess tends to be essentially focused on themselves. Anything relating to the external world has far less impact on their feelings.

It is as though depression robs us of the great thing about sadness: the capacity for compassion. Depression does not make people more altruistic or more concerned about what is happening in the world – indeed, quite the opposite is true. The heightened lucidity of those suffering from depression about what is not right with this base world of ours does not provide them with either the motivation or the energy to change it. Yet another reason not to confuse depression with sadness someone has managed to overcome. Contrary to certain claims, depression does not bring any benefits.

This relative insensitivity can last after the depression has apparently been cured, like a hidden scar. When sad music is played to people who have previously suffered from depression, or when they are reminded of sad memories from their past, it turns out that the less affected they are by this induced sadness (particularly in terms of diminishing their positive emotions), the greater their risk of relapsing into depression.[54] In other words: if someone is incapable of being 'normally' sad, they are still in a fragile state! For this relative insensitivity already indicates a seizing-up of the free movement of feelings: it is normal to feel less happy when listening to sad music or remembering sad memories. The impoverishment of our feelings is therefore an indication of fragility or a risk factor.

Look how the writer Pierre Guyotat describes emerging from depression:

> Once you leave the clinic, it is as though you are entering a gentle depression, a slow healing process: the reward for this passage through death, is, instead of the enchanted palace you thought you had won by the sweat of your dead blood, a disenchanted world, with no features and no discernible colours, dull gazes which no longer see you, voices always addressed to others and not to you, returning from so far away, a daily duty to survive, a heart whose only function is to pump blood, blood which no longer warms the body . . . You must wait. Without anger. Concentrate on sleeping, eating, washing yourself, getting dressed, walking, every single day: all of it virtually on your own, and without even yourself for company: you must keep trying in fits and starts, however clumsy, to take heart once again. Patience, patience.[55]

Emerging from depression

But there are some people who, once they have overcome their depression, emerge feeling a little stronger, as the American writer Andrew Solomon describes:

> However I discovered something I can only call a *soul*, a part of me that I could never have imagined before that day, seven years ago, when hell

decided to pay me an unexpected visit. Almost every day, I experience flashes of despair and each time that happens I wonder if I am losing my footing again. [. . .] These feelings fill me with horror but I know they have forced me to look more closely at life, to find reasons why I should live and to cling on to them. It is impossible to completely regret the course my life has taken. Each day, sometimes courageously and sometimes against all reason, I choose to go on living. Is that not a rare happiness?[56]

Solomon does not claim that he will never relapse, but what he does say is that his depression has in some way enriched him and brought him to a closer understanding of himself.

On a darker and more sober note, the Swedish writer Stig Dagerman wrote:

Here is my one consolation. I know I will have many deep relapses into despair but the memory of the miracle of rescue carries me as though on wings to the vertiginous goal: a consolation which is more than just a consolation, greater than a philosophy: a reason to go on living.[57]

Clément Rosset is more circumspect about the idea of being cured:

The wisest course is to make a pact with evil, instead of trying in vain to eradicate it, and thus to obtain an honourable "stalemate" as in a game of chess.

And this is what William Styron has to say:

Generally speaking, the vast majority of those who experience depression, even in its acutest forms, survive, and afterwards and at least to the end of their days, live no less happily than people who have been spared the disease. Except for the horrific nature of certain memories, a severe depression does not inflict lasting wounds. The fact that a large number – half in fact – of those who are afflicted are condemned to be further affected sooner or later is like one of Sisyphus's torments: depression often recurs. But most victims overcome such lapses, and even deal better with them, for psychologically their previous experience has prepared them to face the ogre.[58]

Can we understand how best to prepare ourselves for the *return of the ogre*? Once we have escaped the grip of the wave of depression and are washed ashore like survivors, worn out and weary like Guyotat, or relieved and wiser like Solomon, what next?

And after depression? The inevitable return of sadness?

On the evidence of the vast majority of cases, and probably of more 'ordinary' people than our writers, scientific research is categorical: depression is potentially a chronic illness, or rather one likely to recur, like cancer. It is not just a question of getting over it; we also need to do whatever is needed to prevent it coming back.

Recurrences of depression are frequent, whether in the form of relapses (the rapid recurrence of symptoms, for example a few weeks or months after a course of treatment ended prematurely) or in the return of the illness (at a later stage, several years after recovery).

After a depressive episode, the patient is vulnerable to this threat of recurrence for a number of months or even years: they are only in *remission*. Statistics vary according to the research, but in general it appears that in the absence of effort or of treatment, 50 per cent of people who have suffered from depression will suffer a relapse at some point, with the figure increasing to 70 per cent for people who have had two episodes and to 90 per cent for those who have had three or more recurrences.[59] That is to say that these statistics would apply if these people did not make an effort to reorganize their way of living or thinking, and more precisely, their relationship with their feelings and moods. Evidence enough in favour of preventive action!

I remember that, when I was a young psychiatrist, we sought to reassure people suffering from depression by promising them they would not have a relapse. For a long time we would say: 'There you are, it's over, no need to worry any more, no need even to think about it, just get on with your life.' And then we would see a good number of these poor patients coming back and being readmitted to hospital over and over again. Subsequently, on the evidence of research on longer-term follow-ups, psychiatrists realized that some of these relapses could be prevented by keeping patients on anti-depressants for an extended period of time, between one and five years, depending on the number of relapses they had experienced, or better still, by prescribing cognitive or behavioural psychotherapies.[60] Today we are also starting to look at advice about lifestyle and personal psychological hygiene, both of which will be dealt with in the next part of this book.[61] As you will have realized, therapists are currently interested not only in helping to cure depression, but also in guarding against recurrences, and even where possible in preventing its onset in people at risk.[62] Given the scale and the cost of this condition, this is a major public health issue.

The question of the scars left by depression is a fascinating one: does depression have the same effect on the brain as a heart attack has on the heart? Or can it simply disappear without trace and without consequence? It would appear that in a certain number of cases, depression may leave 'neuronal scarring', particularly in cases of severe, prolonged or recurring depression.[63] And that this should now motivate doctors and carers to encourage their depressed patients to work on rebuilding their cerebral capacities. A bit like the way that after a heart attack, help is needed to revascularize the damaged cardiac zone. In contrast with what used to be thought (you know, the depressing theory of a fixed stock of neurones acquired at birth and gradually used up afterwards), the brain is an organ with considerable capacity for reconstruction – what is called neuroplasticity.

Various experiments have shown that treatment, with either drugs or psychotherapy, can 'repair' the brain, and correct any possible micro-lesions linked to depression. This is rather like what happens in cardiology: if you have had a coronary thrombosis, once you have recovered the cardiologist does not say 'That's all sorted, we've managed to save you. You're not going to die. Off you go in peace.' He will probably prescribe medication, and also (this should be systematic) a certain lifestyle, with advice on diet, physical exercise, stress management, etc. In a similar way we are now trying to understand what advice we should be giving to patients who have recovered from depression. Such as, for example, psychotherapies focusing on the little residual symptoms of depression, minor emotional dysfunction, fragile emotional states.[64]

One of the most fascinating avenues of research in this area of post-depressive fragility concerns what we could call the 'invisible wounds'. How can this persistent vulnerability be detected in patients who are on the road to recovery, who feel better and whose answers to question-naires assessing depression are often normal? By using what is called *mood induction*, where we induce sad feelings through listening to a piece of music, reading a short text, or watching a film. By doing so, we see evidence, both in the responses to the questionnaires and in the results of functional neuro-imaging, of disturbances which were not evident in the 'calm' state: by activating sad feelings, a complete depressive vision of the world, hitherto simply dormant, has been awoken. And recent research has shown that these little fluctuations of mood can lead to a return of the disease.[65] Hence the importance, yet again, of being able to manage our feelings.

We are currently attempting to find out if certain tests can allow us to predict such risks. After a sad frame of mind is induced, the activation of certain areas of the brain (notably the area around the amygdala) just as emotionally charged words are being memorized indicates that negative words will subsequently be more easily remembered by patients at risk of depression.[66] It is essential to understand that, for fragile patients who have recently emerged from depression, today's dysphoric rumination is tomorrow's depression.

It was not my intention to fill you with gloom by the enumeration of all this data. The micro-mechanisms of recovery from severe depression are more complicated than was first imagined. Staving off depression on a lasting basis also requires much more effort over a long period of time than had previously been thought. And yet in spite of all that, people can indeed recover and live happily afterwards! It is strange that the period leading to recovery, when patients are getting better, has been little studied from a qualitative point of view. We have tended to concentrate either on quantitative scales (which measure the decrease in the number of depressive symptoms under a particular treatment) or on clinical observation (although in general the clinician, relieved at seeing the patient emerge from the tunnel, is more inclined to encourage them to move on rather than to urge them to analyse and dissect the mechanics of their improved state). The few studies that are available show that, at the time of recovery, the negative beliefs are still there and still active (perhaps a little less powerfully), but that the control mechanisms (notably distance and a critical approach) filter them very quickly. Negative thoughts are always ready to launch an attack on our consciousness, but they are immediately passed through the filter of reason and distance.[67]

Put another way, the normal capacity for sadness is restored!

The work of cognitive psychotherapy on sad feelings and moods

This process of 'filtering' negative feelings is used in cognitive psychotherapy for depression,[68] and will prove extremely useful both before and after depressive episodes.[69] It has been demonstrated, for example, that the more patients continue to use and apply the behavioural and psychological strategies they have learned during therapy sessions, the longer any benefits in terms of ongoing emotional equilibrium will last.[70]

A principal element of such strategies, to be integrated into everyday behaviour, involves placing greater emphasis on the way we think, or in other words, on the way we talk to ourselves. More introspection! Depressive thoughts and, to a lesser extent, sad thoughts are like harsh words constantly directed at oneself and at the world. Like a constant murmuring sound which we no longer hear but which we are subconsciously aware of, and which gradually saddens, worries and undermines us.

Amongst the efforts required to avoid falling into this trap, one of the most important consists in paying *particular attention to words*: for example, by defining exactly what they mean. In therapy, if a patient says she does not feel *up to* her job, or her role as a mother, this is what the therapist would say to her: 'You say you think you are a bad mother. I don't know about that personally, but I'd like you to tell me exactly what a bad mother is. What does she do? What doesn't she do? Which bits of that apply to you?' The idea is to prevent biased judgements disguised as neutral statements from going unchallenged. And to keep steering the patient away from generalized opinions and towards precise facts. With a view to gradually helping them to become more vigilant with themselves: 'I *feel* I am a bad mother when my children cry at night and are anxious. But I'm *not* a bad mother: it's just that, at the moment, I'm not quite as available for them as I used to be, and they are aware of that. That is the problem, and that's what I need to address. Instead of beating myself up over it and judging myself negatively.'

Other examples of words which cause cognitive therapists to prick up their ears: incapable, incompetent, selfish, fragile, incurable, serious . . . Patients will be asked to explain in detail exactly what they mean by such terms.

Another classic strategy: *the reattribution of responsibilities*. So, for example, the young mother referred to above blames herself for her children's poor performance at school ('bad mother'). It is important to help her share out that responsibility: not by denying it completely, but by making sure that she does not end up with more than her fair share! We draw a large circle representing a cake which she must then cut into a number of pieces: instead of keeping it all herself, we discuss her husband's share in these poor school results, that of the children themselves (why not!), of any teachers involved, of society in general (which encourages people to work less hard), of the babysitter if there is one. The aim of all this is not simply to shift the blame onto other people but to relieve her of the weight of assuming imaginary and therefore unnecessary responsibilities, and to show that since the problem stems from various sources, various solutions are possible, and more practically, that 'becoming a good mother' is clearly a project as intimidating as it is vague!

Equally, it is important to *reintroduce the notion of continuum* in depressive thought processes, using the technique of the 'graduated scale'. This is in order to avoid the all-or-nothing view, that distortion called 'dichotomous reasoning'. This is at work whenever we find ourselves tormented by feelings with thoughts along the lines of 'It's a disaster', 'It's my fault', 'I'm not capable of doing this job, I'll never be up to it.' In response to which, the therapist will ask 'What do you understand by the word disaster? And following on from that, on a scale of 0 to 100, how would you grade this "disaster"?'

Many of the thoughts we have under the influence of a negative mood turn out to be radical judgements, totally lacking nuances. So, faced with a difficulty, instead of saying 'This is difficult and I'm struggling with it', we say something along the lines of 'This thing is *completely* impossible', 'I'm rubbish', 'I'll *never* manage it', 'It's *always* the same', and other pseudo-certainties. Which is why reintroducing nuance is so important.

Being attentive to your hidden obligations. As we have seen in relation to feelings of resentment, we always harbour subconscious beliefs belonging to three separate categories: 'I should . . .', 'Other people should . . .', 'The world should . . .'. Amongst the beliefs that tend to induce sadness (there are others that provoke anger and anxiety), these are some examples. In the 'I should' category: 'always be well, always succeed in anything I take on, always know how to respond to and sort out problems'. In the 'Other people should' category: 'be loyal to me, not forget about me, be fair, respect me, listen to me, understand me'. And in the 'The world should' category: 'be fair, coherent, gentle'. Such convictions are perfectly legitimate and are the ideals of the majority of people. But the incapacity to accept that sometimes ideals cannot be attained can cause us to suffer, without our necessarily being aware of it: even if consciously we know that the world is not the same as in our dreams, we still unconsciously dream that it is.

Coping with sad feelings and moods

'You cannot prevent the birds of sorrow from flying over your head, but you can prevent them from making their nests in your hair': so says a Chinese proverb.

Controlling our sad feelings is a vital task for people who have previously suffered from depression. But it is also recommended for people who have not experienced depression but who sense they may be vulnerable to it. As for those people who are neither fragile nor former sufferers, I am of the opinion (1) that there are not many of them, (2) that they are unlikely to be reading this book. So, for anyone left, here are a few comments and some practical tips.

Do not over-value sadness

Montaigne already touched on this in his *Essays*: 'I neither like it nor respect it', 'It is always a harmful quality, always insane.' But clearly romanticism has not helped, as Gide observed: 'Our literature, and particularly during the romantic period, praised, cultivated, and propagated sadness; not the active resolute sadness, that makes men rush to glorious deeds, but a kind of flabbiness of soul, which was called melancholy, which gave a becoming pallor to the poet's brow and filled his eyes with yearning.'

Beware of the pleasure of feeling sad

For certain fragile people and in particular adolescents, the taste for sadness can be like the taste for blood. It sometimes seems as though melancholic people are almost like vampires preying on themselves, cutting themselves off from the world and living in a bell jar, wallowing in their sad and toxic feelings, which are never – or only half-heartedly – challenged or questioned.

We need to carry out a kind of cleaning and identification operation on our melancholy states. And, like pulling weeds out of a garden, this little psychological task needs doing over and over again. With the help of a patient, a hairdresser, I invented the expression 'thinning out melancholy feelings'. Which does not mean we should never have any sad feelings but simply that we should prevent them from becoming established and taking over.

Recognizing the first signs of rumination

The symptoms of rumination are always the same: the mind is preoccupied by worries; thinking about these constantly brings us neither relief nor solutions; as a result we can find ourselves 'distracted' in our daily activities (we lose things, we cannot remember if we posted that letter or not, we switch off when people we are close to are talking to us, etc.). An awareness of slipping into this psychological mode is the first stage in fighting it: avoiding (or proceeding cautiously and with great care with) questions like 'Why am I so sad?', which will then stir up and bring to the surface all our limitations and dissatisfactions, all the things that always seem to be lacking in our lives, as in everybody's lives. Instead we need to ask 'how' questions: 'How did my illness start? What is happening to me? How is it affecting me physically? And mentally?' Knowing how to observe the flow of our feelings then becomes invaluable and fascinating. It is all about having an active and productive approach. Infinitely better than sombre ruminations on the *why*.

Accepting imperfection

Perfectionism is a danger which can lead us into battles that are exhausting if we win and depressing if we lose.[71] It tends to have an aggravating effect on many psychological disturbances, including depression.[72] We need to accept that our lives are always going to contain unfinished business. Take a look around you: all those things that still need doing or putting away, all those little jobs around the home, all those people to see . . . Learn to accept that all that is not a sign of failure or incompetence: it is simply proof that you are alive and are living a normal life. If you do not do this, the anxiety will be followed by depression at the prospect of this impossible mass of things you will never be able to deal with. You will end up only seeing all the things 'not done, not done, not done'. Like Clément Rosset in his account of his own depression:

> This reluctance in the face of the slightest effort is often tinged with the paralysing sensation that in any case you will never have enough time to do all that needs doing, nor to find out all that needs to be known. A sensation I refer to in my own jargon as the symptoms CSH and CSS, respectively, borrowed from the Spanish *cosas sin hacer* and *cosas sin saber*: things not done, things not known.[73]

Action is an anti-depressant

It is in our interests to be active when we are sad or depressed. Not only in order to 'pull ourselves together', as those around us exhort us to do. But also because all those little gestures of everyday life (walking, tidying, cooking, taking good care of our bodies, of our environment, exposing ourselves to fresh air, to social contacts) are anti-depressants. Only in homeopathic doses perhaps, but with genuine effect. And all the more so because inaction has a highly toxic effect that is both rapid and tangible. So, even if the direct effect of the action is diluted, faint, slow, it is still preferable to the poisonous effects of inaction! Not easy if you are suffering from depression: when you have fallen out of love with life, when it sometimes disgusts you, forcing yourself to do something is a bit like swimming in water choked with seaweed. We need to struggle on valiantly: eventually we will reach clear water.

Keeping the brain active too

Research is currently being done on what is known as 'cognitive remediation', a sort of brain-gym for people with depressive tendencies.[74] There is also evidence that being exposed to different and changing ideas induces positive feelings, boosting morale and energy:[75] this can be achieved in the laboratory by making people read rapidly through a succession of sentences which express different ideas, inducing an accelerated thought process (*tachypsychia*). And in real life the same effect can be had by taking part in interesting discussions, listening to lecturers who are passionate and knowledgeable about their subject, to radio programmes or intelligent TV programmes, etc. An active brain is good for morale.

Beware of bad habits you are not even aware of having

'Major depression extinguishes the spirit', said Cioran.[76] And vigilance too. In general, sadness drives us to do whatever will nourish it: rumination, withdrawal, depriving ourselves of anything that could distract us or bring us pleasure. If we want to fight against this, we need to recognize this tendency as a symptom of sadness rather than a legitimate need. And certainly not wait until we feel like doing something. Nor should we expect to get any pleasure from this initially enforced activity. In brief: accept the need to be active even if you do not feel like it and do not obtain any immediate benefits. We know it is not easy! But it is an effective way of kick-starting well-being.

And always come back to happiness

Happiness is the only effective and lasting antidote to sadness. Or rather, instead of being an antidote, which would imply cancelling out or getting rid of sadness, neither of which is either possible or desirable in the long term, happiness enables us to form an alloy with it, as when two metals are blended together to form a new composite, different from and superior to the original metals (such as bronze, an alloy of copper and tin). Take, for example, the sadness and the happiness of being a parent: the sadness of seeing your children growing up and eventually leaving home is a very real one; indeed, some parents find this very difficult. Often, as a parent, we experience this sadness even before the situation arises. But if it is accepted and understood, it can also open our eyes and motivate us to enjoy the happiness of time spent with our children more intelligently. To free up more time to spend with them now. Their eventual departure, even if inevitable, is as yet theoretical; it is not the reality of the present moment. The happiness of having them with you now, on the other hand, is real. The pleasure derived from someone's presence is thus reinforced by being steeped in sadness, just as in the past, photographic films were immersed in developing fluid.

The wisdom of sadness

Can sadness be put to good use? In his *Letters to a Young Poet*, Rainer Maria Rilke gives this advice to his correspondent: 'You shouldn't be dismayed if a sadness rises up in front of you.' Yes, we could impoverish ourselves by refusing to accept that sadness. Just as we could also damage ourselves by giving it too much rein. What Rilke teaches us is that there is an art of observing sadness in ourselves, one which is different from observing the world through sad eyes. That there is a huge difference between *thinking* 'I am unhappy' and *observing the thought* 'I am unhappy.' It is the art of watching dark thoughts pass by in the same way we watch the great black clouds drift across the sky.

If we patiently cultivate this art, then sadness could become a friend, who gently reminds us of our limits and our fragility, curbs our delusions and our pride. And who softly whispers in our ear: be happy and enjoy this life, if not . . . it is all too sad!

Chapter 9

Despair

I would not know how to justify my abiding confidence in the future of mankind. It may be that it is not at all rational. But despair is irrational: it does not solve any problems, it even creates new ones and it is by nature a form of suffering.

Primo Levi

If I had been born with a self-destruct button [the patient indicates the exact centre of her chest], I think I would have ceased to exist long ago. All those times when I've been seized with violent feelings of disgust and weariness with life, all those early morning thoughts of suicide, all the betrayals and the trials: at all those times, if that button had existed, if I could have just breathed in, closed my eyes, smiled with the relief of knowing that this was the end, and that it was a gentle one, if I'd only had to press it in order to cease to exist . . . Well, I would have ceased to exist a long time ago. I wouldn't even have reached adulthood. And, in the end, there are so many beautiful things I wouldn't have seen or experienced. What a shame! But it's as though the temptation to commit suicide is part of me, that the monster stirs whenever the dose of suffering is too powerful. If it was easy to do away with yourself, I'd do it. But I don't think I'm the only one who feels like this, and I'm sure that if everybody had such a self-destruct button they could press, there wouldn't be all that many people left in this world of ours.

Doctors and psychotherapists remember with great clarity their discussions with suicide-prone patients. Probably because all of them are steeped in a bath of emotional activation, making them hyper-memorable (emotions make excellent fixatives for memories). And I remember very clearly all (or the majority at least) of my conversations with suicidal patients. Another patient spoke to me one day, with a sad and embarrassed smile, about his dream for a 'euthanasia kit': 'To end it all easily and painlessly, a little tin containing two pills: one anti-depressant to send you off in a last burst of happiness, and one containing poison.' On the same occasion she also admitted using the internet to try and get hold of a gruesome book, well known in its day, called *Suicide mode d'emploi*,[1] a best seller until it was swiftly banned on the grounds that it provided, with a wealth of detail, reliable advice on methods of committing suicide easily and effectively. But the price of this now rare book – several hundred Euros – had put her off. 'I was ready to commit suicide, but not to pay that sort of money! And it ended up making me think about the comic absurdity of the situation! And I'm still here.'

The crepuscular feelings associated with suicide are a strange mixture: despair, weariness of life and desire to die, suicidal ideas, but also feelings of guilt, sudden resurgences of the will to live, vague hopes rekindled, terrible doubts ('And what if I was wrong, and if in the end everything worked out?'), then back to feeling tired of life, to memories of disappointed hopes and sufferings endured. Our minds are in turmoil, everything seems complicated and impossible. At such times comes the temptation of a perfect solution, the only one which eliminates all our problems, and for ever.

Why live? Why die?

'Life is a restaurant which is pokey, bad and expensive. And, in addition to all that, it is too short.'

Woody Allen's words, of course. And of course, words which are more profound than they might seem: we moan and groan, but in the end, for most of us, even though we may indeed have spent more time complaining than celebrating, we will be sorry to leave the stage when the time comes. Good old Woody succeeds in pinpointing our ambivalence towards existence.

To live, to die ... Why do we ask these questions? Do we tend to ask them when things are not going well? Or, on the contrary, when we are at our happiest? I remember a dream I used to have, a dream about the end of the world: it was the Apocalypse, but it was taking place on a beautiful day, when everyone was extremely happy; it was strange and intense, an end of the world without turmoil or agony, but coming suddenly, out of the blue, when everything was perfect. There was what seemed to be an enormous screen filled with blue sky which suddenly went blank.

To live or to die? We often feel uncomfortable with questions like these and see no reason to ask them. But just because there is no obvious answer does not mean the question is pointless. Albert Camus begins his famous work *The Myth of Sisyphus* with these sentences: 'There is only one really serious philosophical question, and that is suicide. To decide whether or not life is worth living is to answer the fundamental question in philosophy.'

Why live?

On the internet there is a site set up by an artist who every day asks different people in the street the same question: 'Why makes you get up every
morning?'[2] I distinctly remember my confusion when she asked me the
question, and how difficult I found it to answer: I had never really given it
much thought. Afterwards I thought how strange it was that I had never
thought about it like that, head on.

So, what is it that gives us the strength to get up in the morning?
Some people object to the question and say that life is the place that has
been assigned to us and therefore we stick with it. It is even possible to
approach the question from a mathematical point of view: even if we
grumble about things, there are still on average more good times than
bad, so 'You just carry on and there you are!' Others are more prosaic:
even if things are tough today, something good is bound to come along
sooner or later: we can at least carry on living out of curiosity; you never
know with life (and as for death, we will find out about that some day
or other). Some of my patients have confessed that the reason they go on
living and do not put an end to themselves is largely out of fear of death.
A fear of death that saves them. Cioran also has something to say on the
subject: 'If, by some miracle, the fear of death were to disappear, "life"
would be left defenceless: it would be at the mercy of our first whim.'[3]
That self-destruct button once again!

But in the end, the most frequent scenario is that we do not even ask the
question: so, it is morning. Well, we get up and that's that. Indeed people
with suicidal tendencies tell us that it is better not to ask it too often. For
as soon as we begin to think about those sorts of questions too deeply, the
thread which attaches us to life can suddenly seem very fragile.

Why die?

How can we explain the temptation to commit suicide? It is not a question
of cowardice in the face of existence: many victims of suicide demonstrated enormous courage in their lives.

Generally people kill themselves to put an end to their suffering, to
abandon their struggle. They seek death as they would a painkiller or the
chance to rest. They take the last wish offered to the dead quite literally:
'May he rest in peace.' They want to *rest in peace*, those two words, *rest*
and *peace*, have a kind of magic; they are so much more attractive than the
alternative facing them: *strive on in suffering*.

In many cultures, suicide was considered a legitimate way of putting
an end to suffering or loss of dignity. This was the case, for example, in
Ancient Greece and Rome. In his *Portrait of Don Juan*, Marcel Jouhandeau
writes: 'It may be there is no such thing as suicide: people do not kill themselves unless they have drifted so far away from who they are that they
no longer recognize themselves: they see a ghost, a puppet, a caricature so

promiscuous that it shames and dishonours them.' To which Montherlant adds: 'We commit suicide out of respect for life, when our life is no longer worthy of us.'[4] It is painful to be no longer able to live according to your own values, with dignity, independence, lucidity, freedom. We turn to suicide because at some point the gap between what we have become and what we were or wanted to be has suddenly become too great. At such a point, suicide seems to offer a solution. Whether it is a good one remains to be seen.

Because, in the end, the big question is about the role of subjectivity in all the decisions and all the moments of despair which lead to autolysis. 'It is not that suicide always comes from madness [. . .] but generally speaking, it is not in an access of reason that people kill themselves', Voltaire wrote.[5] Most suicides are puzzling when viewed from the outside: how many situations appear 'not as desperate as all that'? For suicide can perhaps sometimes be legitimate, for example when someone is suffering from a painful and incurable illness. But in so many other cases, suicidal ideation seems to be associated with feelings which we suspect, rightly or wrongly, but often rightly, would in the end have changed with time. And that it was only a question of waiting.

Feelings of despair

There are indeed some feelings of despair which somehow creep quietly into our lives and show no sign of leaving. They take different forms depending on the personalities, resources and values of the individuals concerned. Initially there are a thousand and one ways of experiencing despair, before rumination gradually ends up making all those contemplating suicide resemble each other.

Feelings of despair are often made up of a mixture of mental suffering, painful lucidity (we feel we have lost the positive illusions which protected or blinded us) and an inability to do anything to change the course of existence. Fitzgerald spoke of the need to 'hold in balance the sense of the futility of effort and the sense of the necessity to struggle'.

There is also an immense sense of fatigue, of loss of life force, that mystery that makes us 'machines for living' (in the words of Paul Valéry) but which is no longer working. This is that feeling of being weary of life which afflicts certain depressed people, worn out by years of relapses. I remember a patient telling me:

> I only have *negative plans* now: not to do anything, not to go out, not to have to cook, not to have to make decisions. Fortunately I went for the ultimate negative in *not* committing suicide! But at the time, I saw each day as just a series of withdrawals and evasions. Everything was being taken away: I was incapable of *adding* anything whatsoever to my life.

Feelings of despair are often imbued with a complex emotional atmo-sphere. Sadness, of course, the extreme sadness referred to by St John of the Cross: 'What we call "night" is the deprivation of the taste for every-thing.' But also sometimes a gnawing anger, against ourselves, against those who have hurt us or who have not understood or helped us, against the world for being the way it is. Or anxiety, with the sense of being trapped, cornered, in a situation from which there is no way out: in such circumstances, suicide seems like a headlong flight, a way of halting the pain and the terror. On that subject, I am fascinated by a little painting by Bruegel in the Kunsthistorisches Museum in Vienna. It depicts the suicide of the biblical King Saul, as he is on the point of being defeated in battle. Surrounded and in desperate straits, both his sons already killed by the enemy, having lost everything, he kills himself by falling on his sword, in a corner of the painting which is otherwise entirely taken up with the clash of the battle. He is dying in despair and terror, to the utter indif-ference of everyone else. There can also be an element of shame in some suicides, a feeling of having lost face, sunk into failure or of having done wrong, like Judas, hanging himself after betraying Jesus. But this shame is often the fruit of what we call 'melancholic' depressions, the worst type of depression, where the victims blame themselves for every possible evil and are racked with an overwhelming sense of guilt.

Sometimes, a far cry from these sudden jolts in our feelings, the sense that 'life no longer has any meaning' manifests itself in feelings of tedium and of emptiness, where, as this patient put it, 'I am in a state of vague unhappiness. I keep thinking: if only my life could just stop now!' People are more often 'pushed' into suicide (by their suffering) than they are 'attracted' by it (apart from imagining, rightly, that it will bring an end to that suffering).

The temptation of suicide: how people become *morituri*

'Wouldn't it all be so much easier if I just disappeared?'

Humans often flirt with despair: this sombre association with dark ideas must be seen as a continuum. It is not a matter of suicidal people on the one side, and on the other those in perfect health whose thoughts never turn to suicide. With a solid barrier between the two sides. Few people have not at some time toyed with the idea of their own voluntary disappearance. The existence of such feelings in the population as a whole is far more common than we might think. More than a third of us have had suicidal feelings at least once in our lives.[6] Although adolescence is a particularly dangerous period in this context,[7] the situation is not hugely different when it comes to adults. For example, a study conducted amongst 700 students showed that 54 per cent of them had had suicidal thoughts at some time during the previous year, that 2 per cent of them had attempted suicide during the same period, and 10 per cent had done so at least once in their lives.[8] The same frequency of suicidal thoughts also occurs in older people.[9]

It is for this reason that we should always be prepared to ask patients if they have perhaps thought about wanting to die. Young doctors are taught to do this, even though some of them are afraid that bringing the subject up might be dangerous, that making the patient think about it might provoke the gesture; as if the patient had not already thought about it themselves! But the question can also be put to friends or people we are close to if we feel there is ground for concern.

There is an identifiable scale of suicidal thoughts, which are not always of equal strength. When a psychiatrist explores these different levels with patients, he or she will ask a range of questions ranging from the vague and fleeting idea ('sometimes I think it would be better if I didn't exist any more') to the minutely detailed plan ('I've thought out exactly how and when I would do it'). The progression is both qualitative (from simply being tired of life to actually wishing to die) and quantitative (occasional feelings that can be dismissed, then constant ideas which are difficult to ignore, and finally obsessions which fill the consciousness entirely). The major concern of those caring for the patients is of course the moment when suicidal thoughts come to a head, when the spiral towards suicide itself begins as people find themselves locked into ideas about death. That moment when the individual begins to 'incubate suicidal thoughts'.

Withdrawal from society and retreat into oneself both play a very significant role. This is the drama of the psychological self-isolation suicidal people find themselves in: once they are isolated and cut off from the world, there are no longer any obstacles to ever more violent ruminations on death. Because these meet with no resistance, no argument need be advanced against them. The case against continuing the struggle to go on living is heard *in camera*. A case against themselves, against their lives, against life in general. At that point they want to 'get off the train', as one of my patients put it, and 'leave behind all those blissfully ignorant revellers'. They increasingly feel they no longer belong to the same world, to the same species as other people. As a result, they no longer want to confide in them, to seek their advice or listen to their arguments. They want to be left alone to ruminate more deeply, without being distracted or contradicted, to convince themselves that life is not worth living, to carry on quietly blaming themselves and drawing up their own gloomy balance sheets: rumination and self-criticism are both closely associated with the existence and intensity of suicidal ideation.[10]

This withdrawal into oneself with its deadly logic is all the more tragic in that, astonishingly, when studied over a long period, suicidal thoughts turn out to fluctuate in intensity. In people who have made multiple suicide attempts, we therefore find considerable instability in their feelings associated with considerable instability in suicidal ideation.[11] And a number of studies have stressed that the less well regulated emotions are (frequent and poorly controlled fluctuations in feelings), the greater the risk of suicide.[12] It is rumination which gradually reinforces suicidal thoughts, endorsing them as a solution and a source of relief.[13] After a while, these suicidal thoughts start to develop an autonomy of their own. It is as though the virus of suicide is embedded in our minds, needing only a further dip in morale to be reactivated once more.[14]

In the final stages of this process, by dint of rumination and isolation, we reach the stage of obsession, where one single preoccupation exists: to do away with yourself. At this stage life is seen only as a burden, as Chamfort wrote: 'Life is a long illness, from which sleep relieves us every sixteen hours: sleeping may ease us: death alone can cure.'[15] Our vision of the world degenerates rapidly. We feel like 'an extinguished sun around which nothing gravitates any more'.[16] We see only two things when we look around us: on one hand the suffering, which is everywhere and insoluble: on the other, THE solution. Let us listen again to William Styron describing this moment in his own depression:

> Many of the artifacts of my house had become potential devices for my own destruction: the attic rafters (and an outside maple or two) a means to hang myself, the garage a place to inhale carbon monoxide, the bathtub a vessel to receive the flow from my opened arteries. The kitchen knives in their drawers had but one purpose for me.[17]

Between two worlds

At this point, we feel a stranger to other people. We have stepped out of their world. Sometimes, without anyone even noticing. Which can, depending on the individual, upset us ('in the end, whether I am there or not makes no difference'), or reinforce our sense of solitude and of the necessity and the legitimacy of suicide ('those around me won't be upset by my absence for long'). This is the moment when we can start to experience strange combinations of contradictory and intense feelings: solitude and jubilation, terror and serenity, doubt and certainty.

There is sometimes a curious *switch* when someone decides to commit suicide: a sense of calm which can sometimes prove deceptive to those around them. We are now in the eye of the storm. A number of studies have explored this paradoxical calm, associated with the sense of relief at feeling escape is at hand.[18] We feel as though partially released from suffering. And, paradoxically, at that point we can re-envisage living again. This is the time when tiny appeals for help to those around can be made, like messengers who have managed to slip past the vigilance of the suicidal intent, and have succeeded in escaping in order to seek help and reinforcements.

A further paradox: as a result of this calmer state of mind, we can once again become sensitive to the little details of existence. Things which seemed a burden are suddenly seen to have touching, or even appealing, aspects. At this instant some individuals may hesitate or change their minds. Life is not any easier, but a little time has passed and that can sometimes be enough. Though not always.

Indeed, we are in great danger in this state, which is in reality a state of *deconstruction* of the self, where we feel a stranger in our own life, as though partially outside ourselves. It is not unlike certain states of depersonalization experienced by people confronting extremely traumatic situations: they participate in whatever is happening but as though it were happening to someone else. In the context of suicide, this state of deconstruction represents an escape from suffering, but it is dangerous because it is an escape into limbo: we no longer feel pain because, in reality, we have begun to cease to exist.

This is strange territory, situated between the desire for death and regret for the life which is ending. It is a crossroads. For some people, this occurs only once, at a particularly painful period in their lives. After that it is as though they are immune to it happening again. For others, these ruminations towards suicide, followed by periods of wanting to live, recur in an endless cycle. But ultimately, does the desire to die come only to those who have wanted to live? This is what Tolstoy felt: 'I did not know myself what it was I wanted: I was afraid of life, strove to get away from it, and at the same time expected something from it.'[19]

The little details which can kill, or save

In these dark moments, poised between the longing for death and the desire to live, the smallest things can make all the difference. Often it is hard to understand this from outside: 'If you really want to kill yourself, it's surely not going to be a little thing like the absence of a rope to hang yourself with that's going to stop you.' Not always perhaps – but sometimes, yes indeed, that is all it takes.

Two examples: the numbers of deliberate overdoses of paracetamol (taken for pain and fever) dropped when they started to be sold in blister packs requiring the tablets to be extracted one by one, rather than in a bottle where you need only open your mouth to swallow the entire contents in seconds.[20] The simple installation of anti-jump barriers on an English suspension bridge, where many desperate people came to end their lives, led to an instant and dramatic drop in the number of suicides, simply by making the jump a little more complicated.[21]

They will commit suicide some other way, but by some other means, you might say. That seems not to be the case!

In the study relating to the barriers installed on the English bridge, for example, did the potential suicide victims find somewhere else to jump from? Apparently not: researchers were careful to check there had not been a 'transfer' phenomenon with more jumps in neighbouring areas;

nor was there any compensating increase in suicides occurring in the same region, but by other means. By forcing them to postpone their gesture, the lives of a good number of people had quite simply been saved.

Another example happened in Great Britain in the 1960s: the town gas used until then was obtained from coal combustion and was very rich in carbon monoxide. Ideal for committing suicide. All you needed to do, as they used to say, was to 'stick your head in the oven'. With around two thousand five hundred suicides per year, this was the favourite method for English people wishing to end their days. When the composition of town gas was modified so that it no longer contained carbon monoxide, the number of suicides overall went down by a third. Just as a result of there not being any gas-related suicides, without any substitution of other means of autolysis! The same thing happened when cars were fitted with catalytic exhausts, since before that a great many desperate people committed suicide with the gases from their car exhausts.[22]

And for some even more precise figures? If you look closely at the statistics supplied by the Californian police force, you discover that out of the 515 people who had been prevented from jumping from a famous bridge (the Golden Gate Bridge in San Francisco) between 1937 and 1971, only 6 per cent went on to commit suicide: a statistic verified by checking their death certificates subsequently. And even if you include deaths registered as accidental, on the assumption that some of them could be suicides in disguise, still no more than 10 per cent of the formerly desperate people had died violent deaths. Admittedly the figure is higher than in the population as a whole, but it still means that 90 per cent of those who had been stopped at the last minute, just as they were preparing to jump, ended up rediscovering the joys of life! Or at least losing the desire to die . . .

There are some other American statistics which are extremely clear: the fifteen states with the highest levels of firearm possession have suicide rates three times higher than those with the lowest levels; where suicide rates by other means are roughly the same. It is not therefore that life is harder in these states, but simply that there are more guns available. And when guns are immediately to hand, then the transition from idea to gesture is so much smoother.[23]

If a man who has just had an argument with his wife picks up a gun in the heat of the moment and kills her, people will say 'If the gun hadn't been there, things might have been different.' They do not say 'Even if he hadn't had a gun, he would have strangled her: the urge to murder had taken hold of him anyway.' Yet we do not reason in the same way when it comes to suicide: instead we tend to think that in their despair, even if the gun was not there, the person would simply find another means to commit suicide. This is often not the case. In spite of the powerful effect of their ruminations, in spite of the strength of the death wish, complicating access to death is effective, and preventing people from killing themselves easily and impetuously is a useful form of protection against suicide.

What makes people vulnerable to suicidal ideation?

Obviously childhood trauma, a significant factor in all psychiatric problems. But also having been exposed to a high number of adversities during childhood: abuse, pathological relationships, violent parental conflict and parental psychopathology all represent risk factors for suicidal tendencies in adulthood.[24]

Witnessing a relative or friend commit suicide, or attempt to do so, is another factor for subsequent risk. This is an account given by one of my patients:

> When I was a little boy, my father's work meant he was away from home almost every week and, in his absence, my mother often attempted suicide. I would sometimes find her in a coma in the morning, before going off to school, and would have to go and fetch the village doctor. We didn't have a telephone so I would ride my bike round to his house. That probably explains why, for a long time, whenever things got difficult in my life the idea of suicide would come back to haunt me. Whenever I was under any kind of pressure, that was the first thing I would think about: finishing everything, finding peace. Fortunately, I never actually did it. It was becoming a father that cured me in the end. It's not that I never have suicidal ideas any more, but just that I know what a waste it would be: I want to see my children grow up.

There are also the suicide epidemics. Social mimicry exists in all areas of behaviour, including suicide. This is not a modern-day phenomenon: in 1787 Goethe wrote *The Sorrows of Young Werther*, the novel that would make him famous, in which the hero kills himself because the woman he loves marries another man. The book was a huge success and apparently provoked a wave of copy-cat suicides in Europe at that time. We do not have figures from that period, but the phenomenon has been studied more recently and confirmed. When a celebrity commits suicide, the knock-on effect is often a significant rise in the number of suicide attempts in the period immediately afterwards, not just in vulnerable people suffering from pre-existing psychological difficulties[25] but also amongst the population in general.[26]

The role of life events in driving people to suicide has also been recognized. The more someone encounters adversity, the greater their risk of succumbing to suicidal ruminations.[27] But the role of adversity tends to be significant only in initial suicide attempts. After that, when subsequent attempts are made, external events are less important. This is when psychological factors take over. At some point, suicidal ideation becomes obsessive and permanent, forming a kind of unconscious reflex of thinking about suicide whenever life becomes problematic and negative moods take over. These are obsessions which are almost detached from reality and which function on the principle of all or nothing: either calm and the absence of any problem or suffering, or the temptation to commit suicide.

Included in these life events, there are bereavements of course, but also disappointed expectations, for example in a romantic or professional context, etc. Amongst this catalogue of disappointed hopes, it is worth pointing out the high suicide rate following plastic surgery.[28] Finally, for older people, the role of illness and the complications of life can be a significant factor in the temptation to end it all.[29]

Two major factors can aggravate these adverse life events: the sense of solitude (real or imagined, 'nobody can or wants to help me') and the sense of helplessness ('There is nothing I can do to get me out of this situation'). But in reality, do life events only serve to highlight our weakness? Cesare Pavese, an Italian writer who committed suicide, clearly thought so: 'People do not kill themselves for love of a woman. They kill themselves because a love, any love, reveals us to ourselves in all our nakedness, our misery, our helplessness, our nothingness.' Then, in the last poems he wrote to the last woman he was in love with: 'Death will come and it will have your eyes.'

Suicidal illnesses

'Depression is a Russian doll where the smallest doll contains a knife, a razor-blade, some poison, some deep water and somewhere high to jump from.'

As his writing suggests, Stig Dagerman, author of *Notre besoin de consolation est impossible à rassasier* ('Our need for consolation can never be met'), suffered from violent attacks of depression. He committed suicide in 1954, at the age of 31.[30]

The existence of the specialized area of psychiatry known as suicidology is a reminder that there are approximately eleven thousand deaths by suicide in France each year, and about sixty thousand suicide attempts. Suicidologists tell us that mental illness is a factor in 90 per cent of deaths by suicide. And that it is often a depressive disorder.[31]

The longer depression lasts, the greater the risk of some kind of suicidal gesture. This may indeed seem logical,[32] yet research shows that, for an equal level of depression, other factors can intervene to drive someone to suicide: notably unemployment, the presence of a physical illness, social isolation and relationship difficulties. What can stop people at the last minute (or not) is having something to cling to, something to look forward to – soon, tomorrow, in a week's time.[33] Here too, it is the little details which count, as this patient explained: 'I just keep clinging to the idea of my grandchildren coming to visit me this summer: I want to see them again and to enjoy them once more at least.' By the time autumn came around, she had recovered from her depression.

Depression is closely linked to suicide risk, but there is undoubtedly an additional vulnerability among depressives who have already attempted suicide. A recent French study demonstrated this: neuronal activity, observed via neuro-imaging, in patients who had suffered from depression but were not currently affected shows that those who also had a history of suicide attempts reacted very differently to hostile or smiling faces, generally indicating a heightened sensitivity to social opinion, and a reduced sensitivity to pleasant social signals.[34] It is not known if this is a case of cause or effect, but the evidence is clear and needs to be considered when we are trying to help such people. And probably explained to them too, to help them towards a better understanding of their own vulnerability.

Multiple attempters are one of the most painful problems of psychiatry. This group of patients, who make one suicide attempt after another, leave those close to them and their carers increasingly frustrated and sometimes close to despair. These *suicide-obsessed* individuals seem already dead in their own heads. They are like transsexuals, who feel trapped in the body of another sex and who seek to escape through surgery, except that these people are trapped in a living body, in a life they no longer want and are desperate to abandon. The temptation of the void is constantly present in them, they only need to heed it.

Biologists claim that these death-obsessed multiple attempters suffer from a specific deficit in serotonin (a neurotransmitter), which moreover is partially independent of the level of depression.[35] Let us hope that we can quickly find a way of treating it more effectively than we do at the moment.

I remember

I have to admit that writing this chapter brought back some odd feelings. *Recovered memories,* as my psychoanalyst colleagues would say, but anyway, a whole pile of memories came flooding back. You never forget the suicides you have encountered in your life.

I remember – I had only recently started working at Sainte-Anne – a young girl who overdosed on the Prozac I had just prescribed for her. I remember the meeting with her parents who came to the hospital to tell me what had happened and to seek some kind of explanation: I was probably the last person who spoke to her.

I remember – I was an intern in Toulouse – a doctor who had been admitted for depression, immune to any kind of dialogue, with a cold smile. He had already made three suicide attempts. I have never had such a strong feeling of being so powerless to help someone, where even the smallest attempt to help was doomed to fail. I remember his wife had just left him. I remember meeting his parents, who were desperately worried. I remember their telephone call announcing his death, a few days after he had been discharged. I remember that they managed to find the strength to comfort me.

I remember the letter from a mother whose daughter had committed suicide. She had asked for an appointment a few months beforehand but I had not been able to see her straight away. Naturally I had pointed her in the direction of various colleagues, but it was me she wanted to see, in the misguided belief that I would somehow be the best person to help her. I remember feeling sick with guilt for many months.

I remember a young woman on the orthopaedic surgery ward and the sunny winter morning when I was called in to examine her. At the time I was the psychiatric liaison (which meant going onto medical wards to examine patients with psychiatric problems). She had jumped out of a window a few weeks earlier. As I was trying to talk to her to find out what was wrong, she looked closely at me and said: 'But I know you!' I stared back: she was my best friend when we were in our first year at secondary school.

I remember the patient who rehearsed hanging himself at some future date by putting his head in the Argentinean lasso he had brought back from his holidays. He never did use it.

I remember medical colleagues who committed suicide.

I remember the statistics showing that doctors were much more likely to commit suicide than other people.[36]

I remember a colleague with a brilliant career ahead of her, no doubt suffering from bipolar illness, who committed suicide a long way from where she lived, after giving those around her misleading information in order to prevent them looking for her too soon. I remember her whole department in mourning.

I remember that old friend from my intern days who committed suicide many years later in a chic hotel room, unable to face up to the compromising rumours that were dogging him. After swallowing the carefully chosen medicaments, he sat himself in an armchair facing the window and smoked a final cigar, washed down with a final brandy.

I remember a GP friend describing the time she jumped from the roof of her building and the strange moment of depersonalization she experienced once she had climbed out onto the roof: how, in a surge of heightened sensory awareness, she paused for a few seconds (or minutes, she was not sure) in order to take in the details of the lead-work on the roof, listen to the distant hum of traffic from the street, watch the clouds drifting past, breathe in the spring air; then the immense jump, which, by some miracle and great luck, she survived. I remember the joy I feel each time I see her. Alive and smiling.

I remember these lines from Bernanos: 'I would really need a friend to talk to . . . along the banks of the Seine, under those magnificent great trees . . . I was slipping, slipping, my friend . . . Until I reached the dark threshold. But you know as well as I do that the call of death is not without its sweetness.'[37]

I remember the suicide of Achille Zavatta, the clown who could no longer face living on dialysis.

I remember the shudder the word 'suicide' gives me every time I hear it.

I remember that only yesterday, I passed two young boys in the street running towards some shop or other and heard one say to the other 'If it's closed I'm going to kill myself.' And I remember that, even though they seemed perfectly fine, I still stopped, turned round and checked that the shop was indeed open. I remember breathing a sigh of relief.

In case of despair and suicidal thoughts

Amongst my patients I have a poor poet, a writer nobody has heard of. An artist who struggles to find his place here on this earth. He has a number of psychological problems, social phobia, depressive and suicidal tendencies, if we want to use the psychiatric terms. I have done my best to help him with some of them. But recently, after the death of his wife, everything fell apart. As it was just before the summer holidays, and he was going to be completely alone, I did my best to cheer him up, giving him the address of a reliable colleague who was going to be around that summer and to whom I had spoken about him. And then, the day before I left, I suddenly felt worried about him and sent him a postcard saying something along these lines:

> Please stay with us. We need you down here. We need people who are poets like you. We need sensitive people in what is sometimes referred to as 'a world of savages'. Imagine a world without poets, a world with only fight-ers, winners, bankers. Imagine a world where the only plants left would be thousands of square kilometres of tomatoes or some other similar plant, growing in pots under plastic. Well a poet is like the little patch of forgotten waste land where wild grasses and flowers bloom in abundance. See you in September. With best wishes.

I was extremely relieved to see him again when I got back. He had done whatever was needed in order to stand firm.

What can we do when the dark days come along, the bad days? It is often thought, even by doctors, that there is not much anyone can do if someone is determined to die. This dismays suicidologists,[38] for in fact there are a great many things which can be done.[39] These may indeed seem trivial given the stakes involved. But I could not care less. If just one of them helps someone, somewhere, there is clearly nothing trivial about them at all.

Look after your feelings

As we have seen in some detail, negative feelings and moods have a strong correlation with suicide risk. Consequently, the ability to regulate these feelings is a crucial measure of personal hygiene to protect against suicidal thoughts.[40] Especially for those who are vulnerable. But surely looking after ourselves and feeling at ease with our lives will require effort on our part? And what if it does? We do not wait for our teeth to start decaying before brushing our teeth. Are our minds less important than our teeth? Cioran, once again, observes: ' I have conquered the appetite for, not the idea of, suicide.' If the ideas about death which come to us no longer find an echo in us, what progress that is! Admittedly, he follows this almost positive remark with a reservation: 'Subdued by so many defeats'.[41] But even so . . .

Cultivate self-awareness

Very important: people with a case history of depression, whether or not they have entertained suicidal ideas in the past, have a normal capacity to resolve problems, except when a sad mood is induced in them. When this happens, those with a history of suicidal thoughts (at a level high enough to be measured) are suddenly less capable of resolving problems, less intelligent in the way they approach them. As though the scar formed by dormant suicidal ideas is reopened by negative feelings and clouds the clarity of their thinking and their lucidity.[42]

A great many studies have shown the link between a sense of being incapable of resolving problems and the onset of suicidal ideas. One of my patients told me that, in periods of his life where he was unwell and not looking after himself, the smallest hitch was enough to bring on suicidal thoughts: being unable to mend a dripping tap, failing to find a buyer for the flat he was selling, having to sit medical exams which interfered with his professional schedule. If he felt the tiniest bit tired or overwhelmed, if he was pressed for time, or if any other little setbacks had prepared the ground, any of these was enough to light the fuse of suicidal rumination. Without our being aware of it, after any experience of failure which leaves us with significant negative feelings, our intelligence tends to seize up. In particular this affects the memory of our past skills and capabilities, and our ability to solve problems, itself largely dependent on the mobilization of our past resources: knowing that we have solved similar problems in the past and remembering how we went about it.[43] Perhaps this is why suicide, which does not solve the problem but makes it disappear, can seem like a solution at such times?

A good deal of research is now beginning to focus on what happens in our brains to make these tendencies so powerful in certain people. This research has identified cerebral dysfunction associated with significant suicidal behaviour.[44] Of course, these dysfunctions improve if treated with anti-depressants, but this shows that we are a long way from considering suicide as proof of lucidity in the face of the world and its problems.

So, let us reiterate once again: the prevention of these suicidal tendencies involves, at an early stage, a reflection on our susceptibility to failure and adversity. And therefore a reflection on the problems of self-esteem, which we will not deal with in detail here.

Avoid being alone

A well-known hymn begins with the words: 'Where is the friend whom I seek everywhere?'[45] Social links are one of the biggest protectors, and the consolation they bring undoubtedly works in several ways. First of all the existence of such links makes it more complicated to act upon suicidal intentions, and we know the extent to which even small delays can prove significant (which is why single people are more vulnerable to suicide). Empathy is also a factor: not wanting to cause suffering to those who love me, not abandoning those who need me. Acting as a brake, perhaps, to the proud solitude of suicide?

Use or seek out humour

Humour directed at yourself, the world and life. Here are two little flashes. Woody Allen: 'I asked this girl if she had any plans for Saturday night and she told me she was going to kill herself. So I asked her what she was doing on Friday night.' Éric Chevillard: 'When I feel in a gloomy mood, all I have to do is tickle my daughter. The dear little thing never refuses to laugh on my behalf.'[46]

Why does humour make us feel better and sometimes even save us? Because regular exposure to it helps us distance ourselves, it teaches us to rub shoulders with tragedy without dramatizing it, and strengthens our links with other human beings: laughter is even better when it is shared.

The importance of faith

Faith (but also all forms of 'spirituality without god') seems to represent a partial protection against the temptation of suicide.[47] This phenomenon does not appear to be linked to any one religion in particular and involves several interlinked processes.

Some of these are internal: faith provides us with a system of beliefs concerning the meaning of our lives and of the challenges we have to face, and it reduces or removes the sense of helplessness and of the absurdity of trying to do anything; it opposes suicide, which is generally not part of our Creator's plan. But there are also external mechanisms: faith usually encourages social links (gathering together with other believers, at least for religious ceremonies, but very often in other circumstances too); it often promotes a lifestyle which excludes a certain number of risk factors (avoiding toxins, for example).

And then there are also the things which are beyond our grasp. In *La nuit* (The Night), Elie Wiesel describes a horrific scene which takes place in a concentration camp. The Nazis have hanged a young boy, but his emaciated body is so light he does not die straight away. All the other prisoners have been forced to watch. Faced with this unbearable torture one of them cries out: 'Where is God?' And another replies: 'He is there.'[48] With us.

Understand the notion of impermanence

On a trip to India, I accompanied my dear friend Matthieu Ricard on one of his visits to Trulshkik Rinpoche, an elderly Tibetan lama in exile and one of the masters of the current Dalai Lama. He was living near Dehra Dun, in the Uttarakhand, an Indian region in the Himalayan foothills. Matthieu had invited me to attend the audience and to have a brief conversation with the lama. When I asked him about suicide, an issue which preoccupied the minds of so many of my patients, he replied by referring to the Buddhist concept of impermanence, which he then explained to me. Nothing is destined to last, neither we ourselves, nor our sufferings. As is often the case in Buddhist philosophy, the concept of impermanence is of course a complex one: it refers to 'the free movement of phenomena' and 'the freedom intrinsic to the real'.[49] It is more than just the idea we are familiar with in the West, originating from the philosopher Heraclitus, that we 'never step into the same river', or the intuitive knowledge that every living thing is destined to disappear, even our distress and our suffering. In suicide we cling to the idea that our suffering will go on forever. Training ourselves to meditate regularly on the impermanence of all things is a way of making us stronger – or less weak – when tempted by suicide.

As I came away from the meeting with the elderly lama, one phrase seemed oddly stuck in my head: 'To commit suicide is to cling on.' Cling on to certainties and hopes, even when they are disappointed or painful ones. The following day, while walking in the nearby town of Rishikesh (where the Beatles took a rather troubled two-month retreat in 1968), Matthieu went off on his own and sat for a long time on the bank of the river Ganges. I never dared ask him afterwards what he was meditating on. Impermanence, perhaps?

There is nothing desperate or hopeless about impermanence. It is not a nihilist feeling. Indeed there is something bright and joyful about it: notably the idea that our suffering is only temporary and will come to an end.

Cherish happiness

This is one of the central messages of the trend for positive psychology: learning to make yourself a little happier can be a form of prevention against sudden surges of despair. This will be particularly effective if the individual has worked at happiness in a realistic manner, which means, as we shall be seeing shortly, learning to extract happiness even from adversity and misfortune. Happiness as a resource and a vaccine against thoughts of death and despair.

The huge question of hope and despair

We are familiar with the famous line from Cioran: 'People always commit suicide too late.'[50] He goes even further: 'I only continue to live because it is in my power to die when I want to: without the *concept* of suicide, I would have killed myself long ago.'[51] And he clarifies the point yet further: 'Only optimists commit suicide, optimists who are no longer able to be optimistic. Why should other people, who have no reason to go on living, have any reason for dying?'

In fact, Cioran turns the question of suicide on its head: it is perhaps life that is worthless, and death that brings freedom. But as this freedom is a certainty, merely a question of time, we need only to wait for it, without hope or illusions. I have never fully understood why reading Cioran comforts me, instead of plunging me into melancholy. Perhaps it induces a kind of paradoxical effect in us, like a lightning conductor? By describing in detail the workings of our undefined despairs and giving them a concrete form, Cioran enables us to understand them better, to embrace them fearlessly, and in the end, to transform them.

Yet is Cioran not too desperate? Does his vision not lead us to a state of *calm despair*, as Thoreau puts it, where hope is abandoned? And yet, the loss of hope – the certainty that the future will bring no solution to the difficulties we face – seems, at first sight, one of the strongest indicators of suicidal behaviour.[52]

In fact, there are two ways to respond to despair.

The first is to cultivate an optimism which is both practical (involving actions as well as thoughts) and lucid (which does not exclude the existence or the power of adversity). For example, by observing and acknowledging the number of times we have survived our 'mini-despairs'! There are numerous examples of these mini-despairs in our lives: all of us have survived disappointments in love, professional difficulties, bereavements, which at the time seemed unbearable.

But there is also another way of interpreting this way of thinking: one that consists in trying to rid ourselves of hope rather than of despair. For any form of hope makes us vulnerable: 'There is no hope without fear', said Spinoza. This gives rise to the notion of 'cheerful despair' advocated by Comte-Sponville, in his book *Le bonheur, désespérément* ('Happiness, desperately'): serenity must exclude any form of hope or expectation. For hope carries in it the seeds of disappointment, anxiety and dependency. We need then to cultivate freedom for our hopes. Not through nihilism, but simply by trying to inhabit the real in a different way. This is what Albert Camus suggests in the pages he devotes to suicide in *The Myth of Sisyphus*: 'It used to be a question of finding out if life needed to have meaning in order to be lived. It now seems, on the contrary, that life is better if it does not have any meaning.' For Camus, the sense of the absurd and the ability to accept this are crucial: 'Simply by being conscious, I can transform what was an invitation to death into a rule for life'; 'Everything slips back into its place and the absurd world is born again in all its splendour and diversity. . . . Now, let's get on with living.'

We need to accept the notion of despair, of absurdity, when necessary. But without allowing it to be linked with the idea of suicide. This is something we have to learn for ourselves, not something which can be decreed. We shall see that meditation is one element in this learning process: by training ourselves to become familiar with emptiness and nothingness, to have no other expectations except that of living the present moment intensely, it enables us to walk on the cliff edge without fear. We are no longer afraid of being sucked into the void, of falling for no reason.

Part Three

Equilibrium

Training the mind

Lucidity: accept your vulnerability but see beyond it.

Put you body in 'a good mood': help it find calm and energy.

Pacify your feelings: keep a tight hold on your mind as you would a sail in the wind.

And do not forget that you live in a strange world: think about changing that too.

The daylight disappears and now
A lamp is lit within the prison
We're all alone here in my cell
Beautiful light beloved reason.
                    Guillaume Apollinaire,
                            In the Santé

Chapter 10

Fragility

Man cries out where the iron gnaws into his flesh,
And his wound forms a sun.

Louis Aragon

'If I stop trying now, I'll drown. I have the feeling – no, I am sure – that all this effort is what is keeping me alive: the effort of working, of smiling, of keeping up the pretence, the pretence of being well, of being just like everyone else. The effort of making the effort. Some days, I feel exhausted by the sheer effort of constantly having to construct barriers and ramparts to protect me from attacks of depression, despondency, revulsion and weariness of life. Of course, there are times when I do not need to think about any of that, when I am not aware of any such efforts, times when I even feel light-hearted: in these rare moments, I am *rewarded* for my efforts and everything is fine. Like in the Netherlands: it is easy to forget that, if the sea-defences collapsed, a huge part of the country would be engulfed by the sea waters which lie calmly out there waiting for just such an opportunity. There must be people there whose job is to inspect the dykes, others whose job is to repair them, so that everybody else can forget all about them. And in the same way, a part of me keeps up these vital efforts to prevent my mind from being submerged by the waves of despair. And the rest of me tries to forget all about it. Is that what is meant by the "threat of depression"? Is my relative well-being merely the result of my constant vigilance? And what if I stop pedalling? Will I simply fall to the ground as my whole little world of illusions collapses around me? There are days when I dream of finding refuge of some kind! Refuge in religion, in its certainties, in the protection of a monastery or of an ashram. I long to be able to drop my guard, to stop having to make all these efforts, to give up, to let go. I need to be protected from existence. More than ever before, I am so tired of my fragility. And what if, in the end, I am just too fragile to survive?'

Fragile people can be broken by adversity or excessive hardship. Broken, or at least permanently scarred by the injuries, left crippled or lame, 'battered by life'.[1] All living creatures are characterized by their *vulnerability*, in other words, etymologically speaking, by their ability to be wounded. All definitions of what it means to be alive include the notion of death: what is living is what can die. But there is no mention of wounds, so much more important to us who are living. After all, once you are dead, that's it. But living with pain, being crippled, lame, fragile, that is another matter.

Three advantages of fragility

'One evening, after work. I am riding home on my scooter. It is dark and pouring with rain and I am on the ring-road with lorries and cars on all sides. I feel like an antelope surrounded by herds of elephants and rhinoceroses. We are all galloping along but if there is a collision, I am the one who will get crushed. Almost every time I get on my scooter, I am conscious that I could die. Not that I can take much credit for my prudence in constantly thinking like this: nearly every day, as I drive round the Paris ring-road, I see someone like me who has been the victim of an accident: ambulances, police, the motorbike lying on its side.'

The greatest advantage of fragility – or rather of the *consciousness* of our fragility – *is that it protects us* from the illusion of invincibility ('nothing can happen to me') and from certain beliefs ('everything will be easy'). For the fragile and sensitive, on the contrary, anything can happen and it will all be difficult. They discover this at an early stage, in the nursery-school playground. There is evidence that being an anxious child or adolescent offers protection against violent or accidental deaths until adulthood.[2] This is hardly surprising given that their excessive fragility makes them afraid of everything and therefore far less inclined to act *recklessly*, for, under duress, they have an instinct for survival, a heightened sense of their vulnerability and the need to be wary of everything, in anticipation and at all times. This is also why the very things which make us vulnerable can also prove to be enriching: for example, we know from studies on the psychology of relationships that an acceptance of being emotionally dependent on a small number of people (those close to us) can paradoxically enable us to face up to life with a greater sense of freedom and autonomy.[3]

Fragility makes us lucid, we just have to be observant: look at a child sleeping, see a friend getting older, be aware of time passing. And suddenly we find ourselves saying, or rather shouting, to ourselves: 'I must stop acting as though I was going to live forever! As though I had endless lives at my disposal! I must stop living as though I were invincible and eternal.' And there we are, nudged towards wisdom by lucidity and fragility. As the philosopher Clément Rosset so brilliantly puts it: 'Real joy is in fact simply a clear but considered vision of the human condition; sadness is the same vision, viewed with dismay. Joy is therefore what

Spinoza might have called an "active mode" of sadness, and reciprocally sadness can be described as a "passive mode" of joy.'[4]

Fragility brings with it a further advantage: *it makes us more aware of the world*. At first we watched it closely, in order to ensure our survival, constantly asking ourselves where the next blow, the next danger, might come from. Then, as time went on, we learned to watch it in a more relaxed way, we continued to enjoy looking at the world even when there was no longer any danger, and we had already learned to cope with it. When that happens there is often a kind of fortuitous 'rebound effect': emerging from our fragility and anxiety, albeit sometimes only temporarily, it is like daybreak after a night of sickness. We appreciate it more fully and more intensely than someone who has slept peacefully all night long.

It has always seemed to me that the joy of living was more intense for fragile people than for . . . than for what precisely? What exactly is the opposite of fragile? Solid? Hard? Strong? No matter. Surely what is more interesting is what comes next, what follows on after fragility, rather than its opposite. What is really interesting is what happens to fragile people who have managed to move on, not by suppressing their fragility (and becoming 'strong') but by learning to live with it, without suffering too much, or too often.

The unequal distribution of fragility: the case of hypersensitive people

Because of specific circumstances in their lives, anyone can be hypersensitive to any given situation or stimulus. But some people are hypersensitive to almost everything: noise, smell, light, crowds, criticism, responsibility, stress . . . Little research has been done on these hypersensitive people.[5] Not surprisingly perhaps, since, as always in psychiatry, research tends to focus, initially at least, on conditions which are likely to have a negative impact on other people. Society is very concerned about the issue of depression (people who are depressed cannot work, they try to commit suicide, and sometimes even succeed), about anorexia (victims horrify others by their skeletal appearance), about insanity (those who are insane refuse to respect rules). It is less concerned about social phobias or bulimia (whose victims are so ashamed of themselves that they tend to hide away or make themselves as inconspicuous as possible to other people). And it is not in the least concerned about hypersensitive people, who are careful to keep out of the way of anything that moves, shouts, draws attention to itself and kicks up a fuss. And who after all are not even ill but merely fragile and – as a result – more susceptible to certain disorders.

To understand what hypersensitivity is, we need to understand that everybody, hypersensitive or not, experiences an optimal feeling of well-being when the amount of stimulation they get from their environment is just right – neither too much nor too little – in relation to their needs.

Depending on the individual, this optimal zone is situated at a higher or lower level. We all have different levels of tolerance to noisy environments, to the smell of smoke or fried food, to crowded conditions and physical proximity, to heat, to arguments and raised voices, to stress, etc.

This level is of course partly a question of habit: we can get used to something that bothered us in the past, though we rarely learn really to enjoy it since our tolerance has its limits. Temperament (largely innate) is also likely to be a factor: we know, for example, that introverts tend to be generally less tolerant of high doses of stimulation, social or otherwise, than extroverts. In other words, they respond more quickly, more intensely, more painfully to such stimulations; they are more likely to find social situations more tiring and more threatening and to need time on their own to recover from them.

This is what one of my patients had to say on the subject:

> I never liked going to night-clubs or to parties. I went because I felt I had to, because it was expected of me, until I realized that I was perfectly entitled not to enjoy those things. And yet I like people and I like to have fun. I just couldn't stand all that noise, the fact that it was impossible to see anything or talk to anyone. For a long time I had to put up with being called a 'wet blanket' or a 'kill-joy' by other party-goers. But after all it's not my fault that I prefer the peace of midday to the din of midnight! It was the same with my career. I started out on completely the wrong track by going into marketing . . . For me, finding myself caught up in this frantic and phoney world was a complete nightmare. I retrained as a midwife. The pay isn't as good, but at least now I feel I can breathe.

Recognizing these differences in sensitivity, rather than denying them, makes life easier. Being capable of asking: 'Are night-clubs really my thing? Or red wine? Or staying up talking until three in the morning?' And, conversely, for some people: 'Are intimate little chats really for me? Or herbal teas? Or long solitary walks which I know are good for me?'

Living with sensitivity

Talking about her life, a patient of mine used the expression 'painful banalities': a reference not to exceptional traumas or events, but simply to all the little hurts any life brings with it. Hurts to which, in spite of herself, she was more sensitive than other people.

Because, where sensitivity is concerned, there are no clear boundaries between what is normal and what is excessive, and because all of us experience periods when we are hyper-reactive and hypersensitive (if we are not getting enough sleep, or are under too much stress, etc.), any analysis of hypersensitivity will contain elements useful to all sensitive people – in other words, to all of us.

Hypersensitivity is interesting because it forces us to think about the advantages and disadvantages of sensitivity: what it adds and takes away, forbids and allows, limits and enlightens. It forces us to seek compromises with existence (problems relating to the over-stimulating, competitive, unstable, overemotional environments which we are often confronted with today). But it also sets us on the path towards the inner life.

Hypersensitive people, however, for whom certain confrontations have a high emotional cost, often face a particular dilemma: knowing when to make the effort to confront the situation, and when to have the lucidity to avoid confrontation. Implicit in living are two major obligations: the need to protect yourself (avoidance of confrontation) and the need to be able to adapt (confrontation). The way in which we balance these two obligations, and the degree to which we take our fragility into account, condition a large part of our lives, situated between the two poles of avoidance and confrontation.

For hypersensitive people, everyday life is not just a matter of coping with the problem of sensory over-stimulation, but is also about their vulnerability to what we generally refer to as stress (excessive pressure and emotional overload). This triggers a whole range of feelings, from irritation ('I don't believe it, they're not going to start smoking again!') to despair ('I'm never going to be able to stay in this new job, these open-plan offices are just too noisy') and including anxiety ('Let's hope he doesn't lose his temper like he did last time, I am terrified of people who shout').

If we examine the 'emotional chronometry' of hypersensitive individuals (the intensity and duration of their emotional reactions), we find that it is often explosive: feelings and moods succeed each other more rapidly and are more intense and longer-lasting. As in the motto for the Olympic Games, '*Citius, altius, fortius*' ('Faster, higher, stronger'), feelings are often more exaggerated in the very people who crave greater emotional stability, a more efficient internal cooling system.

This is why we have to work hard not to be ashamed of a preference for quiet and for soft tones, or to feel that such preferences are a sign of inferiority and incompetence. The present era is not ideal for hypersensitive people, unlike the eighteenth century, for example, or the Romantic era, where it was acceptable to show your feelings. In the West, that changed when the Victorian era came along, with the cult of 'You'll be a Man, my son', from the famous poem by Rudyard Kipling. And yet being sensitive is not the same as being weak. 'Strong' people think that sensitive people are weak and are surprised when they find that they simply want to be left in peace, but are nevertheless capable of fighting back with a vigour all the more powerful because unexpected.

A whole range of other characteristics have been imputed to sensitive people: their conscientiousness, their high levels of concentration (in the absence of external distractions), their ability to spot minor differences, their empathy, their ability to remain still for long periods, their strong reaction to caffeine, and also the high incidence amongst them of allergic reactions and hay fever, etc.[6] All this detail helps to support the probability that biological and cerebral specificities may indeed account for hypersensitivity.

But, right from early childhood, hypersensitive individuals have an extremely rich inner life with intense imaginary worlds. More than other people, they need moments of calm in order to reconnect with themselves. Failing that, they experience a sense of alienation and quickly become exhausted. They find it hard to sustain social situations for any prolonged periods, and need to be able to withdraw from these frequently: during family holidays they seek regular opportunities to go off for a walk on their own or to find a quiet corner in which to read peacefully. This is why artists and poets, the majority of whom are hypersensitive, feature prominently amongst their ranks. In some cases this can result in psychological problems developing as a consequence.[7] For there is also a dark side to hypersensitivity, with the heightened risk of anxiety and depression.

Should we all be on Prozac?

After suffering from depression, hypersensitive people sometimes notice that taking Prozac, or any other anti-depressant acting on serotonin (a neurotransmitter involved in mental stability), helps to bring them greater emotional stability and a calmer state of mind. Not only are they no longer depressed but they actually feel better under the treatment than they did even before the onset of depression. Not surprisingly, some of them are reluctant to stop taking it. Even if the idea of feeling 'chemically' better does not appeal to them.

Which is why a book devoted to the subject, *Listening to Prozac*,[8] generated a huge debate (in the 1990s) about Prozac and the other medicaments belonging to the same chemical family, the selective serotonin reuptake inhibitors (prolonging the effect of serotonin). These drugs are more general regulators of emotion than simply anti-depressants or tranquillizers. Would these substances be used as a kind of food supplement for people subject to painful feelings and moods? It was not the first time in history that psychotropic drugs had been seen as a panacea for painful feelings and moods: the years between 1960 and 1980 had seen an over-consumption of tranquillizers. Remember the Rolling Stones song *Mother's Little Helper*: 'And though she's not really ill / There's a little yellow pill', which described how the young mothers of that time coped with life with the help of little coloured pills, almost like aspirins for the mind, then sold under the names of Librium or Valium, and now called Lexomil or Xanax. But times have changed. If the drugs of the Prozac family are indeed sometimes prescribed over very long periods and even for life in some cases, generally speaking this is in the context of severe illnesses, either anxiety (such as obsessive-compulsive disorders) or depression (recurrent depression), and not as 'psychiatric cosmetics'. First, this would be illegal, and secondly, such treatments can produce some serious secondary effects (on sexual desire for example) if used over a long period.

Those patients who opt to continue taking Prozac describe how this drug (or its equivalents) acts as a regulator of their painful feelings and moods, and, as a result, enables them to avoid relapses into anxiety or depression. They could of course find other ways of regulating their feelings. But they may never have been told about these or been shown how they work or how to use them. All these patients have certainly tried to stop their medication on more than one occasion. They are often ashamed to admit their continued and secret use of the drug to those close to them, for fear of being judged to be self-indulgent or weak. I remember a journalist who was interviewing me about the supposed abuse of prescriptions for anti-depressants, and who ended up admitting that she had been taking them ever since being treated for depression years earlier, and that she was reluctant to stop because they had enabled her to overcome her chronic and paralysing anxiety and depression. But there was no way she was going to mention that in her article. She told me 'On the three occasions I tried to stop, I felt awful, constantly on edge, overwhelmed by the slightest little thing, like a hermit crab without its shell. Exactly the way I was before I started taking them, in fact. Except that then I couldn't imagine ever feeling better.'

The Welsh poet Gwyneth Lewis describes her own fragility in these words: 'Since I was a child, I've lacked an emotional epidermis. This is good for writing – it means I feel things very intensely – but bad for my daily equilibrium.'[9] A little later in the interview, Lewis adds: 'Even if it were proven that antidepressants adversely affected my ability as a poet, I'd still take them. After being a zombie for months, being able to write at all is a miracle, and that participation in the creative discipline, rather than a more objective measure of excellence, is the bottom line for me.' As someone who has suffered very severe depression, she knows what she is talking about.[10]

Such people have therefore often tried first reducing their dose before going on to stopping their medication altogether. Not all of them succeed. In such cases, the advice of psychiatrists – in addition to embarking on a course of psychotherapy adapted to their needs – is to start reducing the dose during relatively calm periods, on holiday for example. And to do so very gradually, reducing the dose by half over half the length of time of the treatment: for example, after a treatment lasting three years, take half the dose for a year and a half; then stop completely and see what happens. As a psychotherapist, what would be my advice in these situations? First of all, avoid such prescriptions wherever possible, especially in cases where the person is a suitable candidate for psychotherapy. And, if a prescription is necessary, in cases where severe anxiety or depression risk causing serious damage, I try, like the majority of my colleagues, to avoid what I call 'orphan prescriptions': never prescribing a psychotropic drug without first taking the time to discuss the vulnerability which led to the illness in the first place, giving advice about how to cope with everyday life, and organizing a follow-up course of psychotherapy. I remind the patient that, in any case, their personal efforts are indispensable if they are (1) to get better, (2) to stay well, (3) to avoid the possibility of a relapse once they stop taking the drugs. And I also urge them to pay attention to the effects the medication has on them: so as try to reproduce them afterwards, but with psychological techniques and efforts.

There is, however, little point in continuing to demonize psychotropic drugs: they are at least preferable to the regular use of alcohol and cannabis. A case of two evils . . . Moreover, long-term studies show that they can be effective in cases of genuine need. So, for example, a follow-up of adult patients in England over a six-year period showed that those who had been prescribed psychotropic drugs at the age of 40 – following psychiatric diagnosis – were better off aged 50 than those with the same diagnosis who had not taken them.[11] Stating the obvious? Not at all: if you do not have access to psychotherapy, a situation which is surprisingly common, and if you have established symptoms, taking appropriate medication over an appropriate period of time is still an acceptable way of helping you in the short term, and of ensuring you remain well in the long term.

How medication modifies our feelings and moods

The effect of selective serotonin reuptake inhibitors (SSRIs) on our subtle psychological dynamics has been studied in detail.

The studies found, for example, that these drugs caused slight modification of personality traits, making people less aggressive, not only as a result of the anti-depressant effect (reducing mental suffering diminishes hostility towards the surrounding environment), but also through a generalized reduction of negative affects. Anti-depressants exert this effect both on people who are not, or no longer, depressed,[12] and on those who are still suffering from depression.[13]

These drugs can also influence our subconscious recognition of facial expressions. When healthy volunteers – in other words, people not significantly affected by either anxiety or depression – were shown photos of faces expressing recognizable emotions (those capable of activating the amygdala, our emotional brain) whilst being treated with anti-depressants, reduced reactivity in the amygdala was observed.[14]

SSRIs also affect memory in 'normal' people, making them recall positive memories more willingly and easily. They have a similar effect on their general perception too: they are more likely to react favourably to adjectives describing a wide range of personality traits, for example seeing stubbornness as a quality rather than a defect.[15]

It is logical then that everything is perceived in a somewhat rosier light: transposed to everyday life, these laboratory results suggest that anyone taking these drugs would notice fewer glum faces around them, and would anyway be less sensitive to these. These people would more easily focus on happy memories and would be more inclined to judge people they encountered in a positive way. A tempting scenario! Well, yes, it is somewhat reminiscent of Aldous Huxley's novel *Brave New World*, in which people were given a drug – *soma* – to regulate their behaviour ('One cubic centimetre cures ten gloomy moods'). And besides, as we have pointed out, there are also a number of side effects associated with these drugs.

But, in fact, 'If these medicaments work, it's because they are correcting a biological deficit, isn't it?', our patients often ask. And that is the problem . . .

Biology of fragility and repair

A considerable number of recent studies have focused on people with a discrete genetic particularity: a short allele on the gene encoding the serotonin transporter. It seems that these are the people who dominate the ranks of the hypersensitive, that is, approximately 10 to 20 per cent of the population.[16] In these people the amygdala tends to respond more intensely than normal to any situations which are emotionally charged;[17] they react to threats with a greater degree of anxiety[18] and, as a result, are more vulnerable to a range of psychiatric disorders, and to depression in particular.[19] In case of confrontation with a traumatic event, the psychological effects are likely to be more significant in these people.[20]

But the most interesting aspect of this epidemiological data is that their fragility is only transformed into illness when they are confronted with adverse life events.[21] In the absence of any such events, their excessive emotional vulnerability will not lead to illness: they will simply be more sensitive than other people, not in itself a significant problem. This interaction between genes and environment is what is known as epigenesis and it is a reminder that in psychiatry, genetics is not strictly deterministic. Only an indication of our potential strengths and weaknesses.

And moreover, not all hypersensitive people will be vulnerable even when they are confronted with difficulties in their lives: there will always be a difference between the fragile people who have learned to manage their fragility (thanks to their past or to self-discipline or personal efforts) and those who have not learned to do so, and who as a result are vulnerable when adversity strikes. Unless they too have made an effort to understand themselves better and to protect themselves more effectively: studies on preventive therapies offered to fragile volunteers confirm the advantages of this kind of preparation.[22]

It is not just a matter of 'major' adversities: we know too that one of the characteristics of psychological fragility is an excessive negative emotional reactivity to the little events of daily life and not just to the major challenges of existence.[23] This fragility in the face of trivial details can sometimes be a pre-depressive symptom, as in this short story where Scott Fitzgerald describes his mental distress: 'But at three o'clock in the morning a forgotten package has the same tragic importance as a death sentence, and the cure doesn't work – and in a real dark night of the soul it is always three o'clock in the morning, day after day.'[24] The tiniest details can thus plunge us into great distress, driving us into a state of collapse where we even frighten ourselves.

Does this mean that hypersensitive people are condemned for life to rely on medication to keep their genetically based fragility under control? The answer is no!

First of all because we know that our cerebral biology is malleable: this is what is called neuroplasticity. All psychological problems are indeed anchored in a biological cerebral reality: when we are depressed or anxious our condition is not the result of some abstract cause but corresponds instead to some kind of cerebral malfunction. But this does not apply only to problems: *all* cerebral phenomena are biological. Moving, feeling, loving: all of these are transmitted via our cerebral circuitry. The same goes for learning to read or to count and to the ability to change. Any regular change, any learning process, gradually imprints itself onto our brains. When we learn to play a musical instrument, we are creating connections between different areas of the brain (such as motor, auditory and visual cortex). And the same happens when we learn to understand and regulate our feelings and moods and the behaviour and thought processes associated with them. Studies focusing on depressed or anxious people have shown that, thanks to the efforts of psychotherapy, we can, to some extent, repair or compensate for dysfunctions in our neurotransmitters.[25] In the same way as medication does. And with lasting effects. Which cannot always be said of medication!

Our pain and our vulnerability, even if in part genetic, can nearly always be improved and 'put right' once we reach adulthood, provided that during our adult years we work on developing our capacity for self-control.[26]

Furthermore, it is highly likely that the more progress scientists make in identifying the biological or genetic causes of sensitivity and vulnerability, the fewer people there will be who can claim to be exempt from any form of fragility: for each of us is fragile in one way or another. The risk of stigmatization, which some people fear will result from advances in our knowledge of such fragilities, will in fact be countered and diluted as they become more universal. As Archytas, a mathematician and philosopher, and friend and master of Plato, observed, 'In the same way as it is difficult to find a fish without bones, it is equally hard to find a man without some kind of pain.'[27]

Getting closer to what matters to all humans

Disability is not the same as fragility: a disability is a permanent defect, either physical (being deaf or paraplegic) or mental (Down syndrome), which will never return to normal. A disability can be compensated for, but not repaired. In spite of this difference, being disabled implies having a close acquaintance with fragility and, as a result, fragile people can learn a lot from those who are disabled.

In his wonderful autobiographical account, the historian Jacques Sémelin describes the experience of going blind, and provides us with considerable food for thought on living with fragility.[28]

Some of his anecdotes are full of joy: running ('when you cannot see any more, you can no longer run') on the beach at Noirmoutier with his 9–year-old daughter, without worrying about tripping over. Some are sad: such as when the same little girl, some years earlier, leaps from a wall into his arms, assuming he will catch her, but tumbles to the ground in a flood of tears because he had failed to realize she was going to jump. He also tells how, in the United States, when he is asked what he needs in reference to his blindness, he knows the unspoken text is 'In order to continue to manage on your own'; and he takes comfort from this absence of pity, and the desire to offer concrete assistance in response to his need for autonomy. He describes how, in order to come to terms with his dependency, instead of denying it, he dilutes it by spreading it as widely as possible: he needs to ask for a lot of help, but not always from the same people. Such as his sessions of 'hitching walks', along the same lines as ordinary hitch-hiking, which bring him into contact with a wide range of people. Yet at the same time he makes no attempt to conceal the problems, as well as the sadness, his disability brings with it: such as the day when a passing tramp called out 'That's tough!' – 'No, it's not that bad' – 'Yes, yes, that's tough!' And when, in the end, he couldn't help thinking the tramp was right. Or the day when his daughter said 'I'm so unlucky to have a dad who can't see.' He does not seek to deny the reality of his situation and the suffering it brings, but is determined not to give in to gloomy ruminations on his plight. And Sémelin quotes one of the most famous blind writers, the Argentinean Borges, writing about his blindness: 'It is not a "complete misfortune" but just one more instrument amongst all the strange ones that destiny and chance hand out to us.'

What else can we do but understand and accept our vulnerability? And accept that we lack the necessary strength? That we all have our weaknesses? By admitting and embracing our fragility we can avoid futile conflicts, saving our strengths for those which are unavoidable. Accepting our fragility helps us to understand that we frequently need to take refuge elsewhere, by withdrawing to some peaceful place, going on retreats, meditating or cutting ourselves off from the world from time to time.

But there is no point in feeling bitter about the 'specifications' which are harsher in our case than for other people. In the end, being fragile simply forces us to do what would do everyone good, but to do it better and more often: to take time to think, to avoid over-stimulation, to find out what we really enjoy, what we really want to do with our lives. All of which is a source of potential enrichment for those who have understood and applied these principles: our fragility forces us – no, helps us – to stay close to what is truly important.

Coping with fragility: artists and artisans

In his magnificent and disturbing *Book of Disquiet*, Fernando Pessoa describes his own fragility, his unfitness for the world, and his retreat into a hypersensitive inner life. Finding it acutely difficult to live in close contact with other people, he describes 'an anguished feeling of being exiled among spiders, and a sudden awareness of my humiliation among real people'. He refers to his feelings of boredom and emptiness as 'a head-cold of the soul'. He depicts his retreat from the world as 'a life of aesthetic quietism, to prevent the insults and humiliations of life and the living from getting any closer than a loathsome periphery of our sensibility, outside the walls of our conscious soul'. Like so many other hypersensitive writers and so many other artists, Pessoa finds refuge and comfort in his inner life.

But what about the vast majority of us who are not great artists, who do not have special talents? Well, we can content ourselves with being artisans. Not artists, but artisans, who use their fragilities and their abilities to try to feel well, to do things well and, where possible, to do good. And also to work quietly on their feelings and moods. To learn to see more clearly through the eyes of the soul. Like Rainer Maria Rilke: 'I am learning to see. I don't know why it is, but everything penetrates more deeply into me and does not stop at the place where until now it always used to end. I have an inner self of which I was ignorant. Everything goes there now. I do not know what happens there.'[29]

Chapter 11

Calm and energy

Don't you know it's plain
That all your nature yelps for is a body free from pain,
And, to enjoy pleasure, a mind removed from fear and care?
Lucretius, *On the Nature of Things*

What does it mean to be well?

Health professionals have definitions of health which can guide our thinking on what 'being well' means. Moreover, the way these definitions have changed over time throws light on the historic evolution of our expectations on the subject of health.

In the past, health was 'life lived in the silence of the organs':[1] to be in good health meant an absence of symptoms, of suffering or of disability. Today the World Health Organization provides us with a more relevant definition: 'Health is a state of complete physical, mental and social well-being and not merely the absence of disease or infirmity.' This new approach to health shows that the focus is shifting towards a sense of well-being rather than simply an absence of suffering.

This view is widely held, given the importance of the body–mind link. Being well means feeling well in both mind and body, simply because mental and physical feelings are linked. Think about what goes on in your body when you are worrying about something (someone you love is very late coming home and you have had no news from them) and about what happens in your body when that person turns up at last: your feelings find expression first in tension and then in relaxation.

In the area of well-being, modern medicine and psychology are also devoting considerable attention and scientific research to developing the capacity for general well-being rather than simply seeking to repair what is wrong. When it comes to feelings, we now know that it is better not to wait for the onset (or the return) of anxious, depressive or angry tendencies, for example, before taking action.

At last we have understood and demonstrated that well-being is the result of a combination of permanent adjustments and personal efforts and that it is an attainable equilibrium. Albeit a relatively unstable one.

So, if we want to 'be well' in the long term, we know that what we are seeking is not simply a state which is only attainable in certain privileged conditions, and in isolation, akin to relaxing in a nice hot bath (we cannot go through life in a foam bath and a peaceful atmosphere). Instead we need to find one which stands up to the confrontation with everyday life, a basal state. It is the search for and the cultivation of this basal state that interests us here.

We are therefore going to examine in more detail these three dimensions of well-being: (1) 'feeling well' as a general state which includes both physical and mental feelings; (2) 'feeling well' as the result of certain efforts; (3) 'feeling well' as a basal state. And indeed, what exactly is the base in question?

The magic formula for well-being: calm and energy

If we accept that permanent well-being is probably not attainable in normal life conditions where we have to face stress and adversity, the question we should be addressing is: what sort of basic state should we be attempting to cultivate in ourselves? What do we need in order to face up to the demands and the vagaries of everyday life? What level of equilibrium should we aspire to?

If you try asking those around you the question 'What does it mean to feel well?' you will probably get a wide range of replies (just as you would for the question 'What does it mean to be happy?'). These will range from 'not being ill' (being well means not being unwell) to 'to being at peace in mind and body' (being well means being in harmony), with a thousand other options in between.

A second stage in your inquiry would then be to ask the same people to describe moments when they did or did not feel well. At this stage, you will gain a little more insight. They will tell you that that 'not feeling well' generally equates to feeling: *exhausted, demotivated, stressed, tired, irritated* . . . And, conversely, 'feeling well' is associated with feeling: *on top form, full of energy, zen, serene, confident* . . . Such intuitive responses correspond to the findings of research on the subject, which also suggest that the ideal to aim for and to cultivate is a mixture of calm and energy.[2]

This may remind some older readers of the electoral slogan of former French president François Mitterrand: 'Quiet strength'. This slogan was widely used during his electoral campaign and probably had a subtly reassuring effect for many voters: when he came to power, the left had been confined to opposition for decades and many people were worried by the prospect of an alliance with the Communist party. Combining the words *strength* ('We are not merely peaceful dreamers only useful when in opposition') and *quiet* ('We are not revolutionaries who are going to turn everything upside down and throw the country into unrest') proved to be a winning concept. And one that also applies to our well-being.

The notion of calm suggests the absence of disturbance and unrest, but without implying passivity or withdrawal. It means being attentive to, but not perturbed by, what is happening around us. As well as a general feeling, calm can take different forms in our bodies (relaxed but not completely switched off) and in our minds (still 'observant' but not yet lulled into sleep). In his *Journal* Jules Renard notes: 'The ideal of calm exists in a sitting cat.'[3] Peaceful but ready to pounce . . .

The notion of energy implies the capacity to act or to envisage action, the sense that action is possible and the conviction that it will be conclusive or useful. Similarly, the general sense of possessing internal energy is both psychological (confidence and pleasure at the idea of doing something) and physical (the ability to begin and sustain a course of action).

The opposites of these notions are, in the case of calm, a state of tension, in which it is difficult to feel at peace both mentally and physically, and for energy, fatigue, the feeling of no longer possessing any inner resources. Both tension and fatigue are states all of us experience on a regular basis.

Understanding calm and energy

By combining these two dimensions, calm versus tension and energy versus fatigue, it is possible to describe fairly accurately the various general or what we might term 'psychosomatic' states that we experience in the course of our daily lives.

Our four major 'body–mind' states

	Calm	Tension (absence of calm)
Energy	Optimal state (the 'quiet strength')	Annoyance
Fatigue (no energy)	Weariness, desire for rest or sleep	Nervous exhaustion, but inability to rest or sleep

In each of us, these dimensions combine in different ways at different times to form four very different basic states: calm and energy (which is the optimum, at least where action is concerned); calm without energy (which is peaceful fatigue, for example when we are about to fall asleep); tension and energy (stress); tension without energy (when we need to relax in order to be able to rest).

In normal conditions, at the beginning of the day, when we have just woken up, we are usually in a state of increased calm and low energy. Then, as the day goes on, our energy levels fluctuate, but so too do our levels of tension: depending on what happens to us, but also on the manner in which we take care of ourselves, at certain moments we feel full of energy and reasonably calm (optimum efficiency) while at others we feel energetic but tense (stress). Quite often, by the end of the day, our energy levels have dropped (onset of fatigue) and we then need to be looking for ways of reducing tension: by relaxing, stopping work, spending time with people close to us, slowing down. All that in order to get ourselves gradually into the state conducive to sleep: calm (low tension) and fatigue (low energy). At that point we can take what is called a 'well-deserved rest'.

These natural cycles can be disrupted by psychological problems. When someone is depressed, for example, there is a chronic energy deficit: energy levels are very low in the morning (to the extent that it is difficult to get up, get dressed, get washed) and scarcely increase through the course of the day. And the sufferer is still tired by evening, in spite of having done nothing (hence the feelings of guilt). When someone is suffering from anxiety, on the other hand, the opposite applies and there is a deficit of calm: tension is high from early on in the day (sometimes their anxiety even wakes them up) and generally stays that way throughout the day, until the evening (leading to sleep problems).

Common errors in the search for calm and energy

Our relationship with these two dimensions of calm and energy is by no means clear cut. Three major misconceptions can be identified.

First, many people tend to confuse the subjective feeling of tension and excitement with energy: by drinking coffee, listening to loud music, smoking tobacco, they feel they are boosting their energy levels, whereas in fact they are also increasing their levels of tension, sometimes to an even greater extent. It is true that the combination of tension and energy also facilitates action, but in the long term there is a high price to be paid in terms of fatigue, given that stress-related fatigue is much more problematic than the fatigue associated with energy.

In fact, these two phenomena – energy and tension – are not necessarily a good combination. We can, and this is clearly preferable, feel calm energy. This basal state (which we are sometimes called upon to abandon temporarily in certain specific situations) is the one best suited to our purposes. Calm and energy enable us to achieve the great classical ideals embodied in the *serene action* of the Stoics, or the *right action* of the Buddhists.

The second major misconception is the notion that being calm necessitates a withdrawal from the world. This is only partially true: withdrawal from the world can indeed bring about a state of calm, but we can also (and this is once again the ideal approach) remain calm and still be in contact with the world: calm in arguments, calm in action. Sportsmen and sportswomen are all too aware of the need to remain calm during competitions in order to avoid making mistakes; but this calm in no sense distances them from the action. On the contrary, it is the best way of staying fully concentrated on it.

The final misconception is the idea that these states are purely a reflection of what happens to me. I stay calm provided people do not annoy me too much; I have energy if they are not too exhausting. Again this is only partially true, and therefore to some degree inaccurate: our levels of calm and energy depend not just on what happens to us but also on what we do (or fail to do) to increase them.

Finally, let us talk about something which is more error than misconception: in order to boost our energy levels we turn to substances like coffee which increase tension as much as they boost energy. And we neglect the more 'organic' means of doing so, such as physical activity. For it is indeed possible to focus on certain activities and attitudes which will help us achieve the optimum combination, the 'magic formula', for well-being, allowing calm and energy to take up more space in our daily lives.

The influence of physical states on our feelings and moods

People often think that a problem is a problem and that, no matter when we look at it, it always remains the same. But we may be wrong to think in this way.

In fact the time of day influences how we feel. In a study in which volunteers were asked to note down their levels of calm and energy at regular intervals over a period of several days,[4] it became clear that an identical problem (for example, a problem with a relationship or an issue about weight loss) was judged as being more serious in the afternoon than in the morning. What is the explanation of this? Generally speaking, our level of calm and energy reaches a peak towards the end of the morning. By the end of the day, on the other hand, there is a build-up of tension (less calm) and a drop in energy levels (fatigue is starting to make itself felt).

In the same study, volunteers also perceived their problem as being less difficult to solve when they were asked to think about it after 10 minutes' fast walking.

In both cases it was clear that these positive changes in judgement corresponded (without participants being aware of this) to higher levels of calm and energy.

What are the mechanisms which cause these physical states to have an influence on our feelings? When it comes to judging our own problems, we know that we tend to extrapolate our future energy on the basis of our current energy levels. So, when we are at our best, we feel capable of resolving a whole range of problems. This explains why sometimes, in a fit of enthusiasm and energy, we take on projects which subsequently appear oppressive once fatigue begins to take hold. Or why we turn down projects proposed at a time when we are feeling exhausted. If our physical states change, our judgement – which we often think of as being purely *rational* rather than *biological* – also changes!

Predictions such as these which are based on our immediate sensations (*affective forecasting*) are extremely important in helping us to understand those feelings based on anxiety and despondency in the face of adversity: if we feel tired when we are carrying out a particular task, we are more likely to think that we will not succeed, assuming that this is a rational assessment, when in fact it is not. It is simply that we are less likely to succeed *in the state we are in at the present moment*. In the same way, if we are tense, we unconsciously feel we will never be able to calm down enough to deal with the situation.

In this way, understanding the fluctuations of these states of calm and energy is the key to understanding most of our feelings, since these depend on these two major physical states. For example, in worry there is both fatigue and tension while in optimism there is energy and calm.

Things we can do to facilitate calm and energy

In preparation for this particular chapter, I asked those around me what they did in order to feel well. Looking at her three children, a mother replied 'That's easy. For my children to feel well they need to eat well and sleep well; and they mustn't be stuck inside, in front of their computer games all day long either.' And that is exactly the conclusion reached by researchers. Except that it took them longer, of course.

Feeling well depends on respecting our natural needs: eating and sleeping. Which seems obvious. If we fail to respect these two basic needs, our bodies will soon let us know. But there are also two others: physical activity and relaxation. These are more easily neglected, all the more so because such negligence is not punished immediately as it would be with eating or sleeping, but more gradually, through a disturbance of our emotional balance, and therefore of our feelings and moods.

We are now going to focus on these two fundamental elements of our psychological equilibrium, and thus of the healthy functioning of our feelings: physical activity and the practice of relaxation.

Physical exercise: 'Put your body in a good mood!'[5]

We have of course known for a long time ('*Mens sana in corpore sano*') that being in good physical shape helps to keep the mind working healthily. And a considerable amount of research has confirmed this view.[6] This applies to everybody: people with existing psychological problems, those who have previously experienced them, and people who hope never to have them!

For those without any specific problems, there is a direct correlation between the number of steps taken each day and improvements in energy level and mood.[7] Approximately ten minutes' fast walking is enough to boost our sense of well-being, and the effect lasts for about ninety minutes. Put more precisely, it seems that exercise stimulates positive feelings and normalizes them, and, to a lesser extent, leads to a reduction of negative moods.[8] Perhaps this explains why the benefits of walking are not as obvious as they might be: when we are feeling low (negative feelings), our expectation is that the negative feelings will disappear rapidly and completely. We tend to focus on this, rather than on the increase in positive feelings, which is subtler and therefore more difficult to identify.

For people suffering from psychological disorders,[9] the benefits, if not instantaneous, are nevertheless spectacular. A considerable number of reliable studies have shown that exercise is as effective as anti-depressants, provided it is practised for forty-five minutes, four times a week over a period of four months. Not an easy matter for someone suffering from depression: which is why they should ideally have access to group gymnastic sessions in the hospital environment which they could attend every day of the week. Sadly, very few psychiatry departments prescribe physical activities to patients; though all that would be required would be a full-time gym teacher and a suitably equipped room. However, the most interesting outcome of this research is the observation that, six months later, those patients who had done exercise were less likely to suffer a relapse than if they had taken anti-depressants.[10] It has also been demonstrated that doing exercise enhanced the effects of taking anti-depressants where these were not enough on their own: even where depression requires treatment, physical exercise offers a booster effect which probably avoids doses having to be increased.[11] In cases of anxiety disorders, it has also been proved that six 20–minute exercise sessions, whether moderate or intense, reduce the tendency to anxiety.[12] In summary, because the list of studies would be a long one, a 30–minute exercise session per day is sufficient to improve temporarily not only the mood, but also the intellectual capacities, of patients suffering from depression.[13]

A number of debates and studies are under way to ascertain the precise mechanism behind these benefits, and to establish whether all patients are affected, or only certain groups. Perhaps the very people who are the least likely to be spontaneously attracted to exercise![14]

On a slightly different level, in what is known as 'chronic fatigue' syndrome, which involves a whole range of feelings associated with the difficulty of taking action, a structured exercise programme is as effective as (and cheaper than) psychotherapy.[15] Which confirms what was already known: in most cases of chronic fatigue where no obvious medical explanation can be found, it is not rest that should be prescribed, but physical activity!

It is worth pointing out that in order to help motivate patients to take up physical exercise, psychotherapists may find it helpful to conduct some of their consultations while walking with their patients![16] From the evidence already cited, this would also help patients face their problems with increased energy and optimism whilst enabling therapists to keep fit and cultivate calm and energy alongside their patients!

In practice, what can be done? Most learned societies or research organizations have come to a similar conclusion. Take, for example, the recommendations made by the French Institute for Health and Medical Research (Inserm):[17] the advice for adults between the ages of 18 and 65 is to do some kind of aerobic activity (walking, jogging, cycling . . .), at a moderate rate, for at least 30 minutes, five days a week. Over the age of 65, the advice remains the same but the activity should be modified to suit the person's physical condition. These activities should be associated with exercises designed to maintain bone density, flexibility and balance and should include muscle-strengthening exercises (resistance exercises: lifting weights or objects, pushing, pulling, hanging from a bar etc.), flexibility exercises (gentle movements of the neck, shoulders, waist, hips), and balance exercises (walking on tip-toe along a line drawn on the ground, jumping from one block to another in a fitness circuit, or standing on one foot while doing slow stretching movements as in tai chi). All to be done at least twice a week for between 5 and 10 minutes for each of these three groups of exercises.

Finally, we must learn to be patient: most studies suggest that positive effects on feelings and morale will only be felt fully after about eight weeks of activity.

Clearly there is nothing particularly demanding about investing in our well-being in this way! And yet many people simply do not do it. A survey conducted by *Baromètre Santé* in 2005 showed that in the week prior to the survey, only 45.7 per cent of French people aged between 15 and 74 had taken part in a physical activity lasting more than 10 minutes. Yet such activities are easy to do, and cost nothing. And they suit our biological identity. As one of my colleagues pointed out when I mentioned this research: 'Well, that doesn't surprise me! We are made to run after antelopes or run away from lions!'

One last point before you get started: there are three different levels of physical effort. *Physical activity*: being active in the course of normal daily life, for example, taking the stairs instead of the lift, or walking instead of going by car. *Physical exercise*, in other words an activity specifically designed to improve well-being: going for a walk or a bike ride, for example. And finally, *sport*, which involves a competitive element either on an individual level or against other people.

Taking part in a sports activity is not essential in health terms; it can of course be extremely beneficial, but in some cases, for example if taken to excess or when injuries occur, it can also be harmful.[18] Being more active

in the course of everyday activities is beneficial but the benefits can sometimes be 'polluted' by the psychological or physical context: if we run
for a train or race down the corridors of the underground, the benefits of
the physical activity may well be outweighed by the stress or irritation
involved. For the majority of people, opting for some kind of enjoyable
exercise, however gentle, appears to be the best way of benefiting from
the effects we have just described. Being conscious of the fact that we are
making our bodies work as we exercise is an important factor which is
underlined in a number of studies we shall be referring to. Consequently,
if we choose not to 'force' our bodies to the level of sport, or are unable to
do so, we can instead simply intensify our mental presence in whatever
exercise we are doing. The mind must be engaged alongside the action.

Relaxation: calming the body

Another simple and cost-free activity (though requiring a certain amount
of initial training) is relaxation.

Why do we need this too?

First of all, because each time we are confronted with a stressful situation the result is a discreet tensing of the muscles, a tension which often
tends not quite to return to normal, because other difficulties or other
stressful tasks need to be dealt with, and because our minds, capable of
remembering and anticipating, will continue to store the anxiety even
after the situation is resolved. As a result we continue thinking about the
problem and, because our body reacts in the same way whether we are
thinking about something or actually experiencing it, it continues to tense
and contract as though we were in the situation all over again.

This is why any relaxation method will focus on getting us to do a
number of little exercises of 'mini-relaxation', with a view not to achieving total relaxation, but simply to helping 'reduce the pressure' and
easing some of the muscular tension which accumulates throughout the
course of the day. In practice, this means focusing on how our body feels
in order to detect at a relatively early stage the onset of any muscular con-
tractions in the sensitive areas (usually the shoulders and neck, but, for
some people, the jaw) and to work on relaxing the muscles in these areas.
For those who find it difficult to detect this kind of tension, the simplest
approach is to assume there will be some, and to take one or two minutes
to relax your body every hour (by breathing deeply, adjusting your position, stretching where possible, and gently working the muscles of the
neck and shoulders). This can and should be done at any time, regardless of where you are (in public transport, waiting for the traffic lights to
change, in a waiting room, during breaks at work).

A second reason why relaxation is essential is that we need prolonged periods of relaxation and recuperation. In heat-wave conditions,
the associated problems and dangers are caused not only by the very

high temperature reached during the day, but also by the fact that temperatures do not drop enough during the night, with the result that our systems are unable to recuperate fully: days that are too hot followed by warm and sticky nights are the worst combination. The same applies to the stress in our daily lives: we need to get rid of it in the evening and at night, by reducing our level of tension substantially and durably. Failure to do so can lead to experiences like this one:

> Before his depression, my husband went through an awful period of *burn-out*. I would see him come home from work every evening totally exhausted and at the end of his tether. But the worst thing was that he just could not relax, even at home: he was still anxious, absent, incapable of playing with the children, or of showing any interest in them, or of chatting to me. He would vaguely watch TV but all the time he was just brooding over his anxieties and thinking about the next day. When he went to bed, he found it difficult to get to sleep, tossing and turning in the bed and sighing as though he was suffocating. In the night he was constantly restless, starting and kicking out in the little sleep he managed to snatch. And of course there were the nightmares when he would shout out and sit up in bed. And when morning came, he would wake up already anxious and tense all over, ready to start worrying all over again.

In practice, it is advisable, particularly during stressful times, to try to do relatively deep and prolonged relaxation exercises (approximately ten to thirty minutes) to restore physical, and therefore psychological, calm. Clearly this is not always easy, given that the periods in which we are most subject to anxiety are also the ones when we are pressed for time. Finding time to relax at the end of the day is essential, however – even more important than watching television or losing ourselves in a good book.

The essence of relaxation is simple: when the body starts to have its own reactions above and beyond feelings and moods, when our muscles tense up or our breathing feels constricted, we need to breathe deeply, relax, get our bodies into a state of rest. Not to get rid of the tension, but to ease it, to calm it down, so we can observe what is happening to us: being aware of our anxieties as we relax makes them less oppressive. Doing this repeatedly and frequently means gradually depriving them of one of their sources: if the tension in the body stops responding to the tension in the mind, any contraction will be quickly banished.

I am not going to give details here of all the various research which for some considerable time has demonstrated the clear benefits of relaxation in anxiety,[19] as well as its importance in the treatment of depression[20] and recurrent anger problems.[21] The methods involved are generally extremely simple and are used by the majority of psychotherapists.[22] But, of course, as with all the other methods referred to, regular practice is the only guarantee of success.

Resorting to stimulants

We are all the same: we all prefer short cuts.

In the quest for higher energy levels, the short cuts mostly involve coffee and sugar and, when calm is required, tranquillizers and sleeping pills. But there are also the anti-depressants mentioned in the preceding chapter, as well as alcohol and tobacco or cannabis, which will be discussed in the next chapter.

Let us start with what looks the most harmless: sugar. Sugar produces the sensation of an instant energy boost, because of the surge in glycaemia it provokes,[23] but the problem is that after the initial surge, our energy levels drop even further. Swallowing sugary drinks and eating sweets or bars of chocolate when we feel 'a sudden energy dip' is therefore a poor investment over the course of the day. It is worth pointing out, moreover, that these famous 'energy dips' are purely an invention dreamed up by the fast-food industry. On the basis of hyperglycaemia, a genuine, though rare, phenomenon, advertisers have succeeded in generating a subconscious thought process in many people, making us think that we often have (sometimes true) energy dips, that these are caused by hyperglycaemia (by no means always true, given that there are many other reasons for this subjective feeling), and that the solution is to reach for a sugary snack (a genuine catastrophe from the point of view of both diabetes specialists and psychiatrists). The worst of it is that taking sugar for what we take to be an energy dip creates more of a problem than it solves: by so doing we are laying the foundations for a genuine energy dip later (and this one may indeed be due to hyperglycaemia). What is more, even if sugar appears to boost our energy levels, it seems that it also increases psychological stress. Indeed, for some researchers, cutting down simple sugars which are rapidly absorbed can lead to a reduction in depressive symptoms.[24]

Coffee does indeed stimulate energy levels, but it also increases tension. This happens immediately for occasional coffee drinkers and after high doses for regular drinkers.[25] This is why coffee has an adverse effect on sleep quality, particularly for people suffering from anxiety.[26]

It is not my intention here to emphasize the considerable effectiveness of *tranquillizers* and *sleeping pills* as a means of inducing the state of calm necessary for sleep (most of them also have a muscle-relaxant effect), nor the fact that this effect is rapidly undermined by regular use (leading to tolerance): the real value of such products is therefore in occasional use, in response to specific difficulties arising in someone's life.

It is of course preferable to avoid using these various substances to regulate our feelings and physical states on a regular basis. We should turn instead to more natural strategies. Psychiatry can be *green* too![27]

Informed efforts

Clearly, feeling well requires a certain amount of effort. And of course, the first challenge to such efforts in terms of both physical activity and relaxation is to stay the course. It is helpful to plan time for these activities in advance and to stick to the schedule, but also to make sure our chosen activities are relatively enjoyable.[28]

Another important factor is our state of mind during any of these activities, as demonstrated in two now-classic studies.

The first of these was based on a gymnastics programme for forty-eight young adults who were monitored over a period of ten weeks. Half the group were told that the programme was intended to improve their psychological well-being. This was not mentioned to the other half, who were simply told that the research was looking at the biological impact of physical exercise. At the end of the ten weeks, the two groups had made the same progress in terms of their physical condition, but the group who had been told to expect improved psychological well-being did indeed show improvements in this area.[29]

The second study focused on a group of eighty chambermaids working in big American hotels. Half of them were told that their work, which involved a considerable amount of physical exercise, complied with the recommendations on that subject made by the Department of Health, and were given detailed information on how and why this was so. The other half were not given any particular information. Neither of the two groups was instructed to modify the way they did their work. After four weeks, the 'informed' group had the sense of having worked their bodies better, and, more significantly, tended to have lost weight (an average of 800 grams), have lower blood pressure, and have a reduction in body fat levels and in waist measurements.[30] All that, as a result of being told that what they were *already* doing was good for their health! And having it properly explained to them.

The benefits of physical activity clearly operate through two pathways, one strictly organic, the other psychological. Being conscious that the exercise we are doing is good for our morale and for our health makes it even more effective! We shall examine this in more detail when we deal with the question of engaging in activities mindfully.

Clearly an informed effort is both more enjoyable and more effective than one which has no particular sense. It is like the story of the stone cutters, often attributed to Charles Péguy: in the Middle Ages, three men were breaking up stones. The first one looked miserable and when passers-by spoke to him, he replied 'This tough job is the only one I know how to do.' The second seemed indifferent, and said: 'I just do my job in order to feed my family.' The third smiled, as he explained 'I'm helping to build a cathedral.' If our modern studies are correct, he should have lived to be older and happier than his fellow workers.

What is the point of feeling well?

Feeling well is not an end in itself. Or rather, we should not seek to feel well merely *in order* to feel well. Moreover, a few years after putting out the famous definition of health referred to at the beginning of this chapter, the WHO declared: 'Health is, therefore, seen as a resource for everyday life, not the objective of living. Health is a positive concept emphasizing social and personal resources, as well as physical capacities.'[31]

Not the objective of living . . .

Of course, being well is not an obligation. But our interest in it lies in the fact that it can help us have an impact on the world. Once again we come back to our quest for calm energy: calm to help us accept the world's faults (and at the same time our own) and energy to change them.

Chapter 12

Regulating feelings and moods

With some people, you get the impression they've never used their mind.

Georges Bernanos

If we do not understand our feelings, we will end up being pushed and pulled in all directions by them. We will react like children under their influence. Instead of being a source of richness, they will be a hindrance; instead of helping us, they will confuse us. What we call maturity stems, far more than from our intellectual abilities, from this emotional dimension, this capacity to perceive and calm our inner movements.

Why not just accept our feelings as they are?

After all, these are natural phenomena. And anything natural is bound to be good, is it not? Why not accept happiness when it comes, reconcile ourselves to sadness when it appears, and leave it at that?

First of all, because not everything natural and spontaneous is good: aggressive impulses, sudden fits of depression or spiralling anxiety are indeed natural in certain circumstances but that does not make them good. And in any case, it is never a good idea to give in to something blindly.

And then, because on this rudimentary basis – accepting our feelings as they come along – we would end up with only a rudimentary inner life. And one which would depend solely on external events: where these are favourable we will generally feel good, and where they are not, we will tend to feel bad. There is nothing absurd about that, but it is nevertheless somewhat limiting: our lives could be so much more interesting.

We will see that the ideal way of relating to our feelings does not involve opposing their natural movement, for example by forcing happiness into our lives and rejecting unhappiness in any form. Instead we need to focus on improving this natural movement: making the most of our moments of happiness rather than wasting them; 'shortening and easing' unhappiness. For our sufferings, as we have said before, have an instructive side as well as a destructive one.

An ability to regulate our feelings is indispensable for our personal equilibrium, since all too often these feelings rush in on us in a crowded tumult, transforming our minds into a busy crossroads which nobody is supervising and which everybody wants to get across at the same time. The result is that traffic backs up, horns are sounded, tempers fray, no one is moving, time and energy are wasted, pollution levels rise. In other words: an impossible situation. So what can we do? Carry on as we are with all that chaos in our heads? Or, instead of trying to control everything, simply try to introduce a little bit of order, so as to be able to see what is happening and what can be done?

Various metaphors are used to illustrate exactly what regulating our feelings involves. There is the metaphor of a boat on the river: we drift with the current (our feelings) but keep our hands on the tiller so we are still capable of steering our boat; this means we can moor on one side of the river to explore the territory (negative feelings) or on the other to take on provisions (positive feelings). Then there is the metaphor of the policeman at the crossroads referred to above: his job is to make sure no feelings stop for too long in the middle of the junction and to ensure all of them can keep moving, coming and going, doing whatever they have to do but without interfering with anyone else. The policeman is responsible for keeping the traffic moving, for the unrestricted flow of our feelings, each with its role to play. But he does not prevent any of them gaining access to the crossroads of consciousness. Another comparison: if neglected, our feelings resemble a 'primeval' forest, left to its natural state and therefore completely inaccessible to humans, who can no longer explore it. It is not a question of transforming our feelings into formal gardens where everything is neatly marked out, trimmed back and carefully tended, but into properly managed forest, with paths and occasional clearings and where the intention is to respect the forest while keeping it accessible. A forest is a beautiful, fascinating and sometimes disturbing place. We do our best not to get lost, but it would be a pity not to be able to walk there. This is the very essence of the regulation of feelings and moods.

What is the reasonable goal of regulating feelings?

In the past, there was one particular feeling which was considered extremely pernicious in the Western Christian world. It was called *acedia* and was a kind of sadness, a melancholic apathy which affected monks in particular, and which, from the descriptions given by ancient writers, resembled a state of depressive despondency and apathy:

> The demon of acedia attacks the monk round about the fourth hour, and lays siege to his mind until the eighth hour. [. . .] It makes the sun seem slow

to rise. [. . .] It inspires horror of the place in which he finds himself, of his condition of life [. . .] the idea that there is nobody who can comfort him.

It is said that, in his struggle against acedia, St Rodolphe used to hang by his arms from ropes fixed to the roof of his cell, reciting the Psalms as he swung to and fro.[1] Since these heroic days some progress has been made (even if, as we shall see, the association between physical activity and psychological strategies is still relevant today).

There are three main goals in regulating feelings and moods: to see more clearly what is going on inside us, and create an inner atmosphere of relative peace and coherence, which means we are more able to turn our attention to the external world, without being constantly drawn back into ourselves by our ruminations; to experience more frequent happy moments; to be less aware of our suffering.

Being attentive to our feelings and moods helps us gain better knowledge of ourselves and therefore better control over our lives. For our own personal equilibrium we need to have a clear vision of our capacities, our needs, our motivation, our weaknesses. This is why it is so important, in the context of *intelligence of self*, to understand and to regulate our feelings.[2] If we fail to do so, sooner or later our state of inner confusion will be transformed into mental suffering. For example, as a result of the phenomenon of remanence we have mentioned earlier: that tendency for a negative feeling to persist beyond whatever originally provoked it. Good regulation of feelings allows us to pay attention to a feeling which refuses to go away, helping us to understand and alleviate it so as to prevent it from contaminating other feelings which follow in its wake, in the same way that anxieties or problems associated with our work can prevent us from enjoying time with children or a partner. Failing to pay attention to a feeling which is causing concern is a little like not hanging up after a phone conversation: the line will then remain engaged and no incoming calls will be able to get through.

We saw in the previous chapter how we can, through physical exercise and relaxation for example, encourage and nurture in ourselves a stable emotional base (calm and energy). We are now going to reflect on how, when confronted with destabilizing events in our lives, we can deal with the sudden changes in our feelings these can provoke and succeed in gently restoring equilibrium once again, having learnt some useful lessons from the period of instability we have been through. *Regulating our feelings means asking this question: what can I do about what I am feeling, without trying to run away from it or deny it, without seeking to suppress it?* But on the contrary, by using it to understand and move forward.

My favourite cousin, who sometimes finds herself at the mercy of her feelings, told me, on one occasion when we were discussing all this: 'Sometimes there are days when I would really like to get these feelings of mine under control!' But there are also days when we should simply enjoy them; others still when we need to focus on trying to understand them. In short, regulating our feelings is not about wanting to keep them constantly under control or to sterilize them, but simply about seeking to clarify (what is confused), calm (what is too agitated), reorient (what has headed in the wrong direction). Broadly, it is about limiting our negative feelings (but not simply limiting them: it is also about no longer being afraid to give them their rightful place), of developing, enjoying and reliving our positive feelings (but without wanting them to last forever: understanding that they cannot always be the same). This is what is referred to in psychology as 'the hedonic balance', a sort of mathematical calculation of our feelings which corresponds to the following equation:

$$E = 2\,PF/1\,NF$$
(E for equilibrium, PF for positive feelings, and NF for negative feelings)

Researchers and therapists consider that 2 is the ideal ratio in terms of emotional equilibrium: about two thirds of positive feelings to one third of negative ones.[3] This ratio combines the energy of positive feelings with the vigilance of negative ones. We have already referred to the benefits of negative feelings: anxiety which opens our eyes, anger which drives us to take action, sadness which forces us to reflect, despair which reminds us of the meaning of life. The same is true of feelings which are a mixture of both: guilt makes us re-evaluate our behaviour, nostalgia helps us appreciate the past and makes us less inclined to waste the good times to come. If instead of dominating our emotional landscapes, these negative or mixed feelings are understood and integrated into predominantly positive feelings, then our inner life will be more productive than it would be if either the negative or positive poles dominated absolutely.

Finally, it is worth remembering that the equilibrium of the emotional balance is one of the most important factors in terms of existential satisfaction, our feeling of long-term well-being.[4] This is the case in cultures the world over.[5] Hence the importance of taking an active rather than a passive approach when it comes to the equilibrium of our feelings.

Some theoretical reminders on the regulation of feelings

A considerable amount of research has been devoted to the process of regulating feelings. The findings demonstrate the importance of that process to our general well-being,[6] but they also emphasize its complexity.[7] Let us nevertheless start by attempting to simplify matters . . .

Generally the regulation process is somewhat like a thermostat on a boiler: once the desired temperature is reached, the thermostat continuously compares the actual temperature with the programmed temperature, and the heating or air-conditioning systems are activated accordingly.

Regulating our feelings is a similar process, though obviously more sophisticated.[8] We could describe it in terms of a 'thymostat' (from the

Greek word *thymos,* meaning 'mood'). Based on whatever feeling seems appropriate at a given moment, we compare what we are currently feeling and attempt to adjust it, by acting either on the situation we are in (for example, by leaving the room, if we want to stay calm in an argument) or on ourselves (by telling ourselves to calm down in the same situation). We then assess whether that action has been successful in bringing about an appropriate change in our feelings, and so on.

The same model of regulation applies to positive feelings. If being happy is the desired state of mind, we will try to get as close to it as possible, through strategies such as a heightened awareness of moments of well-being, or by attempting whenever possible to place ourselves in situations or with people which do us good, etc.

Mistakes and problems in regulating feelings

Although the regulation of our feelings is clearly more subtle and complex, this simplified model of a thermostat serves to identify at what stage problems and errors can occur in the process.

The first stage is in the choice of the benchmark feeling: it is therefore necessary for us to have clearly defined goals. And these will also depend on our values and on our existential choices: for example, wanting to remain calm during an argument implies placing your personal well-being and respect for others above the need to defend your interests; being determined not to make yourself ill over missing a work deadline implies putting your own health at least on a par with your professional success; opting for a happy life requires giving up a certain number of other sources of satisfaction (financial or narcissistic), which might bring pleasure but not happiness.

There is also a certain amount of variation between different people: generally speaking, extroverts will choose to experience more intense and therefore more clear-cut feelings than introverts, who prefer their feelings to be more nuanced and often more of a mixture. Each person therefore sets their own 'thymostat' differently.

In all cases, in the absence of any clear idea of what we wish to achieve, we will tend to have feelings combining tendencies innate in all humans (irritation when dealing with frustrations, worry in situations of uncertainty, sadness when faced with loss) and reflexes from our own personal history (we will, for example, reproduce what our parents did, or what certain feelings allowed us to obtain when we were children: sulking in order to be comforted, shouting to get our own way). In other words, a somewhat stereotyped and limited range!

This stage also depends on our motivation for regulating our feelings or even simply taking an interest in them. We know that paying attention to our feelings is already an indicator of general and emotional well-being.[9]

The extent to which we believe we can control our emotions also plays an important role. In a study focusing on students during their first year at university, those who regarded their emotions and feelings as flexible, adaptable and responsive to their efforts were in a much better state at the end of that demanding first year, requiring so much adaptability.[10] Being convinced we can change and adapt to situations does indeed help us to adapt better and cope more easily.

The second stage lies in the sensitivity of our 'comparison' mechanisms and more broadly in our perception of both our mental and physical states. In the previous chapter we referred to the frequent confusion between stimulation and energy, which can lead to us drinking more coffee or listening to louder music in order to be 'more awake and more efficient', whereas in fact these strategies will tend to over-stimulate us, and end up making us perform less well when the tasks facing us become more complex,[11] since stimulation is only helpful for simple tasks. Similar confusion can affect people suffering from anxiety, who often confuse physical tension with mental unease. And bulimics, who find it hard to distinguish between the desire to eat in response to painful feelings and genuine hunger. Equally, pessimists cannot always differentiate between their current state of fatigue and their capacity to accomplish a task once they have had a chance to rest. Finally, in our quest for positive feelings we can sometimes confuse satisfying material needs – which simply means gratifying the artificial desire to buy something – with happiness. In conclusion, discernment in the context of our feelings remains indispensable if we are to be able to evaluate where we stand, and see whether we are on the right course. Which is why a certain level of ability and, even more importantly, an introspective approach are crucial.

The third stage is about having strategies for repair, where, for example, the absence of carefully thought-6out strategies leaves room for reflex strategies, generally poorly conceived and often problematic because of their focus on avoiding suffering (running away from a situation or numbing discomfort with alcohol, cannabis or tobacco).

How we go about regulating our feelings: a brief overview of strategies

There are of course a vast number of ways of regulating our feelings.

More often than not, we are not particularly lucid ourselves about the existence of these mechanisms, and about what improves, or the opposite, our internal emotional climate. One researcher, for example, compared our existence with that of laboratory rats placed in an immense cage containing hundreds of levers: pulling these levers produced results which were sometimes agreeable (making it warmer, providing food or company) and sometimes disagreeable; these results were sometimes immediate, some-times not, etc.[12] The rats of course found all of this rather confusing, and this somewhat resembles what happens to us in life (which is not always clear or logical) if we do not make some efforts at introspection.

A good way of understanding these mechanisms is to say there are four main stages in our regulation process: (1) the selection and the modi-fication of situations (choosing to put ourselves in a given situation, or, conversely, avoiding it); (2) the deployment or withdrawal of our attention (choosing to concentrate on the situation or the experience, or mentally avoiding it by daydreaming, thinking about something else, rumination); (3) psychological efforts (understanding, reassessing, stepping back from the situation); (4) implementing certain modes of behaviour, which more-over often initially involves controlling the reactions or automatic reflexes triggered by the emotions of the moment (breathing deeply instead of panicking, saying what is wrong instead of bottling it up).

An example of an automatic reflex would be responding to sadness by becoming withdrawn, experiencing the desire to hide away in a 'place of pure solitude where all consolation is refused', as Pessoa put it. Of course, the implication behind the choice of strategies corresponding to these four stages assumes that we have identified that something is going on in us! Rather than simply relying on our reflexes.

It is also worth emphasizing the importance of the state of mind in which we use these regulating strategies: for example, listening to music when faced with problems can happen in a variety of different contexts. Is it simply a way of distracting ourselves and helping us think about other things? Or is it to help us relax so we are able to think more constructively about the problem we are facing? Is it cheerful and stimulating music intended to provide us with the necessary energy to do something about the situation? Or is it sad music which will intensify our rumination?

More generally, it appears that the difference between strategies which are largely effective and those which are less so is conditional on an ability to accept the experience of having feelings, particularly unpleas-ant ones: are we prepared to feel sadness, anxiety, resentment and more general psychological pain, *before* wanting either to resolve them or to run away from them? Given that our automatic reaction to painful feelings is initially to run away from them.

Some ways of running away from our disagreeable feelings

There are all sorts of ways of running away from our inner experiences.

We can suppress our feelings and try to ignore them

For example, if we are worried about the health of someone close to us, but the anxiety is painful in itself, we can take refuge in work. Or quite simply refuse to feel this anxiety, by persuading ourselves too soon that 'it isn't serious, there isn't really a problem, it will all be all right' even though, in our hearts, we are thinking the opposite. But chasing these worrying thoughts away as soon as they come knocking at the door of our minds is of course doomed to failure and even causes a rebound effect: the thoughts and the pain come back incessantly.[13] In the most extreme cases, we can even experience a process of 'dissociation': if the emotions are too powerful – too much fear, too much anger – it can seem as though what is happening is actually happening to someone else, rather than to us; or that we have somehow stepped out of ourselves and are watching what is happening 'from outside'. These are no delirium-induced situations, but an automatic reflex on the part of our consciousness to avoid the impact of so powerful an emotional charge. In general, therefore, this tends to apply more in extreme situations (like traumatic events, assaults, violence). However, for some ultrasensitive people, this can also happen in the course of what other people would regard as 'normal' days, but during which the excessively vulnerable person will frequently lose touch with reality. Throughout his work, the writer Pessoa describes the numerous and subtle sentiments of depersonalization, like this moment of slight sensory dissociation: 'I hear, without hearing, the voices of the packers at the far end of the office, where the warehouse begins, and without seeing I see the twine used for parcels, double knotted and doubly strung around the volumes wrapped in heavy brown paper.'[14]

We can try to transform our feelings

I remember a detailed discussion with a patient in which we talked about the resentment she felt towards her husband, and how this made her feel guilty since he was really quite a 'good husband': behind her resentment lay a mixture of sadness (according to her, he had lied to her, when he was wooing her, by making himself out to be deeply romantic, which turned out not to be entirely true), of anxiety (she was not sure she could bear to grow old with him), of disappointment, etc. Setting out these initial feelings during the consultation enabled her to calm her irritation, and even more importantly, gave her more courses of action than the secondary feelings of resentment. Most of our feelings of resentment are derived from other, more deeply hidden feelings: in fact resentment and feelings of anger are the ones which, as we have seen, make it easier to shift the problem onto someone else and therefore avoid having to do any soul-searching ourselves. Once again, it is all about avoiding pain.

We can chemically alter our moods with alcohol, cannabis, tobacco, etc.

We know of course that alcohol is used as a way of improving the way we feel, particularly by people who lack the motivation and effective strategies to do so by other means.[15] Alcohol acts on our feelings in multiple ways. For example, it causes a 'psychological myopia' in which our psychological perception narrows so that it focuses on only one thing at a time, thus removing our capacity to step back and put things into perspective: this theory explains why alcohol can make us 'stupidly' happy, if we start our drinking in a positive state to which we will stick against all the odds; it can also make us stubbornly inconsolable if we are drinking in a gloomy frame of mind.[16] Alcohol is also associated with the capacity to reduce our self-awareness, with the particular advantage of making us feel less concerned than usual about the various worries which would normally trouble us.[17] The desired effect in such circumstances is a sort of 'escape from the self', an avoidance of oneself, fuelled by the pain of being who we are, in parallel with the escape from the world sought via the myopia effect (if someone is very short-sighted, they can only see what is immediately in front of them). Moreover, research focusing on why people drink alcohol systematically shows that a desire to influence feelings is top of the list of reasons put forward: people seek above all to 'forget about their worries' and to 'feel better'.[18] Inevitably we drink more on days when we are feeling low: negative feelings are one of the major causes of relapses in ex-drinkers (particularly amongst men – relationship issues are a more important factor for women). But all of this is to no avail, since, unfortunately for drinkers, research also indicates that alcohol makes things worse in both the short term (once the immediate effects wear off) and the long term (once an addiction is established) with an enormous resurgence of negative feelings, sadness, anxiety, irritability, etc.[19]

Tobacco is also frequently used as a means of regulating both mental and physical feelings, very often by people who lack effective strategies for regulating their feelings.[20] It enables smokers to boost their energy levels and reduces feelings of tension.[21] But it can also lead to the problems of physical toxicity and addiction we are already familiar with. Generally speaking, smokers turn to tobacco as a means of reducing their painful and negative feelings.[22]

Finally, regular use of cannabis is a similar process: more and more young patients who are anxious or sub-depressive resort to one or more joints at the end of the day to calm their feelings and be able to relax and get to sleep. Just as their older fellow sufferers consume their trusty litre of wine each evening with exactly the same aim.

Some scientific data on the suppression of feelings

The crucial question hinges on whether we should embrace or avoid disagreeable feelings: since they are disagreeable, why should we not simply ignore them and wait for them to go away?

In everyday life, it is sometimes preferable not to worry about situations which would anyway tend to improve regardless of any efforts we might make: if it rains on the day we had planned a picnic, thinking about other things is an appropriate way of countering our disappointment and gloom.[23] In the same way, if a particular political or social news story is troubling me, avoiding over-exposure to news programmes which endlessly feature catastrophes I can do nothing about is a logical strategy to adopt.[24] And in a similar way, it appears that when faced with extreme situations such as the loss of a partner, initially avoiding very painful and damaging feelings can be a way of coping psychologically, especially if this strategy of avoiding negative feelings is combined with a determined effort to seek out positive ones:[25] while we are in a fragile state we take steps to avoid being overwhelmed with suffering, and we do not forget to live and to allow ourselves to be comforted, in spite of everything.

In general, however, systematic escape strategies, whether they take the form of some kind of distraction or the suppression of negative feelings (and the underlying realities of these), tend to be counter-productive, and there is strong evidence associating them with the chronicity of all sorts of psychological problems.[26] Studies have shown that they intensify sensations of physical pain,[27] anxious[28] and depressive[29] thoughts, that they distort our general sense of well-being and our relationships with other people[30] and reduce the frequency of positive feelings.[31] And that, often, the suppression of our disruptive mental states leads to a rebound effect: they tend to come back with a vengeance.[32] All this needs to stop! Of course, this tendency to suppress our feelings is often rooted in the past: for example, being brought up in an atmosphere where there was little encouragement to express them, or living through extremely painful experiences such as physical violence or abuse.[33] We now think that these generalized tendencies to suppress what we have experienced only alleviate suffering in the short term and are inadequate in the longer term, in terms either of limiting negative feelings (there is generally a rebound effect of whatever has been suppressed) or of developing positive ones (in the long term, any happiness must have understood and assimilated negative feelings).

How to accept and regulate our negative feelings

We cannot hope to be successful in regulating our feelings unless we accept them in the first place. Generally speaking, most scientific psychotherapies are beginning to integrate this principle.[34] There is even a completely new approach currently centred on this notion of emotional acceptance and known under the acronym of ACT: *acceptance and commitment therapy*.[35] This term is a reminder that acceptance only makes sense as a precursor of action, rather than a substitute for it, which would simply be resignation.

The metaphor most frequently used to help patients understand this notion of acceptance is simply the idea that we cannot leave a place unless we accept that we arrived there in the first place. If I want to stop constantly feeling sadness or anger, instead of wanting *not* to feel them when they come along, I need first of all to be able to accept those feelings fully and lucidly; to 'go to meet them' instead of running away from them; to experience them and pay close attention to them when they present themselves. This means resisting the natural tendency to embrace what is pleasant but reject anything unpleasant. This purely hedonistic attitude can only function for certain specific and limited situations; not for complex life experiences. Of course, embracing our painful feelings presupposes an ability to avoid the two pitfalls of either suppressing them or being overwhelmed and submerged by them. But the stakes are high: acceptance brings with it the possibility of seeing our suffering gradually diminish in a lasting way. It also offers us the opportunity to be enriched by our experiences, instead of simply getting through them without wanting to engage with them and emerging unchanged.

We must therefore sometimes be ready to stop wanting to rectify our emotional experiences or correct our feelings. And, instead of simply trying to change how we are feeling, we should aim to change *our relationship* to the feelings that come along.

Take the example of boredom. An evening where boredom strikes, when we say to ourselves: 'I am so bored!' By refusing to accept this boredom we end up focusing on it all the more, telling ourselves this is not the way things should be, that we are unlucky, that it is all pointless.

We could of course disguise our boredom with alcohol. Why not drink? True, that might at least provoke some positive feelings, but in reality it will not bring us much relief. And, if we drink too much, boredom will come back again, bringing with it those old drinking companions: sadness, resentment, disgust, world-weariness . . .

We could take refuge in rumination, in reviving memories of previous experiences of boredom and negative opinions about ourselves ('I'm bored to death here'), about other people ('They are so boring, they don't make the slightest attempt to be interested in me'), about the world ('Everything is futile'), etc.

Finally we could replace our boredom with anger, directed either at ourselves ('What am I doing here?') or at other people ('What makes them think they are so interesting?').

None of this will have much effect, and in addition, it will prevent us (1) seeing that the evening might also have some entertaining or interesting aspects, (2) actively seeking to identify and cultivate these, given that, unless we regulate our boredom, we will be stuck in the position of passivity brought on by rumination, waiting for situations or people to *be* interesting, instead of helping to *make* them interesting. But since these ruminations activate increasingly negative feelings, we are unlikely to take initiatives. Then we end up sulking or withdrawing into ourselves, and then nothing interesting can happen to us at all; and even if it *became* interesting, we would have reached a point of no return, of dishonesty, of denial.

The only possible way forward is to say to yourself: 'OK, I'm feeling bored. That's already enough negative feelings. No point in adding any others. So what can I do about it? Do I politely say goodbye to my hosts and mutter some kind of excuse about having to leave? Do I make one final attempt to find someone entertaining? To liven up the evening? Or do I set about regulating my feelings by doing something about my boredom? But whatever I decide, I must do it without moaning or sulking: my boredom is quite enough on its own!'

If we accept them, our negative feelings (1) become paradoxically less painful, (2) become a useful source of information about a whole range of different situations and our reactions to them, (3) can enrich our experience, since they are a reflection of real life, (4) show us that we can survive our difficulties. The attitudes involved in acceptance also encourage us simply to do whatever is best, without complaining or moaning. According to how we are feeling, we decide what to do, or not do, but without making things worse for ourselves. For acceptance is an alternative to avoidance, not to action.

Indeed it is sometimes felt that this notion of acceptance encourages a sort of passivity, a *new-look quietism*. Quietism (from the Latin *quies*, 'peace of mind, tranquillity') refers to a seventeenth-century mystical Christian movement which encouraged its followers to seek a state of complete passivity, which would enable the soul to be completely immersed in God, thus allowing God to act in it. Accepting everything as it comes, in order to elevate the soul? This is not of course the message intended here: we are in the domain of psychotherapy where the goal is well-being, not getting closer to God.

Moreover, it is certainly no coincidence that these therapies centred on acceptance are based on behavioural therapies, in which patients are encouraged to take some kind of action. Put in simple terms, the idea is to encourage a lucid and clear-sighted commitment to action based on the vital information provided by our feelings. In order to avoid such misunderstandings, in psychotherapy we should perhaps talk in terms of *welcoming* our suffering, rather than *accepting* it: the word *acceptance* is subconsciously too closely linked with the notion of submission, suggesting that we should accept everything; whereas the word *welcome* reminds us that we remain active and discriminating in our welcoming.[36] Which is, of course, the goal.

Research on the effectiveness of acceptance

The above reflections are not of course a purely theoretical view or a declaration of intent: a great deal of research has been carried out over many years, both in experimental psychology (in laboratories) and in clinical psychology (in real-life situations).

Generally speaking, accepting psychological suffering allows us to control it more effectively.[37] Research has also been conducted on physical suffering, but this is a separate subject and too vast to be touched on here. Let us merely point out that, not surprisingly, the same elements recur, for acceptance also has a physiological impact: it can lead to speedier recovery in terms of heart rate, for example, when a personally painful situation has been recalled.[38]

When we examine the mechanisms involved, acceptance does not, initially at least, diminish the frequency of disagreeable thoughts. Instead it affects the way we react to such thoughts: they still come to mind, but we are able to step back from them, because we accept their presence rather than simply keep saying 'no, no, not them!'[39] Acceptance means looking in detail at what is painful, rather than judging it undesirable from a distance: if we ask volunteers to imagine various unpleasant things happening to them (having an argument with a friend, failing a job interview) from two different standpoints, one ruminative ('Why has this happened to me?') and the other experience-based ('If that happened to me, what exactly would I feel, what state of mind would I be in?'), we discover that the second mode – close to acceptance – is emotionally less uncomfortable, but also leads to a positive 'delay' effect: volunteers who have practised acceptance tend to be less upset when they fail in a subsequent task.[40]

Research also exists showing the effectiveness of these acceptance-based approaches not only in volunteers with no known illness, but also amongst patients suffering from anxiety and depression,[41] bulimia,[42] obsessive-compulsive disorders[43] or chronic pain,[44] etc.

In conclusion, acceptance can be learned: it is not just a case of understanding what it is and deciding to apply it (although this is an indispensable first step), but also about regular training and practice: a study showed, for example, that in terms of the capacity to tolerate a small amount of physical pain, simple explanations and recommendations to accept the pain were notably less effective than a small amount of mental training in advance.[45]

How to increase positive feelings

Accepting what is disagreeable does not, however, exempt us from aspiring to positive feelings as often as possible. We shall look at this in greater detail towards the end of this book when we deal with the broader question of happiness, but here are a few indicators to be going on with.

We have seen how *physical activity* boosted the sensation of energy which is the basis of numerous agreeable feelings, such as confidence, curiosity or optimism. Practising a physical activity each morning – and sometimes first thing in the morning for vulnerable patients who are going through a difficult period – is often extremely useful.

Here, for example, is what Clément Rosset wrote about his own depression:

> As for me, I cannot fully express the horror that I feel for about an hour on certain mornings just as I am about to get out of bed. I suffer, but for no specific reason; nothing in the images or thoughts which go through my mind in my half-awake state accounts for the pain I feel. Yet they are accompanied by an absolutely indescribable surge of suffering.[46]

And Cioran described his experience in these words: 'For many years now I have woken up in the morning with the sensation that my brain has been replaced by a vast steppe.'[47]

Studies on mood regulation tell us that it is often pointless to spend *too much* time in moments such as these trying to find out 'why' we are like that, or attempting to relativize our suffering or our problems mentally. The best solution in these circumstances is probably just to get up and do half an hour's walking or gymnastic exercises. Yes, I know this is not very subtle from a psychotherapy point of view, and that it requires more time than the split second required to swallow a tranquilizer! In any case it is a third option to either putting up with the pain or drowning it in medication. But 'professional ruminators' over-estimate the effectiveness of mental activity and tend to scorn concrete solutions to some extent (they do not always, for example, try out suggestions made to them, rejecting advice with an 'it won't work' instead of trying it out 'just to see').

Another crucial issue is *social interaction*. A sound capacity for emotional regulation enhances the quality of social contacts,[48] logical enough given that we are more willing and able to turn to others if we have got our personal feelings under control. The opposite is also true: seeing people and socializing puts us in a better mood. What is referred to as 'social sharing of emotions' has also been widely studied:[49] common sense tells us that talking about our worries to people we are close to will do us good, and this is indeed the case, particularly where feelings of anxiety and sadness are concerned.[50] But sharing positive feelings also allows them to have increased impact on our well-being, enabling us to 'capitalize' on them, as researchers say.[51]

In an entertaining study, volunteers were asked to spend a few minutes chatting with strangers of the opposite sex. When their feelings before and after the exchange were analysed it was found that the experience of encountering an unknown person produced a slight increase in well-being. And the same was found to be true for other volunteers who were asked to chat for a few seconds with their girlfriend or boyfriend but as though they were meeting them for the first time.[52] The researchers assumed, logically, that meeting people you wanted to make a good impression on slightly improved our feelings: socializing satisfies a fundamental need for recognition and allows us to verify our social acceptability. Speaking in order to please is good for morale.

Another interesting outcome of this study is that it shows that those who took part in the experiment completely under-estimated the impact that the social interaction had on their morale when they were asked to evaluate its importance in advance. In general, this under-estimation of the emotional benefits of the situations we encounter is classic in social psychology:[53] we over-estimate our stability and our imperviousness to our environment and we see ourselves as far more imperturbable than is actually the case! In reality we are indeed highly *perturbable* and we may as well recognize and accept the fact.

Being active and socializing are undoubtedly two of the most common inductors of positive feelings and amongst the easiest to apply to everyday life because of the simplicity with which they can be implemented. But there are also many others. For example, *doing – and mastering – simple tasks,* which are easy and familiar, induces a positive mood, identifiable by a smile, or the beginning of a smile, measurable by a facial electro-myogram (EMG) of the zygomatic muscle.[54] Yes, after a while that must become boring, but we should not under-estimate this little mechanism whereby 'things that are easy are enjoyable and good for the morale'. This undoubtedly lies behind the attraction of the card game Patience or of certain leisure activities with predictable results. In any case, it is better to do simple things we can do well than to ruminate or do nothing at all, or to embark on ambitious but doomed actions and projects which will leave us feeling low.

It is worth noting that certain strategies are not equally effective for everyone. And that often they are inadequate when there are psychological problems. In a study, a sad film was shown to three different groups of people – those suffering from depression, those who had previously suffered from depression and a third group who had never been depressed. After the film they were asked to deal with the negative emotions it had provoked by *recollecting happy memories*. This was successful only in the group who had never been depressed. It did not work at all for those who had previously suffered from depression, and left those currently affected in a slightly worse mood.[55]

The right attitude to regulation of feelings

Let us conclude. The quest for a better balance of feelings does not of course amount to some kind of 'emotional consumerism', which would consist in keeping only the 'good' feelings, the enjoyable ones, and methodically getting rid of any others. In order to feel good without losing something of ourselves, we need to have a profound acceptance of what we are and what we feel. But without forgetting that suffering can impoverish us even more than the mental 'air-conditioning' involved in maintaining a steady mental state. And that the regulation of our feelings is not just about what we do with our feelings but also about our attitude and motivation in doing so (to forget, calm myself down, move on, gain better understanding of the world . . .). And finally we must not forget that we can influence our feelings not only with our minds, but also with our bodies, or with the minds of others through our social contacts.

The run-over cat

On my way to work one morning, not very long ago, I noticed a poor cat which had been run over and was almost completely flattened, lying between the second and third lanes of the four-lane motorway. It was stone dead, in the midst of what must have been, in those last few moments, a complete hell (perhaps it is a hell for us too but we no longer notice it). The sight of that poor, flattened little corpse triggered an extraordinary surge of feelings in me. I thought about how it would have panicked when it found itself there, thanks to some absurd error of orientation, or frantic escape from pursuit. How, in that hostile and terrifying environment of concrete and tarmac, with not a living thing in sight, it must have been panic-stricken as all those steel monsters roared past, disgorging their blasts of polluted air. If only it had stayed close to the edge of the parapet, and run along the protected zone until it came to an exit, it could have survived. But it was all too ghastly, too threatening, too unfamiliar: the animal panicked and tried to get across, to reach the other side. On certain days, when I am a little lost in my feelings, when life is a little hectic, when I feel the panic of anxiety or sadness creeping up on me, I feel like that cat. And then I remind myself how incredibly important it is to work at remaining as lucid as possible. Miaow.

Chapter 13

Curing ourselves of the disease of materialism

Nothing of what he possessed enriched him.
Éric-Emmanuel Schmitt,
Odette Toulemonde et autres histoires

'A Saturday morning, in the local supermarket. Perhaps I am tired, perhaps simply preoccupied because of various difficulties in my life, but doing my shopping feels different. A mixture of vertigo, of nausea and of bewilderment at the sight of this profusion of merchandise, at the artificiality of everything around me, the neon lights, the mood music. The overwhelming amount of choice makes it impossible just to find something quickly amongst the twenty different varieties of mayonnaise, thirty kinds of olive oil and a hundred flavours of yoghurt. People are dropping fruit and vegetables on the floor; nobody seems bothered by all these foodstuffs being wasted and trampled under foot. When I leave the supermarket, the shopping mall brings a second wave of depersonalization: I feel as though I am floating weightlessly like an alien in what is – horror – a hub of life, a place where people go for a stroll with their families, their friends or on their own: under the neon lighting, amongst all that junk and fake, all those temptations to spend when outside the sun is shining and you can breathe fresh air and liberty, and all for free. I find myself reeling; I am struck by this vision of a strange and inhuman universe, but one designed to tempt me. And then the guilt at being there myself, with my trolley, and criticizing it all: after all, I am here too under the neon lights, in spite of all the excuses I might come up with (I only come occasionally; I've never enjoyed it, etc.). I am in no position to give myself any airs or to feel superior or to judge people. Instead I should try to understand. Why am I in such a state when I am surrounded by people who seem perfectly at ease? Is it me who is not well, who should go home and lie down? Or is it them, who do not even notice any of this any more?'

No, no, do not go home and lie down but keep your eyes open! You need not only to be attentive to your feelings, but also to be on your guard:

your equilibrium and your sensitivity are constantly under threat from the pollution of materialism.

The example of diabetes as a societal disease

Recently some diabetes specialists with whom I was working on the psychology of diabetic patients told me about the epidemic of obesity and of 'type 2' diabetes (a form of diabetes linked to excessive weight) which, after taking the United States by storm, is currently sweeping across the entire world.[1] This calamity is the result of a number of factors. These include sedentary lifestyle, but also the modification of our dietary habits: we eat badly and too much, consuming too much food that is bad for us (too salty, too sweet, too fatty), but easily available.

Type 2 diabetes is therefore an example of what are known as 'societal diseases', diseases which result from our way of life. But is this not an inevitable consequence of an affluent society? In other words, is it not the profusion of food, its omnipresence, the ease with which it is available, that are the problem? To some extent, this is indeed the case. But there is more to it than that.

This society of profusion is also a society of incitement, of temptation. Temptations which are all just so many destabilizations because they become implanted in our minds. Some explanation is necessary.

Broadly, this is what happens. (1) Eating is a basic need. (2) Our societies (or certain market forces at work in our societies) distort this need in order to sell their products more effectively. They exaggerate and magnify its importance: for example by telling mothers that their children need to eat a good breakfast (with the implication that they need sweetened cereal, not just bread) if they are to perform well at school. (3) Our societies usually respond to that need by over-satisfying it: the huge portions served in fast-food outlets, promotions offering three for the price of two, too many varieties of foodstuffs,[2] etc. (4) Our societies make it too easy to satisfy the basic need by making sure that food is always visible and within easy reach. (5) Our societies interfere with the satisfaction of the need: by adding flavour enhancers which encourage people to eat more, or by promoting the fashion for TV meals, encouraging us to eat without paying attention. (6) When the need is inactive (I am not hungry), our societies persuade us to revive it ('fancy a little something?') so that we end up eating all the time: before (just in case), during (because it's time), after (pure greed: it's so delicious). (7) Our societies create a preventive need: 'Watch out for that sudden drop in energy.'

It is not just that too much food is being produced (for the rich countries only): it also needs to be disposed of rapidly, which is why we have to be manipulated to that end. Why are we encouraged to consume *junk food* instead of simpler foodstuffs? Because it is more profitable to sell biscuits or ready-meals than fruit or vegetables and to market highly sweetened fizzy drinks rather than water.

Where does this lead? To an epidemic of obesity and of cases of type 2 diabetes, with all the attendant complications (cardiac, vascular, renal, etc.). No doubt also to increased rates of certain cancers caused by the disruption of insulin production and the activation of inflammatory mechanisms. But also to a range of psychological problems: bulimia, diet-related obsession (for, as we are also urged to be thin, people are driven crazy). What is happening here is a destabilization of our feelings as a result of this constant mental manipulation: as soon as the slightest thing goes wrong, as soon as an unpleasant feeling (solitude, stress, boredom . . .) comes along, we can turn to food. It is so easy; food is waiting with open arms.

Impulse buying

The phenomenon is even clearer with impulse buying (where someone suddenly decides to buy something they had not intended to buy, and which generally they do not need). The impulse purchase is a response to an inner state of uneasiness or tension, which is temporarily eased by the act of buying something. This is why impulse buying can become an addiction (like alcohol, tobacco, food): we get into the habit of regulating our feelings, particularly the unwelcome ones, by resorting to a certain way of behaving or to a substance. And since it works (though not for long), we keep doing it.

One of my patients told me about the stock of objects discovered in his grandfather's home after his death. These were presents he had bought for his grandchildren, but had never given them, perhaps because he did not see the children often enough, or because he had forgotten he had bought the presents or where he had put them. He simply piled them up, like little tokens of love: he would think about his grandchildren, he missed them, so he would buy something for them and that would make him feel better, at least while he dreamed about the moment when he would give it to them. Elderly people living alone are often victims of telesales: I remember the story of the old lady whose home was found to contain dozens of unopened packages, including an exercise machine, an exercise bike, a giant plasma screen, kitchen gadgets, etc. The sympathetic smiles of the only friends she had, the TV presenters, brought her so much pleasure . . . But many younger people, even more exposed to the profusion of things to buy, are also victims of the 'shopping frenzy'.[3]

Not surprisingly, studies show that impulse buyers are people who have significant difficulties in regulating their emotions and feelings.[4] Such people buy in order to counter their negative feelings (approximately one third of impulse purchases), but also, curiously, when they experience a sudden burst of positive feelings, in moments of euphoria and good humour (two thirds of cases), as a way of 'making the most' of these feelings and trying to prolong them.[5] A logical finding, given that the majority of these compulsive buyers have significant anxiety and depression issues, and 25–50 per cent of them have already suffered from depression.[6]

But these compulsive buyers, aimlessly spending in order to regulate their feelings, are only the outriders, the first to be targeted by this organized bombardment of our feelings. We are all victims. It may be less obvious, but we are all nevertheless affected by the same disease.

The materialistic society

The rampant materialism of our society constitutes a major threat to our psychological well-being, and, insidious though it may be, exacts a significant cost in terms of mental health.[7]

Materialism can be defined thus: (1) possession, power and social status represent the highest values; (2) we value *having* rather than *being*, *doing* rather than *living*, *showing* rather than *appreciating*; (3) consumption is seen as the solution to our needs and the cure for our stress.

All societies are inevitably based partly on materialism (which also brings with it a number of lateral benefits we shall refer to later). But it is particularly evident in our contemporary society, with first the 'consumer society', from 1960 onwards, and then, from the 1990s, the 'society of hyper-consumption', as the sociologist Gilles Lipovetsky called it.[8] The latter is characterized by an ultra-professionalized exploitation of human needs which is no longer content simply to satisfy those needs, but also seeks to stimulate them and create new ones. The result, as Lipovetsky points out, is a 'capitalism engaged in a programme of perpetual stimulation of demand, of the commercialization and endless multiplication of needs', which is obsessed with 'commercializing all experiences wherever they occur, at all times and at all ages'. We can now add a new dimension: that of cynicism. There is increasing scientific evidence of the damage caused by this pressure to consume, yet commercial forces continue to pollute our minds. It is exactly the same scenario we have seen with the tobacco industry, in which cigarette producers, perfectly aware of the carcinogenic nature of their products, continue to the bitter end to make the maximum profits, leaving millions of dead or diseased people in their wake.

For the sole preoccupation of this type of capitalism is to preserve or increase the 'gross national appetite', and to stimulate consumption, which keeps growth steady and brings in profits (for the shareholders).

Materialistic societies are no longer satisfied with simply responding to our needs but instead constantly try to create new ones. So, in traditional 'advertisements' a product was promoted as a means of satisfying a specific need (food, clothing). Modern publicity sets out to do the same thing, but it also seeks to create non-existent needs (yoghurt drinks), or to associate a product with an enviable lifestyle: coolness, luxury, status, distinction, popularity, love (all of which can be attained simply by drinking a particular brand of coffee, or wearing a certain clothing brand[9]). Our society has access to sources of information and organizations (marketing departments and advertising agencies) whose sole purpose is to boost our consumption endlessly. Hence what are called 'trend-spotting agencies', whose role is to 'predict' consumers' needs and expectations, and who effectively validate the efforts of brands to transform what was the 'height of fashion' one year into something completely 'naff' the next.

Materialism as a disease

The psychological impact of these powerful mechanisms is discreet, because gradual, yet palpable: the end result is that we are slowly transformed into *impulsive fools*. This disease of civilization could be called the MZSSE disease: mind-numbing zap-crazy self-centred and stressful excess.

There we are: obese with goods, food, objects; with our freedom and our capacity to think for ourselves curtailed; ready to switch our attention to something else as soon as we encounter a problem – check my e-mails, grab a bite to eat, do a spot of shopping, just for a change; self-centred – 'Because I'm worth it', 'I should never have to hang around with nothing to do', 'I'm *amazing*, since that's what presenters and politicians keep telling me on TV'; and, ultimately, stressed, unhappy, frustrated, dependent, no longer understanding who or what we are. And once again eagerly grabbing at whatever false solution the market comes up with next: consumption as a cure for our problems.

We need to recognize and understand that the profusion surrounding us is debilitating: it reduces our intellectual and emotional capacities. It channels our energies towards what is useless and sterile. Shopping, often the favourite pastime of many people, does not offer us any enrichment in terms of personal development. Far from it! On the contrary, spending a long time looking for the 'bargain' and the 'best price' is quite simply a waste of energy which might be needed for other more important decisions in the future.[10]

This profusion of objects, of activities, of possibilities, apparently so rich, can in fact lead to a breakdown of our mental capacities through over-stimulation, trying to do too many things at once, and lack of concentration. Materialism prevents us from engaging in concentration, reflection or introspection: through zapping (multiplicity of choices requiring no effort) and through access to activities requiring no mental input (video games, constant music). Our concentration is constantly interrupted and solicited: advertisements in public places and during TV programmes, interruptions in the form of e-mails, telephones, texts.

Advertisers, keen to sell us machines which supposedly help us communicate with other people, would have us believe these are all about maintaining contact. But, at a certain level, these contacts are completely empty, as conversations overheard on mobile phones in public places all too plainly demonstrate.

One example of this invisible pollution is the multiplication of camera angles on television.[11] The speed of the images, the multiplication of different shots, obey a certain commercial logic (keeping viewers captive in order to hold on to their audience, i.e. their advertising profits). There is a word – zapping – for what the different channels fear, but none exists for this multiplication of shots – *stupidizing fragmentation*, perhaps? All of this is all the more pernicious because by not naming the evil, there is a risk it will pass unrecognized. The end result is a useless simplification of thought processes, and an impoverishment; not that the long and the complex necessarily mean richer, but simply that they are sometimes necessary. And, once again, this wretched habit of not focusing our thoughts, of not developing our concentration. Of becoming psychologically unstable, as though living in a goldfish bowl, incapable of even the slightest introspection or reflection.

Impulsive fools, we said. We have seen the justification for *fools*. Now let us look at *impulsive*. That action brings relief is a well-known principle: we can lower our stress levels by doing something, and in this way successfully distract ourselves from unwelcome feelings. What is wrong with that? But if we do so *systematically*, we will never understand or learn anything about life. Except simply how to obtain relief.

Our stress, our anxieties, our sudden fits of the blues can all be temporarily banished by *doing* something. Since most of us have non-manual jobs, in urban environments, and since shopping and eating are now amongst the easiest things to do in our society, what can we *do* with our bodies when we feel tense? There is sport, of course (which explains its current popularity), but that needs effort and space. That leaves us with the easiest of all – eating and shopping. Everything tempts us towards these. Consumerism encourages us to avoid painful experiences (no need to suffer! if you feel like buying something, buy it! if you feel like eating, eat!) rather than seeing them as a useful source of information on what is wrong in our lives, and inspiring us perhaps to find an alternative rather than simply running away from them in our headlong race towards the checkout.

It is exactly the same scenario we described in relation to diabetes and food: (1) uncomfortable feelings; (2) the availability of a source of distraction (eating, checking e-mails, playing a computer game, phoning someone); (3) running away from the painful feeling; (4) feeling better; (5) but by doing all that, we have understood nothing and learned nothing.

Instead we have simply made ourselves dependent on a way of regulating any feelings which revolves round buying things or consuming goods. It is an inefficient and expensive way to take care of ourselves:

filling our brains with emptiness, our stomachs with junk and our ward-robes with useless stuff, as a way of compensating for the fluctuations in our feelings. But why do we keep falling for it? It is all down to the genius of marketing and publicity. These professions attract brilliant people who are paid extremely well, far better for example than teachers, who do an infinitely more important job. But it also works because these messages ('Don't worry, just buy it') are lodged in our psychological needs for 'elixirs for oblivion': life is often hard and being able to forget about it sometimes does us good. But not wanting to accept that it is hard puts us in moral danger, whereas accepting its difficulties in order to approach it in a different way can save our souls.

The disease of materialism reduces our positive feelings

The studies are unanimous: the more pronounced a person's materi-alistic tendencies, the lower their level of personal well-being, and the greater their risk of suffering from psychological problems. This applies particularly to adolescents[12] and students,[13] probably because these are particularly vulnerable groups of people who are more powerfully exposed to social and advertising pressures about what they must *have* in order to *be* someone worth knowing, and because they are less clear about what constitutes a happy and interesting life. But of course all of us are affected to some degree.

In an interesting study conducted over a period of nineteen years and involving about twelve thousand people, it was shown that the more someone expressed materialistic values and goals at a given time, the more likely it was that when researchers looked at that person's life twenty years later, they would find evidence of damage in terms of the quality of private life and sense of happiness.[14]

This no longer applies only to Western countries but to the whole world, in so far as Western values and lifestyles have conquered the planet. This was shown in a study carried out in the United States and in South Korea (both highly materialistic countries) in which large numbers of people were asked about satisfying events which had occurred in their lives during the previous week, month and six-month period, and this information was then correlated with their perceived levels of well-being: the reactions were the same for both Koreans and Americans, in that the more the events were associated with materialism (money, luxury, social recognition . . .), the lower the level of well-being was likely to be as a result, in contrast with less materialistic events (meeting people, walks, practising a leisure activity . . .[15]).

From a psychological point of view, the consumerist quest can corre-spond to an aspiration for increased material security, linked either to a difficult and insecure childhood, or to material values cultivated within the individual's own family.[16] More generally, we tend to become more materialistic when faced with situations of uncertainty.[17] In such circumstances we regulate our anxieties by clinging more tightly to values of possession and success, to the detriment of the construction of the less material matter of our happiness.

The disease of materialism increases our negative feelings

There is a considerable body of research on the theme of *Too many choices, too much stress*.[18]

Let us return to the supermarket: a single product (milk, dark chocolate, apple juice . . .) is systematically available in dozens of different options. Is this a good thing, as we are led to believe? No! This abundance of possible choices leads to pointless stress:[19] there are already enough important decisions to be made in life without the need for any more. Again, such abundance is problematic for certain psychological types (those combining depressive tendencies and perfectionism): a study demonstrated, for example, that 'maximizers', who always want to make the best choice in different life situations, are often caught out by this sort of situation, whereas 'non-maximizers' (who could also be referred to as the 'that'll do fine-ers') quickly understand that the *best* choice does not exist, or that, in any case, it is better to stop at the first acceptable choice you come to, and keep your brain on form for what really matters in life.[20]

Brands and shops are beginning to realize that this abundance of choice can be counter-productive, since research shows that although people *say* they prefer to have the widest choice possible, in reality their purchasing behaviour is adversely affected when there is too much choice: for example, people will buy less jam if they have a choice of twenty-four varieties instead of six.[21]

But this problem of choice is itself also exploited by brands in order to increase sales: this is what is known as *branding*, or the power of a name. *Branding* takes advantage of the stress caused by too much choice, by offering an apparent solution: 'Don't stress over trying to make the right choice, come to us and buy a designer label!' It is simply a different poison, and a more expensive one.

Ah, I almost forgot: the more choice people have in making a particular decision, the more likely they are to regret their choice if they subsequently feel it is an unsatisfactory one.[22] Oh yes, this obsession with 'making the right choice', with 'not being had', is exhausting and wearing. And all that to what effect?

To experience even more negative feelings: for example the frustrations of broken promises of happiness. Buying does not make us happier, or not for very long. But this materialistic society would have us believe that achieving an objective opens the door to happiness. Even without our necessarily being aware of it: for example, in these romantic films which end just as the couple finally begin to get rid of the obstacles that were preventing them from getting together. In fact that is precisely when the hard work begins in earnest. Whereas we are led to believe that it is all over, that the main goal has been achieved. And yet it never happens quite like that in our own lives! Which is why we can find ourselves assailed with doubts and frustrations: 'And what if this isn't the right person? Because it's not like it is on the television . . .'

More seriously, the materialist pollution of consumerism depends on the promise of small moments of happiness shown in adverts, which are always along the same lines: we associate an eternal and legitimate 'value' (enjoying time with people close to us, or with friends, bringing pleasure to someone or to ourselves, enjoying happy moments) with a product (coffee, car) that we are being persuaded to buy.

As a result, false hopes are raised and frustrations are created which people then attribute not to these manipulations but to their lives: they will then try to change either the physical circumstances (move house, find a new job or a new partner) or psychological ones (go to see a shrink, who will attempt to repair the damage).

The disease of materialism pollutes our minds

'We cling to things not only with our hands but also with our minds.'[23] The disease of materialism slowly but surely weakens our capacity to regulate our feelings. Even the most common ones, like sadness: it has been shown that the sadder someone is, the more they consume as soon as their thoughts are steered towards egocentric preoccupations.[24] Which means that in a society which flatters our ego and offers us an abundance of things to buy, the reflex will be even stronger.

The ease and speed with which we can consume, the possibility of doing so many things at once, the opulence we see around us, are all obstacles to slowing down and reflecting on things, painful as that can sometimes be: they interfere with our sense of identity, which, illusory as it may be, is nevertheless precious, and with our capacity to reflect on ourselves and to regulate our feelings. The result is total confusion: our feelings are all over the place, disoriented, superficial, dissatisfied, at the mercy of every passing commercial distraction in our environment. This is not richness but pollution, an invasion not just of our behaviour as consumers but of our minds. It is similar to the effects of plastics or pesticides, gradually building up in our systems.

Materialism snatches us from what constitutes our identity and our humanity: the alarm was raised by poets long ago. But no one listens to poets these days. This is what Stefan Zweig wrote on Rilke:

> More and more it seems a wonder to me that we had such immaculate poets amongst us in our youth. And that is why I ask myself repeatedly with a kind of private anxiety: will it be possible for such personalities, completely

devoted to the lyric art, to exist in our time, in our new forms of life, which drive men out murderously from all inner contemplation as a forest fire drives wild animals from their hidden lairs?[25]

Or our dear Thoreau, who went to live in the woods at Walden for a whole year: 'I believe that the mind can be permanently profaned by the habit of attending to trivial things, so that all our thoughts shall be tinged with triviality.'[26] And also: 'When he has obtained those things which are necessary to life, there is another alternative than to obtain the superfluities, and that is, to adventure on life now.'[27]

Or Nietzsche: 'Is it not the case that all human institutions are intended to prevent us from feeling our lives, by means of the constant dispersion of our thoughts.'[28]

And that was back in the nineteenth century. It was probably then that things started to get really out of control:

> You know the Navajo women, when they weave a blanket, leave a little place for their soul to come out, at the end: not to weave their soul into it. – I always think England has woven her soul into her fabrics, into all the things she has made. And she never left a place for it to come out. So now all her soul is in her goods, and nowhere else.[29]

What would they have made of our era? Poets and novelists as always were the first to see the problem. It is there, now, on a vast scale, all around us and inside us. It is, as Cioran said, 'The nightmare of opulence. Incredible accumulation of everything. A sickening abundance.'[30]

Stuffed, but starved of real nourishment

Work more – and see less of your children, your partner, your friends?

Earn more – to buy things you do not need?

Play music constantly – to forget definitively what silence is like?

In all illnesses associated with abundance there are hidden deficiencies: obese people, for example, are often deficient in fat-soluble vitamins, folates and zinc.[31] Our minds suffer from deficiencies too, even when we think they are being nourished and stimulated. Materialistic lifestyles distance us from getting the basic nourishment we need.

It is not only hypersensitive people who need silence, calm and time for reflection: all humans need these things. And yet today, silence needs to be a deliberate choice, a decision to be taken, and even more crucially, adhered to in our daily lives.

We have become obese with over-stimulation, we have to be occupied permanently and must never be bored: 'The time just flew' has become the success criteria of leisure moments. But as a result we are less aware of existing, because it is the sense of time passing that gives us the sense of existing, of having a *past*, and not just *memories*. This is troubling. So, in order to feel we are living, we set about filling our lives with artificial feelings: lots of music, lots of films, lots of reading, lots of fun and entertainment. Some of it phoney and poor quality: television, for example, with its pre-recorded laughter and the fake outpourings of celebrities who are all over each other even though in reality they detest each other. Or computer games: children – who have grasped all this – have this to say about people who spend their time playing games rather than living: *they should get a life*.

'Man is thirsty for truth, but is he seeking a spring – or a trough?'[32] We need to be wary of what is too easy – salespeople have understood that we are tempted by the easy. Instead we should be making the effort to open our eyes. If we start to be aware of our real needs, and of how we can genuinely satisfy them, we will feel better and our societies will be better places.

Here, for example, is what the English writer Alain de Botton says: 'Why then, if expensive things cannot bring us remarkable joy, are we so powerfully drawn to them? [. . .] because expensive objects can feel like plausible solutions to needs we don't understand. Objects mimic in a material dimension what we require in a psychological one. We need to rearrange our minds but we are lured towards new shelves.'[33] It is what Epicurus called 'vain opinions'. Commercial companies have every interest in perverting the hierarchy of our needs (having rather than being), or in fallaciously associating themselves with them in a duplicitous way (having in order to be). Which accounts for our impulsive consumer behaviour. We are looking for something and we think we have found it in whatever is put in front of our eyes: we buy a 4 × 4 to satisfy our need for freedom or recognition. A beautiful sofa because we are looking for friendship and time to spend talking to those we are close to. Expensive beauty products to make us feel more attractive. Useless toys to show our children we love them. But are we really sure these purchases will add to our happiness, create it or facilitate it? What if the opposite were true and they threatened or prevented it?

The materialistic lifestyle does exactly that: it palms its junk off on us, crowding out our real needs. This system has understood that humans need social bonds so it sets out to transform places of consumerism into 'places of conviviality'. We sometimes refer to supermarkets and department stores as the 'temples of consumerism'. In reality these are not temples, but public spaces, forums. Which is worse. At least in temples only the faithful come to pray and to receive communion, whereas everybody comes to chat in the forum.

From social animal to commercial animal: the materialistic disease and the pollution of social bonds

Numerous studies have linked materialism to problematic values such as financial success, social status, obsession with physical appearance.[34]

Why are these values problematic? Because not only do they undermine personal well-being, but they also lead to major social tensions and rifts. Not only do they cause a problem of psychological malaise, but they also pollute relationships.

First of all, materialism is based on the cult of money and the commercialization of all goods and services. Money affects us much more than we like to think. This has been proved in a series of experiments,[35] in which people were primed to think about money, without it being overtly referred to: for example by asking them to complete money-related phrases or to sort Monopoly banknotes; or by positioning them next to computers showing a screen saver with images of banknotes. They were then exposed to a number of different situations and their reactions were observed and compared with those of people who had not been primed in the same way (who had, for example, been exposed to neutral phrases or objects with no connection to money). When someone from the 'money group' was asked to pull up a chair close to someone in order to talk to them, they left a greater distance between the two chairs. When they were asked to choose a leisure activity, they tended to opt for a solitary activity which did not involve other people. Faced with a difficult task, they waited longer before seeking help. When asked for help (the experiment was designed so this would happen), they gave on average half as much time as the other group. And when they were asked to pay back a little of their money, not surprisingly, they gave half as much. Even that apparently innocuous mention of money was enough to modify significantly – and without their being aware of it – a whole series of social responses. As the philosopher Peter Singer observed on this subject, 'It would be a mistake to assume that allowing money to dominate every sphere of life comes without other costs.'[36]

Research has of course also been conducted on the possession instinct. In one study, volunteers were given small objects worth approximately five dollars (mugs, pens, etc.).[37] Then a sort of auction was organized in which each of them tried to buy or sell the objects: on average participants refused to pay more than four dollars (therefore under-valuing them) for objects belonging to other people but were not prepared to sell their own objects for less than seven dollars (as though the fact that they were *theirs* somehow increased their value).

Materialism affects human relationships.[38] Particularly because it often leads to a sense of self-esteem which is unstable, vulnerable and self-centred and which depends on the attainment of objectives.[39] Look, for example, at all those adverts which flatter our egos in the wrong way, giving us an inflated view of ourselves, urging us to enjoy certain 'privileges'. The slogan '*Be yourself*' is of course another example of flattery and a shameless lie. '*Be yourself*' does not mean, in advertising language, 'Cultivate your intellectual autonomy or increase your lucidity, your emotional intelligence.' Its message is simply 'Don't wear the same clothes as other people, or else wear them before other people do and then reject them afterwards', etc.

Tim Kasser, a psychology professor who specializes in the ravages caused by materialism, describes a little experiment he regularly conducts on students attending his university lectures.[40] He asks them this question: 'Do you think you are all unique or all alike? – All unique! – OK, put your hand up if you're wearing jeans!' And 75 per cent of students put their hands up. Not quite as unique as all that, then. He could just as easily have said 'if you're wearing Gap', or, in front of an audience of executives, 'if you're wearing Ralph Lauren', etc.

It is the triumph of marketing to make us all look the same but at the same time give each of us the feeling we are unique and free. But why must we be made to feel there is something wrong with being like other people? It is not difference at any cost which should be valued (as it is in our society, which places a high and sometimes even absurdly provocative value on eccentricity), but tolerance and an acceptance of difference, where it exists.

Our materialistic pseudo-liberty is no better than that of caged animals. We have become like farmed animals or creatures in a zoo. Fed, stuffed, looked after, but pacing sadly up and down in our cages neurotically. And psychologically vulnerable.

The media, naturally part of this materialistic society, and indeed a spearhead of it, play a large part in this mental pollution. Through television series,[41] for example, featuring people, often Americans, who have thrilling, varied and intense experiences and who enjoy lifestyles superior to those of most of their audiences. One effect of their massive popularity is to provoke a desire for emulation: I want to have whatever they have, to live as they do. And ultimately, to suffer the same problems as they do.[42] Because, in the end, this emulation gives rise to feelings of boredom and dissatisfaction (the result of comparing their lives to our own). Contaminated in this way, we subconsciously seek to emulate these worthless models. The desire to imitate is not in itself problematic. It is after all one of the ways in which we can learn and progress. But the models on offer are simply incarnations of the worst aspects of materialism. They provoke mimetic desires driving us to accumulate possessions, to seek domination and competition. Whereas in fact we are an animal species with no need for all that and we should get rid of these instincts for domination.

The disease of materialism and the pollution of the space around us

The disease of materialism also disturbs our relationship with nature. Back in the nineteenth century, Thoreau had already understood where America with its current values was rapidly heading: 'If a man walk in the woods for love of them half of each day, he is in danger of being regarded as a loafer, but if he spends his whole day as a speculator, shearing off those woods and making earth bald before its time, he is esteemed an industrious and enterprising citizen.'[43]

Various studies have shown that people alienated by materialistic values are more inclined to use up the earth's resources more quickly. One of these showed how, in a simulation game about the exploitation of forests, students with materialistic tendencies used up the resources more quickly in order to obtain greater initial profits.[44] Not surprisingly, materialistic values lead to a reduced commitment to ecologically sound behaviour.[45] However, this is a book about psychology, not ecology, so we will leave it at that, and conclude with this little comment by Éric Chevillard: 'So this is what human activity amounts to: extracting gold from the mines only to bury it in the garden.'[46]

Towards a reasoned materialism: kill the beast or keep it on a leash?

Clearly a materialistic society has some positive advantages: our material needs (electricity, running water, bathrooms . . .) are certainly well provided for and our lives are consequently pleasanter and more comfortable than those of our ancestors. For example, we now have the chance to discover new places (tourism) and the opportunity to travel (being able to see loved ones no matter how widely scattered).

Materialism is not necessarily to be condemned *per se* and neither are the spoils it brings: slow pace and concentration are not *intrinsically* better than speed and the ability to do lots of things at once. But it all depends on the context: in our society, for example, with its emphasis on possession, accumulation, acceleration, doing lots of things at once, we should be aiming to value and practise simplicity, austerity, slow pace and concentration so that these eventually become automatic and an intrinsic part of our lives.

There is no point idealizing the past: previous generations had their faults too. People were rendered almost mindless with boredom and monotony, individuals were stifled by collective constraints (family, neighbourhood, society). But today things have reached the other extreme, with over-stimulation and a horror of boredom, and an excessive emphasis on the individual over the group. We need to invent new kinds of society, instead of putting up with the existing situation or longing to go back to the old one.

And for that to happen, we need to make progress within ourselves: it is when material progress advances at a faster rate than psychological and spiritual progress that humans suffer.[47] When the biggest investments a society makes are those destined to produce more and to increase consumption, and where there is no counter-investment to improve people's personal equilibrium, then the world is in moral danger. That is when we need to start fighting and grow in our heads and in our behaviour.

Resistance through conscious awareness

Understanding the influence materialism exerts on our moods and feelings is an important starting point. This is often achieved through the use of subliminal techniques such as priming, an extremely efficient means of inducing moods without our being aware of what is happening.[48]

Priming is a very strange process: anyone can, for example, be subconsciously made to feel older just by being asked to complete sentences with words such as 'old, alone, dependent, cautious', with the result that they subsequently walk more slowly.[49] All this happens on a basic level, without our being fully conscious of what is influencing us: for example, men find plumper women more attractive when they are feeling hungry![50] For priming can reflect what is going on in our minds: if we are hungry ourselves, we are less severe in our judgements of other people's impulsive behaviour towards food, etc.[51]

The technique of neuromarketing aims to make people buy more:[52] we have known for some time, for example, that music stimulates buying behaviour. But there are also dozens of similar studies: we buy more if we do our shopping when we are hungry, and less if we do it on a full stomach; the sound of a beer can being opened or a fizzy drink being poured makes us want to buy the drink in question. And simply displaying the sign 'credit cards accepted' resulted in shoppers spending more.[53] The appeal of the word *credit*, no doubt.

Priming, like any other manipulation technique (influencing someone without their being told directly), is not *good* or *bad* in itself. It can just as easily be used in a good cause: in an experiment carried out in a hospital context, people were invited to help themselves to tea or coffee in exchange for a contribution to be left in an honesty box. If a photo of a person's face apparently staring at the giver was put on the box, the amount of money contributed was considerably greater than it was if the photo was of a bunch of flowers, for example.[54]

A clear consciousness of our feelings and moods increases our chances of being aware when this priming has taken place, of understanding its origins and being able to think about diffusing it rather than falling into the trap. But this clarity of mind needs to be cultivated: it certainly will not fall from the sky in a society which resorts to such methods. It is also against the background of our intrusive, disruptive, distracting society that the need for some kind of meditative technique is at its most urgent: in the interests of our mental stability.

But, in addition to all that, we must also keep reminding ourselves that we are easily taken in by the illusion of freedom: the basic principle of any kind of manipulation is to give us the impression of acting of our own free will.[55] And our consumer society takes maximum advantage of this: we do more of our shopping in self-service stores than in traditional shops (where you need to ask a salesperson). In Sweden sales of alcohol increased by 10 per cent when self-service was introduced in the stores authorized to sell it, where previously people had needed to ask for what they wanted, rather than being exposed to a proliferation of products within easy reach.[56]

Resistance: individual action

We need to free ourselves from two great modern evils: 'TMD' and 'TBD': TMD as in *too much disorder*: the disease of *too many things*. And TBD as in *too busy disorder*: the disease of having *too much to do*.[57] The antidote to these lies in Thoreau's historic slogan: 'Simplify!' More of less and less of more! Owning less and doing less have now become contemporary necessities.

Own fewer possessions and, even more importantly, replace them with experiences, replace gifts with time spent together. I remember once, when I was travelling to a conference, finding myself gazing at a display of toys in an airport shop window. In the space of a few seconds that teddy-bear and those dolls had turned into primers inducing guilt feelings with regard to the children whom I had 'abandoned' to go and work in some far-off destination, and whom I would not be able to kiss goodnight that evening. Suddenly I felt a strong urge to buy them something, not necessarily just so they would forgive me for being away, but also to ease the pain I was feeling at that moment and as a way of communicating with them. The toy shops which fill our airports exist in order to persuade over-worked executives to buy a toy for their children. Clearly, in doing so, they are satisfying their need to have a good relationship with their children and keeping everybody happy. But not necessarily in the best way. Another way would be to spend less time in airports and more time with the children. Or, instead of buying a new toy, deciding to spend the following Sunday going for a bike ride or flying a kite with them. And doing it.

Stop buying and start enjoying things!

All the studies carried out on this subject show that enjoyable experiences have a more lasting influence on our sense of well-being than buying equally enjoyable purchases: in the long term, doing is better for us than having,[58] and going to a concert will make us happier than simply buying the recording of the same music. We know too that becoming absorbed in an activity we do well is an important source of personal well-being, especially if it counts as an *autotelic* activity, in other words one which is a goal in itself. Like walking for the sake of enjoyment and not just as a way of getting somewhere. Or playing with your children or reading them a story because you enjoy doing it, not because they need to be calmed down or occupied.

Becoming less attached to objects requires a considerable degree of consumer vigilance. The need to ask constantly, for example: do I really want this thing? Do I really need to buy it? Do I really need something to eat or another helping of food? To turn on the TV, or the radio? To buy that magazine? Or are these simply reflexes, habits, or worse still, a response to the priming I am targeted by all day long? How can we be sure? By waiting a while, by letting any possible needs and desires I may have clarify themselves; by resisting the *'omnia illico'* reflex ('everything, now') materialism has implanted in us all.

We can also conduct experiments in non-consumption: by going to the supermarket after a good meal, exposing ourselves to this vast array of foodstuffs and thinking about what we would have bought if we had been hungry at the time. In the crusade against impulse purchases, systematically boycott anything placed near the checkout or on gondola ends in shops. And boycott products which advertise intrusively, or in an unscrupulous manner, promoting destructive values (flattering egos, impulse behaviour, the taste for privileges). By repeating aloud: 'I will never buy that!'

Going on retreats in places with a spiritual association, such as monasteries or ashrams, is also a powerful way to experience a simple life, recalibrated to its essential elements. For, in all cases, the difficulty is of course the same as with any other resolution: that of moving from thought to deed. And from deed to regular practice.[59]

The same applies when it comes to TBD, the *too busy disorder*: whereas 'time management' guides have long urged us to do more in less time, today the trend is in the opposite direction: if you feel you do not have enough time, it is not only because you are failing to manage it properly (which is possible), but also because you *genuinely* have too much to do! We need to understand that one of the most powerful factors of well-being in existence is the sense of having time at our disposal, time to do what we enjoy, or to do nothing whatsoever.

Resistance: social and political action

Étienne de La Boétie, a close friend of Montaigne, reminds us in his tract *The Politics of Obedience: The Discourse of Voluntary Servitude* that tyranny is based on the consent of the slaves as well as the power of the tyrant.[60] The question of 'political' commitment in its broadest sense also applies to protecting our feelings from the intrusion of consumerism.

We can decide to judge our politicians, of both sexes, on their attitudes to materialism. We can talk to teachers and head-teachers in an attempt to keep the consumer society out of our children's schools: why, for example, are televisions increasingly appearing in the covered areas in French school playgrounds? Why are pointless toys sometimes handed out at Christmas time? Should schools be involved with promoting consumerism? We can also question why the best-paid jobs – those most highly esteemed in a materialistic society – are often the most socially toxic. The most highly rewarded are not inventors, engineers, health workers, teachers. But advertisers, marketing designers, commercial bankers, *traders*. It is not the people doing the jobs who are to blame: our professional choices are more often the result of luck or necessity than a reflection of our own values. But these careers simply create inequalities and instability rather than goods or happiness. Moreover, in the medical profession, which jobs are the least well paid? In France the answer is general practitioners, paediatricians and psychiatrists: social bonds, child-hood and feelings and moods. Symptomatic, or what?

Another example of the intrication of social, political and psychological issues is to be found in the current French debate on Sunday opening hours for shops. An unlimited opening would be a step towards increased materialism: more free time and family time would thus be centred on consumer activities. The Christian 'Sunday as a day of rest' is not a purely religious one: it has social and psychological benefits too. For its part, the Jewish community encourages its members to respect the weekly rest-day of the Sabbath: no working, trading, TV, computers, telephone, etc. But, instead, time to focus on social relationships and family (and of course to pray). This is an issue of religious authority but also of good sense and well-being. Islam takes a different standpoint, since for Muslims, Friday (which in Arabic means *meeting, gathering*) is a day of intensified prayer, rather than simply an obligatory day of rest.

The political dimension of the relationship with materialism is more and more often debated in the very heart of those scientific and medical communities interested in the notions of happiness and well-being, par-ticularly since the work of Daniel Kahneman, Nobel prize-winner for economics in 2002 with his study of the psychological factors behind economic decisions.[61] This was, for example, reflected in the recent dis-cussions on the notion of the GNP, gross national product (production of wealth), as an indicator of the progress made by a country: it has been observed for some time now that an increased GNP is no longer asso-ciated with an increased level of GNH, or gross national happiness, a concept launched in all seriousness by Bhutan at the UN.[62]

In Great Britain, Tony Blair's New Labour party (which after his depar-ture reverted to being simply the Labour party, situated on the centre left) declared its intention of counteracting the negative psychological effects of capitalism: these moderate reformists were addressing issues neglected by the traditional left.[63]

As a result, Richard Layard, an economist who worked as an adviser for Tony Blair, struck by the high levels of psychiatric illness in Western popula-tions, pressed for political measures to ensure that psychological well-being was taken into account in political and economic decisions.[64] For him, the rise in individualistic attitudes, the erosion of trust in others, society's tol-erance for 'dishonest' behaviour (if you find a wallet, keep the money) are more prevalent in societies where the collective happiness index is at its lowest.[65] In Layard's view, encouraging people to work longer hours makes no sense whatsoever and is detrimental to the level of collective happiness. Increased productivity comes at a high price given the psychiatric illnesses and family and social breakdown associated with it. He too is pressing for the establishment of some kind of index of 'gross national happiness'.

Richard Sennett, like Layard a teacher at the London School of Economics, reaches a similar conclusion: we need to rethink our attitude to work in order to take into account the negative effects it can have on the individual, and in doing so encourage a more balanced professional career, an expansion in public services and a restoration of the prestige of manual work and craftsmanship.

Finally, Richard Wilkinson, doctor and epidemiologist at Nottingham, has much to say about the psychologically destructive effects of social inequality: the more unequal a society is, the higher levels of ill-health are likely to be. Even when the effects of this inequality are taken into account (poor people have worse diets, or less access to health-care, etc.), even taking into account those people excluded from the health system and living below the poverty line, societies based on the *winner–loser* system (like the United States and Great Britain, both adept in ultra-liberalism) are extremely toxic in terms of the physical and mental health of their citizens. As a result of the same mechanisms as those identified by Layard: the weakening of social relationships, the lack of confidence in other people, a growing reluctance to help others, a reduced sense of security.

Look to your minds and your weapons, citizens?

But let's lighten up occasionally

Clearly the subject of materialism is a crucial issue in terms of our personal equilibrium, and one which concerns me deeply. Yet there is no point in being too pure and self-righteous about it: we are all consumers and, at certain times, glad of it. And, as we have seen, not everything is *bad* in the consumer society. There is no harm in an occasional impulse buy or in indulging in some unnecessary consumption. 'Oh dear!', one of my friends commented, after reading this chapter, 'You should at least say that it's OK to let go from time to time, to eat sugary things and fall for some ridiculous promotion on a supermarket display. Otherwise, life isn't much fun, if everything is completely under control the whole time!' I agree. But let us keep an eye on the proportions: a hint of consumerism diluted in a solid mixture of liberty and mistrust of materialism, rather than the opposite.

Stone Age thoughts

More than fifty years ago, in 1964, Joseph Delteil, one of my favourite writers, published a little book called *La cuisine paléolithique*.[66] It was a time when materialism was in its early days and full of confidence in its capacity to create a better future. Delteil, a bright-eyed old fellow dressed in an ancient, threadbare velvet jacket, who was living a cheerful existence near Montpellier, wrote, in an astoundingly prophetic voice:

Modern civilization: that is the enemy. It is the era of the caricature, the triumph of artifice. An attempt to replace human beings with robots. Everything is corrupted, polluted, false, all nature is distorted. Look at these steel-covered landscapes, the polluted atmosphere of our towns (lungs the colour of soot), the skies and their birds riddled with insecticides, the fish poisoned even in the depths of the ocean by nuclear waste, the steady and ubiquitous rise in carcinogenic substances, the unbelievable speed of every-thing, the hellish din, the tremendous panic of nerves, hearts, minds, mass production, mass production, I tell you ... This is industrial life, atomic life. The great crime of modern man! Yes, all this is simply a cry: Help! Fire! Madman! Assassin!

Another of my favourite authors, Louis-René Des Forêts, had this to say: 'Overabundance has nothing to do with fertility.'[67]
What more is there to add?

Part Four

Awareness

Going further

You will carry on now.

Now you have understood and accepted that your life is happening here, at this precise moment.

That you need to love yourself, that you can love other people, and be loved by them, without trembling or clinging to them.

That happiness is tragic, intermittent and indispensable.

That you can sometimes be wise, and sometimes not.

You can go ahead.

In tranquillity.

Tranquil bird on inverse wing bird
Nested in mid-air
At the border of gleaming memory
Abase your other eye
Neither to sun nor earth
But to the oblong fire gaining intensity
To the point of the entire day

One day
One day I awaited myself
I said to myself Guillaume it is time
Finally to know myself.

Guillaume Apollinaire,
Procession

Chapter 14

Living mindfully

Someone with nobody inside
Romain Gary

A sudden moment of awareness, of illumination. It came one day, a few years ago, when I was attending a psychiatry conference. We were in the middle of working with a number of colleagues on a plan to introduce a university diploma course. The conference had been very intense and, after a few days of it, I was beginning to feel a little tired, a little weary of talking and listening and of being fully immersed in psychiatry. At one point, I looked up to glance though the huge skylight of the room where we were working. Outside there was a beautiful winter sun looking all the more wonderful because I was stuck in the conference, in those stuffy rooms and open spaces full of people, bustle and noise. I found myself wishing I did not have to be there any longer, and I wished even more that I didn't have to be involved in this university qualification project, even though I knew it would be beneficial for students and rewarding for those involved in setting it up. A phrase from the American writer Thoreau popped into my head: 'It is in the woods that I would like to find man.' That did it. From that moment on, I was overwhelmed with an irresistible urge to quit all that artificiality (electric lights, intercom announcements, escalators) and to go and walk in the woods. I heard myself announcing my intention of withdrawing from the project. The intensity of the light had saved me: I left the room, I quit the conference, and – for real this time – I headed off to walk in the woods with a strange and slightly absurd impression of rebirth.

It was a period when I was doing a lot of meditation. I try to meditate regularly, but at certain times it takes on a greater importance either because I have more time for it or because my need for it is greater. At such times I am hypersensitive to the intensity of the present moment. I am quite capable of prioritizing needs which rationally should not be given predominance. How can certain professional commitments be compared with a walk in the woods, for example? Yet in such periods, such reactions fail to strike me as even the slightest bit incongruous. And the strangest thing is that I rarely regret (never, in fact, but that may also be because I do not *want* to regret) any decision of this type. Because in the end these are not spur-of-the-moment ideas, or impulsive notions, but simply an obvious truth which has been hatching for some time and which suddenly bursts into the open. Making time in our lives to walk alone in the woods is just as important as working on professional projects and successes.

But how can we remain aware of our needs, as often as possible?

How can we be sure we are not missing out?

Often we miss out on our lives

So often, we end up not being fully involved in what we are doing! Missing out on it somehow.

Missing out on happiness. All those Sundays when we spend the whole time thinking about Monday instead of enjoying the opportunity to relax and spend time with people close to us. Then the Mondays when we regret not having made the most of our time off, and, as a result, end up unable to concentrate on what we should be doing, and finding it difficult and unsatisfying. Which in turn leads to delays, complications, unhappiness, and a new wave of unpleasant feelings.

Missing out on all those unimportant little things. All the times when we fail to listen to what someone is telling us, or are distracted, elsewhere. All the times when we cannot remember where we have put something. All the times we end up going somewhere without thinking, as though on 'automatic pilot'. When we arrive and realize we have walked or driven in a kind of parallel state, another universe: not in the real world but absorbed in our feelings.

Missing out on the big moments. How many weddings, celebrations, 'big moments' have passed by with us in a distracted state, thinking about everything except what is really important: the present moment. All because our minds are so cluttered with so many things and so many worries that we are incapable of either controlling or putting aside.

Sometimes it almost seems as though our entire lives are drifting past like that, out of our control, somewhere ahead of us, out of reach. And we just run along behind, trying to catch up, scurrying to pick up a few bits and pieces, to make some kind of coherent construction out of it all after all, by sticking together memories, photos, scattered thoughts. We are victims of remanance: the preceding moment devours the present one. Or of anticipation and anxiety: the instant to come dominates our thoughts. The present moment no longer exists: it is lost in oblivion.

But what if missing out on the present means we are missing out on life?

How we end up missing out on our lives

There are so many different ways of running away from our lives and not being present in the moment.

We can take refuge in actions, whether useful or not, becoming 'enslaved to action': always doing something instead of stopping to think and to feel. Of course we need to act and to do things in our lives. But are we really aware of all those times when doing means running away? Of those times when we throw ourselves into doing something not because we really need to but to avoid having to feel something? Planning what to do can also be another way of escaping, leaving us 'bogged down' by things to do, always thinking about later, afterwards, tomorrow. And finding ourselves taking to absurd lengths this phrase coined by someone or other (dozens of celebrities must have said it, and most people must have thought it): life is what goes on while you are doing pointless things.

We can also take refuge in rumination, or in dreams or hopes, living our lives wrapped up in our imaginings and our hopes, without ever stepping outside to breathe the air of a lighter life, lighter because free of expectations, devoid of any intention other than that of feeling and observing what it is to live in the present.

We can take refuge in certainties. Always judging and deciding what is right and what is wrong, for ourselves and for other people, at home and in society. In other words, becoming inflexible, turning into machines programmed to judge everything. By always wanting to pigeonhole our opinions and our experiences, by modifying and distorting them, we end up out of reach of reality, incapable of being moved, of changing. We reject anything that is different or unexpected, condemning it with comments such as 'It exists, of course, but it is contemptible, devoid of interest, pointless.' Yes, of course such an attitude is comforting: reality can often be disturbing. But thinking like this is impoverishing too: reality is what nourishes us.

We can – because life is complicated and beyond our comprehension, and also because it is often painful – *be too wrapped up in ourselves,* and fail to be aware of what is going on around us. Failing to listen to what the other person is saying in a discussion because we are convinced they are wrong, or because we are concentrating too much on what we want to say to them and make them hear, we who are right. Seeing only our own pain and misery and forgetting that they are shared by almost all human beings. Looking at other people only in order to compare them with ourselves ('Am I better? Am I worse?') and always bringing everything back to ourselves, to that 'miserable little pile of secrets', as André Malraux put it.

We can be victims of repeated raids on our concentration. Our era is characterized by 'raids on our attention': the interruptions of advertisements,
telephone calls, texts or e-mails, but also our habit of being constantly
'available', now a given of modern life. Of course being unavailable and
out of reach can be problematic, but our readiness to drop everything in
order to respond to the slightest demand is surely itself an absurdity. It
can certainly result in a fragmentation of our concentration: the possibility
of 'zapping' as soon as there is something we do not like and therefore of
switching our thoughts to something else will end up leaving us with no
ideas whatsoever. We have already seen how these constant attacks on
our powers of concentration can end up disturbing both our inner equilibrium and our feelings and moods, and, in the long term, this can have
damaging effects.

We can refuse to let things be. And instead, lock ourselves into a problem,
or a pseudo-problem, refusing to let it drop until we have resolved it.
We call this 'neurotic perseverance', which is a fairly explicit psychological term. Here is a little example, given by a psychologist friend in
his book on consciousness:[1] spending two minutes looking for your
keys is appropriate behaviour, spending two hours looking for them
is much less so and spending the whole day searching is no longer
appropriate at all. It is better to accept we have lost them, give it some
time or find some alternative solution rather than just going on looking
for them. We end up transforming many perfectly benign difficulties
into huge existential problems. The lost keys become the temporary
incarnation of my misfortune and of my destiny as a miserable creature
thwarted by fate. Yet life can go on, even if some of our problems remain
unresolved!

*Or, as we have seen, we can try simply to refuse to accept the pain of certain
moments in life.* Simply refuse to experience suffering, or unpleasantness.
Then, when painful feelings come along, our reaction to them is that
of a surgeon: we eliminate the problem by making deep incisions and
removing everything. In order not to feel those feelings of sadness or
anxiety that creep in when I let go a little, or when I am doing nothing,
I avoid letting go or doing nothing. To protect myself from unpleasant
feelings, I force myself to feel *nothing* at all. I armour myself. I harden
myself. I deprive myself of the taste of life because, in the past, it was
bitter.
    Such strategies will not change our lives, if indeed they need changing.
They will just keep us going, *holding on*, until we die – some pessimists
might say that is not so bad – or until the inevitable explosion is triggered
by a crisis or by the onset of depression. Not present, not conscious, so
how can we be happy? The best we can hope for is sometimes to find
some comfort and satisfaction and not be too unhappy.

The result: 'You're almost dead in life'

The list of ills is a long one. Having the constant feeling of not being in step with your life, of not feeling 'at ease' in your life. Being riddled with a sense that you would be better off elsewhere, but without being convinced you really would be (and knowing all too well you almost certainly would not). Always wanting to *escape*: but it is we who have locked ourselves into ourselves! We would only succeed in moving the cage. Fitzgerald had this to say on the subject: 'The famous "Escape" or "run away from it all" is an excursion in a trap.' Having the nagging feeling you are not in the right place but never succeeding in finding the right one. And ending up wondering if there even is a right one for us.

Being filled with feelings of ennui, of non-fulfilment, of dissatisfaction. Feeling a sense of emptiness. Leading 'lives of calm despair', as Thoreau called it. Often being plunged into gloom and subject to fits of depression brought on by the pointlessness of daily life, by its colourlessness.

Being dragged down by a vague sense of suffering. Genuine mental suffering, but without clear or specific causes. The hardest to treat in psychotherapy. Perhaps psychoanalysis is the only way of bringing relief, provided the principle is acceptable: in analysis there is no knowing where the process might lead, or how, or if it will indeed leave us feeling better. Even if on the contrary psychoanalysis sometimes just ends up leaving people feeling submerged in themselves. Or if sometimes it can seem as if it is just the passage of time which has brought relief, when it finally comes; and that it has more to do with the wearing down and gradual fading of the pain rather than liberation from it. But no matter, if some kind of relief comes out of it.

Feeling overwhelmed. By waves of despair, crises of anguish, surges of anger, coming from somewhere deep inside us, we know not where. Then they are over, without our understanding why, and we are left with the sense that nothing has been resolved. We have simply emerged, slightly relieved, with the vague sense that another wave will soon break over us and suffocate us. When it comes, we will struggle with it, seeking refuge in action, work, alcohol or anything else which might calm us down or distract us. Then it will begin all over again, an endlessly repeated cycle. We will end up like Sisyphus, condemned never to be at peace and in the end not even content to be alive.

We can also lose our efficiency and our productivity at work or our ability to face up to and solve everyday problems. But given everything we have mentioned above, do we really care that much about efficiency? In any case, we are certainly not going to set huge store by this soulless and joyless efficiency: we would rather have an efficiency capable of embodying and reflecting our enjoyment of life, our pleasure in being something rather than nothing, in being alive rather than dead.

For the worst thing is life without consciousness. And worse even

than this are those moments when we become aware that we are living
unconsciously. Modernity exacerbates this phenomenon, but in reality
this is an eternal problem of human life, and that is why these verses from
the Roman poet Lucretius, a contemporary of Spartacus, still sound a
chord in us today: 'You're almost dead in life, although you walk / And
breathe.'[2] As do these words from our contemporary, Éric Chevillard,
when he speaks of those 'pointless days', those days 'when the nerves are
not plugged in, when I struggle just to lift a wing. In the evening, before it
too fades away, my shadow makes my mark on the attendance register.'[3]
Why are we not present, why do we not live more consciously? Why all
these bitter feelings, like so many alarms and backfire kicks associated
with the sense of living an empty life?

How can we live more consciously?

Often, we only become aware of what matters to us when we encounter
some kind of crisis in our lives. The kind of crisis that knocks us to the
ground and shakes up our habits and our convictions. Crises when we
are simply 'fed up': fed up with this job, this life, this family, this society.
Or crises of 'meaning', life's 'time-outs'.[4] We find ourselves wondering
'What's it all about?', 'This isn't how I saw my life.' We experience surges
of anxiety, of depression or anger. Followed by feelings of bitterness and
inadequacy, of perplexity, or by existential nausea. Could this suffering
and the temptation to react in an extreme way be avoided if we paid more
attention, at an earlier stage, to our feelings? We often get the feeling it
would have been better if we had thought things over more carefully and
understood them better: but life is just so complicated!

How can we know if we were right to make this or that choice in our
lives? Sometimes it is better to feel rather than to know something is right:
but in order to *feel* it, we have to be completely in touch with reality. For
example, if we are in a relationship with someone, we should be really in
a relationship with that person. And not with the person we would like
them to be, with the constant refrain of 'Why isn't he (or she) different?'
Once we have really accepted the other person, then we are in a better
position to decide if this is indeed the life we want, if this is the right
person or not. Or indeed to decide that it is possible for things to change
and to do whatever is required to bring that about.

We need to accept things as they are, to live in the real world; then
make a decision and act accordingly. And not to refuse to accept things
as they are, to dream of things which cannot be, to run away from reality;
then suffer and put up with things as they are or do something absurd
and impulsive.

Illness can make us more conscious. Does illness speak? Does it have
something to say about our lives? Many arguments and theories seek
to explain our illnesses on the basis of our existential malaise.[5] And a

considerable amount of research is currently focusing on this body–mind relationship. The link is unquestionably there but we are only in the initial stages of really understanding what it means. And in the meantime, there is little point in speculating too much. However, there is always an important element: even if the illness is *only* the result of poor management of our lives and of our moods, it can nevertheless provoke us to reflect more deeply, helping us to understand what is wrong in our lives. In serious illnesses, the ones which are truly 'life-threatening', as doctors say, the ones of which patients say 'It was touch and go' (cancers, leukaemia), we suddenly find ourselves reassessing the way we have lived our lives up until then and the priorities we have chosen and valued. At such moments, the illness is not teaching us anything, or at least nothing new. It is simply helping us see more clearly things we already knew: that it is important to make the most of life while we can, that nothing is more important than spending time with people we love, etc. Illness merely opens our eyes to all of that. And that is an enormous step.

Our eyes can also be opened in a less painful way, through the simple and natural events life brings: having children, travelling, meeting people, being in love . . . These recurrent moments in our lives, which we accept and enjoy, help us to understand what matters, not in an intellectual way, but in terms of experience. They make us more aware, unlock our consciousness, help us to focus on the fundamental things in life.

And sometimes much simpler moments can tear the veil even more radically, in a way that is both gentle yet brutal . . .

Moments of illumination

It is a journey on a dismal train on a rainy day. We are reading peacefully, thinking about what is to come. And, suddenly, we are overwhelmed with strange feelings, of inadequacy or of sadness, feelings which makes us aware that what we are experiencing is perhaps not quite normal, not completely anodyne. A little voice whispers in our heads: 'What are you doing there?' Then another: 'Just forget it, go back to your reading.' We are on the point of returning to all those little banalities which were going through our minds when the first little voice comes back again: 'Hey, you. I'm speaking to you! What exactly do you think you're doing there?' So we give up trying to run away and start listening to ourselves and thinking.

A September day, a leaf from a plane tree that falls with inexorable grace, spiralling irregularly – twenty centimetres to the right, a sudden change of direction and ten centimetres to the left, a leisurely half-turn, a rapid but harmonious change of direction. The leaf is dead. I stop to observe its fall. It drifts past my nose, brushes against my heart and falls right into my hands, which somehow opened of their own accord. Why am I torn from my thoughts by a leaf? Why am I touched and moved? Why this sense of harmony, this impression of everything being in place? Later a friend will tell me I could have interpreted this as a sinister omen, a reminder that everything, including me, must die. But no, it was quite the opposite. The falling leaf made me aware of the eternity of all things.

You are walking in a park, one winter morning, on your way to work, your head full of worries about your health. You see two women out for a run, chatting cheerfully, looking the picture of health. You are suddenly conscious of a whole surge of different feelings: envy ('It's all right for them, they are in perfect health'), irritation ('a pair of housewives who have nothing better to do than keeping themselves fit'), sadness ('if only I were not ill'), anxiety ('how is it going to end?'). All these ideas start going round in your head, but you carry on walking, breathing in the cold air, savouring the smells of the park and the town, all mixed up together. You do not try to fight off these feelings, but simply wait for them to go of their own accord. And they disappear without your really understanding why or how. Peace has returned just because you are once more living in the present moment.

The bell ringing in a nearby church one day when I am working in my office. Ding . . . ding . . . every five seconds. Someone has died. How can I go on working? I stop for a few minutes and get up from my desk. I take some deep breaths, aware that I am alive, thinking about the dead person. Otherwise, where is our sense of humanity? Vague memories of those theories reminding us that human civilization arises from the way we honour the dead.[6] I think about the day when a hominid, a mother no doubt, placed some flowers in the hands of her dead child, before covering the body with leaves. At that moment, she became human. She still lives on in me now as I stand here behind my chair, feeling odd, breathing a little more deeply, looking through the window at the constantly changing March sky, and thinking about this dead person whom I will never know. I remember Ernest Hemingway's novel For Whom the Bell Tolls, with the epigraph 'And therefore never send to know for whom the bell tolls; it tolls for thee.' These words were written by the English poet John Donne, and are preceded by the phrase 'Any man's death diminishes me, because I am involved in Mankind.'[7]

You are waving to a friend who is leaving in a taxi, in the pouring rain. Suddenly, you feel touched by the intensity of the moment, totally absorbed in the present. You hear every sound in the street, you feel every drop of rain, you see everything clearly, unhampered by thoughts or judgements. You are simply saying goodbye to a friend who is leaving. You watch her face through the raindrops on the taxi window; you hope all will be well. Time seems to have slowed down. You are struck by the immense fragility of our lives, by the immense importance of relationships and affection. You feel like running after the taxi to hug and kiss her one more time, to make a better job of it this time. But you feel no trace of anxiety or melancholy. It is just that you have understood something. Something you might have forgotten in five minutes' time, especially as you know you have a busy day ahead of you. But you feel a sense of peace because this instant will leave its mark on you forever. You know that.

At the hospital. I'm rummaging through the secretaries' bin, looking for an envelope which had contained a letter from a patient. Having read the letter in my office, I realized there was no address on the letter, which was a request for an appointment. Patients who are distracted or disturbed sometimes do that. Quick, find the address on the envelope so as not to have to ignore this sad cry for help! I rummage in the bin, sifting through lots of old bits of paper, a couple of used paper tissues, some slightly sticky coffee cups. Bah . . . There are lots of envelopes, of course, but where is the one I am looking for? The nurses and secretaries laugh at the sight of me bent over the bin. I find it funny too but I have no sense of embarrassment about what I am doing. Strangely it is as though there is a little voice in my head saying: 'It's OK. You are just doing your job and you are exactly where you should be, rummaging about in the dustbins of suffering; carry on looking for a bit longer.'

You think about Pascal and his *Memorial*, those feverish notes he always carried around with him on a scrap of paper and which were found after his death in the lining of his coat. You think about that moment of fire and faith that he experienced, on Monday 23 November 1654, 'between half-past ten in the evening until around half-past midnight'. When he was struck by grace, '"God of Abraham, God of Isaac, God of Jacob", not of philosophers and scholars.' Not reflection or cogitation, but a revelation, 'Certainty, certainty. Sentiment, Joy. Peace.' Pascal dropping to his knees under the violence of what he is experiencing and understanding. 'Joy, joy, joy, tears of joy.' Who trembles as he understands, 'Renunciation total and sweet.'

I recall my shock on first reading 'La lettre de Lord Chandos', the famous short story by the Austrian writer Hugo von Hofmannshal, in which a man is explaining to a friend (the philosopher Francis Bacon) why he has decided to retreat from the world and to give up writing and much more besides. 'In those days I, in a state of continuous intoxication, conceived the whole of existence as one great unit.'

> Since that time I have been leading an existence which I fear you can hardly imagine, so lacking in spirit and thought is its flow [. . .] It is not easy for me to indicate wherein these good moments subsist; once again words desert me. [. . .] A pitcher, a harrow abandoned in a field, a dog in the sun, a neglected cemetery, a cripple, a peasant's hut – all these can become the

vessel of my revelations. [. . .], filled to the brim with this silent but suddenly rising flood of divine sensation.

The significance of this text has been endlessly analyzed (notably the inadequacy of language to convey the complexity of any form of experi-ence) with the result that it is inevitably simplistic, just as it is for Pascal, to quote only these few words from it. But they say so much, and so powerfully!

Understanding moments of illumination (the lessons of awareness)

These moments when we step out of the box, when, gently or abruptly, we abandon the reflexes and habits we have acquired, are so important! It is like turning off the main road when driving somewhere by car, aban-doning the route we had planned: these are experiences of illumination. We had fallen asleep or been lulled by the humdrum routine of the pre-dictable and the usual. In reality we were absent both from ourselves and from life. And then suddenly here we are, jolted out of this reassuring and predictable monotony.

Such experiences occur relatively commonly in our lives. But often we are in danger of not paying attention to them. We need to have left space for our vulnerability, our receptivity. They cannot happen if everything is kept under lock and key, padlocked, barricaded behind possessions, preoccupations, obligations, actions.

In general, these experiences follow a recognizable pattern: a particu-larly receptive state (for all sorts of reasons: fatigue, melancholy, serenity), a small detail which somehow stands out from an otherwise ordinary moment in life, and the sudden realization that something special and inexpressible is happening, something which is both problem and solu-tion, question and answer, and even something beyond all that. But it is something we cannot immediately put to use as such. Because it is not yet explicit; clear but not explicit: the experience does not tell us what to do, but simply that we must – or will have to – do something. Or nothing, as the case may be. And also, because the sense of illumination, of sudden awareness, cannot necessarily be put into words. And if it is a phrase which bursts in upon our consciousness (sometimes these moments are like a cry uttered by 'something' within us), it may be a long time before we can fully understand its implications. The moment of illumination is a flash of intuition. It can sometimes be accompanied by a physical jolt, a corporal response: we can feel light, or heavy, different from the way we felt only a second before. We almost always feel as though time has changed its pace: the sense of time standing still, a kind of psychological slow motion.

The poet Christian Bobin speaks, for example, of 'a state of calm upheaval'.[8] It is a state where extremes can be brought together easily: clarity and perplexity, lightness and depth. We sense some kind of revelation. Yet in reality it will be days or weeks before we can really understand everything, unravel everything. Sometimes it may take an entire lifetime.

These experiences of illumination and awareness exist in many different cultures: they are called *Satori* (awareness of the knowledge of truth, intuitive vision into the heart of things) in Zen Buddhism, in which, in contrast to Nirvana, they are regarded as a transitional state. Christians speak of an Epiphany, in which a divine manifestation enables us to see something previously hidden from us. In Buddhism,[9] Enlightenment describes the state attained by someone who has freed themselves from passionate or intellectual distractions, who understands the transitory nature of reality and can experience the state of tranquillity, achieved through the quelling of passions and the elimination of their causes. The existence of such experiences in all traditions demonstrates the universality of this psychological phenomenon, which gives rise to a multiplicity of explanations, often linked to mysticism (which is an approach to the divine based on experience rather than rationality). This is what André Comte-Sponville had to say on the subject: 'The mystic is someone who sees truth face to face: he is no longer separated from what is real by speech (this is what I call silence), nor by want (what I call plenitude), nor by time (what I call eternity), nor finally by himself (what I call simplicity, the Anatta of Buddhism).'[10]

These experiences of awareness are therefore experiences of freedom and of access to another dimension than that of everyday existence, or perhaps to the only dimension of everyday life: the intensity of the present moment.

The consolation of the present moment, in the face of distress

We generally think of these moments of illumination in terms of openings, of flights, of taking off. But are they not also – and above all – returns to earth? They bring us back to what is important in our lives: the feeling that we are alive, or mortal, that we are alone or loved. They bring us back to beauty or to violence. To the meaning or the absurdity of our lives.

And, because they force us to focus on what is important, they can be even more significant: we can sometimes 'extricate' ourselves from misfortune by being exposed to grace. Or rather than 'extricating ourselves', find ourselves suspended in a state of grace, raised above our suffering.

I was talking about such experiences one day with a friend who told me how one morning when he was feeling low, a Mozart string quintet (K593) had had this effect on him: 'As I was listening, everything melted away. My melancholy had disappeared. Incredible.' Another friend described what had happened to him when his father was dying:

When I realized he was dying, I felt the need to listen to the aria 'Casta diva' from Bellini's opera *Norma*. And I had that sense of awareness that you've described, of being disturbed and soothed at the same time. After that, every time I felt upset, I just kept on hearing that tune in my head, right up until his death. It did not drive out my pain but it made it bearable. It reminded me, I suppose, that this was a story about life and death and therefore something to be *accepted*.

I remember one day reading this phrase of Pascal Quignard: 'Only music can reach into the depths of pain.' And this is what Cioran had to say about it: 'It makes our unhappiness a little better.'[11] In other words, it can throw light on our experience of misfortune or of suffering, making it clearer or easier to bear.

But feelings of melancholy or mourning are the 'ordinary' sufferings which affect every individual. There are also some extraordinary experiences which demonstrate that awareness does not only happen, and indeed this is far from being the case, in privileged circumstances.

The Austrian psychiatrist Victor Frankl, who escaped from the concentration camps, had this to say:

One evening, when we were lying on the bare earth floor of the hut, completely exhausted after a hard day's work, clutching our bowls of soup in our hands, a friend suddenly came running in, urging us to go out onto the assembly ground, in spite of our exhaustion and the freezing cold outside, so as not to miss a wonderful sunset.[12]

The Russian writer Evguénia Guinzbourg recalls a memory from the Gulag, when she was taken out of her cell to attend a political tribunal where she knew she might be condemned to death: 'Through the windows I could see tall dark trees: I listened with emotion to the fresh and secret murmuring of the leaves. It was as though I was hearing it for the very first time. How that rustling of leaves moved me!'

The solution of mindfulness

How do such experiences come about, whether in moments of drama or of simplicity? And to what do they owe their existence? These sudden illuminations cannot of course be summoned to order. They require a particular mental state, an ability to keep our minds open to everything around us and to everything that exists, and not merely to the things we are preoccupied by or to what is on our minds or in front of our eyes. In psychotherapy this state is called *mindfulness*. We can experience it through the practice of what is called 'mindfulness meditation'. Shortly before her departure for Auschwitz, Etty Hillesum wrote this: 'I will be wary of hanging the anxieties that the future inspires in me like so many weights onto the present day. And that needs a certain amount of train-ing.'[13] An inspiring summary of what we are striving to achieve.

Mindfulness means being open to the experience of the moment we are living, without any kind of filter (we accept whatever happens), without judgement (we are not concerned whether it is good or bad, desirable or not), and without expectation (we are not hoping that something will happen).

Mindfulness is therefore a simple presence – *just being there* – but one which is extremely difficult to achieve. More often than not, our atten-tion is only partially focused on what we are experiencing. And we make an effort to concentrate on certain aspects (which seem important to us at the time) rather than on others (which we esteem to be of secondary importance). When Evguénia Guinzbourg was moved by the murmuring of the tall trees in the wind, she could have considered that experience to be of secondary importance given the gravity of the situation she was facing and the possibility of being condemned to death. But no, she was in a state of mindfulness, and the murmur of the trees was at that precise moment the most important thing on her mind. Was she simply running away from a situation too painful to bear? Was this a *defence mechanism*, as psychoanalysts would say? I think not. More a case of infinite lucidity. For mindfulness can be interpreted as the highest level of acceptance: an integrative wisdom, in which all detail is absorbed into the whole. At the moment when I might be about to die, who can say that it is not supremely important to hear the murmur of the wind for the very last time?

In psychology, consciousness is the combination of awareness (this receptiveness to all the stimulations which come to us from our sur-roundings) and of attention (the capacity to focus on one aspect of what is happening). Mindfulness is therefore an optimal integration of all of that: presence, but an intense one, and openness, but to everything. It could also have been called 'total awareness'.

It is not a blind form of passivity and acceptance: it allows us to live in the present but with a certain flexibility, with the option of withdrawing from it, if we so wish, and in any case, being fully aware of it.

The capacity for mindfulness is present in every individual. It probably depends on a natural aptitude for concentration and receptiveness (the two need to be linked and synchronous) but it can also be acquired or devel-oped through practice and training. Until recently, such training was not highly valued in the West, where priority tended to be given to action and systematic intervention. We place more value on winners than on wisdom.

Learning to meditate?

In this era of globalization, psychotherapy cannot escape the great melting pot of ideas and systems. Various forms of meditation have indeed been practised at all times and in all cultures, but what we refer to as meditation in the West involves a deep and largely rational reflection, whereas in the East it tends to be centred on contemplative techniques, as we saw in reference to experiences of awareness.[14]

Mindfulness meditation, as used in psychiatry, psychology or medicine, is undoubtedly the first clear example of *world therapy* (rather as in cooking or music): it combines the foundations of Buddhist meditation with more obviously Western elements of stress management or cognitive therapy.[15]

The aim of this psychotherapeutic approach, 'secularized' and stripped of its religious elements, is not to bring us to awareness for the sheer beauty of the experience, but to help us find other ways of dealing with our problems. It is a way of helping patients experience calmer feelings and get over a range of difficulties such as depressive relapses or severe anxiety associated with serious illness.[16] Or of enabling them to overcome personality disorders.[17]

Therapies based on mindfulness take the form of a series of simple exercises intended gradually to help us 'keep our mind in the here and now'. We sit down, close our eyes and we discover . . . that our mind goes off in all sorts of different directions! We do not let this trouble us, we accept that this is normal, it is simply how our minds work, how our lives have accustomed them to function; and, moreover, this active mind, constantly looking around for things to do and to think about, actions to trigger, often serves us well. So we do not let these wanderings, usually so useful, trouble us. But now they are indeed distracting us. So, we stay calm, and we begin again.

There are of course a great number of variations and developments on this basic approach: we can focus on our breathing, on the sounds we can hear around us, the sensations from within our own bodies, we can observe the flow of our thoughts, their comings and goings, the direction they want to take us in. But without following them. Instead, we bring ourselves back to the exercise: *simply being there*. And we do all of this with an inner attitude of calm and kindly curiosity: not judging, nor rejecting or introducing thoughts. Simply accepting everything, observing everything.

Often, these journeys deep into ourselves can be painful: the very fact of being there in our living bodies makes us aware that we are not at ease in this body, that it is painful, tense, that our breathing is troubled. It is at that point that we realize that we normally run away from all these sensations by taking refuge in action, or by seeking distraction.

Sometimes we suggest exercises which seem strange to patients, such as *the exercise for both ears*: the patient kneels down, closes their eyes, lets their breath come and go peacefully, adopts a state of mindfulness (accepting everything that comes into their minds and their senses without imposing any filters) and focuses on the sounds they can hear. They note them, not trying to work out what they *mean* (if these engine noises are disturbing them, if the footsteps they hear might be someone about to open the door of the meditation room) but concentrating on what they *are* (loud or soft, high or low, one-off or repeated, getting nearer or fading away in the distance, observing whether they sound different in the right or left ear, then how the brain organizes the synthesis between them, etc.).

Why do such exercises improve my inner peace, my capacity to live better? Because they bring me a better understanding of how my mind works: how it constantly tries to get away (to think about other things), to judge ('this exercise is ridiculous'; 'and it's getting on my nerves, I just can't do it'), how it goes off in all sorts of different directions at once (constantly distracted by other thoughts). Mindfulness meditation will enable me to accept that all this is normal, that going off in different directions is simply what our minds do. And that this exercise of patient refocusing on whatever it is I have chosen to observe (sounds) is a multifaceted training in accepting, feeling, looking more deeply into things. There will in any case be other kinds of unusual exercises: tasting raisins, walking slowly in a state of mindfulness, etc.

Since this book is not intended to be a treatise on meditation, I will simply refer readers to some classic texts on the subject which explain it in more detail.[18]

Three points need to be made at this stage.

The first is that meditation is essentially practical rather than mystical, and that we need to 'demystify meditation', in the words of Matthieu Ricard, that great meditator.[19] For Matthieu, and he knows what he is talking about, meditation is essentially a form of mental *training*. A training which is essential if we are not to let our minds go to waste, and in order to enhance our well-being: 'We learn everything in life, so why shouldn't we learn to make our minds work better?'

The second point is that meditation can be non-religious. In spite of being an integral part of all the great religious traditions. The meditation used by therapists is clearly exempt from any religious dimension. But not from a spiritual one: a 'spirituality without God' is of course possible, as André Comte-Sponville demonstrated so clearly, reminding us that we are by nature 'ephemeral beings who open on to eternity'.[20]

The third point is that meditation is evidently not a form of escape from reality. On the contrary, it encourages a serene confrontation with *all* reality. As Lucretius urges: 'Rather, to look on all things with a mind that's free from care.'[21]

Benefits of meditation

The reason we medical staff are so interested in meditation is because it offers practitioners multiple benefits. The official line of the various schools is not to expect anything from meditation. Simply to do it and see what happens. I have always found this total absence of expectation difficult. At least in the long term. Perhaps I am just too much of a Westerner. Of course I know that one should not expect too much from a particular session (as opposed to relaxation, where we expect to be relaxed): more often than not, we will not feel any clearer or more serene afterwards. Sometimes indeed, meditation sessions will simply have taught us how difficult it is for us to meditate at the moment. But this does not matter: we had to do it, as the musician must practise his scales, the sportsman do his exercises, the monk his prayers, in full understanding of why they do so. I fully recognize that it is very good for us Westerners to renounce any immediate expectations. And that tolerating, or rather wholeheartedly accepting, sessions which are difficult or which seem to have 'failed' probably increases our tolerance of imperfection and failure in our lives in general. Which, given the world we live in, is an extremely beneficial practice, an indispensable vaccination.

But, all the same, when it comes down to it, we can have very high expectations of meditation, in the long term, and provided we understand that it is something we have to work at. Here is what meditation can bring, but – hush – without us expecting it.

Meditation helps us to understand the nature of thought. In reality we do not *think*: our mind produces thoughts, which we choose and select, or which force themselves on us. We simply submit and choose. We cannot keep up with their production, we can only follow on behind them. Meditating makes us more aware of that: our brain like a tap gushing thoughts, constantly turned on, for better or worse. And meditating helps us to make better choices, and to be less passive, in this flow of thoughts. The more regularly we practise meditation, the less likely we are to ruminate.[22]

Meditation enriches feelings and moods and helps regulate them more effectively. Meditation helps us to be more aware of our feelings, to have a better understanding of the links between our feelings and our physical sensations. It also helps us to detect how our physical state (tension, pain, hunger, fatigue) influences our feelings. As a result, the practice of mindfulness can, for example, be useful when we have decisions to make (particularly in complex situations) because it enhances our ability to recognize 'somatic markers', those little physical sensations which are a source of intuition.[23] That little twinge you feel when you are on the point of saying yes even though you really want to say no, or the feeling of unease when someone is lying to us or trying to impose a decision on us, or the uncomfortable sensation when we make a decision which seems logical but which we are unhappy with: we are better able to lend an ear, or rather our whole body, to all of that. Similarly, it is likely that meditation, by facilitating cerebral synthesis,[24] also facilitates the processes of problem solving, consciously or unconsciously: the mechanisms whereby, once we have calmly thought about a question, the answer comes to us a little later.

Meditation improves our capacity to concentrate for study or reflection. Even if that is poles apart from its original purpose, which was not at all intended to boost our performance. Mindfulness probably helps us to be more creative, by making us less self-critical. And it helps us to think in a completely open way: to take everything into consideration before reaching a decision.

Meditation is associated with well-being and, for those who practise it, seems to be associated with an increase in positive moods, and a decrease in negative ones. It is clear that living mindfully helps us be more aware of the little joys of everyday life. The overall effect on our feelings is particularly interesting given that the selective attention to the *positive* is not the objective of mindfulness meditation, which simply advocates observing and embracing *all* feelings: but the simple fact of observing in a benevolent way, which then enables feelings to be scrutinized and examined closely, seems enough to re-establish their balance in a positive way.[25] And in this way meditation also facilitates the natural processes by which our sufferings are healed and assimilated: when we are troubled, we just sit down, close our eyes and give ourselves over to mindfulness of the present moment.

Meditation facilitates changes of attitude and opinion. Because it leads to openness, curiosity and an acceptance of things as they are. It facilitates tolerance of difference and an understanding of other people more effectively than just education: for education tends only to be useful to people who are already adaptable and receptive. Research has shown, for example, that a particular form of psychotherapy based on acceptance and mindfulness (which we have already referred to) had a positive effect in changing prejudices.[26]

Meditation helps us to appreciate life. Not only because it makes us less likely to be dragged down in ruminations, which we are able to identify more quickly. But also because it helps us to appreciate the good moments, by making us more deeply present in them. The most entertaining research on this subject was based on chocolate tasting: participants who were made more attentive to what they were tasting got more pleasure from the experience than those who were offered some other form of distraction at the same time.[27]

Meditation as treatment

Because of all these benefits, meditation has been used in medicine to help patients cope with pain and illness, but also more widely in psychiatry to treat psychological disorders. There is currently a considerable body of convincing research on the subject, even though the level of proof still needs to be improved.[28] If we study the literature closely, we see that it is often research carried out by charismatic pioneers in the field: would the results be the same if these practices were more generalized? We would expect this to be the case, but in any case it is clear that the passage of time continues to bring further confirmation on a regular basis.[29]

In order to initiate patients into the practice of mindfulness, a number of protocols have been developed to adapt the technique to medicine and psychotherapy: in particular there are MBSR (mindfulness-based stress reduction) and MBCT (mindfulness-based cognitive therapy) . These programmes are currently proving extremely effective in the prevention of depressive relapses and of chronic depressive states, perhaps not surprisingly, given that these are patients who have developed strong tendencies to rumination,[30] as well as in the prevention of recurrent anxieties.[31] All this is logical given the numerous automatic pilots and programmes of pathological emotions and feelings in anxious patients and those in remission from depression. But meditation has not been evaluated in the acute stages of these illnesses: it is likely that it would be harder, or even impossible (the exercises are by no means simple and, even more critically, need to be done regularly), and that it is legitimate to see it as a method for preventing relapses and a means of maintaining good psychological health. Which is of considerable significance. And very useful, since professionals often find it difficult to know what advice to give patients following cure or remission.

Living mindfully, in practice

'Instead of being here with my body, somewhere else in my head and deaf to my heart, I am gradually learning to be fully engaged in every activity, no matter what it is.'[32] The object of learning to meditate is to modify one's relationship with the everyday: it is not simply about having a tool at your disposal, but also about developing a new frame of mind. This frame of mind can be summed up in the following words: as often as possible, as regularly as possible, live the present moment fully. Do what you need to do, but do not forget *also* to live in the present. There is nothing new about the programme. Montaigne mischievously rebuked an imaginary character: '"I have done nothing today." – What! Haven't you lived? That is not only the fundamental but the most illustrious of your occupations.' We may sometimes be doing nothing, but we are always living. In his marvellous essay *N'oublie pas de vivre* ('Do not forget to live'), Pierre Hadot also reminds us of this wonderful saying, coined by Goethe, for whom the *memento vivere* was a central theme.[33] Here then are some points to think about to make sure we do not forget to live.

Learn how to wait: there is no such thing as wasted time, only time lived

Instead of getting irritated in queues, waiting rooms, traffic jams, remind yourself that there is no such thing as wasted time, only time lived. Living is a chance we have been given, and an experience that will one day be taken away from us. Instead of always wishing to be elsewhere, later, otherwise, let us be here. Completely. From now on, in the queue, in the waiting room, I focus on my breathing, I am aware of what is happening in my body. Because I cannot 'do' anything, I can 'be': be there, be who I am, think about Montaigne and Goethe and many others besides who understood all this centuries ago. I can do other things with my mind than be irritated by the wait (for example if my e-mails are slow to come in or if my internet page takes a long time to load). It is true that the impatience of Westerners was a factor in their progress (although . . .). But this progress outran our wisdom, and ended up gaining the ascendency over us, turning us into slaves. Let us free ourselves from futile feelings of impatience. And keep any others, if there are any.

Be present in everyday life, in the little gestures

When I am eating, when I am cooking, tidying up, doing little jobs around the house, fixing things . . . Not be thinking that I could instead be doing something better, more important, more urgent. That may be true, and, in that case, there will be a time to think about that and to decide how to organize my life differently. But, in the meantime, there is no point in polluting my present with all that. I am conscious of being alive. I fully inhabit whatever I am doing at this moment: I am trying to eliminate gradually that sense of doing things 'while I'm waiting' to get on with something else. When I read a bedtime story to my child, even though I still have work to do, or e-mails to send, or still have not had dinner: I make myself focus on the here and now. I am with my child, and the most important thing is to be completely and utterly with him or her. To make sure that, while I am telling the story, I am truly telling it, for that child. And not thinking of other things, or wishing I were somewhere else. That moment, like every other moment in my life, is a chance and a blessing. If I am not present in these moments, I will regret it later. As in Apollinaire's poem 'Le voyageur': 'You will mourn this time of weeping / which will be gone too soon / as all the hours go by.'

Learning to stop

Stop abruptly, in the middle of an activity. And observe what is happening in us, in our bodies and our thoughts. I often make myself do this exercise when I am under pressure: when there are too many things that need doing in my life, too many demands I have to meet. Like everybody else, I feel overwhelmed. So, when the sense of urgency is at its greatest ('A few minutes? A few seconds? Quickly, do something, act, speed up, *gain* some time!'), I simply stop. I force myself to breathe calmly, to focus my mind on an important detail: the sky, the clouds, my breathing again, the face of someone I love, an idea from something I have recently read and the effect it had on me. I force myself away from what is *urgent* to breathe in what is *important*. Then, I start running again, of course. But I feel like a whale which has got its breath back again, before diving once more down into the depths to look for food. We need to stop and let our minds breathe, especially when we are in a hurry.

Identifying the automatic pilot

I understand what this is: it is this mental programme which is triggered in those routine gestures requiring no attention. When I am brushing my teeth, taking a shower, getting from once place to another, doing certain tasks, eating, I do not need to engage all of my brain. I can let these things happen of their own accord, automatically: that is the job of the automatic pilot.

The automatic pilot has certain advantages: it is a way of saving energy by reducing the investment of consciousness. There would indeed be little point in putting *all* my consciousness and *all* my heart into cleaning my teeth *every* morning (although my dentist has indeed pointed out the importance of brushing *all* of them).

Yet the system has its disadvantages too: for example, at certain times, it can facilitate the opening of another automatic programme, that of rumination. If I am not present in what I am doing, at times of stress or irritation or depression, I can find myself vulnerable to rumination ('Hey there! Come on! There's nobody in! There's plenty of room!'). All those activities normally done on automatic pilot can then be invaded by rumination: I ruminate whilst cleaning my teeth, going to my office, working . . .

The automatic pilot can also cause me to be absent from what is going on: I end up falling down the stairs with my tray because I was thinking about something else, thanks to my stair-climbing automatic pilot: or else I cannot find my keys, because it was not me who put them down somewhere, it was my automatic pilot for tidying (who did exactly as it pleased).

Mindfulness encourages and helps me switch off these automatic programmes on a regular basis (not all the time, but regularly).[34] To choose, occasionally, to be mindful of cleaning my teeth, or going upstairs, or eating, etc. Really to do whatever it is I am doing even if it is *only* the washing up. Even putting out the rubbish, mindfully, is good for the soul.

Disobeying unconscious injunctions

From my past, from society. I learn to recognize all the 'command centres' lurking inside me. Do I have to get angry and stressed when I cannot find a solution to a problem? Do I really have to read a magazine while I am sitting in this waiting room? Read my e-mails every day? Stay at work so late? Is it so important to avoid 'wasting my time'? Pessoa, great dreamer and great chronicler of the wanderings of the human mind, talked about remaining 'faithful to a forgotten pledge'[35] with reference to these moments in which we perpetuate reflexes learned from the past, but which may now no longer be relevant, or at least should no longer be automatic.

Changing your pace

Try some 'slowness' therapy. We need to recognize that in our lives there have to be some periods of 'fast time' and others of 'slow time'. As modern life often imposes more of the former, we need to allow ourselves the latter, on a regular basis. Walk more slowly along the street. Stop more often to look around. Keep some free time in our timetable, and allow ourselves to do nothing in it.

Protecting the continuity of our experiences

Whenever possible, be wary of interruptions. Often this applies particularly to our working environment: not keeping your e-mail page open while you are doing other work on your computer, switching off your mobile phone. Setting aside a period of at least two or three hours in the working day when you will not answer the phone or reply to e-mails or texts. Research has demonstrated the extent to which interruptions reduce our efficiency at work, even comparing them, in terms of the effects on our IQ, to the act of smoking a joint of marijuana.[36] And, unlike marijuana, the interruptions tend to have a stressful effect. So let us grant ourselves the free luxury of uninterrupted concentration.

Introducing small shifts in our everyday routine

For example, by being alone in a room at an unusual time when either you would not normally be there or you would be busy doing something, or by being in a different part of a familiar room. For example, alone in your child's bedroom; lie on their bed to see what they see, on the ceiling and all around them, when they are in bed. Or stand for a time, breathing calmly, in an entrance or hallway you would normally pass quickly through. Let your feelings flow: memories, sounds, thoughts, anticipations, the past and the present mixed together.

Ask yourself if you really want something

Do you really want to watch TV, read this magazine, have another helping of food, wine, coffee? Or a cigarette? Do you *really* want it, or is it just a reflex, a habit? Or a *need*, because you are feeling low, because you are trying, without having to think about it too much, to sort out another problem, because you feel sad, ill, alone, a failure, unloved . . .

Do not insist on resolving the problem immediately, if you either do not have time or are in danger of ruminating over it. But do something to stop it taking control of this moment of our lives. By saying to ourselves: no, I don't really want that. So I'm going to do something else. Breathe deeply, walk, for example, in a fully mindful way. We never do it enough.

Make time to appreciate nature

'Really to see the sun rise or go down every day, so to relate ourselves to a universal fact, would preserve us sane forever',[37] wrote Thoreau. The sky, the countryside, the rivers flowing by, springs, sea shores, hills and mountains, the rain falling, the wind blowing: all these can help us. Look for opportunities to seek out the healing power that contact with nature can bring. Take your suffering (or your joy) as an offering to nature, let it be absorbed into it. Without doubt, being confronted with some element of eternity, something which existed long before us and will survive long after we have gone, but which we are part of, originate from and will return to, helps us unconsciously to recalibrate our suffering.

Mindfulness as a way of reconnecting with ourselves and with the world, with our animal nature, and with our status as a living creature and as part of the universe. As a way of experiencing a transitory abolition of what separates us from our surroundings, an experience we will emerge from with renewed tranquillity. Lucretius, once again, points us in the right direction: 'This dread, these shadows of the mind, must thus be swept away / Not by rays of the sun nor by the brilliant beams of day, / But by observing Nature and her laws.'

Pause before answering a question

Sometimes the mindful life brings about some unexpected responses or requests. For example, having the courage to say, when we are asked certain questions: 'That's difficult, if you don't mind, I'll need a little time to think about it.' And stopping to think it over. Instead of replying at once with an off-the-peg thought which may not be particularly relevant. Why do we not do this more often? Not just because it is considered impolite to make other people wait. Not just because we are not convinced that waiting and thinking it over will really help us find the answer unless it was already stored conveniently in our memory. Not just because we are afraid the other person might think us odd. No, we reply straight away because that is how it is, that is what people do, and what we are used to doing. But then that means we will never stray from the beaten track, that we will never be surprised or enriched by a question! That our answers will only ever be ones that have already been given somewhere else! That the question will not really make us really think! Thinking is not only about looking for answers.

In reality we often end up doing this retrospectively, saying to ourselves: that's odd, that question intrigued me, disturbed me, touched me. But sometimes we would be better off noticing that at the time and discussing it with the other person. But it takes time to think more carefully.

Reconnecting to our senses

A classic meditation exercise: stop what you are doing in order to look, listen, feel, touch, enjoy, smell . . . And try to be simply a 'pure presence'. Mindfulness is thus often achieved by paying attention to and embracing everything our senses bring us.[38] Complete immersion in the sounds we can hear. Connecting with matter through touch. The dissolving of the internal/external boundary through taste: what a strange thing it is, when we really think about it, this food which comes from outside us and which enters and is absorbed within us. The animal connection to the world through smell. And the rapture of vision, that window open to the world. Take regular notice of all the riches our senses bring us.

Cultivate a capacity for presence, for contemplation

When we are confronted with an event, a thought, a memory, an important moment, before taking action or saying anything, simply suspend that urge to act, and instead breathe deeply and become conscious of what it is we are experiencing. Like the minute's silence (often shrunk to a few seconds) in certain ceremonies or in sports stadiums. Do this regularly during the course of our days, which always go by too quickly. In the morning, at work, stand for a few minutes by your desk and think about the meaning of what you have to do. Are you ready to do it wholeheartedly and serenely? Do it just as you are about to sit down to a meal. Or meet a friend. When I see a patient, I always make myself remember how important our meeting is, not to motivate myself and put pressure on myself, like a sportsman or sportswoman eager to win their match, but in order to focus my thoughts, my emotions and my energy as much as I can in preparation for our session together. For our mutual benefit. Since that is what we are here for, let us really be here, and really focus on it.

Make time for moments of deliberate awareness

Ask yourself 'What is happening to me at this precise moment? What is this situation? These objects? What feelings are going through my mind?' Or else 'What if this was the very last minute of my life, the last second? Or the first? What if I had to describe it to a blind person, to someone who is no longer with us, to an alien?' Go deep inside yourself to see exactly what is going on there.

Embrace adversity

Mindfulness also helps us to approach adversity differently, encouraging us to practise the acceptance we have already referred to. It is the metaphor of a swimmer caught by a strong current and swept out to sea (as in the 'baïnes', a kind of lagoon in the Landes region of France) and not knowing what to do. He should not panic, or try to swim back to the shore: he will only exhaust himself and risk drowning. He should simply continue swimming, not trying to get anywhere in particular, but just in order to remain on the surface, accepting that the current is stronger than he is. Acceptance is about not letting yourself be dragged under, but about swimming with the current. The current stops after a while: the swimmer will be washed ashore a few kilometres further on. This is active acceptance, often the only solution at certain times in our lives. Of course we also need to have other, more energetic, more aggressive attitudes at our disposal too. And sometimes refuse to accept. But acceptance should also be part of our survival kit.

Accept difficult moments

Understand and accept that suffering is part of human life. Accept it sincerely, and not with a distracted or hypocritical 'yes' whilst secretly hoping it only applies to others and not to us. Put this book down and ask the question in all earnestness: am I prepared to accept suffering in my life? And to accept it for those I love? For my children? Or do I dream instead of a world without suffering? Even if I do not want it to exist, suffering is there, it will come at some stage, and come back again. It is perhaps for that reason that, for some people, it is better to aim for consciousness rather than happiness (though it seems to me that the two are not incompatible). As Camus wrote, 'I no longer seek to be happy now, but just to be conscious.'[39]

Switch from 'doing' mode to 'being' mode

What all these efforts gradually teach us is the importance of regularly making space in our lives for moments where we focus on *being* rather than *doing*. Therapists using mindfulness techniques refer to the *doing* mode as opposed to the *being* mode. In the 'doing' mode, we are always struggling to reduce the discrepancy between things as they really are and as we feel they should be. In the *being* mode, we start by accepting what is, and by observing it attentively and, if possible, favourably. We do not seek immediately to change our thoughts but instead to modify our relationship to those thoughts. In the 'doing' mode, when a worry enters our minds it is accompanied by a painful feeling of pressure because of the necessity of finding a solution. In the 'being' mode, we start by considering the worry for what it is: a thought which comes into our mind. We tell ourselves that we will not try to resolve it straight away, but instead we will really listen attentively to everything it is telling us, and examine whether what it is telling us is right. To feel what it is doing to us, to understand exactly what effect it is having on our bodies. To examine it tranquilly, attentively. In other words to 'de-dramatize' it a little. We need the 'doing' mode as well: without it, we would never get anywhere. But we cannot manage without the 'being' mode: without it, we would end up so exhausted, stressed and demoralized that we would be constantly asking ourselves what on earth we were doing struggling in this way.

Do nothing

'True happiness is the conscious state which is totally detached, with no objective, where consciousness enjoys the immense absence with which it is filled.'[40] Doing nothing: the ultimate luxury? Yes, the supreme luxury of this era of agitation and of pragmatism. This fascinating and productive era. But which we can only fully enjoy if we also know how, at certain times, to do nothing. I remember one day, while I was working on this chapter, passing the bedroom of one of my daughters and noticing that she appeared not to be doing her homework, which I had asked her to do. I challenged her: 'Hey, my friend, what are you doing?' 'Um, er, nothing . . .' And just as I was about to reply 'What? What do you mean? What about your homework?', I remembered what I was writing about, and I found myself saying instead 'You're doing nothing? Excellent!' That made her laugh. I must remind her about it in a few years' time: perhaps it brought her a moment of illumination.

Living mindfully: is there anyone in there?

Living mindfully simply means living a normal life. But in a constant state of openness and sensitivity. With a constant readiness to embrace both the banal and the extraordinary. Living consciously is life here and now. Complicated, confusing, imperfect, rickety. We sometimes tend to think that life, the *real* life, the *good* life, will begin only when all our problems have been resolved. No, it is already here, hidden beneath our problems and our dissatisfactions. We must be ready to embrace happiness and grace. I am very fond of this phrase by Maître Eckhart: 'God often comes to visit us, but most of the time, we are not in.'[41] Surely I can take three minutes, three times a day, to check who I am, and be able to say *yes* to the question: 'Is there anybody in?'

Yes, I am here. Alive. Present.

Mindful . . .

Chapter 15

Compassion, self-compassion and the power of gentleness

But when he saw the multitudes, he was moved with compassion on them, because they fainted, and were scattered abroad, as sheep having no shepherd.

Gospel of Matthew

Louise, aged 12, when her grandfather was dying of cancer. One night, when I went to give her the usual goodnight kiss, she admitted that every night, once we had turned out her bedroom light, she would hold her breath for several minutes. She was convinced that every second she managed to keep doing so would give her grandfather one more day of life. She told me she had lost count of all the time she had gained for him, but she knew it was a lot, and she was happy to think it was helping him. She added that she was not completely sure if it was really helping him, but she thought it probably was. She was the only one of the three sisters who was brave enough to go and see him before he died, when he was extremely weak and very thin, and looked rather frightening. During her last visit, she was so kind to him, without any solemnity, without trying to play the perfect grieving granddaughter, but simply being her normal funny and lively self. I was deeply affected by what I saw. Neither her sadness nor her compassion prevented her from simply enjoying chatting to the grandfather she loved so much.

We need gentleness and the strength of compassion.

The more lucid we are about the world, the more we accept seeing it as it really is, the easier it is to accept that we cannot encounter all the suffering that is encountered in the course of our lives unless we have this strength and this gentleness. It may indeed not be enough, and we will need other energies as well, but without the lively and joyful energy of compassion, we would find ourselves wanting to run away from the violence of the world instead of getting closer to it with a view to easing it.

All the hurt that we see around us, that psychotherapists encounter in the privacy of their consultations, can be attributed to a lack of love, and is caused or exacerbated because of that. A lack of gentleness, of understanding, of kindness, of goodness. Past experiences of these lacks, which caused us pain; present ones which reopen those wounds. The healing process will be linked to compassion in all its forms and all its expressions.

It is as simple as that.

We need gentleness

Gentleness towards others, and to ourselves, is rooted in compassion, that feeling of 'pity aroused by the distress of others, with the desire to help them'. And which is a form of love, as Fénelon noted in his *Dialogue des morts:* 'Compassion is a love which grieves over the misfortune of the person we love.' Compassion means 'to suffer through the sufferings of others'.[1]

Although compassion is at the heart of any relationship between patient and carer, and therefore something that concerns me as a doctor closely, it never occurred to me that it could, in its different forms, be not only an essential element of any form of treatment, but also a means of enhancing personal well-being. My discussions with Matthieu Ricard and my readings of his Buddhist masters opened my eyes to this possibility. In Buddhism there is the stated wish that all living beings should be freed from their suffering.[2] Compassion is therefore central to many meditative practices.

Compassion is an attitude and a sentiment which is both wider and more positive than the pity which we can feel in the face of another person's suffering. Pity involves an element of distance which is absent in compassion. This makes it closer to the original Christian notion of 'charity': a joyful and unselfish love of our neighbour, whoever they may be. The joyful and happy dimension of compassion is an indispensable one: how else could we cope with the constant presence of suffering, its universality and intensity? We need joy to stop our hearts from break-ing. Another Christian term for compassion is *misericord*: which literally means 'having a heart sensitive to misfortune'. Its proactive dimension is also a fundamental element: compassion cannot be simply an emotion or an intention. It must take the form of action. This is what we call good-ness, or kindness: the desire quietly to make things better for someone, without any kind of ostentation; the wish to spare them unnecessary pain, or at least to ease it; this message of simple affection and cheerful respect for other humans.

Compassion is always disinterested, it is not – ever – an investment in expectation of some kind of return. If that were the case it would end up, sooner or later, leading to bitterness or resentment. Total disinterested-ness, with no other expectation than the feeling of having done the right thing, of being at peace, of having done our 'duty as a human being', according to Marcus Aurelius.

But we have suffering and abuses in ourselves. Which is why we also need self-compassion, to be compassionate towards ourselves. Why add to the sufferings life brings us? Compassion means wanting the best for *all* humans, ourselves included.

Lack of compassion for ourselves (and its impact on our feelings)

Lack of self-compassion is a great source of suffering, since it adds to the problems already present in our everyday lives. Moreover, this lack of self-compassion is often associated with feelings of self-resentment, of shame and guilt which in turn cause a sort of 'suppuration of suffering': the absence of compassion hinders the process of repair and healing of our psychological wounds, because we do not offer ourselves any comfort, but also because we do not accept comfort from others. These auto-aggressive feelings also prevent the passage of time from having a soothing influence, for they keep making us return to supposed failures or omissions from the past, endlessly reminding us of what is wrong with us. They prevent us from recognizing, accepting and respecting our suffering.

This can take the form of attacks of self-criticism; the violent *self-attacks* which we see in so many psychological problems,[3] in the guise of an insidious and constant self-persecution – thinly disguised as objectivity and fact: blaming and denigrating yourself, running yourself down over the slightest incident. 'I start off being annoyed with myself, feeling responsible, guilty, pathetic; then once I have calmed down, I try to think about it more carefully; more often than not I continue finding things to reproach myself with, but a little less violently, whereas at the beginning I would be ready to do myself harm or to jump out of a window.'

In cases like these, specific sessions on self-compassion are necessary in psychotherapy, and these generally prove effective.[4] In fact, these *self-attacks*, whatever their intensity, represent mental habits of aggression and self-depreciation which assert themselves in us automatically.[5] The notion of habit applies not only to our behaviour but also to our thoughts and feelings. A mental habit has four characteristics: it is automatic, it is repeated, it happens without our realizing it – at least initially (we do not see them, or are no longer aware of them, or notice them too late when they have already become established) – and it has an impact on us (our feelings and our behaviour). As a result, if we are to lose the habit of self-criticism, we need to work hard to root out these reflexes; first of all to weaken them, and then, with the help of time, to hope they will disappear as a result of no longer being summoned. The first stage in this task is to develop a regular awareness of the existence of negative thoughts: the more they pass unnoticed, the greater their impact will be. And, when they are painful, we are more inclined to want to run away from them, thus allowing them complete freedom to act.

These self-deprecatory habits can of course be rooted in our past,[6] but they can also occur after an episode of depression, and in such cases should not be under-estimated. A study carried out amongst adolescents suffering from depression showed, for example, that those who had the highest level of self-deprecatory thoughts when they were experiencing dysphoric feelings – in other words, whenever they were feeling down – were most likely to experience chronic depression.[7] These habits persist even after the depression is cured, like the 'depressive scars' in adults who have previously suffered depression: when describing a recent dysphoric experience, people who had experienced depression had more self-deprecatory thoughts than those who had never suffered from depression. And this, even where levels of dysphoria were identical: in spite of appearances, not all fits of the blues are the same. Those experienced by people previously affected by depression were more likely to contain the seeds of self-loathing, that accumulation of negative feelings about the self which is central to depressive suffering, prolonging it and causing recurrences.[8]

The deficit of self-compassion also exists in all of us when we experience certain forms of sadness: in moods of guilt or remorse for example. Long before psychiatrists, philosophers had identified this phenomenon. Montaigne wrote: 'Of all our infirmities, the most savage is to despise our being.' And long before that, our beloved and mysterious Lucretius had this to say: 'Each man is running from himself, yet still / Because he clings to that same self, although against his will, / And clearly can't escape from it, he loathes it.'

I remember the strange dream described to me by a patient who was in fact making progress in terms of self-compassion. He was better, but this dream was backward-looking in terms of his psychological reality. Instead of being premonitory, it was *post-monitory*. A haunting dream, harking back to past events like a scar. I should point out for the benefit of my compassionate readers that, in spite of this dream, he did not suffer a relapse.

> It was a dream in which I was in a desperate state, rolling on the ground, trying to do myself harm. But not even managing to do so. Which made me feel even more desperate because, in the dream, I felt that I deserved these blows, and that I absolutely must inflict them on myself. I kept telling myself: you deserve it, you deserve it! And I tried to hit myself, harder and harder, to really hurt myself. I was determined to hurt myself. So there I was, tossing and turning, kicking out violently in the bed, until I ended up waking myself up and was left feeling totally puzzled by the whole thing. It wasn't a nightmare: I didn't feel any terror, I wasn't sweating, and my heart wasn't pounding. It was a chill sort of dream, where the dominant theme was: hurt yourself, you deserve it. And yet I hadn't done anyone any harm recently!

Do not inflict harm on yourself. Ever. Life will take care of that . . .

You must have compassion for yourself

Be compassionate with yourself.

Self-compassion means being attentive to your sufferings (instead of ignoring them), looking for ways of easing them (instead of seeking to punish yourself or make things worse), showing yourself kindness and understanding (instead of being distant, hard, scornful or violent).

What is self-compassion based on? It is simply about considering it normal to look after ourselves; about understanding that what happens to us and what we feel is a universally shared human experience (so it is pointless to blame ourselves or to punish ourselves); about learning to accept failures and problems (not judging ourselves too quickly, not over-identifying with our problems and with the shifts in our feelings).

It is clearly associated with equanimity (*even-mindedness*): a number of studies show that treating ourselves kindly is generally extremely good for our psychological well-being.[9] It also plays an important role in resilience, the capacity to rediscover a taste for life after violence and difficult times. In the long term, in other words, in the context of real lives and not just in psychology laboratories, this element is a decisive one: self-compassion simply enables us to make regular self-repairs in the face of adversity, because we are its ally rather than its enemy and its persecutor.[10]

It is undeniably implicated in the successful treatment of certain depressions, when patients stop persecuting themselves, notably by no longer comparing themselves to other people. At this point in their recovery, they progress from a vulnerable state of preoccupation: the restoration of self-esteem (convincing themselves that they are not inferior to others), to a secure stage, that of self-compassion (the realization that all this talk about being better or worse than others is of no importance and that we just need to concentrate on looking after ourselves until we are ready to start looking after others once again[11]).

When studied closely, the capacity for self-compassion generally means putting less emphasis on failure (which is logical), but also on success: in their lives, some people seem to have given priority to distancing themselves from pressure and criticism and are determined not to get upset because they have lost out in certain competitive social situations.

Certain patients are uncomfortable when we talk to them about showing compassion to themselves: 'Is there not a risk that it would involve an abdication of responsibility, and a self-complacent or self-pitying attitude?' This seems not to be the case. Indeed it appears to be perfectly compatible with a good psycho-social adaptation and a good level of functioning.[12] And on the contrary, self-compassion generally brings with it a greater sense of personal responsibility (we take responsibility for any problems there may be, instead of suppressing or denying them) but without at the same time becoming overwhelmed by guilt.[13]

Concepts close to self-compassion

Patients who find it difficult to understand self-compassion can be forgiven: it is not necessarily a concept our minds are familiar with. However, it bears resemblance to a number of other concepts.[14]

Self-esteem: 'I have value and skills.'

There are both similarities and differences between self-compassion and self-esteem.[15] Self-compassion focuses more on comforting and respecting yourself as a person than on performance and social recognition. On the sense of belonging and of being connected with others ('We all suffer from the same wounds in the same way') rather than that of difference ('We are all trying to make a place for ourselves'). But rather than comparing them, we can simply regard self-compassion as a major element of good self-esteem. Stable self-esteem, which is what we should be aiming for, is also self-compassionate,[16] since this stability can only be achieved through self-compassion: it depends on the way we console and encourage ourselves after failures and difficulties. Without this kindliness, we would be more inclined, on any subsequent occasions, to try to avoid the pain of another failure by running away. If we have consoled ourselves, it will be easier for us to try again, bearing in mind what we have learned from the experience.

A high level of self-esteem but one which lacks this self-compassionate element will not offer such effective protection from the risk of depression: in the context of major adversity, all the forces that drive us to perform could instead become self-destructive ones. A number of studies have demonstrated that instability of self-esteem, rather than its level, is a stronger predictor of subsequent risk of depression.[17] And self-compassion is a very good way of stabilizing the ego. Moreover, studies also show that being accepted for what we are proves to be much more beneficial in terms of self-esteem than being accepted for what we have *done* and what we have *succeeded in*.[18]

Self-acceptance: 'Even imperfect, and even if I were worse than I am, I deserve to exist and to be loved.'

Self-acceptance is probably closer to the idea of self-compassion: it is about having a calm relationship with yourself, embracing all the characteristics of your personality, both 'positive' and 'negative' ones. It means seeking to accept yourself for what you are, in a kindly way. And when you see something you wish to change about yourself, doing it without violence, patiently: you are able constantly to embrace your difficulties, your slowness to change, because you know (there again through the feeling of belonging to the human race) that change is difficult. But this kindliness towards ourselves allows us to save our energy for the efforts involved in change, rather than wasting it on pointless and painful anger against ourselves.

Self-compassion: 'I don't have to be hard on myself when I am suffering, or punish myself when I fail. At such times I deserve attention and sympathy like all human beings.'

Compassion always distances itself from any notion of judgement, whether we still rely on it, as in self-esteem, or whether we are beginning to free ourselves from it, as in self-acceptance. It prefers a more 'caring' approach in the sense that it seeks to reduce our pain and desires our good. Only compassion is capable of avoiding veering into guilt (the sense of having done something bad: judging our behaviour) and shame (the sense of being contemptible: judging ourselves in general). It does not rule out guilt or shame completely, but only when these are in excess: self-compassion allows us to accept the wound, as a sort of reminder, and encourages us to examine it closely, to see what can be done.

Compassion and self-compassion

Are there links between self-compassion and compassion?

Exceptional individuals remind us, and demonstrate through their own lives, that compassion is even more important than self-compassion, and is its source. Etty Hillesum, for example, says 'I keep discovering there is no causal connection between people's behaviour and the love you feel for them. Love for one's fellow man is like an elemental prayer which helps you live.'[19] Compassion which *helps us live* . . . It is no coincidence that it is to be found at the heart of all the major religions. St Augustine wrote, 'If charity is missing, what is the good of all the rest?'

Indeed, peace of mind needs compassion, otherwise it is merely detachment. For what purpose? But, conversely, compassion needs equanimity, because otherwise it will simply bring too much pain. For most ordinary humans, long-term compassion, as opposed to occasional or exceptional forms of it, requires a minimum of personal well-being: too much suffering renders us incapable of compassion. Excessive and uncontrolled personal suffering therefore tends to result in people distancing themselves ('I am too vulnerable, I'm already in enough trouble myself, I already have too many worries of my own, I can't even manage as it is') or resentment ('they don't deserve my compassion'). Studies have looked at what happens in the case of hostile feelings: anger tends to make us judge people more negatively, whereas sadness makes us judge situations in a more negative light.[20] There is also evidence that depression leads to a deficit of compassion.[21] If we have too much sadness in us, it will clearly be difficult to feel the joy and the energy needed for compassion.

Obviously these two steps, the quest for inner peace and that for compassion, should not be opposed to each other, and should, on the contrary, be managed in unison. It is not a case of compassion – caring for others – on the one side, and self-compassion – caring for yourself – on the other. In reality, compassion also involves taking care of ourselves. And self-compassion to some extent means taking care of others, who, in the future, will need us.

Stories of compassion

In his last sermon, given at Memphis on the eve of his assassination, Martin Luther King referred to the parable of the Good Samaritan, the story of the man who stopped on the road to Jericho to take care of a stranger, the victim of an attack by robbers, after two other passers-by had ignored him:

> That's a dangerous road. In the days of Jesus it came to be known as the 'Bloody Pass.' And you know, it's possible that the priest and the Levite looked over at that man on the ground and wondered if the robbers were still around. Or it's possible that they felt that the man on the ground was merely faking. And he was acting like he had been robbed and hurt, in order to trick them, to set them up so he could grab them more easily. And so the first question that the Levite asked might have been: 'If I stop to help this man, what will happen to me?' But then the Good Samaritan came by. And he reversed the question: 'If I do not stop to help this man, what will happen to him?'[22]

That says it all: when faced with a challenge, to whom do my thoughts turn?

The birth of compassion in children. My eldest daughter, Faustine, told me about her Latin teacher who is also a poet, and who publishes a poetry review.[23] Describing the difficulties the teacher has to keep it going (you do not need me to tell you that poetry reviews do not attract a huge readership), Faustine added, genuinely touched: 'The poor thing!' It was the first time I had seen her express compassion towards an adult outside the family. She was growing up.

Once day, I parked my scooter on a pavement in Paris, stupidly thinking: 'It won't bother anyone, pedestrians can get past easily.' I had only gone a few steps when I saw a blind woman almost trip over it, her white stick caught in one of the wheels. Deeply ashamed, I rushed over and offered to help her. She asked me to lead her to the nearest bus stop, at the end of the road. She could have asked me to take her anywhere whatsoever and I would have done it, so guilty did I feel. Then for a long time afterwards, I felt troubled, overwhelmed with feelings of sadness, of anger towards myself. These feelings certainly did their job: they got their painful message across, and imprinted it in my mind. I had understood. Now, whenever I park my scooter, even if it takes me a bit longer, I try to avoid parking it on the pavement, and if I do end up doing so (in Paris, it's not always easy), I always check: if a blind person needs to get past, can they do it without tripping over the bike?

I was taking my youngest daughter, Céleste, out to a little Japanese restaurant in our neighbourhood. In the street, an old lady was struggling to carry a heavy shopping bag. We offered to help her and accompanied her to the building where her flat was. On the way there, she told us about growing up in that neighbourhood, about how everything has changed, how she had lived on her own for many years now. Céleste listened to her with rapt attention. I could tell from her expression (and from the questions she asked over the next few days) that in those few moments she had understood what it meant to grow old. And why we should offer to help elderly ladies. There are times when I feel Céleste's compassion is excessive, or at least overwhelming. The minute I look slightly anxious or sad, she starts worrying: 'Are you OK, dad?' Sometimes I would prefer her to be a bit more self-centred, because I am worried she will suffer as a result. But I also know that her attitude will bring her more happiness than it does suffering. One day, Maya, a friend of hers, tore her brand new coat at school. She was worried and upset as her mother was very strict. So Céleste, aged nine, came up with a plan: she took the coat home so that her own mother could mend it that evening. She gave her coat to Maya so that she could say they had swapped coats at school: if her parents told her off because of that, it would still not be as bad as if she had come home with a torn coat.

A former patient of mine in Toulouse sent me an invitation to a private viewing (she is an artist). I could not attend as it was too far away and too complicated. But all afternoon, I felt slightly bothered about it. I made myself stop to think carefully about what was going on. No, this did not feel like guilt. Then I understood: I had a very clear picture in my head and what was bothering me was the idea that not many people would turn up for the private viewing. Compassion tinged with sadness. But look here, old boy, I said to myself, your compassion is theoretical and pointless: she has lots of friends, she is an extrovert, there will surely be plenty of people, even if you cannot make it! In spite of that, I still sent her a little note.

Franz Kafka and his endless torments, compassionate to an almost obsessive degree. When his father, a rough and violent man, insulted and scolded his employees, it was Franz who felt compassion and remorse on his behalf: 'And even if I, insignificant creature that I am, had licked their feet, it would not have made up for the way in which you, the master, had berated them.'[24]

Yet another story about blindness. A young boy who was working as an instructor in a children's summer camp had a little blind girl in his group. On one occasion when they had gone on a walk to a beautiful place, he described the scenery for her, at her request. She was thrilled and asked him all sorts of questions, and he, forgetting himself, got quite carried away in his description of the beauty of the scene. Then, abruptly, silence: she stopped talking. He realized what had happened. He had done such a good job of trying to make her see through his eyes that he had ended up reminding her of the fact that she could not see for herself. In his desire to help, he had caused pain.[25] He had no reason to regret his actions: he was right to do what he did in describing the landscape and making it come alive for the little girl. And yet, sadness. Compassion.

My dear friend Alexandre Jollien, a tender-hearted and sharp-minded philosopher, told me the story of a man who was rescuing starfish stranded on the beach: a passer-by pointed out that his action would not do much good, given how many of them were stranded there. Putting a few of them back in the sea would not change anything. 'Yes, yes', the man answered, 'That's true. But for the ones I put back in the sea, for those, it changes everything.'

The impossibility for you from now on of causing prolonged or repeated harm except out of haste or clumsiness. The guilt as sadness at having made someone else suffer. The intolerable idea that someone, somewhere could have a grudge against you, because you have caused them harm; even a stranger; even a bastard. The very clear awareness of the absolute need to break the chain of suffering.

Compassion in practice

How can we bring about a gentler world without it being a feeble one which has given up any hope of changing and developing? Simply by cultivating compassion. The compassion we have described above: the acceptance that suffering exists, the desire to alleviate it in others and in ourselves, and the commitment to doing so in a state of contentment. Self-compassion and compassion for others call for the same efforts, and I have made no attempt to separate them in what follows. In my view, the two are extremely close and where this is not the case, they are still complementary, the one helping and preparing the ground for the other.

Show interest in the sufferings of our fellow humans even when all is going well for us

Happiness is a resource to be shared and redistributed, in order to bring more kindness and gentleness into this world in which opportunities for suffering abound. A large number of studies have shown that personal well-being, far from making people self-centred, naturally inclines them to want to help other people.[26]

Remember that suffering when things are going badly for us

Not in order to say: 'Don't complain, there are people worse off than you', but rather: 'Other people are going through exactly what you are facing.

And people have suffered in the same way in the past and will do in the future when you are no longer there. This suffering is shared and is part of our human condition.' Suffering is not eliminated, that is not the aim, but is as though diluted in something greater than we are.

When adversity strikes, do not seek to re-evaluate yourself but to console yourself

One study, amongst so many others, demonstrated this:[27] volunteers were asked to think about a recent unpleasant event which had affected their self-esteem (triggering feelings associated with a sense of failure, humiliation and rejection). They were then encouraged to restore their morale by focusing in one case on self-esteem and in the other on self-compassion. Those focusing on self-esteem were instructed to write a list of all their qualities and an explanation of why they were not entirely to blame for what had happened and why the event did not show them in their true light. In the second case, the group focusing on self-compassion, still in writing, were asked to emphasize the fact that the event in question was one that many others had experienced and come through, and then to write the sort of consoling comments that one might offer a friend, but addressed to themselves. In this note they were to distance themselves from the event by describing it in a detached and non-critical way. The results clearly showed that, when the event was subsequently referred to, the participants in the 'self-compassion' group experienced fewer negative feelings than those in the 'self-esteem' group. With moreover a small paradox: they felt better in spite of the fact that they had accepted greater responsibility for the event; clearly this result was not due to a survival mechanism such as denial ('It's nothing to do with me, it's not my fault, in any case it isn't really a problem, etc.'). Of course, there is nothing to prevent us using both strategies: consoling ourselves and boosting our self-image. But focusing simply on self-esteem only enables us to get ourselves back on our feet again ready for the next challenges; introducing an element of compassion as well is a reminder that we should always distance ourselves from the violent and dehumanizing aspect of all the challenges life brings, or that we sometimes think we see in it.

Experience compassion through gratitude

By being constantly attentive to the efforts others have made to enhance our lives. This is achieved through focusing on gratitude: when listening to music, think for example about Bach, who, instead of going fishing or for a longer walk with his children, sat down at his desk to compose all these metronomic wonders which, centuries later, bring us such pleasure. Rejoice in the fact that he existed, in the work he did. For compassion must also make us interested in other people, including those who are not suffering, and in their achievements. It must make us experience the joy of being human, and feel gratitude for those who have enabled us to experience this joy. The same is true when it comes to ourselves: we need to develop our self-compassion, recognizing and understanding our suffering, but also our awareness of all the good things, great and small, that we have done for other people. Awareness of the thousands of smiles, of words and of comforting gestures: the ones we were conscious of, and the ones, even greater in number and more wonderful, that happened without our realizing that they were doing someone, somewhere, good.

Cultivate kindness and tolerance

Looking in a favourable way at other humans creates space for compassion in ourselves: when someone irritates or disturbs us, before we react, or at least once we have done so, we need to remember to think about the damage or the weakness which provoked the behaviour we are now affected by. And then, tolerating other people's imperfections, understanding where they come from, will have a *boomerang* effect on our own imperfections, and on our capacity for self-compassion. But the most interesting and the most wonderful aspect of this mental gymnastics – 'understand before judging' – is that it makes our own lives more agreeable. Being astonished and even moved by the strangeness, excesses or inconsistencies of other human beings will enable us to live in a world which is less oppressive, more understandable and more accessible. This is one of the elements of wisdom, which we shall be referring to shortly. And, as always, none of this excuses us from taking action; it simply helps us act in a measured way. This is the essence of kindness: before we mock or criticize, we are moved. Then we can indeed mock afterwards, or judge, if we really must, if it has to be done. But it will be with tender humour rather than cruel irony. Judgement and not punishment.

Meditate on compassion

'To this end, Buddhist texts advise us to cultivate four particular thoughts or attitudes and to extend them to all beings, in every direction, without limit. These are altruistic love, compassion, joy in the happiness of others and equanimity.'[28] These four attitudes are intended to balance each other out. Altruistic love (wanting good for everyone) can be balanced by equanimity (this should not depend on our personal attachments, and should not only include those we love or those who have done us good). Joy in the happiness of others can be balanced by compassion: in order to avoid an unrealistic euphoria, think of the suffering those people have gone through or which awaits them in the future. And so on. Regular practice of meditation exercises on compassion and the attitudes associated with it allows these to be kept in our minds as living values. It also makes it easier to move from thought to deed. And finally it helps us feel better: these meditation exercises on compassion probably indirectly 'strengthen' the way positive emotions are activated.[29] Further research is currently being conducted to assess the value of approaches based on self-compassion in psychotherapy.[30] I feel reasonably confident about the results.

Have mantras for self-compassion

In Buddhist and Hindu traditions, the mantra is a very condensed phrase which is regularly repeated until the speaker becomes immersed in it. The word comes from Sanskrit and roughly translates as 'tool for the protection of the mind' (*manas*, 'arm or tool of the mind', and *tra*, 'protection'). We can make use of personal mantras such as 'Take care of yourself', 'Don't harm yourself', 'There's no point in punishing yourself', 'No double punishment', 'Do what you need to do', 'Don't hate yourself.' Obviously there is a risk of such phrases seeming somewhat naive or rigid, but in practice, they can act as little automatic reminders whenever our inner demons fill our minds with contrasting phrases, 'self-destructive mantras': 'You're useless', 'It's a complete disaster', 'You'll never manage', 'You don't deserve it', etc. Having kept these little 'self-help' mantras in our minds during meditation sessions can also help to turn them into reflex responses available when we need them. This is not about turning into robots but is simply a way of reducing the impact of the other reflexes, imposed on us by our past, while we take the time to think calmly about what is happening. As far as I know, this approach has never been scientifically validated (or invalidated). However, a large number of my patients seem to have adopted it spontaneously: 'Now I have a little voice in my head telling me not to do myself harm.' Victor Hugo said the same thing in a more solemn way in his *Contemplations*: 'We are all followers / Of some profound word.'

Have available mantras of compassion for others too

As part of the same process, in order gradually to challenge our reflexes to judge or be aggressive, remind yourself: 'People do what they can', 'A violent person is someone who has problems or who is scared', 'Take a few deep breaths before you reply.' And for those close to you: 'This person loves you, even if they are behaving aggressively towards you.'

Introduce exercises to expand compassion progressively

It is easier at first to concentrate on being sensitive to the sufferings of people we love, then try to feel compassion for people we know, and finally to include people we do not know. In the same way, we can train ourselves to be compassionate towards people who are kind to us, then towards those who are neither especially kind nor especially unkind to us, then to those who have harmed us and who continue to do so. The aim of compassion is to spread as widely as possible. There is no point in trying to be a saint: feeling compassion is like forgiveness, which we have referred to earlier: it does not mean we have to accept everything. It is simply a question of understanding that our good, and that of the world, cannot be based on resentment and on a refusal to see the suffering around us. Not even the suffering of one single person, as Marcus Aurelius reminds us: 'A branch cut off from another branch to which it adhered, cannot but be separated from the whole tree; thus a man, disunited from any man with whom he was connected, has fallen off from the whole community.'[31]

Practise gestures of active kindness: comfort and consolation

During group therapy sessions like those run by our small team in the hospital where I work, I have always been struck by how sensitive the participating patients are to the compassion and kindness they receive: what touches and helps them most of all, and what they still talk about years later, is the atmosphere of understanding and compassion in the group work, the little words or gestures coming from those in the group or from the therapists which demonstrate respect for their sufferings and difficulties, but without any trace of pity, and in the context of encouraging them to action, which is the aim of our therapies (which I would define as humanist-behaviourist). Gentleness and kindness are powerful motors for lasting psychological change. Interiorizing these experiences of emotional sharing seems to me to be immensely restorative (in the case of past suffering) and energizing (for future efforts). It is not necessarily enough on its own, since other efforts will also be needed, but it is nevertheless inspiring: 'This gentleness is possible; I can seek it and create it in my life.' For a while, psychotherapy distanced itself from the notion of consolation, although in reality it cannot exist without it. Hence my dismay when, as a young psychiatrist, I discovered psychoanalysis and its rejection of involvement in any process of comfort and consolation. At that time, psychiatry had lost its way somewhat by borrowing the stance of neutrality, even if 'benevolent', from the context of psychoanalytical treatment (where it does indeed have its place). For those who are suffering, neutrality is interpreted as coldness. I therefore branched out into other approaches, determined that my work would in no sense resemble this line from Musset: 'You pity me without consoling me.' Consolation without pity: that seemed to me a preferable goal! Consolation is contained within compassion: we need energy and joy to console, and consoling implies encouraging some kind of action. But feeling sorry for someone seems to me to be more about pity, and pity does not generally urge people to change things.

Daily exercises in kindness

Cultivate gestures, or words or glances which do a little good. 'A little sweetness in a world of savages', in the words of an advertisement which appeared some years ago (for chocolate, if I remember correctly). When you are driving, stop at every pedestrian crossing as soon as there is a pedestrian in sight, even if you are in a hurry, even if they have stopped to let you pass. You will see them hesitate (a driver who stops when he or she doesn't have to!) and often make a little sign of thanks as they cross. There is nothing very complicated about it.[32] Or you could decide to give some money to *every* beggar you come across at least for a few days each month. Just give it a try, you will see, it need not cost you very much. See how it feels to do away with feelings of hesitation ('Should I give something? Or not? Why this one rather than someone else?'). Or of guilt ('I should have given him something'). See what it feels like to look someone in the eyes as you give, to smile, to show you are glad to be giving, instead of giving without making eye contact, begrudgingly. A minuscule gesture, in the light of all the misery in the world? Yes indeed. Like this image from a poem by André Breton: 'A star, nothing but a star / lost in the night's fur cloak.'

The ecology of compassion

Today, humans are slowly acquiring an ecological conscience towards the planet: the smallest plastic bag we throw away is harmful; and the smallest discarded bag we pick up is good, even on a microscopic scale. Being careful in this way is not particularly demanding, nor is it a heavy responsibility to bear, particularly given the immense benefits it brings to us all.

The same argument applies to developing a universal compassionate conscience too: we are responsible for the spread of compassion, kindness and gentleness, through our everyday behaviour. We are each of us responsible for the human climate which reigns on this earth. Compassion and self-compassion make for better societies. One reason for this is that they deactivate the urge for domination and differentiation, and put the individual back in a fraternal and non-hierarchical perspective, based on similarity and collaboration between individuals, rather than domination and competition. Compassion is a tool for equality and fraternity.[33]

And finally, compassion is the universal remedy for all our injuries, which are all essentially injuries or disappointments associated with love or relationships. All our sorrows are the sorrows of love, with a large *L* or a small *l*. And the only effective remedies are – also – the remedies of love. That is why Thoreau wrote in his journal: 'There is no remedy for love, but to love more.' Love more, not necessarily the same person. In spite of all our disappointments and sufferings, we should never give up on love or stop wanting to love. Yes, there is indeed only one cure for love: to love more.

Tirelessly.

Chapter 16

Happiness

Too many speeches on happiness
Brothers and sisters,
Too many maxims
And too many rhymes
Contradicting each other
It is only in heaven! – No, on earth!
So I have decided
To do without them.
                    (Quotations, not happiness)

At the end of his masterpiece, the long philosophical poem *On the Nature of Things*, Lucretius tackles the question of death and the necessity of accepting that we must give up everything which has made us happy in this life: "'No more happy welcome-home, no waiting wife to miss you, / No pitter-patter of little feet as children race to kiss you, / Touching your heart with wordless tenderness. Alas, no more / Can you provide for them, you can't keep danger from their door. / Unlucky man! One dark day snatched these joys of life from you," they cry.'[1]

This image of the Roman father, dressed in his toga and returning home, delighted to see his children running to greet him and to be reunited with his wife, has tranquilly endured for many centuries. Such is its power that I am still deeply moved by it each time I read it. The scene goes back more than two thousand years, but the happiness and the feelings it evokes are ones we still feel today. And in those few lines, as usual, Lucretius says it all and makes us feel it all: the eternal aspiration of all humans towards happiness, its tragic and poignant nature, its fragile beauty. And, because of all that, its absolute necessity.

It only remains for us to reflect on the legacy of Lucretius: let us think about the master's words.

What is happiness?

Happiness is 'feelings of joy and pleasure mingled in varying degrees, the full satisfaction of the deepest desire'. Let us examine some of the components of happiness in more detail.

Satisfaction, of course, because happiness has a hedonistic dimension, linked to the satisfaction of our desires and needs. Hedonism, in which pleasure is the supreme good, is embodied in this saying by Chamfort: 'Enjoy and give pleasure, without doing harm to yourself or to anyone else. That I think is the whole of morality.' His phrase reminds us that happiness is based on a multitude of small satisfactions with life, those anonymous 'little pleasures', none of which would be 'memorable' in isolation, but without which a happy life would be an impossibility. An ability to welcome these micro-moments of happiness is the indispensable base for our general happiness. This is not, however, enough.

There is also the sense of *plenitude* or *fulfilment*. Happiness is the goal of all human endeavour: when we want to be loved, to excel, progress, to enrich ourselves, it is because we think and hope that this will make us happy. We suppose that this will at last enable us to achieve that restful sense of plenitude in which we will no longer aspire to anything except living and savouring the present moment. This dimension of fulfilment is important: it reminds us that there is nothing more important than happiness, that it needs to be placed at the very pinnacle of what we should respect, aspire to and pass on to others. We experience that sense of fulfilment when we feel happy, through the feelings of harmony and the sense of belonging which envelop us at such times. Pain isolates and drains us. Happiness links us to others and makes us feel fulfilled.

Finally there is *awareness*. For we can spend our entire lives missing out on happiness. Not because the requisite conditions are missing from our lives, but because aspiring to happiness implies being conscious of happy moments when they occur. Conscious both of their existence and of their significance. Without that awareness we will only experience lost happiness, happiness after the event, as in Raymond Radiguet's poem 'Les adieux du coq': 'Happiness, I only realized it was you by the sound you made as you were leaving.' Being conscious of happiness is what enables it to transcend well-being: it raises our sense of well-being (feeling relaxed, calm, enjoying wonderful things) towards something on an even higher plane.

But this consciousness, which enables us to experience the plenitude of happiness, and allows us to feel the brief intimations of immortality that it brings, is also what makes us aware of its transient and therefore tragic quality. And consequently we are caught between the extremes of happiness, with on the one hand its trivial, even sometimes slightly foolish character, arising from its tenderness and simplicity, and on the other its awe-inspiring, intimidating and grandiose nature in bringing us face to face with the essence of life and death.

Between the grandiose and the minuscule, I have chosen, in the course of the following pages, to approach happiness through the apparently trivial channels of smiles and feelings. This is where we see it in its most human form. And where it is closer and most accessible to us, where it is most apt to help us change. Which is, after all, our aim, is it not?

Feelings of happiness and the meaning of life

Most research on what it means to have a happy life shows that this sentiment is more closely associated with frequent and repeated small-scale experiences of happiness, with snatches of 'little' moments of happiness, rather than with major emotional experiences and intense moments of joy.[2] It is the weaving together of all those agreeable little moments which form the fabric of our happiness: moments spent with someone close to us, a walk in a beautiful setting, stimulating reading, music which moves us . . .

Many different feelings are associated with happiness: elation, light-heartedness, confidence, strength, harmony, fulfilment, inner peace, serenity; the sense of belonging, of belonging to a brotherhood, and all the feelings associated with relationships with other people. Happiness is rather like an Impressionist painting: all these positive feelings are minuscule brush-strokes, but there are also, as we shall see, the darker strokes of negative feelings, which mean that the end result is not just a rosy haze after all. Indeed it is *never* a rosy haze, in real life at any rate. The Romantic poets are there to remind us of this, as in these lines from Chateaubriand:[3] 'Dances begin in the dust of the dead, and tombs open beneath the footsteps of joy.' Again that proximity between happiness and tragedy: there can be no enduring happiness which is unconscious or carefree.

Which is why there are limits to the notion that happiness can be seen as an accumulation and a repetition of pleasures. We must also see happiness as the result of a life full of meaning. These two approaches complement and reinforce each other, and even more importantly, are mutually necessary. Happiness depends on happy moments, but it is more than just that: it is also about the integration of these happy moments into a vision of our lives which brings it meaning. However, except in exceptional cases, the construction of a life full of meaning requires energy, perseverance and confidence. Where else can we get this impetus and this perseverance, except from the pleasure of existing, from these positive feelings which, as we have seen, help us to have a unifying vision of all the moments of our lives?

This is what science demonstrates today: positive feelings facilitate the sense of personal coherence, and help us to make sense of our lives. Thanks to positive feelings, we are able to see the whole forest rather than just isolated trees.[4] And we are also able to hear the forest growing and not just the falling tree. Studies which compare the frequency of positive feelings and the experience of meaning in life conclude that a close link exists between the two:[5] one of the best predictors of our sense that our lives have meaning at any given moment is the presence, at the time the question is being asked, of positive feelings.

Moreover, when we are confronted with a task, our positive feelings enable us to distinguish more clearly what is meaningful from what is not, by giving us heightened pleasure when the task is meaningful, but a sense of perplexity when it is not; where negative feelings would leave us less disheartened by a meaningless task. In an experiment on this issue,[6] volunteers were asked to read a spiritual text and were asked either to reflect on the significance of the text (meaningful task) or to count the number of times a particular diphthong featured in the text (relatively meaningless task). The mood they were in affected their judgement of the tasks: the more positive this was, the more acutely they were aware of the presence or absence of meaning. Being in a good mood does not make people less intelligent, but appears instead to give us an enhanced and discriminating opinion on what is important in our lives.

Alongside these studies emphasizing the important role positive feelings play in giving us the sense that our lives have meaning, there is also, conversely, research demonstrating that giving meaning to one's life is an important tool for personal stability, especially in adversity, and that it enables us to return to normal more quickly after difficult events.[7]

But, as promised, let us leave aside the big questions and instead return to the minuscule ones.

Minor details, or not so minor?

Take the class photo: remember, all of you grouped together, on two or three rows of benches with the teacher in the middle of the front row; the photographer tells us to smile, and there it is! A souvenir of our younger days! A slightly yellowing photo, in which some people are smiling, others not. Could those smiling adolescent faces be an indicator of happier adult lives? Curious as it first seems, this was exactly the question asked by a team of researchers.[8]

In one of the many 'cohort follow-up' studies popular in America in the 1950s and 1960s, researchers set out to compare the facial expressions in a class photo with the subsequent life outcomes those in the photo would experience. An odd idea indeed! How, in the space of a split second, as the camera shutter clicks, could the expression on our face be an indication of what the rest of our lives would hold? But no question is too odd for science.

Using their year-book photos, taken between 1958 and 1960, 141 female students aged about 20 at the time were followed up over a period of thirty years, at the ages of 27, 43 and 52. The researchers were surprised to discover that those who smiled most on the photo (the decoding system was a strict one carried out by external observers who did not know the young girls in the photo) turned out to be those who (1) according to their responses to questionnaires at the time the photos were taken had the lowest scores in terms of negative emotions when the photo was taken; (2) years later were the most often happily married, and living what they perceived to be happy lives.

Puzzled by these findings, the researchers set about checking that there had not been error or distortion: for example, whether there was a link between the desire to please or to make a good impression (what is called 'social desirability) or with physical appearance (which might make a face more attractive and therefore appear to be smiling more than was really the case). But no, the smile on the photo was simply a reasonably effective indicator of the subsequent capacity for happiness of the young girls in the photograph. On average, at any rate: of course some of the grumpy ones ended up happy, and some of the smiling ones unhappy. But taken together, the smile was more than just the expression of momentary feeling: it reflected a lasting attitude.

I remember my own reactions to this study. Initially perplexed, I checked which university they had attended. Ah, Berkeley! So at first I thought to myself, these Americans must be kidding! Californians, into the bargain, whose obsessive smiling even irritates other Americans, like the New Yorker Woody Allen. Then, anxiety: I started to think (desperately trying to remember my own class photo) that it was pretty depressing for the ones who were not smiling. Then finally, a note of exhilaration: come on, smiling is easy enough! If it is really that important, surely that has to be good news. Try it, right now: see how easy it is!

In the end, it is all more logical than it seems: the smile on the class photo is associated with feeling good, both in general and at that particular moment (being happy to be there rather than in the classroom!), and also with the capacity to smile in social contexts, and with wanting to make a good impression. As there is also the notion of facial feedback, which we shall be examining shortly (smiling puts us in a better mood than sulking), and the fact that smiling makes us more popular, we can quickly see that gradually what seems to be a mere detail can acquire importance over a period of years. A detail which ends up being extremely significant. Smiling attracts (without guaranteeing them) good things, or at least better things than not smiling. It is therefore as simple as that. Just as walking puts us in a better mood than not walking (again without guarantees). There are plenty of other little things too. So, the smile is not just a *marker* which indicates we are feeling good, it is also an *inductor*, making us feel good, or at least somewhat better.

It is important to point out that the study only focused on female students. Generally speaking, girls have relatively stable facial expressions: if they tend to smile easily anyway, that will be reflected in the class photos year after year, whereas boys' expressions usually vary more over a period of time. For my part (I am sure you will do the same), I went and looked at those photos: my expression varied considerably over the years, from the photos where I looked serious to those where I was clowning around; but I often had a slightly worried smile. And when all is said and done, that is a fairly close indicator of my feelings about life: smiles and anxieties!

Be that as it may, other studies have been carried out to look at what photos of young men could tell us about their future, particularly in terms of future leadership qualities. And the results showed the exact opposite: the less the males smiled, the more chance there was that they would be leaders in the future. This was particularly striking in a study conducted in the most prestigious military school in the United States: at West Point, you are more likely to be promoted and to have more children if you refrain from laughing in your class photo![9] Of course, being a military leader and fathering lots of children may not be everyone's life goal, but it is still an interesting piece of research nevertheless.

All of this also throws light, at the same time, on our social stereotypes: in the 1950s and 1960s, we were interested in knowing if women would be happily married and if men would be leaders. But does this sexism not still exist today? Happiness is for women, honour for men.

Smile and grit your teeth

We referred above to a phenomenon familiar to those specializing in emotions: *facial feedback*, which means that the act of smiling slightly increases our positive feelings.

This means that the little photocopied message seen in so many offices and reception areas, 'Smiling uses fifteen muscles but sulking requires forty. Give yourselves a rest: smile!', is based on well-researched neuropsychological data. In my view, carrying out studies like this on the impact of smiling on our feelings is what science should be about: motivated more by curiosity ('what if there was something in it?') than by any desire to censor or judge *a priori* ('too ridiculous to be true!').

The most entertaining studies of this sort involve volunteers watching cartoons with a pencil clamped either between their teeth (try it: you will find that it forces you to pull a face resembling a smile) or between their lips (the grimace turns into a sad expression). The images seen whilst smiling, even in a somewhat forced way, are deemed to be funnier than those seen with the corners of the mouth turned down.[10] Life is sweeter when we are smiling than when we are scowling.

In the light of these studies, we can see more clearly how 'being sulky' can be an active act of defence: it is not that we *cannot* feel in a good mood, more that, on some occasions, we do not *want* to be in one. Because that is not how we want to see life: it *ought to* be sad. Because we want to punish other people: by showing them that what they have done to us will stop us enjoying our lives. Or else because we want to show that we are in charge, a leader, a dominant individual (remember the research on the class photos of young men): because we have so many responsibilities and worries, we adopt the serious mask of the *person-who-has-lots-of-responsi-bilities*, in contrast with the smiling faces of the carefree and irresponsible.

It is worth noting, moreover, that in this context our feelings are closely linked to what is going on in our bodies. Following on from these studies, the same team asked volunteers to assess how satisfied they felt with their lives, using questionnaires which they had to fill in either in a standing position, leaning on a high desk (position of 'pride'), or forced to slump uncomfortably over a low table ('depressed' position): not surprisingly, the upright position produced most responses indicating satisfaction with life.[11] All these studies point to the conclusion that the way in which we inhabit our bodies has a real, even though moderate, effect on our moods. Even the way we breathe plays a role in our emotional equilibrium,[12] which is why, for patients suffering from anxiety and depression, it is important to include breathing exercises in treatments based on relaxation and meditation. And this also explains the importance oriental masters attached to the posture to be adopted during meditation exercises ('straight and dignified') and in daily life in general. Yes, it is indeed a reminder of our childhood, 'stand up straight and smile at the nice lady'. Except that this time, it is science speaking.

We must not ac-cen-tuate the positive!

Or at least, not all the time, not any old way.

I am obsessed by the psychology of happiness. As a psychiatrist: it is an interesting tool for the prevention of relapses in my patients. And as a human being: I feel so much better when I am happy than when I am unhappy that the choice is easily made. But, generally speaking, I do not like slogans of the type 'We must think positively!' I never tell my patients to think positively, or certainly never like that. Even though, deep down, I think we probably do need to think positively and consider anyone already doing so to be in the right. But such injunctions to look on the bright side raise two questions: (1) if being positive means denying the existence of problems and of suffering, if it means refusing to allow them to exist in our lives, then the remedy is worse than the disease, as we have already seen; (2) it can sometimes be obscene to put it like that: 'Trying to get closer to happiness' seems a dignified and serious effort, compatible with grief and suffering, whereas 'thinking positive' seems to me to be a mission without dignity or realism.

So we should avoid trying to be positive in a blinkered and mechanical way. But, by the same token, we should not allow ourselves to sink into distress and to add to our sufferings by abdicating responsibility for them. What should we do, then? Accept, feel, observe, and then, in spite of everything, smile.

'One mild and grey September morning, my doctor calls me to give me bad news about my blood tests – my condition is slowly deteriorating. He reassures me and, indeed, there is nothing to make me shriek with terror, I am not going to die imminently or even in the next few months, but nevertheless it feels as though some inexorable process is moving forwards. Different feelings come over me: sadness, anxiety about the future, disappointment (at every check-up, you hope for a small miracle). At first I abandon myself to a little period of rumination, which I quickly see is taking me round in circles and getting me nowhere. Next, comes the temptation to think about something else, to seek some kind of distraction. I try reading a magazine, doing a bit of work. But, not surprisingly, it fails to work. How can you manage to think of other things when you have just been reminded that you are mortal? So I sit myself down, I take some deep breaths, then I decide to go out for a walk, on my own, peacefully. To accept the bad news: "Whether you like it or not, that is the reality, there is no getting away from it." I focus on calming myself down, on my breathing, on concentrating on the present, on not judging my situation as awful or unfair, on not thinking about what might happen. Not now, not in the heat of the emotion. I am going to give consideration to what I can do. And I mean do: not imagine, brood over or fantasize about. I shall look for new information on the internet, prepare my list of questions for the specialist who is treating me. I shall remind myself that I am not the only person who is ill. In the meantime, I resolve to live well. To make sure my illness is no more than that: an illness. To make sure I am very much alive. And not just someone who is about to die, or someone locked in a living death of anxiety. In the end I even manage to smile, gently and peacefully. How strange this smile is, rising from within me like a hidden truth: what else is there to do except live and smile?'

Smile in your head

Another study on the role of the smile, both facial and mental.[13] Yes, you can smile *in your head*, and it can even be seen and measured.

In this study, volunteers are shown funny or sad films (to put them into a cheerful or sad mood). Then they are asked to speak for five minutes about all the positive or negative feelings they are currently experiencing in their lives, to someone who listens to them in silence but attentively and in a sympathetic way. During the session, which is filmed, the presence of smiles is recorded, as well as the quality of those smiles: 'true' or 'false'? In fact, the 'fake' smile is easily identified by researchers specializing in the expression of emotions: rigid, stiff, it has nothing to do with any inner state, or with anything other than the desire to play the game of social conventions. At the other end of the scale, the true smile (the so-called 'Duchenne smile', named after the French nineteenth-century neurologist, Duchenne de Boulogne, who discovered it, and who inspired some of

Darwin's work) affects the whole face and not just the mouth, and notably involves the periorbital muscles, which are virtually impossible to contract voluntarily in a symmetric fashion. It also corresponds to a specific cerebral state, which can be identified with the appropriate equipment.[14]

One year later, the volunteers who had expressed real smiles had a higher level of well-being and social integration. But that was only if they had smiled *sincerely* and *after the sad film*: the smiles after the funny film, whether true or false, did not have a predictive role on the person's psychological well-being one year later. This is logical: the capacity to smile even in sadness is the external indicator of deeper psychological capacities: preserving some element of gentleness and some capacity for happiness in yourself (these needed to be true smiles) in spite of feeling low. Whereas the smiles produced in response to a cheerful film, even if they are *genuine,* do not throw any light on our inner selves: they are simply the result of the circumstances.

It is likely that the effects of smiling can be explained by two mechanisms: an interpersonal effect (smiling brings more social advantages, and therefore boosts our well-being) and an intrapersonal effect (smiling also has an internal function and impact). We smile at life, at the mess we are in, at the future. And when we really smile, *à la Duchenne*, it is not only to neutralize our negative feelings, but also as a sign that we have taken on board the complexity of existence.

'I put on my good-mood mask', a patient told me. And he added, 'And some days, I manage to forget that it is only a mask, and the taste of my life approached in this way, a smile on my lips, gradually makes me feel better.' It was the philosopher Alain who wrote: 'Just as the strawberry tastes of strawberry, so life tastes of happiness.'[15] But to experience that taste, we have to open our mouths, by smiling. So, let's smile and take a bite.

'Smiling in the rain': more than just a pose or a meaningless slogan

During my partner's funeral, in spite of being in floods of tears, I kept trying to smile in my head. Not because I was trying to *cancel out* the pain, but as a way of *associating* it with happiness: I felt it was important, in the violent grip of sadness, to remember happy moments, to gently readjust my feelings, to enrich them. To focus them on the facts: on the joy of having shared so many happy moments with her, of knowing that she had had so much happiness in her life, of seeing all the people who loved her gathered here, not just to pay their respects but as a way of simply celebrating, once again, that she had shared happy times with these people.

We all know the song 'Singing in the rain'. In our lives there is no obligation actually to sing in the rain, but a bit of smiling might be not a bad thing: 'Smiling in the rain'! On condition, as we have already made clear, that it is not just an artificial pose, adopted for the sake of the audience, or just a facade, with no genuine feeling behind it. But rather, a sincere attitude, stemming from genuine feelings.

A beautiful and moving study,[16] conducted amongst recently widowed women (approximately six months after the death of their partners), found that those who managed to smile sincerely when remembering their dead partner would often turn out, two years later, to have coped better with their bereavement. Probably because, in spite of their sadness and the absence of the other person, they are able to remember beautiful things and happy moments. Here too, this protective element of the capacity to smile in spite of sadness only applies if the smile is genuine and corresponds to authentic feelings.[17]

This capacity to *smile from within* even in the violent grip of sorrow is intellectual rather than subconscious, contrary to what sad and pessimistic people like to think. But of course it needs to be a free choice, freely put into practice. Something that is triggered in response to a life event, even sometimes the result of a moment of awareness. Followed by regular practice in the context of everyday life: getting into the habit of smiling (or of being receptive to positive feelings) when confronted with minor problems, making an effort not to allow our anxieties to stop us appreciating beauty or enjoying good times with those close to us, forcing ourselves to extract moments of grace from the dull daily grind, no matter what our constraints and obligations may be (I am not even referring to anxieties or suffering).

> It was only by having children that I learned to cherish, in spite of all the little obstacles and delays, the five minutes my son spent playing the piano, every morning just before leaving for school. He had got into the habit of playing through the little tunes he learned in his lessons, while waiting until I was ready to take him to school. And I slowly began to realize how precious those moments were and to understand that they were unique, moving and short-lived (and indeed by the following year he had got fed up with the piano and had stopped playing). Gradually I got into the habit of sitting down somewhere out of sight and listening with a smile in my head, but without letting him necessarily be aware of what I was doing: I didn't want to transform these moments into mini concerts where he would have had to show off his talents or entertain me.

Finally, let us remember that positive feelings, whether associated with a smile or not, are not only agreeable and necessary in terms of giving meaning to our lives, but also serve to limit the effects of stress and negative feelings.[18] For example, when volunteers who had been put in disagreeable situations were shown a funny or enjoyable film, their cardiac rhythm returned to normal more rapidly than if they were shown a sad or neutral film.[19] It seems that so called *resilient* subjects are particularly good at doing this, seeking out restorative experiences after encountering problems.[20] This may seem logical enough but is in fact a useful strategy for regulating feelings: when faced with difficulties people are often inclined to withdraw into themselves and to stop seeking any gratification from their surroundings.

This point about resilient subjects is an important one: positive feelings are not there to *cancel out* worries, or to blind us to them ('life is *only* beautiful'), but to give us the strength to cope with them when they come along, or to recover afterwards. As we have seen from the research on happiness, the importance of these small-scale pleasant feelings, repeatedly scattered throughout our daily lives, turns out to be greater than that of huge surges of joy occurring in isolation. And their effect is further reinforced, as we have seen, by an awareness of how necessary and significant they are.

The half-smile

When it is too hard to smile, we can try a half-smile . . .

The teaching of the Buddhist master Thich Nhat Hanh encourages the use of the 'half-smile': not in reality 'half a smile', but a discreet smile, at once both slight and profound, a facial expression which corresponds to a tranquil serenity and an acceptance of reality. When my Buddhist friends first told me about this half-smile I was somewhat incredulous (let us just say it made me smile myself, which was already a good thing). But in the end I understood that this was a genuine tool for inner homeostasis: 'I smile to myself out of kindness towards myself, to take good care of myself, to give myself love. I know that if I do not take care of myself, I will not be able to take care of others.'[21] The inspiration clearly comes from the smile of the Buddha, which can also be a source of perplexity, as Thich Nhat Hanh himself observed: 'In my novice days, I could not understand why the Buddha could have such a beautiful smile when there was so much suffering in the world. Was he not disturbed by that? Later I came to understand that the Buddha [. . .] was able to smile at suffering because he knew how to deal with it and transform it,'[22]

Just a half-smile to keep our melancholy, our anxieties, our resentments under control.

The right to be unhappy

Of course we have the right to be unhappy. Even more than a right, it is our destiny: misfortune and adversity are very much part of existence, and will inevitably find their way into our lives. But the insistence on a *right to unhappiness*, as though this were a fundamental freedom, is more surprising.

Indeed, when we say we prefer happiness and that we wish to encounter it more often, certain people feel threatened, as though they feel their *right to unhappiness* might be taken away.

At first, I found this irritating. Then I understood their anxiety: they were worried they would find themselves under some kind of 'obligation'. Their anxiety stemmed from the fear of being subject to a dominant ideology, or in democratic terms, what would quickly be referred to as a dictatorship; in this context, one of enforced smiles and happiness. Hence their imprecations against happiness, like those of the prophet Amos in the Bible, where the sixth verse begins with a resounding 'Woe to them that are at ease' and ends with 'and the banquet of them that stretched themselves shall be removed'.

In reality the danger lies less in a possible dictatorship and more in a real inequality.

For the expression of happiness and good humour seems to confer a distinct social advantage to smiling people over sullen ones. This is partly unfair, but partly morally justified: what about all the efforts smiling people have gone to in order not to trouble other people with their worries? Or in an attempt to remain open to happiness? And their sensitivity to others, not causing them to recoil from our scowling mask of sadness?

If, from time immemorial, the company of smiling faces has been preferred to that of sombre ones, there is good reason: they often 'contaminate' us, especially if the smiles are light and discreet, if they indicate a *receptive attitude* to happiness and to communication, rather than being put on for effect.

And contamination in the reverse direction also exists, hence the sense of isolation that gradually affects people who are morose and depressive. Studies on this subject demonstrate (1) that contact with sad people increases negative feelings in everyone, (2) that in addition, it has a negative effect on positive feelings in those who feel most 'connected' to other human beings.[23] Showing your sadness therefore causes everyone to suffer and stifles the joy of altruistic and compassionate individuals.

But let us go back to our first observations: is being unhappy, more than a right, not also a need? Are negative feelings essential to us?

> Every Monday morning, I go off to work feeling sad and anxious, and every Monday evening, I come back feeling relieved. The week has begun and I know I can cope with it. And strangely, those Monday evenings are perhaps the best evenings of the week, on a par with Fridays. As though the fact that I felt at my lowest that morning made the sense of relief even more precious.

In fact there is an additional reason for not suppressing or banning negative feelings: they serve to emphasize the positive ones. Moreover, it has been shown (and we are all familiar with this) that the higher the level of well-being, the less positive events actually contribute to it.[24] This is what I call the 'democracy and hot shower' effect. When we live in a democracy, voting is not as joyful as it would be if it were the first vote on emerging from a dictatorship. When we are used to having access to a hot shower every morning, we no longer shout for joy about it, unless the boiler has been out of action for an extended period. When we are used to living with a sense of well-being, the causes of our happiness become *commonplace*, the positive becomes *normal*. When that happens we need either to reactivate our awareness, and feel our inner happiness by making a conscious effort ('count your blessings each day'), or else be on the receiving end of a little dose of misfortune to recalibrate ourselves (on condition here too that we make the effort). Happiness – and this is definitely not poetic – obeys, in this sense, the same laws as money: the more we have, the less having *more* makes us happy. Whereas when we do not have very much (because we are poor or because we are a child) we would be delighted with a few tens of Euros more.

We can also regard this 'recalibration through adversity' as a useful health regime for our happiness. It would, for example, be in our interests, when we feel good, sometimes to go back over negative experiences from the past. Not to ruminate on them all over again, not to minimize them and therefore to mock ourselves (which might sometimes be a good thing), but in order to accept them, put them into perspective, examine them more closely, and reinterpret them in the light of our current joy. Then gently return to present happiness. In his book *Looking for Spinoza*, the neuroscientist Antonio Damasio reminds us that the philosopher advocated this kind of exercise for our general well-being: 'Spinoza recommends the mental rehearsing of negative emotional stimuli as a way to build a tolerance for negative emotions.'[25] If Spinoza says so, how can we ignore the advice of a genius?

Accepting happiness as a tragic experience

Human happiness is linked to a twofold and integral process of our consciousness. The first aspect of this process is concerned with well-being: happiness as a conscious sense of leading an agreeable existence, in favourable surroundings.

The second is concerned with death: we are all *morituri, those-who-will-die*, and even more importantly, we are conscious of our mortality. This happiness is therefore our antidote to the obsessive fear of death, since it offers us intimations of immortality, the sense of time stood still, stopped, even absent. But at the same time it is also a powerful and destabilizing message of transience: ultimately happiness fades and humans die. In one of his poems, Nietzsche wrote 'For all joy wants eternity – wants deep, wants deep eternity!'[26]

Happiness is therefore a 'tragic' sentiment in that it is associated with those moments when we become aware of a destiny or fate hanging over us. Tragedy means fully accepting the adversity that is part of the human condition: suffering and death. And happiness is the response to this tragic question: how can we live with that knowledge?

André Comte-Sponville wrote that 'tragedy is what resists reconciliation, finer feelings, blind or bleating optimism'.[27] Ouch! He goes on: 'It is life as it really is, without justification, without providence, without forgiveness.' All right, all right ... And finally he emphasizes: 'It is the feeling that reality can be taken or left, combined with the joyful willingness to take it.' Whew, we can breathe again. In another text he adds, 'As for those who claim that happiness does not exist, that only proves they have never been really unhappy. Those who have known unhappiness know all too well, by comparison, that happiness also exists.'[28] The pragmatics of happiness and unhappiness are experienced in the flesh.

Yes, life is tragic, the world is tragic. Yet we prefer to smile even so and to go on, with lucidity, than to remain frozen in a rictus, incapable of experiencing delight. Indeed, perhaps happiness is not tragic but simply *weighed down* by tragedy, and this ballast is what gives it its value, its savour, what serves to remind us of its pressing necessity. An English friend of mine told me that when her children were small, she regularly experienced hideous nightmares in which Nazi soldiers or barbarians burst into schools and massacred the children inside them; or broke into her home and killed both her and her family. She explained that at first this made her question the very notion of happiness because it introduced a feeling of guilt into her current happiness. Then, when she thought more about it and worked on it, she was able to integrate it into her happiness: the existence of horror did not mean she should not be happy, but simply added some more serious notes to the tone of her happiness, like an instrument on which the tuning has been altered.

Another philosopher, Clément Rosset, has this to say: 'All acquiescence to reality lies in this mixture of lucidity and joy, which is the tragic sentiment [. . .] sole dispenser of what is real, and sole dispenser of the strength capable of accepting it, which is joy.'[29] Aspiring to happiness in an enduring way, to a happiness which does not involve shutting ourselves away from the world in a gilded castle, or deadening our feelings with alcohol, drugs, video games or relentless work, means accepting the world in all its tragedy. Happiness is not a speculative bubble to withdraw into, based on the gamble of a universe made for happiness. Our knowledge of our feelings helps us to understand that: there can be no such thing as a perfectly regulated interiority, but simply a living one, where feelings associated with suffering emphasize the necessity of feelings of happiness.

Another reason for accepting this tragic dimension of happiness lies in its fragility and transient nature. When we become accustomed to a certain frequency of happy moments, we clearly suffer more if we are deprived of them. Happiness is like love: experiencing happiness fully and passionately lays us open to experiencing its disappearance in the same way. But such sad feelings are far more enriching than locking ourselves into defence mechanisms which would consist in taking the preventive action of never allowing ourselves to be carried away by happiness, of not making any effort to make it part of our lives. Coming after moments of joy, our feelings of sadness can be productive. But if they keep on coming, without the indispensable breathing space of happiness, they will more often prove to be sterile and destructive, urgently requiring new defence mechanisms (denial, cynicism, pessimism) or new means of escape (making ourselves insensible to problems by hiding behind something, such as certainties or drugs).

Sadness is therefore all the more powerful, its sting all the sharper, if we are happy. Sadness following in the wake of misfortune is less painful. As in the biblical parable of the rich man becoming poor, where the rich man is depicted as being more deserving of pity than the poor man who has known nothing else. This seems scandalous to us at first, but then is seen to follow a certain logic, relating to the nature of the suffering experienced, a suffering associated with a change in status, one of the forms of suffering traditionally recognized by Buddhism.[30] For example if we usually live on good terms with other people, any conflict with them will clearly cause greater immediate suffering. If we do not see them very often, or if our relationship with them is not very good, then our defence mechanisms will protect us from the suffering associated with the loss of a relationship. Inadequately, of course: we will still suffer and have unexplained mood swings, linked to the chronic lack of social bonds, sudden bouts of despair or world-weariness. The sadness felt after an argument is a healthy one: it is proof of our normal proximity to small happinesses. And, even more importantly, it is fruitful: it provides us with the motivation to restore happiness. Its absence ('we got angry with each other but I couldn't care less') indicates that two things are missing: sadness and happiness. It suggests a curbing of sensibility which is an illusory attempt to make us independent from an essential psychological need. The happier I feel, the less tolerant I am of conflict. But also the happier I am, the more strength I have to seek to resolve conflicts, to negotiate, to forgive, to apologize, to rebuild, rather than to run away from them.

A reader whom I respect and value highly, and with whom I was discussing this tragic dimension of our happiness, remarked (she attributed the saying to Alain) that very often in our lives we are only happy *in spite of* something: in spite of pain, of illness, of adversity . . . And she added: 'Positive psychology is certainly no simple matter!'

Accepting happiness as a fleeting experience: the subtle and poignant happiness of last times

This strange feeling that sadness is sometimes just a worn-out joy, a happiness which has had its day.

If we cling too tightly to it, our happiness can turn to sadness. We need to accept when it is time to move on, to abandon this now dead happiness. Accept that we will leave behind us the corpses of our moments of happiness, great or small. Accept that they will only survive in the form of memories. And learn not to cling too tightly to these specific memories, to these moments, but instead to the notion of happiness itself.

The intensity and the pain of happiness therefore lie in its transient nature. Our personal experience gives us evidence of this, but there is also a considerable amount of research. When, for example, a group of volunteers are asked to imagine they are in a place they love, but for the last time, their feelings will indeed be positive, but more subtle and mixed than those of other volunteers who were simply told to imagine themselves in such a place, but without any other instruction.[31] The richness and the subtlety of our emotional experience of happiness come less from the big, obvious forms of happiness (which may even sometimes be slightly 'foolish', basic, straightforward) than from the existence of these feelings associated with our awareness of the finite nature of our happiness, of its mortal and perishable nature. It is this awareness of the fleeting dimension of happiness which also allows the experience of the present moment to expand to broader temporal horizons: this is why a single moment of happiness can give us a taste of eternity.

This is also why being receptive and attentive to complex feelings is so crucial if we are to be able to experience more happiness, and of a more refined nature. It is a little like cultivating and developing taste: we would all be better off moving on from standardized tastes ('international' wines, predictable ready-made meals, chain restaurant cooking) to a greater diversity and more refined flavour. Long live 'green', complicated, mixed happiness, as opposed to industrial, clean, sterilized happiness!

Other studies show that, generally speaking, the more conscious we are that time is limited, even in a banal, non-dramatic way, such as in a laboratory experiment where we are asked to complete a task on a limited time scale, the more likely we are to seek out and prefer meaningful activities.[32] A good way of recycling our existential anxieties (and one we recommend to our patients): the more anxious I am, the more I need to focus on what really matters in my life, in order to do something about it, get closer to it, enjoy it in the present.

All that is of course linked to a heightened consciousness of the passing of time. As we get older (but, for some people, the phenomenon has always existed), we become more aware that certain forms of happiness will not come around again. For example, happiness associated with ageing parents, children growing up, or during the last years of school or university with friends we will soon be leaving behind.

In our lives there are many last times we are unaware of: the last time we see a certain friend, or place, or hear a certain voice. Such unawareness is fortuitous and makes things considerably easier for us. If we advanced through our lives obsessively asking ourselves the question 'Is this the last time I have done, or experienced, or seen that?', it would be unbearable. But when we reach a certain age, the inevitability of these 'last times' becomes more real: we can no longer ignore them. One of my patients spoke to me about her emotion at living through her *last* pregnancy, at cherishing the *last* child still at home. Another told me about her last great love affair as a *young* woman, 'before the menopause', because for her 'from then on it would be the love affairs of an old lady'.

Thus, as we advance in age, we begin to experience meetings, journeys or events which we know perfectly well will be the last ones. Does that necessarily condemn us to unhappiness?

Happiness and ageing: happiness as a way of understanding life and the statistics on the peak of happiness

When one of my uncles was approaching his eightieth birthday, he decided to do a series of farewell trips to see his 'lifelong friends': childhood friends, work colleagues, former neighbours, and of course cousins and relatives. He wanted to make the trips while he was fit enough to do the travelling involved and even more importantly while he could still enjoy them. When I asked him (cautiously, so as not to offend him) about the element of sadness that might underlie these reunions, this is what he had to say:

> Yes, it will also be very sad. But that sadness will be swept aside by the happiness of meeting up again, by sharing memories of good times, and also by the fact that these will be good moments in themselves, in the present, not just in the past. We are still alive, so there is still room for happiness and emotion. Indeed, I am already enjoying myself in advance just by planning the trips. For me, the passing of time makes me want to enjoy the time I have, and not to weep over the past.

The poignant happiness of these final times is undoubtedly amongst the most beautiful and complex I can personally imagine. And this is borne out by statisticians of the Insee, the French Office of National Statistics.[33] In a study based on the analysis of a series of opinion polls, these demonstrate that, for the majority of people, the sense of psychological well-being slowly declines from the age of 20, reaching a minimum level between 35 and 45 (the period when incomes are, however, generally at their highest), then gradually creeps up again, reaching its peak in our sixties.

Some people are surprised by these statistics. Yet, in reality, they make sense: in our present-day societies, we reach the age of 60 in good physical shape, with a guaranteed income (for the time being) thanks to the pensions regime, and without any of the anxieties and stress of the mid-life years (building up your career, trying to buy somewhere to live, taking

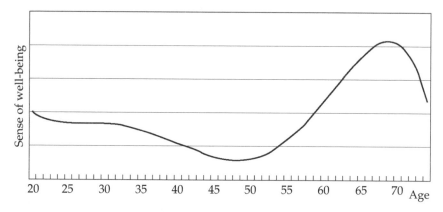

Changes in the sense of well-being throughout life
On average, an individual is significantly less happy between the ages of 45 and 50 than
around the age of 20, and considerably happier at around 65.
Field: metropolitan France
Source: Eurobarometer, 1975–2000

care of the children's education . . .). Plus by this stage, we are in a better position to know what makes us happy, as other studies have shown.

For example, one study found that, between the ages of 18 and 94, positive feelings do not decline with age.[34] It is important to point out that these data were obtained through *sampling* (that means long-term sampling), in which people's feelings and moods are assessed at regular intervals over a relatively long period; this approach is more reliable than a single, snapshot assessment, which is more susceptible to distortion from one-off, random life events. The capacity to experience happiness (in the moment) therefore remains comparable at different ages in life. But we also find that the periods of positive feelings are more likely to last longer in older people! Small-scale happinesses seem to become more stable with age.

As for negative feelings, these reach a peak in the middle years of life, compared to those experienced by younger and older people: this confirms the link, already referred to, between these negative feelings and existential stresses, which are particularly important at the time in our adult lives when we are trying to construct our everyday existence, our future and that of any children we might one day have.

Other studies show how ageing can increase our aptitude for happiness thanks to mechanisms similar to wisdom: for example, the ability to view the past as a sort of apprenticeship and ongoing training for the future. By doing so, we come close to the essence of the matter: it is not ageing itself that is fortunate, but the fact of having lived and lived to the full, with all the experiences involved and the opportunity to reflect on them, to enjoy them and be enriched by them.[35]

We also find that for many people, language use changes with age: we use more positive and fewer negative words, we refer to ourselves less and we use more verbs in the future than in the past.[36] We show a spontaneous and automatic preference for positive images and words as we get older and we remember them better: they stimulate our amygdala (the zones responsible for analysing emotional information) more powerfully than negative images or words.[37]

In short, the process of maturing and of ageing, which we are sadly so terrified of in an era where everyone wants to stay young at any price, brings with it a considerable potential for increasing our happiness. Why should we insist on 'staying young' at any price, as our society encourages us to do? We would do better just trying to stay in good working order and attaching more importance to becoming wise.

The drop in negative feelings ends, however, at around the age of 60, and they subsequently tend to increase gradually. This is when the problems specific to old age come into play, such as those associated with reduced physical capacities and with the approach of death, now no longer just an abstract notion but instead something made real to us by the increasingly frequent deaths of those close to us. At this stage, extra effort is needed if we are to continue to live happily.

Fortunately, our capacities to experience these subtle and multifaceted feelings and moods (like melancholy, the 'happiness of being sad', as Hugo called it) increase significantly with age.[38] This is considered to be the result of a useful psychological ability to accept life as it is, a complicated mixture of positive and negative, often even in the context of the same event or the same period.[39] So, for example, on an occasion such as the wedding of one of our children, or the moment they leave home, we see the coexistence of these dimensions of joy (seeing their destiny being realized) and of sadness (understanding that their future will now happen without us and perhaps far away from us).

Can we increase our capacity to feel happiness?

Heredity and the past are highly significant factors in terms of our aptitude for psychological well-being.[40] And when it comes to happiness, the same inequalities apply as for any other aspect of human existence (beauty, health, intelligence . . .). But, as with those inequalities, a certain amount of regular effort allows any discrepancies to be reduced considerably. Here too, the same things apply as in other areas: beauty is largely genetic, but this does not apply to charm; health is also a matter of genetics, but this can be compensated for by healthy behaviour; intelligence is also partly inherited, but the humility to work in order to do well is not.

The same is true of happiness, and analysis of the major scientific studies appears to show the following distribution: approximately 50 per cent of our aptitude for happiness depends not on ourselves but on our genetic make-up and our past; approximately 10 per cent is only

marginally influenced by us, since it is to do with the material environment in which we operate (democracy or dictatorship, grey, gloomy
country or sunny one, countryside or suburb . . .); but about 40 per cent is
the result of our regular efforts.[41] Which is not bad at all.

Moreover, the 50 per cent which is not, or no longer, influenced by us *a
priori* consists for the most part simply of tendencies acquired in the past,
like reflexes and automatic pilot systems which are triggered spontaneously. They are certainly powerful tendencies, but ones we can learn to
modulate. After all, as primates, we have inherited biological tendencies
to yell and lash out if anyone annoys us, or to just take something if we
want it: and most of us manage to control such tendencies most of the
time! In the same way, once the desire to harm someone, or to make ourselves miserable or to shun happiness, has begun to germinate in us (and
it can sometimes be difficult to prevent that happening), we then have
some room to manoeuvre so as to be able to disobey these 'orders' from
our past, even if, from the start, 'life has not always been kind to us'.[42]

Why this little detour into the genetics of happiness? The better to convince you not to be fatalistic in this context: we can always increase our
happiness.

Making ourselves happy: reasons and arguments

I once met a professor of happiness: in all seriousness, this psychology
colleague had the dream job of teaching the psychology of happiness to
students at Harvard.[43] Listening to one of his lectures, I was amused and
extremely interested by his use of the economic term *emotional bankruptcy*,
which reminds us that our human mind can fail just like a business. In
order to remain solvent, a business has to make profits: over the long
term, if not all the time, receipts need to be greater than outgoings. The
same is true of our minds: as long as pleasant feelings are more frequent
or more meaningful than negative ones, we will feel our lives are worth
living. When the opposite applies, things become more difficult.

Which is why, for those who want to maximize the 40 per cent of happiness which depends on them, it is worth working at it. We can decide
to *work* at our happiness. It is what Spinoza called 'seeking joy by order
of reason'.[44] And, contrary to what many people think or claim, many
changes can be made.[45] By the same token, the efforts required to drive
the changes are beneficial *in themselves*. It has, for example, been shown
that people who are involved in some form of personal development live
better and longer lives.[46] Our efforts to find happiness will in themselves
do us good. As Jules Renard said, 'Happiness lies in seeking it.'

So what do we need to do? What are the tricks? In reality, you already
know everything there is to know. Most people know *perfectly* well what
is important for their happiness, intuitively at least. When they are forced
to think about it, usually because of some drama in their lives (a serious

illness or the death of someone close), they do not 'discover' what happiness consists of, but simply realize that they should have done something about it at an earlier stage. The construction of happiness is achieved not through discoveries (of what we did not know) but through realizations (of the importance of what we already knew). Here is a little example: in a study of young mothers, it became apparent that the time spent with their children was not, according to real-time information about their emotional responses, very rich in positive moods.[47] For the simple reason that they were not with their children 'in their heads', because they were trying to do other things at the same time (housework, shopping, telephone calls . . .) which their offspring were preventing them from getting done. This created the following paradox: time spent with their children was sometimes difficult and dominated by negative feelings. Even though children are our most precious gift, at the time we often perceive them as a source of complication and stress because, when we are with them, we want to be doing other things too.

Putting happiness into practice is, more often than not, a matter of common sense.

Making ourselves happy: practical tips

There is indeed a wisdom of happiness. Close observation shows that most of the advice for a happy life is universal and often goes back a long time.[48] And that it is based on very simple steps. Which makes it easy to caricature or denigrate. But surely we have the right to dream of happiness and gentle pleasures! In any case, those who do dream about them have always struck me as being more appealing than those who mock them. And have always seemed to be better off. But of course, when we are told that we can be happier just by practising and following certain rituals and that it is just like cleaning our teeth, something which needs to be done every day . . .

Positive thoughts in the evening

This is a classic exercise in positive psychology. It consists in asking yourself each evening before falling asleep what good moments you have had that day. Often people who are advised to do this exercise look initially not for *good* moments but for *great* moments, intense pleasures. In fact it is just simple little moments of happiness that need to be recalled, in a straightforward way. There are a number of studies proving the benefits of these exercises.[49] Benefits which seem greater still when people are asked to focus these positive thoughts on feelings of gratitude: to what extent are other people responsible for these good moments I have experienced? Think of the direct gestures which I have benefited from, but also all the indirect ones: the people who created and maintained the path I walked along, those who wrote and played the music I listened to, grew the fruit I ate . . .

Support each other in the good times

No, it is not a mistake, you read correctly and it is indeed 'in *good* times'. We tend to think that support should be given to those we are close to at difficult times in particular. Indeed it should, but that is not enough. In an original approach, researchers set out to study the respective importance of support in both difficult and easy times.[50] Young couples (who had been together for two years on average) were invited to take turns speaking to each other sometimes about positive events, sometimes about negative ones. By filming these conversations, the researchers were able to assess the way each person supported and listened to their partner. The events had to be of a personal nature: they did not include holidays they had taken together (for the positive ones) or financial worries they had faced together (for the negative ones). These were personal events which the other person was not directly part of (professional or academic success, good times shared with friends or associated with leisure activities . . .). When these couples were reassessed a few months later, it turned out that the most accurate indicator of their satisfaction at being together was the support they had got from their partner when they talked about their personal happiness, even if it did not directly concern them! This was more important than the support they received when they talked about things they were worried about. A little counter-intuitive, given our notion of the couple designed to confront adversity! However, though it may indeed also apply to adversity endured together, taking pleasure in your partner's happiness even if you are not directly responsible for it, or not part of it, is good for the couple. Particularly for men, moreover, with their eternal need for recognition; women were more equally divided in terms of positive and negative support. Demonstrating altruistic love for one's partner as a way of cementing the relationship seems a logical enough process, after all! We already know that sharing emotions in a relationship is a good way to regulate them:[51] reducing the negative ones (as a result of support) and increasing the positive ones (talking about these enables us to fix them more firmly in our memory, and to turn them subsequently into more powerful and more available resources with which to face future adversities).

Research along similar lines includes studies showing that cultivating positive moods within a relationship leads to better post-stress recuperation, whether psychological or biological.[52] Clearly, it is really worth putting some effort into sharing good moments together!

Knowing your needs in term of happiness

The ingredients for happiness are multifarious and sometimes contradictory: solitary happiness, social happiness, happiness derived from activity and from seclusion, busy and calm happiness. They are the same for everyone, but the proportions vary from one person to another. And for the same person from one day to another, or from one time of life to another. For some people, it may be a question of 70 per cent solitary happiness and 30 per cent social happiness, for others 90 per cent social happiness and 10 per cent solitude. Yet we tend to lock ourselves into certain habits in terms of happiness rather than trying to vary them. Or else to content ourselves with the commercial forms of happiness on offer to us. Once again, evidence of a failure to be fully conscious of our needs. We need to reflect frequently on what we enjoy.

Never lose sight of your priorities

Think back to that study showing that the main source of stress in the everyday lives of mothers was their own children. Because they found themselves submerged in and stressed by the everyday priorities: getting to school and work on time, preparing the meals, tidying the house, etc. It is the old story of the fundamental difference between what is urgent and what is important. Certain things are often seen as urgent: doing the shopping, the housework, getting the car fixed, helping the children with their homework, cooking, working . . . Then there are the important things: laughing with people close to you, seeing friends, watching clouds move across the sky . . . Generally speaking, the urgent things are noisy and demand our attention; they are hard to ignore. Whereas the important things are silent and can easily slip quietly from our memory. But neglecting them will gradually bring us a deep sense of frustration or of emptiness, which we will not necessarily immediately understand. Until, that is, we finally get it: how long is it since I gazed at the stars? How long is it since I went for a walk in the woods with my children? How long since I spent a Sunday afternoon chatting to my friends in front of the fire? A long time? Hmmm . . . could that be what is wrong with me?

Praying?

This is not only for believers. All the studies on the subject tell us that this religious practice is good for the health of both body and mind. Provided, that is, that it is a joyous and freely chosen religion, rather than a sinister and oppressive one. 'The prayer of a sad man never has the strength to reach God.' This saying is quoted by Cioran,[53] who attributes it to a second-century agnostic. And he goes on to add: 'As we only pray when we are in low spirits, it could be concluded that no prayer has ever reached its destination.' So let us also, and even especially, pray in joy; pray to say thank you and not just to ask for something. But prayer can also be relevant for those who aspire to a 'spirituality without god'.[54] Smiling in adversity, deciding to take delight in living, turning to others even when we are unhappy, all of these have always seemed to me to be a subtle form of spirituality. And contemplation can also take place without prayer. Etty Hillesum, though deeply religious, wrote in her journal: 'There is such perfect and complete happiness in me, oh God. What he called "reposing in oneself." And that probably best expresses my own love of life: I repose in myself. And that part of myself; that deepest and richest part in which I repose, is what I call "God".'

Make happiness one of your personal values

In order for something to make us happy, it needs to match our personal values. This seems logical. But we can also reactivate what makes us happy from a distance, through our memories. And here too, we remember a mood steeped in emotion all the better if these emotions are linked to our values.[55] If we value power, we will remember our successes better. If it is money we cherish, we will of course remember the profits and rewards obtained in the course of our lives. And if it is happiness, the memory of good times will come back to us easily. And, as happiness is good for our health, which cannot be said of the taste either for success and competition, or for money, we would do well to adopt it as one of our values, if we want to improve our well-being.

Is happiness contagious? Let's infect those around us!

Perhaps the best thing about all these little ways of seeking happiness is that they are contagious: by making ourselves a little bit happier, we also make those we meet and spend time with happier. A considerable number of studies on this subject were already in existence, but a large-scale study looking at 5,000 people over a twenty-year period has now confirmed their findings.[56] What wonderful news! It shows that happiness is quietly contagious, and is transmitted through our social network: a happy person *contaminates* others as far afield as the third circle of his or her acquaintances. That means that your happiness will benefit your friends and your friends' friends and that its influence will still be perceptible in the friends of your friends' friends. It will not go much further than that, of course: happiness does not obey the laws of homeopathy. A warning, however: in order for this induction effect to work, the person you affect must live near you (one or two kilometres maximum) and must be someone you encounter on a regular basis: your happiness will not benefit those who live far away from you or people you do not see often enough.

Scholarly analysis of the results of this survey confirmed that this was indeed the result of a cause-and-effect mechanism: this explains why we tend to find more happy people in the company of happy people, not as a result of 'like attracts like' (happy people cluster together because they share the same view of the world and have the same tastes), but because of the induction of happiness in others. We already knew how this worked, but it is the first time this has been demonstrated on such a wide scale: emotional contagion (by means of smiles and little remarks), increased frequency of acts of kindness and of sharing, less conflict and aggression. All these things increase the well-being of those around us (and our own too, when we associate with a lot of happy people).

This contagious effect of happiness comes as no surprise to psycho-sociologists: there is also evidence of other forms of social contamination associated with less desirable phenomena, such as obesity[57] and smoking,[58] but also depression.[59] But nevertheless these new findings are a great source of pleasure: now nobody can continue to claim that happiness is selfish!

Remembering lovely things? Yes, but in the way animals do

Quite spontaneously, we like to remember good things. And when we no longer remember them very well, we tend to embellish our memories, or at least the majority of us do (90 per cent of people, the remaining 10 per cent being probably sub-clinically depressed), because embellishing the past puts us into a better frame of mind.[60] What studies also show is that it not useful to *reflect on* our moments of happiness immediately after they occur in order to try and understand the mechanisms behind them, but that it is better to *relive them*, if we want to prolong the effect. Rather than dissecting and picking over our happy moments, it is better to enjoy them in an animal way, primitively and elementally, or in a 'palaeolithic' way, as Joseph Delteil would say.

Welcome surprises in our lives

Another argument against dissecting our happinesses too quickly (what a strange idea anyway; better to feel them even more intensely, or insist on savouring them and lingering over their minutest details): the unexpected and surprising play a role in our little moments of happiness.

This was demonstrated by an amusing piece of research conducted in the USA:[61] passers-by were stopped in a library and offered a card with a dollar coin attached to it. The person offering the card would say, 'Hi, this is for you, have a good day.' To make sure this did not seem too strange and suspicious, the donor ostensibly proceeded to do exactly the same to other people a short distance away. The message on some of the cards was very clear: 'We are an association for the promotion of gratuitous acts of kindness[62] and that is why we are doing this'; but some were less clear. When the beneficiaries were questioned a short time afterwards, research-ers found that a degree of uncertainty about the origins of this dollar which had dropped from the sky prolonged the pleasure of receiving it. Mysterious, surprise presents are the best ones!

This is all the more interesting in that, in this kind of research, if people are given the choice, they always prefer to know where good things come from, and predict moreover that such knowledge will make them even happier. Error: the pleasure is greater if it is combined with a small element of surprise. Yet another argument in favour of mixed moods.

All the more so as we have access to studies showing the negative role of excessive expectations in terms of happiness and well-being: these expectations often result in disappointment. So, for example, listening to music in an attempt to feel happy whilst listening will inevitably spoil the pleasure.[63] Again, frankly, what kind of idea is that?

'As sad as a Christmas tree on the 6th of January'

I love the instructive sadness of days after a celebration: tired, still full of emotion, we are in a receptive state for feelings and moods. Sadness and nostalgia? Yes. Anxiety about normal life resuming again? Of course. But also the certainty of past happiness. And of happiness to come. What would you have preferred? For Christmas not to exist at all? The sadness that overwhelms you now is not a *punishment* for having tried to escape from your condition as an unfortunate mortal, not a *call to order*, but simply the echo of this fragment of intense and joyous life you have just lived through.

Waking up happy?

'I wake up every morning with a secret sense of joy; I behold the light with a kind of rapture. For the rest of the day, I am happy.' Lucky Montesquieu![64] Personally, I hardly ever wake up in the morning with a secret sense of joy. But no matter; I still like to work at it nevertheless, with a certain amount of obstinacy. I had been doing just that for years, when one day I stumbled upon this phrase which delighted me: 'the obstinate determination to be happy'.

And that is exactly what it is.

And it works.

Often.

Chapter 17

Wisdom

Man does not possess wisdom. He can simply strive for it and love it, which is already praiseworthy enough.

Emmanuel Kant

I like the idea of wisdom. I like it naively, probably in the way you can like a concept you do not know very much about. Today's philosophers are eager to warn against the idea of wisdom, questioning its utility and why anyone should seek it. They urge us all to mistrust anyone purporting to be a sage.[1] 'He who would play the angel acts the beast', said Pascal. In a similar way, our era appears to suggest that anyone seeking wisdom must be either mad or naive. Finally, the term 'wisdom', like 'happiness', has almost become a rude word, used only by idiots, the ignorant, the stupid or those out to exploit human naivety.

Yet, most of us see wisdom as a path we would like to follow: not so we can call ourselves 'wise', but in order to become – after a good deal of personal effort and with the benefit of life experience to enable us to be sure – 'wiser', which is not the same thing. We want to feel ourselves gradually making progress towards something better so that our mistakes and our wanderings will have had a purpose in that they will have helped us to approach the ideal; in other words, a diminution of suffering.

Moreover, we are under no illusions about the enormity of the task, and are instinctively prudent when it comes to wisdom. Which of us would dare to call ourselves completely wise? Or feel we would always be wise? Which of us would see wisdom as anything other than a transitory state?

Yet why should we give up seeking to be wiser?

What is wisdom?

One of the finest definitions is perhaps that of André Comte-Sponville: 'Maximum happiness in maximum lucidity.'[2] Wisdom is a way of seeking happiness which tries not to deny reality.

Here is another definition, from the Zen master Daisetz Teitaro Suzuki: 'knowledge looks towards the outside [. . .] wisdom looks towards the inside'.[3] *Towards the inside*: wisdom cannot exist without self-knowledge, a humble and demanding knowledge. That is why nobody dares to call themselves wise in the hearing of those who know them. We can always get away with it in front of an audience who do not know us intimately, but not with those who live with us on a daily basis: they have witnessed us failing to be wise on so many occasions! But accepting that, rather than trying to hide it, is surely in itself wisdom, is it not? On this subject, I remember a little cartoon in the *New Yorker* in which the wife of Confucius – the ultimate wise man – was scolding her husband about his many sayings prefaced with 'the wise man said'.[4] The cartoon does not include his reply, but the partners of 'wise men' could certainly tell us a thing or two about the difficulties of being wise all the time!

One last definition, whose author I am afraid I have forgotten but which I found jotted down in one of the notebooks where I store all my mental bric-a-brac: 'Knowledge means expanding your self-knowledge. Wisdom means knowing how to use it.' Wisdom is not simply a discourse, but also a practical matter. It is judged not on the brilliance of the tone or the rhetoric, but on how it is applied 'in the field'. Or rather, along the way, as Proust wrote in *In the Shadow of Young Girls in Flower*: 'We do not receive wisdom, we must discover it ourselves, after a journey through the wilderness which no one else can make for us.' He echoes Montaigne's view: 'Even if he could become learned with other men's learning, a man can never be wise but by his own wisdom.' Wisdom is not something which can simply be taught, it also requires regular practice. Like music or sport, or indeed any other kind of learning. These practice sessions will enable us to obtain the discernment which is an integral part of wisdom: the best precepts of wisdom are not necessarily applicable at all times and in all places. But in order to know that, we need to have tried them.

There are therefore three stages in our quest for wisdom: that of knowledge, in response to the 'what?' question. Then that of practice, in response to the 'how?' question. And finally that of discernment, based notably on the 'when?' question.

Seeking wisdom is of course an extremely ancient quest: Pythagoras is said to have invented the term *philosophos*, in other words *he who loves wisdom*, out of modesty, to avoid laying claim to the title of *sophos*, the already wise![5] Wisdom is therefore a value and a goal: it implies that we are taking steps to get closer to it, that we are setting off on our journey. But towards what?

What does wisdom consist of?

The philosophic tradition tells us that wisdom is made up of various 'ingredients': tranquillity of mind, *ataraxia*; inner freedom, *autarkeia*; the sense of a joyous unity with reality, *amor fati*.[6]

We can also echo Marcus Aurelius in stating that it is based on three practices:[7] vigilance over thoughts (not *control* or *command*, but *vigilance*: being the watchman at the gates to our minds, noting everything that comes in and goes out); acceptance of events imposed by fate (not *submission* or *abdication*, but accepting that what is, shall be; then examining what can be done); the duty always to act in the best interests of the human community (selfishness and wisdom are incompatible).

In reality, philosophical knowledge and practices relating to wisdom are infinitely varied. It is worth noting simply that the 'precepts' of wisdom tend to be drawn more from the ancient philosophers than from the modern ones. For, as Pierre Hadot observes, whereas 'ancient philosophy offered people a lifestyle, modern philosophy, on the other hand, is primarily about the construction of a technical language reserved for specialists'.[8] Hadot also reminds us that, for the Ancients, someone could be regarded as a philosopher even if they had never written, or even taught, anything, simply by behaving like a wise person. And anyone at all could try to be one in their own way, at their own level. A reassuring idea.

From the point of view of any psychologists interested in this subject, particularly behaviourist or cognitive psychologists,[9] wisdom is an *integrative* capacity,[10] a kind of 'auditing system' of the management of our knowledge, perceptions and memories which will help us face the inevitably complex problems of our everyday existence.

Amongst the criteria for what constitutes wisdom from the point of view of research in positive psychology,[11] two are non-specific: *having knowledge and having experience. Knowledge* helps us understand complex or disconcerting situations better: knowing – because I have read the research or been taught – that shy people can be aggressive when they force themselves to ask for something gives me the wisdom not to feel threatened by their aggressive behaviour. And *experience*, like knowledge, provides me not only with certain useful indications, but also with the appropriate reflexes: if I have already had to calm angry people down, I know how to listen to them first, without allowing them to go beyond certain limits, and let them see I want to resolve what they perceive as a problem, etc. If I have already done that, I will not be 'lost', and can avoid reacting in too emotional or rigid a manner. But knowledge and experience, though useful to wisdom, are not specific to it, since they are in fact a necessary part of all human activity.

Three criteria are, however, more specifically associated with wisdom: *contextuality*, first of all, which means being able to take account of the context, before reaching a conclusion or choosing a course of action; André

Comte-Sponville points out, for example, that it is not the same to be wise in Auschwitz as it is to be wise in a Parisian living room. There is a wisdom of peaceful times and a wisdom of adversity, and the two are not necessarily identical. Or at least the latter has already proved its worth whereas the former has yet to do so, but has at least the merit of existing and the virtue – perhaps – of preparing us for future adversity.

The second criterion is the *relativism of values*: accepting that what seems appropriate and pertinent here and now will not necessarily be relevant in another time or place. Wisdom is the capacity to *transpose* your thoughts onto other people, other places and other times.

Finally, the third criterion is *tolerance of uncertainty*: wisdom means not having too great an appetite for certainties and cut-and-dried opinions, all too often called into question by the facts. I remember a phrase from Michel Foucault: 'Peace to facts and war on generalities.' *Words of wisdom* in biblical terms!

Wisdom is not only a matter for our intellectual capacities, it is also affected by our moods. Thanks to the work carried out by Damasio, we understand the extent to which our emotions and intuitions, even when subtle and discreet, play a role in the processes through which we understand, judge and take decisions on a daily basis.[12] And how they can therefore disrupt or facilitate such processes. Sound regulation of emotions and moods is generally considered to be an important component of wisdom.[13] For example, it helps to develop the capacity for discerning negative moods which could interfere with our understanding and intelligence. But there is also the need to cultivate compassion.

In a discussion we had, Jean, a cousin of mine who was in the process of getting divorced, admitted to feeling bewildered: 'I don't know if I'm right to destroy everything like this.' Bewildered, but also extremely angry with his perhaps future-ex-wife: too angry to see clearly in the midst of all his prevarications. In an attempt to nudge him towards wisdom (it is always easier to nudge other people in that direction than to steer yourself), I said to him:

> Whatever you do, do it calmly. Think about the consequences. Don't hate her, or do her harm, or speak ill of her. Even if she is hostile towards you and insists on telling everyone about your problems, she's only doing so because she's feeling bad and suffering and because she's panicking at the thought of you leaving. Try to make sure you remain compassionate to her. Apart from that, do what you have to do. Try to minimize your resentment and focus on being compassionate. It is the only way for you, 'bewildered' as you say you feel, to really know where you want to go, without being distracted by overpowerful emotions. It is your sense of resentment which is stopping you from feeling this elusive intuition you are desperately looking for, the intuition to guide you in your choice of going ahead with the divorce or getting back together again. The more you have it in for her, the more deeply you'll

end up getting bogged down with resentment and the less clearly you'll see things. If you need to leave, just leave. But not out of resentment, not with that alibi of hatred. Preserve a bit of compassion: it is the only thing which will help you see things clearly.

To date, Jean is again living with his ex-future-ex-wife, and they are back on speaking terms. I have no idea what role our conversation may have played. But I am glad it took place.

Whom and what is wisdom for?

Wisdom is not permanent equanimity: the clear-sightedness and the empathy it brings can also, conversely, cause us to react even more strongly to a situation which the wise person clearly understands the significance of. Wisdom involves understanding to what extent certain subtle details mean something: being wise means being deeply sensitive to all the little signs of goodness, all the little scenes of humiliation. And then taking action. It is not there to drive us towards a huge renunciation or to a retreat from the world like that described in this witty piece by Cocteau: 'The wise thing would be to go on sleeping until we reach the terminus (death). But, alas, the journey is fascinating and we take such an interest in what should be no more than a passing distraction that it is hard, when the last day comes, to pack our bags.'[14]

It serves on the contrary to help us resolve the difficulties, problems and riddles of human life: bereavements, separations, injustices, conflicts, diseases, death, divisions . . . All those events which require a little more strength and lucidity than usual. But it is not only a matter of what used to be called *reversals of fortune*: we also need wisdom when things are going well, for our successes, our happiness, our *strokes of luck*, if we are to enjoy them wisely without getting carried away.

And finally, we need to be able to call on wisdom in all our daily actions and not just when we are coping with extreme circumstances. This is why we need to train ourselves to understand and apply wisdom when things are calm, so that we can draw on it in more stormy times too. It is why we should not under-estimate even *small* manifestations of wisdom, those ordinary efforts to be wise.

Practising wisdom will help us in our own lives. But, inevitably, our moments of wisdom, when they occur, will also be useful to other people, to those who happen to be listening to us, or watching us at that time. At some points in our lives, we end up, rightly or wrongly, being a source of wisdom for someone. A sage, or an anti-sage, for that matter, because we can also learn, from watching others do things, what should definitely not be done.

Learning wisdom from the great masters?

Long ago there were masters of wisdom who conveniently assumed that role.

Nowadays, prudence takes precedence. For good reasons: some of these masters were not as wise as all that. And for bad ones too: a certain relativism in the face of knowledge and wisdom (a relativism according to which nothing is true or good *in absolute terms*) could be taken to extremes, and result in us giving way in the face of every opposing view.

The modern position of 'I have nothing to teach you, nothing to pass on to you' troubles me, because it seems more selfish, lazy or 'fashionable' than genuinely humble. It reminds me of the story told about Socrates and Antisthenes: the latter, who had chosen to live free from all kinds of constraint, particularly material ones, demonstrated this brave choice of lifestyle by always wearing a worn old coat, full of holes. This coat was famous throughout Athens, and symbolized the consistency of his philosophy: 'I live what I preach.' He would sometimes remind richly dressed people of this as they paraded about in the agora, greeting them by ironically shaking his coat to show off its holes. One day he decided to do this to Socrates, who was walking nearby dressed in a new coat. It is said that Socrates stared at Antisthenes and his coat for a long time, without speaking. Then, as he walked away, he said 'It is your vanity I see through the holes in your coat.'[15] Thanks to Socrates, I often seem to see, behind the humility of the 'no advice to give' attitude, the pride of someone wanting to show that they are simply too wise to give advice.

In short, for all these reasons, the notion of having masters of wisdom has become a complicated one. We are currently happier with *experts*, who can offer us 'cold, hard' knowledge in a particular area. Yet we long to have wise men or women, we need models to inspire us in how to live our own lives: it is almost a psychological need.[16] Consequently, we continue to search for wise people around us.

A survey of 'the fifteen wisest people' conducted amongst students in North America produced the following ranking:[17] Gandhi came out on top, followed by Confucius, Jesus, Martin Luther King, Socrates, Mother Teresa, Solomon, Buddha, the pope ... Then things took a nose-dive with the appearance of Oprah Winfrey, the famous American talk-show presenter, who may indeed be genuinely wise – who knows? – but whose place in the hit parade would appear to owe more to her media appearances than to the strength of her wisdom. Nevertheless, out of this cheerful and heterogeneous mixed bag of names a certain number of truths emerge: without really knowing very much about it, we spontaneously associate wisdom with compassion and with a commitment to bringing about change. Not a bad way of looking at it! What the 'wisdom top fifteen' also teaches us is that wise men and women tend to be a rare breed, not easily accessible and often belonging to past eras. So whom should we turn to? To everybody!

Small masters of wisdom

Each human being can speak the words or adopt the behaviour of wisdom at certain times in their lives. Observing the wise acts or the wise words of humanity as a whole is almost as good as blindly following certain masters, whose reputation for wisdom may not necessarily prove to be consistent throughout their lives.

Moreover, one of the most interesting aspects of current research in this 'psychology of wisdom' previously mentioned is that it focuses on observing wisdom expressing itself, rather than endlessly holding forth on what it is.

In order to represent this process more clearly, here are two examples of responses given in a survey on wisdom,[18] one of which is considered wise, the other less so. Those taking part in the survey had to give their opinion on the following case: *a young girl of 15 wishes to get married immediately*. No more information than that. What do you think?

An example of a response deemed lacking in wisdom:

No, it's not a good idea to get married at 15. She needs to be told that this kind of marriage is simply not possible.

An example of a response deemed to be a wise one:

On the surface, it is simple enough. In general, marriage at 15 is not a good idea. But at the same time it is something a lot of young girls think about when they fall in love for the first time. And then, there are often situations in life where you can't argue for a 'general' approach. Maybe, in this case, there are particular circumstances. Maybe the young girl has a fatal illness and hasn't long to live. Or she's just lost her parents. Or she lives in another country, with a different culture. Or at another time in history?

We see that the wise response takes a more distanced view of the situation and more importantly, in view of the degree of uncertainty and the lack of information available, takes account of the many possibilities of the case before reaching any conclusion: the need to know who this young girl is, what her precise circumstances are, etc. On an everyday level, that could equate, for example, to listening to and understanding those we are talking to before trying to judge them. Obvious? Hmm . . . In practice, for many of us, listening to someone is simply a matter of preparing our responses and our arguments.

Wisdom therefore implies a certain degree of self-transcendence: the ability to detach ourselves from our immediate interests and our opinions and see them as a personal viewpoint rather than universal truths.[19]

Close observation of everyday attitudes we perceive to be wise is therefore a good source of instruction. A little girl (aged 6) sees her two older sisters (aged 8 and 10) quarrelling about who will get the best seats in the back of the family car: the ones next to the windows, rather than the middle seat. Realizing that the argument is going round in circles, and that the parents are beginning to get angry, she makes a personal *sacrifice*: 'I'll go in the middle for the first part of the journey.' Even though she too prefers the side seats. The reasons behind her gesture are multiple and interesting. To what extent is her decision based on sensitivity: 'I hate arguments. They make everyone miserable'? On intelligence: 'They are putting our parents into a bad mood and when the parents are in a bad mood, journeys are never very nice'? And on wisdom: 'In the end, all this fussing about where you sit is absurd. There's nothing wrong with being in the middle'? Should the parents worry about 'the younger child putting herself out for the sake of the older ones'? Or should they be delighted that she has this capacity to show such wisdom? Indeed, a short while later, once the conflict has died down, she will gently negoti-ate some permutations with her sisters, resulting in her not having to stay in the 'bad' seat for the whole journey. And in the end, she will have made the emotional saving of avoiding a conflict, while still managing to find a solution everyone is happy with.

Another lesson (I love receiving lessons in wisdom): a few years ago I was contacted by a medical press agency and asked if I could produce a substantial piece of work on depressive illness. It was a Thursday, and the deadline for the work was Monday, which meant I would need to spend the entire weekend working round the clock. Of course, given the urgency and the scale of the work, it was very well paid. After a good deal of hesitation, I decided to turn it down: my weekend was already fairly busy with family commitments and having to cancel all of those seemed to me both frustrating and complicated. Instead, I offered to pass on the work to a colleague at Sainte-Anne, emphasizing the financial benefits of the deal. He listened politely, then, once I told him when the deadline was, he replied, without a moment's hesitation, that the answer was no. Adding with a smile, 'Personally, I would be ready to pay that amount *not* to have to do the work under such conditions!' In the end, we managed to find a young single colleague who had the time and the energy to do the job but who would not have to inflict suffering on anyone else because she was ruining her weekend with two sleepless nights and quantities of caffeine. But the wisdom of that first colleague made me think for a long time afterwards: without the slightest hesitation, he had opted to fill his weekend with the enriching effects of happiness rather than of money.

How to choose our masters of wisdom, great or small?

'I do not have anything personal to say about wisdom. If I possess it, it is purely in the form of an uneasy impulse which constantly drives me to seek it in individuals reputed to have acquired it definitively.' This was the response of a prudent man, asked what he thought about wisdom.[20]

The first recommendation in the quest for masters, even transitory ones, comes from the Latin sage Seneca:[21] 'The road is a long one if one proceeds by way of precepts but short and effectual if by way of personal example.' The example or, in other words, the practical demonstration given by the master is the best proof of the value of a recommendation of wisdom. The contemporary philosopher George Steiner also reminds us of this:[22] 'In German *deuten* signifying to "point to" is inseparable from *bedeuten*, "to mean" [. . .] In regard to morality, only the actual life of the master has demonstrative proof. Socrates and the saints teach by existing.' And he adds, 'The only thing which can be fruitful is a living instruction, a teaching by and of the entire soul, of the whole person, of life.'

A second recommendation, this time from an Indian master, the Buddha: 'You must accept my words, not out of respect for me, but having carefully considered them.'[23] Put another way: do not listen to me, but test my ideas, evaluate my teachings by putting them into practice. That is why those masters who accept being recognized as such always insist that their teachings are only the *beginning* of wisdom.

The 'great platitudes'

The Talmud, principles (IV, 1): 'Which is the true sage? It is he who does not scorn lessons from anyone.' Then (in V, 7):

> Seven things distinguish the sage from he who is not: (1) He does not speak in the presence of the one whose wisdom exceeds his; (2) He does not interrupt when someone is speaking; (3) He does not answer too quickly; (4) He asks questions methodically and fairly; (5) He deals with questions in the order in which they were asked; (6) When he does not understand something, he says so; (7) And he pays homage to the truth.[24]

For my part, I love reading such precepts, feeling their echo in me, and especially knowing that they were devised, taught, put to the test, all those years ago. Yet some people see them as no more than a series of banalities and generalities.

Most of the wise advice emanating from all times and all places does indeed have a simple and obvious side to it: some people have called these the 'great platitudes'.[25] *Great* because, after all, they were thought up by great minds, and have retained their relevance over the centuries. *Platitudes* because indeed, when we read them, we do not necessarily feel we are discovering anything new. But ultimately this is as it should be, since these are precepts to apply on a daily basis, which need to be simple if they are to be put into practice by ordinary humans. For wisdom has the vocation of being a universal value and practice and not an elitist one. Which is why, as Marcus Aurelius observed, we need to have access to 'brief maxims to help us live'. Whether these come from the Stoics or

Zen, or Tao, words of wisdom will always go beyond what they appear to mean initially. This becomes apparent when we try to apply them on a daily basis: we quickly discover that this is no easy task. We move on from what was merely a platitude in words to what becomes in action an exercise in wisdom. So let us put the great platitudes into action, before we judge them to be so dull.

Wisdom in practice

There is nothing abstract about being wise! Managing not to get angry if we have just missed our plane or our train; being able to enjoy spending time in the evening with our family or friends without allowing that pleasure to be spoiled by worries about work; smiling inwardly when the shelves we were attempting to put up collapse for the third time . . . All these moments are opportunities to test our level of wisdom, or to measure how much progress we still need to make in order to attain it and improve our lives. If wisdom has indeed been an object of research in psychological science,[26] it is simply on the premise that it may bring benefits in terms of mental health, and that it is possible to develop it (which was also the belief of the Greek and Roman philosophers). Here are some observations – commonplace rather than grandiose – on the subject of this 'practical psychological wisdom'.

Listen to your feelings and moods, especially when they are uncomfortable and unpleasant

Turning a deaf ear to your feelings means losing sight of wisdom. They are a sharp reminder of reality, which wisdom cannot exist without. Let us listen to our guilt, which might perhaps be telling us that we went a little too far, so locked in our convictions were we. Let us listen to our sadness, which reminds us that something is wrong in our lives: either because of what is happening to us, or because of what is missing. Let us listen to our irritation: it shows us that something is bothering and frustrating us: but is it life which is causing us to suffer in this way or is it our own expectations? Accepting that we are sometimes disturbed by our feelings means accepting that we may not perhaps have made the right choices, or that our view of reality is not always accurate. And that is one of the components of wisdom. It is better to feel like this than to hope that wisdom will allow us to avoid pain, anger, sadness or anxiety. Conversely, amongst the advantages of our gradual advance in age, and therefore, *a priori*, in wisdom, comes a clearly defined improvement in our capacity to read our feelings and moods and to regulate them, even in advance: it has been shown that the older an adult is, the better they are at savouring planned moments of well-being in advance, and at the same time, the less likely they are to worry in advance about possible difficulties.[27] Which amounts to a significant piece of ordinary wisdom.

Accept sadness and feed on it, rather than letting it feed on us

Wisdom does not prevent sadness. Indeed, there is plenty of evidence that sadness and wisdom share a very old and very deep companionship. We have spoken of the book of Ecclesiastes in the Bible, in which is stated 'In much wisdom is much grief.'[28] The wiser you are, the more you are likely to suffer; but the greater capacity you have to heal yourself. In a study where short sad films (about bereavement or illness) were projected in front of an audience of volunteers whose levels of wisdom had been previously assessed, it was observed that the individuals previously assessed as being wise felt sadder after watching these films.[29] Wisdom does not protect us from sadness – that is not its purpose. On the contrary, it is rooted in both our sad and painful moods (for lucidity and prudence) and also, of course, in our positive moods (for energy). It needs to have felt the fragility of all things and of all judgements. In order to be wise, we have to have been wrong and to have suffered disappointment, to have had some of our dreams shattered. In short, we have to have lived a little rather than have spent our lives running away or protecting ourselves.

Never consider wisdom as a stable and established state

There are no 'wise men or women', there are only people seeking wisdom, those doing their utmost to attain it, and who know that the only way to do so is to keep striving towards it on a regular basis. I remember, for example, the very wise comments of a political journalist: 'I do not believe in objectivity but in mastering subjectivity.'[30] The phrase is very pertinent to our judgement in general because in our everyday lives we are constantly pulled in the opposite direction to that of wisdom: the rapidity and subjectivity of our opinions, the comfort of our convictions. And again we see the importance of humility in our efforts: we cannot make our faults disappear but we can learn not to be taken in by them as often. Let us accept, therefore, wisdom that is incomplete, intermittent and changing according to our moods and our energy levels.

Wisdom requires effort: just make the effort

Wisdom is incompatible with lazy thinking: if we adopt the 'ready-made' thoughts of our circle, of our time, of people who impress us with their intelligence or their prestige, we are not wise, but merely accepted by all those who are making the same mistake as we are. The only solution is to work on the principle that everybody can make a mistake, even the most brilliant. There should not be any sacred cows. As Coluche said: 'The fact that lots of people are wrong does not make them right!'[31]

Frequent other people

Is the wise man solitary? Not necessarily. And indeed: rarely! This is what the rabbi Pauline Bebe has to say:[32] 'The solitary, the loner, the egoist, the misanthropist cannot be wise. It is through close contact with other people that the spark of goodness is kindled and humanity advances.' She adds, 'Wisdom therefore means transforming any confrontation into a learning process.' Wishing to be wise on your own displays a singular lack of wisdom! For it is not only about our brushes with other people, but also about the ties of affection and affiliation. In a charming paradox, it has been demonstrated that accepting and recognizing what we owe to other people, instead of making us more dependent, actually increases our independence.[33] Wisdom means never forgetting the extent to which we are linked to all other human beings. And it is this very thought which will give us the energy to understand them, at all times, and sometimes to know when not to follow them.

Keep an open mind

Wisdom is not only expertise, it is also openness and curiosity: in other words an acceptance of the unknown, of the disturbing, of the surprising, of what at first sight offends or disconcerts us, and in the face of which we have the wisdom not to jump too quickly to conclusions. It also requires love and kindness to enable us to listen to and welcome the words of our neighbours. Their words and much more besides. An example of the wise man in action: when travelling across Europe, Montaigne regretted not bringing his cook with him. Was it because he did not appreciate local cooking and would have liked the cook to concoct tasty little dishes from the south-west for him? Nothing of the sort! Indeed, the opposite was true: he would have liked his cook to learn some foreign recipes so he could have delighted his friends with new dishes on his return home.[34] The spirit of openness and wisdom are sometimes present in these little details. Moreover, in studies on this subject conducted amongst ordinary individuals, a readiness to accept the new appears to be a necessary element of wisdom.[35]

Always be prepared to be wrong

Wisdom does not prevent us making mistakes (wise people probably make just as many as the unwise, out of curiosity and open-mindedness), but it helps to ensure we only make them once (or only a few times, or not too often!): the wise person learns from his or her mistakes. Ultimately wisdom is perhaps the art of the aftermath: instead of moving on to some-thing else, we first take time to reflect on what has happened, without being afraid that doing so will destabilize us or cause us to suffer.

Wisdom also means being constantly prepared to say 'I don't

understand', because we consider this to be a fundamental right of being human, because we know that it is precisely by doing so that we will understand. I treat many patients who suffer from feelings of being imposters, like the patient who, at school, always pretended to have understood, whereas in fact, just like the others, that was clearly not always the case. As a result she went through her schooling like a little ghost, trembling with fear that her pretence would be discovered. We worked on this in our therapy sessions. At the end of this, she had overcome her fears. But it seems to me too that this was not merely about the retreat of those symptoms: by dint of examining her fears and through exercises designed to reduce and deflate them, she had acquired a bit more lucidity about the fact that often these fears came from her, had become a bit more relaxed about what other people might think of her and the possible consequences of that, and a bit more fatalistic about the idea that there could also be some people who might look down on her. In short, she had acquired a little more wisdom. No therapy would ever claim to make a patient wiser. But we must acknowledge that some patients are able to 'benefit' from what they have done in therapy to become wiser.

Be wary of certainties and of 'always' and 'never'

We have seen the extent to which our allergy to uncertainty played a part in our feelings of worry and anxiety. I remember one day hearing the actress Judith Godrèche saying 'It was a long time before I was able to *lose* confidence in myself.'[36] The wisdom of Judith! When we sense uncertainty, we prefer to replace it with certainty, even if exaggerated or misplaced. Yet wisdom is not about being certain, but about tolerating our uncertainties. We examine them, reflect on them, but we accept their existence and the evidence in front of our eyes.

Be warned, sometimes not wanting to get involved or to express an opinion can be the result of laziness rather than wisdom. In the name of relativism, for example: 'Everything has the same value: so I have nothing to say, and I will not take a stand.' Being wise also means having the courage of your convictions, in the full knowledge that you might be wrong. But with the knowledge too that without conviction, no action is possible. And that in that case the world will never change. That is why wisdom is closer to science than to faith: it accepts and even, to some extent, loves being wrong. As long as it brings deeper understanding (and understanding our mistakes is already better than not understanding anything at all).

Accepting complexity and uncertainty. And acting anyway

Wisdom when we do not have recourse to dichotomy, that categorization of the world into two halves (good and evil, friends and enemies, desirable and undesirable . . .), to enable us to think and act in a more complex way: helping our enemies, recognizing that someone we do not like is right, etc. Wisdom when we accept leaving some questions unanswered, but here too without necessarily giving up on taking action: it is the same principle as that of faith, where we act according to our convictions ('I don't know if I am right about this, but I've decided to be kind to people all the time') and not according to our certainties ('It always pays to be kind'). Wisdom when we are capable of relying on 'provisional hypotheses' in order to act: 'I don't know what they think, so I'm going to act as if they liked me, and see how they react', rather than 'As long as I am not sure, I'm not doing anything.'

Love simplicity

In most traditions, wisdom is equated with simplicity. For a reason Paul Valéry understood perfectly: 'What is simple is always false. What is not is unusable.' There are, indeed, two sorts of simplicity: one is poor, the other rich; one is about idleness, the other about acquiring depth; one stays firmly on this side of complexity, the other goes beyond it. The first form of simplicity has not taken time to reflect: it is nothing but gratuitous or all-purpose platitudes and assertions, with little or no foundation. It can, moreover, hide behind learned-sounding jargon, behind the 'false depth' mocked by Paul Valery. The second form of simplicity is one which arises as the result of a quest, of careful reflection, and of repeated practice, shared with others. This is the simplicity Leonardo da Vinci described as the 'supreme refinement'. And faced with simple wise advice, the intelligent approach is not to say 'That's too simple' and to stick to arguments of principle, but to have the honesty to try: 'Did I do it or not?', and to reach a conclusion based on the facts, rather than sticking to judgements.

Always be ready to recognize your limits

Read one day in an article in the *American Journal of Psychiatry*: 'A wise man once said that a conclusion is simply the place where someone got tired of thinking.'[37] We think we are simply reading a psychiatric text and stumble on one of these wise little maxims which are good for the soul.

Build on your indiscretions as a foundation for wisdom

'He who lives without indiscretions is not as wise as he thinks.' La Rochefoucauld's maxim is deliberately striking and memorable. But it is also profound because it allows us many avenues for reflection. What does it mean for you? Personally it reminds me of these words from Svâmi Prajnânpad, an Indian spiritual master: 'Do not seek to suppress your desires. That inevitably leads to disaster.'[38] Our private stumblings are like so many reminders providing us with constant opportunities to test our resolutions to be wise. And after all, so many of the tales of the sages sound like tales of the insane! Like this one, which I often tell my timid patients, when we are working on self-assertion. We are in Athens, around 350 BC. The philosopher Diogenes is standing still in front of a statue towards which he has been stretching out his hand for hours. A crowd is starting to gather and the passers-by are calling out to him 'Diogenes, why are you doing that?' To which he replies 'To accustom myself to rejection.'[39] Madman or sage?

Regard wisdom as a form of humanism

Humanism is the school of thought which takes the individual and their personal fulfilment as its overriding goal and value (other examples of values: the market, truth . . .). Humanism is not a blind faith (that would be unwise given the imperfections of human nature) but a pragmatic loyalty, willed rather than believed.[40] Wisdom is a form of humanism because it favours and advocates values which are universal and 'universalizable', in other words from which everyone can profit: love, intelligence, peace. There are other possible values: power and domination, for example. But, as Tzvetan Todorov remarks; 'Not everyone can be victorious at the same time, but everyone can live in peace: this value can therefore be universalized, unlike the aspiration to supremacy.'[41] Love, openness, respect, listening are the values of wisdom and they are universal ones: all human beings can be wise together.

Change ourselves in order to change the world

One final argument to encourage us to practise wisdom. This remark from Etty Hillesum: 'I do not believe we can put right anything whatsoever in the external world that we have not first put right in ourselves.'[42] If we want the world to be a wiser place . . .

Emotional people who want to become wise

In an interview the actress Julie Depardieu once said, 'I am an emotional person who wants to become wise.'[43] All of us are with her on that. We want to grow in wisdom. We want the wear and the sadness of passing time to be accompanied with joy and illumination. We want the awareness of all our imperfections to be accompanied with acceptance and the tolerance of these imperfections. We want to feel cohesion and clarity within ourselves. Without needing in any way to deny our feelings and moods, whatever they may be. We want to feel we are making progress, however slowly. To feel that tomorrow we will reach the foot of the mountain: we have made our way towards it, walking steadily and advancing gradually. We are only at the bottom, the very bottom, but we feel we can already make out the summit.

Conclusion: see you tomorrow, life

It is an autumn evening and I have just finished writing this book. I am falling asleep.

As always, a drift of odds and ends, fragments of half-dreams and of half-thoughts, goes through my head. Quotations mixed up with memories. Words I have heard or phrases I have read? Things said. Scenes lived through. But when? It is windy outside, woooosshh! I can hear the trees sighing in the woods.

Here comes Lucretius. He has the features of my friend André Comte-Sponville, but I stay calm. He goes past, staring into the distance, one arm raised, the hand held open: 'It is always night somewhere. And a sun is always rising above the horizon.'[1] I want to repeat the phrase aloud, I love its rhythm. But I don't. I sense I am too sleepy to speak. A question hovers in my head for several moments, or several seconds. Just a question, for which I don't even seek an answer: when, exactly, does the night begin and the day end?

A few waves of sleep. They slip back for a moment and a glimmer of consciousness returns. I remember hearing, this afternoon, an interview with an author whose book I have not read, and who said this: 'I always wondered when "the rest of my life" would begin. It's at that moment, when you know that from now on, everything will be merely repetition, that the rest of life begins.'[2]

I can hear music. A sirtaki. The one from the final scene of the film *Zorba the Greek* (remember: 'Teach me to dance, will you?'). I see, in black and white, Zorba dancing on the beach.[3] I remember all those months and months – whole years perhaps? – spent in Greece when I was a student.

I am walking my daughter Louise to school, as I do every morning. We are chatting and she tells me that one of her friends ran away yesterday afternoon. She did not go far and came back a short while later. Louise then reveals that her older sister, Faustine, had told her about her own intentions to run away, a few years ago, when she was seven or eight years old. She had prepared a little bag with some chocolate biscuits, spare underwear and a flute. Louise had asked her 'Why the flute?' – 'So

I can play it in the metro and get money.' – 'But you don't know how to play it!' – 'It doesn't matter: they'll feel sorry for me and will give me some money anyway.' I love these little childhood stories. But no, they are adults' stories. It is the same thing.

Pessoa, in a Lisbon street, with his sad gaze, his hat and his little moustache: 'Peace, yes, peace. A great calm, gentle like something super-fluous, descends on me to the depths of my being [. . .] It's not the mild and languidly cloudy day. It's not the feeble, almost non-existent breeze, hardly more perceptible than the still air. It's not the anonymous colour of the faintly and spottily blue sky.'[4] I too feel strangely peaceful. I feel my whole body breathing, right down to my toes.

Two words: 'Serenity conquered.'[5] Serenity conquered: that would be a good title for my book, wouldn't it? It's getting darker and darker here.

I am becoming calm at last, yes, calm.

See you tomorrow, life.

See you tomorrow.

Notes

Chapter 1 Feelings and moods: towards understanding

1. Pessoa, F., *The Book of Disquiet*, London, Penguin, 2002, p. 377.
2. Proust, M., *In Search of Lost Time. Vol. 6: Time Regained*, London, Random House, 2000, p. 223.
3. Damasio, A., *The Feeling of What Happens*, London, Random House, 2000.
4. Polivy, J., 'On the induction of emotion in the laboratory: discrete moods or multiple affect states?', *Journal of Personality and Social Psychology*, 1981, 41, pp. 803–17.
5. For all definitions the author uses *Le grand Robert de la langue française*, Paris, Dictionnaires Le Robert, 2001. In order to remain as true as possible to the original text the translator has used a range of English dictionaries.
6. See the collection 'Le Parnasse de la viole', from Alia Vox. E.g. Marin Marais, *Pièces de viole du seconde livre*, 1701, by Jordi Savall et al.
7. Proust, M., *Remembrance of Things Past. Vol. 1: Swann's Way*, London, Random House, 2010, p. 13.
8. Quoted by Charach, R., in his review of *Poets on Prozac: Mental Illness, Treatment and the Creative Process* (Baltimore, Johns Hopkins University Press, 2008), *American Journal of Psychiatry*, 2008, 165, p. 1617.
9. Silvia, P. J., 'Interest, the curious emotion', *Current Directions in Psychological Science*, 2008, 17, pp. 57–60.
10. In his delightful blog *L'autofictif*, entry dated 1 October 2008, http://l-autofictif.over-blog.com.
11. Woolf, V., letter to Hugh Walpole (1932), in *The Letters of Virginia Woolf. Vol. V: 1932–1935*, London and New York, Harcourt Brace, 1979, p. 142.
12. Quoted by Assouline, P., in his blog *La république des livres*, 18 September 2008: 'Une affaire d'assurance'. See http://passouline.blog.lemonde.fr/livres.
13. The expression is one used by Simone Weil, with reference to God.
14. Comte-Sponville, A., *Dictionnaire philosophique*, Paris, Presses Universitaires de France, 2001.

15. Richardson, R. J., 'On emotion, mood, and related affective constructs', in Ekman, P. and Davidson, R. J. (eds.), *The Nature of Emotion: Fundamental Questions*, Oxford, Oxford University Press, 1994, pp. 51–5.

16. Rimé, B., *Le partage social des émotions*, Paris, Presses Universitaires de France, 2005.

17. I recommend the version of *Âmes mortes* illustrated by the painter Marc Chagall, published in 2005 in Paris by Éditions le Cherche-Midi.

18. Thibon, G., *L'illusion féconde*, Paris, Fayard, 1995.

19. The effects of premenstrual syndrome are reasonably stable throughout life (Bloch, M., Schmidt, P. J. and Rubinow, D. R., 'Premenstrual syndrome: evidence for symptom stability across cycles', *American Journal of Psychiatry*, 1997, 154, pp. 1741–6), do not seem to be associated with an increased risk of psychological problems (Kendler, K. S., Karkowski, L. M., Corey, L. A. and Neale, M. C., 'Longitudinal population-based twin study of retrospectively reported premenstrual symptoms and lifetime major depression', *American Journal of Psychiatry*, 1998, 155, pp. 1234–40) and can be improved by the intermittent use of anti-depressants (Freeman, E. W., Rickels, K., Sondheimer, S. J., Polansky, M. and Xiao, S., 'Continuous or intermittent dosing with sertraline for patients with severe premenstrual syndrome or premenstrual dysphoric disorder', *American Journal of Psychiatry*, 2004, 161, pp. 342–51).

20. Nezlek, J. B., Vansteelandt, K., Van Mechelen, I. and Kuppens, P., 'Appraisal–emotion relationships in daily life', *Emotion*, 2008, 8, pp. 145–50.

21. Research cited in Damasio, *Feeling of What Happens*, p. 295.

22. See Billand, C., *Psychologie du menteur*, Paris, Odile Jacob, 2004.

23. Frijda, N. H., 'Moods, emotions episodes and emotions', in Lewis, M. and Havilland, J. M. (eds.), *Handbook of Emotions*, New York, Guilford Press, 1993, pp. 381–403.

24. Rimé, B., 'Vulnérabilité: impact des épisodes émotionnels', in Rouillon, F. (ed.), *Vulnérabilité et troubles de l'adaptation*, Paris, John Libbey Eurotext, 2008, pp. 55–68.

25. Watson, D., *Mood and Temperament*, New York, Guilford Press, 2000, esp. p. 15.

26. Hergueta, S., 'Les animaux meurent aussi', in 'Apprivoiser la mort pour mieux apprendre à vivre', *Le Nouvel Observateur*, special edition 62, April–May, 2006, pp. 16–17.

Chapter 2 Feelings and moods: the pain and the pleasure

1. Grandjean, D. and Scherer, K. R., 'Unpacking the cognitive architecture of emotion processes', *Emotion*, 2008, 8, pp. 341–51.

2. Comte-Sponville, A., *Le miel et l'absinthe*, Paris, Hermann, 2008, p. 37.

3. Pessoa, F., *The Book of Disquiet*, London, Penguin, 2002, p. 405.

4. Huston, N., *Professeurs de désespoir*, Arles, Actes Sud, 2004.

5. Schrauf, R. W. and Sanchez, J., 'The preponderance of negative emotion words across generations and across cultures', *Journal of Multilingual and Multicultural Development*, 2004, 25, pp. 266–84.

6. Dijksterhuis, A. and Aarts, H., 'On wildebeests and humans: the preferential detection of negative stimuli', *Psychological Science*, 2003, 14, pp. 14–18.

7. Öhman, A., Lundqvist, D. and Esteves, F., 'The face in the crowd revisited: a threat advantage with schematic stimuli', *Journal of Personality and Social Psychology*, 2001, 80, pp. 381–96.

8. Hajcak, G. and Olvet, D. M., 'The persistence of attention to emotion: brain potentials during and after picture presentation', *Emotion*, 2008, 8, pp. 250–5.

9. Unkelbach, C., Fiedler, K., Bayer, M., Stegmüller, M. and Danner, D., 'Why positive information is processed faster: the density hypothesis', *Journal of Personality and Social Psychology*, 2008, 95, pp. 36–49.

10. Zeigarnik, B., 'Das Behalten erledigter und unerledigter Handlungen', *Psychologische Forschung*, 1927, 9, pp. 1–85.

11. Post, R. M., 'Transduction of psychological stress into the neurobiology of recurrent affective disorder', *American Journal of Psychiatry*, 1992, 149, pp. 999–1010.

12. Baumeister, R. F., Bratslavsky, E., Finkenauer, C. and Vohs, K. D., 'Bad is stronger than good', *Review of General Psychology*, 2001, 5, pp. 323–70.

13. See Watson, D., *Mood and Temperament*, New York, Guilford Press, 2000, esp. 'Situational and environmental influences on mood', pp. 62–103.

14. Gasper, K. and Clore, G. L., 'Attending to the big picture: mood and global versus local processing of visual information', *Psychological Science*, 2002, 13, pp. 34–40.

15. Tipples, J., 'Negative emotionality influences the effects of emotions on time perception', *Emotion*, 2008, 8, pp. 127–31.

16. Fredrickson, B. L., 'The role of positive emotions in positive psychology: the broaden-and-build theory of positive emotions', *American Psychologist*, 2001, 56, pp. 218–26.

17. Chrétien, J.-L., *La joie spacieuse: essai sur la dilation*, Paris, Éditions de Minuit, 2007.

18. Raghunathan, R. and Trope, Y., 'Walking the tightrope between feeling good and being accurate: mood as a resource in processing persuasive messages', *Journal of Personality and Social Psychology*, 2002, 83, pp. 510–25.

19. Schwarz, J. and Pollack, P. R., 'Affect and delay of gratification', *Journal of Research in Personality*, 1977, 11, pp. 147–64.

20. Fishbach, A. and Labroo, A. P., 'Be better or be merry: how mood affects self-control', *Journal of Personality and Social Psychology*, 2007, 92, pp. 58–173.

21. Trope, Y. and Neter, E., 'Reconciling competing motives in self-evaluation: the role of self-control in feedback seeking', *Journal of Personality and Social Psychology*, 1994, 66, pp. 646–57.

22. Briñol, P., Petty, R. E. and Barden, J., 'Happiness versus sadness as a determinant of thought confidence in persuasion: a self-validation analysis', *Journal of Personality and Social Psychology*, 2007, 93, pp. 711–27.

23. Goetz, M. C., Goetz, P. W. and Robinson, M. D., 'What's the use of being happy? Mood states, useful objects and repetition priming effects', *Emotion*, 2007, 7, pp. 675–9.

24. Schwarz, N. and Clore, G. L., 'Mood, misattributions and judgments of well-being: informative and directive functions of affective states', *Journal of Personality and Social Psychology*, 1983, 45, pp. 513–23.

25. Schwarz, N. and Clore, G. L., 'Feelings as phenomenal experiences', in Higgins, E. T. and Kruglanski, A. (eds.), *Social Psychology: Handbook of Basic Principles*, New York, Guilford Press, 1996, pp. 433–65.

26. Daniel Kahneman, quoted by Löwy, L., 'La nouvelle économie du bonheur', *Mouvements des Idées et des Luttes*, 2008, 54, pp. 78–86. I have not been able to find the original text.

27. Thayer, R. E., 'Problem perception, optimism, and related stress as a function of time of day (diurnal rhythm) and moderate exercise', *Motivation and Emotion*, 1978, 11, pp. 19–36.

28. MacDonald, B. and Davey, G. C. L., 'Inflated responsibility and perseverative checking: the effect of negative mood', *Journal of Abnormal Psychology*, 2005, 114, pp. 176–82.

29. Jones, F., O'Connor, D. B., Conner, M., McMillan, B. and Ferguson, E., 'Impact of daily mood, work hours, and iso-strain variables on self-reported health behaviors', *Journal of Applied Psychology*, 2007, 92, pp. 1731–40.

30. Tice, D. M., Bratslavsky, E. and Baumeister, R. F., 'Emotional distress regulation takes precedence over impulse control: if you feel bad, do it!', *Journal of Personality and Social Psychology*, 2001, 80, pp. 53–67.

31. See a review of these studies in Zemack-Rugar, Y., Bettman, J. R. and Fitzsimons, G. J., 'The effects of nonconsciously priming emotion concepts in behavior', *Journal of Personality and Social Psychology*, 2007, 93, pp. 927–39.

32. McFarland, C., Buehler, R., von Ruti, R., Nguyen, L. and Alvaro, C., 'The impact of negative moods on self-enhancing cognitions: the role of reflective versus ruminative mood orientations', *Journal of Personality and Social Psychology*, 2007, 93, pp. 728–50.

33. Pizzagalli, D. A., Bogdan, R., Ratner, K. G. and Jahn, A. L., 'Increased perceived stress is associated with blunted hedonic capacity: potential implications for depression research', *Behaviour Research and Therapy*, 2007, 45, pp. 2742–53.

34. Quoted by Momus, E., *Je hais les écrivains*, Paris, Éditions du Rocher, p. 69.

35. Verhaegen, P., Joormann, J. and Khan, R., 'Why we sing the blues: the relation between self-reflective rumination, mood and creativity', *Emotion*, 2005, 5, pp. 226–32.

36. There are many studies on this theme of creativity and mental illness. See, for example, Andraesen, N. C., 'Creativity and mental illness: prevalence rates in writers and their first-degree relatives', *American Journal of Psychiatry*, 1987, 144, pp. 1288–92; or else Ludwig, A. M., 'Mental illness and creative activity in women writers', *American Journal of Psychiatry*, 1994, 151, pp. 1650–6. Note also the abstract in French of Brenot, P., *Le génie et la folie*, Paris, Odile Jacob, 2007.

37. Friedman, R. S. and Förster, J., 'The effects of promotion and prevention cues on creativity', *Journal of Personality and Social Psychology*, 2001, 81, pp. 1001–13.

38. Hirt, E. R., Devers, E. E. and McCrea, S. M., 'I want to be creative: exploring the role of hedonic contingency theory in the positive mood-cognitive flexibility', *Journal of Personality and Social Psychology*, 2008, 94, pp. 214–30.

39. De Dreu, C. K. W., Baas, M. and Nijstad, B. A., 'Hedonic tone and activation

level in the mood–creativity link: towards a dual pathway to creativity model', *Journal of Personality and Social Psychology*, 2008, 94, pp. 739–56.

40. Hayes, S. C., *Get Out of Your Mind and Into Your Life*, Oakland, New Harbinger, 2005.
41. Van Dijk, W. W., Ouwerkerk, J. W., Goslinga, S., Nieweg, M. and Gallucci, M., 'When people fall from grace: reconsidering the role of envy in *schadenfreude*', *Emotion*, 2006, 6, pp. 1156–60.
42. Goleman, D., *Surmonter les émotions destructrices*, Paris, Robert Laffont, 2003, pp. 218–23.
43. Celli, N., *Le Bouddhisme*, Paris, Hazan, 2006.

Chapter 3 Rumination and losing control

1. Cioran, E. M., *Cahiers 1957–1972*, Paris, Gallimard, 1997, p. 433.
2. Tiedens, L. Z. and Linton, S., 'Judgment under emotional certainty and uncertainty: the effects of specific emotions on information processing', *Journal of Personality and Social Psychology*, 2001, 81, pp. 973–88.
3. Wenze, S. J., Gunthert, K. C. and Forand, N. R., 'Influence of dysphoria on positive and negative cognitive reactivity to daily mood fluctuations', *Behaviour Research and Therapy*, 2007, 45, pp. 915–27.
4. André, C., *Vivre heureux: psychologie du bonheur*, Paris, Odile Jacob, 2003.
5. Koster, E. H. W., De Raedt, R., Goeleven, E., Franck, E. and Crombez, G., 'Mood congruent attentional bias in dysphoria: maintained attention to and impaired disengagement from negative information', *Emotion*, 2005, 5, pp. 446–55.
6. Caseras, X., Garner, M., Bradley, B. P. and Mogg, K., 'Biases in visual orienting to negative and positive scenes in dysphoria: an eye movement study', *Journal of Abnormal Psychology*, 2007, 116, pp. 491–7.
7. Holmes, E. A., Lang, T. J., Moulds, M. L. and Steele, A. M., 'Prospective and positive mental imagery deficits in dysphoria', *Behaviour Research and Therapy*, 2008, 46, pp. 976–81.
8. Neher, A., *Notes sur Qohélet*, Paris, Éditions de Minuit, 1951.
9. All biblical quotations are from the King James 2000 Bible, Cambridge Edition, unless otherwise stated.
10. Cottraux, J., *La force avec soi*, Paris, Odile Jacob, 2007.
11. Cioran, *Cahiers 1957–1972*, p. 961.
12. Miranda, R. and Nolen-Hoeksema S., 'Brooding and reflection: rumination predicts suicidal ideation at 1–year follow-up in a community sample', *Behaviour Research and Therapy*, 2007, 45, pp. 3088–95.
13. Papageorgiou, C. and Wells, A. (eds.), *Depressive Rumination: Nature, Theory and Treatment*, Chichester, Wiley, 2004, p. 22.
14. Lyubomirsky, S. and Tkach, C., 'The consequences of dysphoric rumination', in Papageorgiou and Wells, *Depressive Rumination*, pp. 21–41.
15. Raes, F., Hermans, D., Williams, J., Bijttebier, P. and Eelen, P., 'A "triple W"-model of rumination on sadness: why am I feeling sad, what's the

meaning of my sadness, and wish I could stop thinking about my sadness', *Cognitive Therapy and Research*, 2008, 35, pp. 526–41.

16. Moberly, N. J. and Watkins, E. R., 'Ruminative self-focus and negative affect: an experience sampling study', *Journal of Abnormal Psychology*, 2008, 117, pp. 314–23.

17. Papageorgiou, C. and Wells A., 'Positive beliefs about depressive rumination: development and preliminary validation of a self-report scale', *Behaviour Therapy*, 2001, 32, pp. 13–26.

18. Raes, F., Watkins, E. R., Williams, J. M. G. and Hermans, D., 'Non-ruminative processing reduces overgeneral autobiographical memory retrieval in students', *Behaviour Research and Therapy*, 2008, 46, pp. 748–56.

19. Rippere, V., 'What's the thing to do when you're feeling depressed? A pilot study', *Behaviour Research and Therapy*, 1977, 15, pp. 185–91.

20. Wells, A., Welford, M., King, P., Papageorgiou, C., Wisely, J. and Mendel, E., 'Chronic PTSD treated with metacognitive therapy: an open trial', *Cognitive and Behavioural Practice*, 2008, 15, pp. 85–92.

21. Nolen-Hoeksema, S., Stice, E., Wade, E. and Bohon, C., 'Reciprocal relations between ruminations and bulimic, substance abuse and depressive symptoms in female adolescents', *Journal of Abnormal Psychology*, 2007, 116, pp. 198–207.

22. Smyth, J. M., Wonderlich, S. A., Heron, K. E., Sliwinski, M. J., Crosby, R. D., Mitchell, J. E. and Engel, S. G., 'Daily and momentary mood and stress are associated with binge eating and vomiting in bulimia nervosa patients in the natural environment', *Journal of Consulting and Clinical Psychology*, 2007, 75, pp. 629–38.

23. Franko, D. L., Mintz, L. B., Villapiano, M., et al., 'Food, mood and attitude: reducing risk for eating disorders in college women', *Health Psychology*, 2005, 24, pp. 567–78.

24. Greeno, C. J. and Wing, R. R., 'Stress-induced eating', *Psychological Bulletin*, 1994, 115, pp. 444–64.

25. See Baumeister, R. F. and Vohs, K. D. (eds.), *Handbook of Self-Regulation: Research, Theory and Applications*, New York, Guilford Press, 2004, notably the chapters by Sayette, M. A., 'Self-regulatory failure and addiction', pp. 447–65, and Hull, J. G. and Slone, L. B., 'Alcohol and self-regulation', pp. 466–91; also Curtin, J. L. and Lang, A. R., 'Alcohol and emotion: insights and directives from affective science', in Rottenberg, J. and Johnson, S. L. (eds.), *Emotion and Psychopathology: Bridging Affective and Clinical Science*, Washington, DC, American Psychological Association, 2007, pp. 191–213.

26. Gwaltney, C. J., Shiffman, S. and Sayette, M. A., 'Situational correlates of abstinence self-efficacy', *Journal of Abnormal Psychology*, 2005, 114, pp. 649–60.

27. Pine, D. S., Cohen, E., Cohen, P. and Brook. J., 'Adolescent depressive symptoms as predictors of adult depression: moodiness or mood disorder?', *American Journal of Psychiatry*, 1999, 156, pp. 133–5.

28. Selby, E. A., Anestis, M. D. and Joiner, T. E., 'Understanding the relationship between emotional and behavioral dysregulation: emotional cascades', *Behaviour Research and Therapy*, 2008, 46, pp. 593–611.

29. Watson, D., *Mood and Temperament*, New York, Guilford Press, 2000, p. 103.
30. Tice, D. M., Bratslavsky, E. and Baumeister, R. F., 'Emotional distress regulation takes precedence over impulse control: if you feel bad, do it!', *Journal of Personality and Social Psychology*, 2001, 80, pp. 53–67.
31. Midal, F., *Quel boudhisme pour l'Occident?*, Paris, Seuil, 2006.
32. Ricard, M., *Plaidoyer pour le bonheur*, Paris, NiL Éditions, 2003.
33. Rilke, R. M., *Letters to a Young Poet*, London, Penguin, 2011, p. 51.

Chapter 4 Introspection

1. Hume, D., *A Treatise of Human Nature*, 1739; *An Enquiry Concerning the Principles of Morals*, 1751.
2. McGaugh, J. L., 'Significance and remembrance: the role of neuromodulatory systems', *Psychological Science*, 1990, 1, pp. 15–25.
3. Damasio, A., *The Feeling of What Happens*, London, Random House, 2000, p. 285.
4. Ibid., p. 286.
5. Ibid., p. 313.
6. St Augustine, *Confessions*, Oxford, Oxford University Press, 2008.
7. Jerphagnon, L., 'La conscience mise à nu', *Le Magazine Littéraire*, 2002, 409, pp. 24–6.
8. Montaigne, M., *The Complete Essays of Michel de Montaigne*, Charleston, SC, Forgotten Books, 2008, vol. 2, p. 522.
9. Comte-Sponville, A., *Dictionnaire philosophique*, Paris, Presses Universitaires de France, 2001.
10. Rousseau, J.-J., *Discourse on the Arts and Sciences*, 1750.
11. Pajak, F., *Le chagrin d'amour*, Paris, Presses Universitaires de France, 2000, p. 323.
12. McFarland, C., Buehler, R., von Ruti, R., Nguyen, L. and Alvaro, C., 'The impact of negative moods on self-enhancing cognitions: the role of reflective versus ruminative orientations', *Journal of Personality and Social Psychology*, 2007, 93. pp. 728–50.
13. The best French text for personal work on this subject is Emmons, R., *Merci! Quand la gratitude change nos vies*, Paris, Belfond, 2008. Fine preface by the philosopher Alexandre Jollien.
14. Edwards, M., *De l'émerveillement*, Paris, Fayard, 2008.
15. Mansfield, K., *Selected Stories*, Oxford, Oxford University Press, 2008, p. 142.
16. Entry for 11 May 1894.
17. Pennebaker, J. W., *Opening Up: The Healing Power of Expressing Emotions*, New York, Guilford Press, 1997.
18. Lepore, S. J., 'Expressive writing moderates the relation between intrusive thoughts and depressive symptoms', *Journal of Personality and Social Psychology*, 1997, 73, pp. 1030–7.
19. Sloan, D. M. and Marx, B. P., 'A closer examination of the structured written

disclosure procedure', *Journal of Consulting and Clinical Psychology*, 2004, 72, pp. 165–75.

20. Sloan, D. M. and Marx, B. P., 'Exposure through written emotional disclosure: two case examples', *Cognitive and Behavioral Practice*, 2006, 13, pp. 227–34.

21. Gortner, E. M., Rude, S. S. and Pennebaker, J. W., 'Benefits of expressive writing in lowering rumination and depressive symptoms', *Behaviour Therapy*, 2006, 37, pp. 292–303.

22. Lyubomirsky, S., Sousa, L. and Dickerhoof, R., 'The costs and benefits of writing, talking and thinking about life's triumphs and defeats', *Journal of Personality and Social Psychology*, 2006, 90, pp. 692–708.

23. Jacques Van Rillaer mentions, however, in his work *Psychologie de la vie quotidienne* (Paris, Odile Jacob, 2001, p. 67), the example of the Swiss writer Amiel, author of a diary with 14,500 printed pages, who ended up admitting himself that his *Diary* had turned out to be a rather unproductive affair.

24. Niederhoffer, K. G. and Pennebaker, J. W., 'Sharing one's story: on the benefits of writing or talking about emotional experiences', in Snyder, C. R. and Lopez, S. J., *Handbook of Positive Psychology*, Oxford, Oxford University Press, pp. 573–83.

25. Mirabel-Sarron, C. and Blanchet, A., 'Analyse des discours de patients déprimés', *Psychologie Française*, 1992, 37, pp. 277–89.

26. Niederhoffer and Pennebaker, 'Sharing one's story'.

27. Pennebaker, J. W., 'Writing about emotional experiences as a therapeutic process', *Psychological Science*, 1997, 8, pp. 162–6.

28. Watkins, E., 'Adaptive and maladaptive ruminative self-focus during emotional processing', *Behaviour Research and Therapy*, 2004, 42, pp. 1037–52.

29. Sloan, D. M., Marx, B. P., Epstein, E. M. and Dobbs, J. L, 'Expressive writing buffers against maladaptive rumination', *Emotion*, 2008, 8, pp. 302–6.

30. Langens, T. A. and Schüler, J., 'Effects of written emotional expression: the role of positive expectancies', *Health Psychology*, 2007, 26, pp. 174–82.

31. Jean-Louis Chrétien in *La joie spacieuse : essai sur la dilation*, Paris, Éditions de Minuit, 2007.

32. Maître Eckhart, *Conseils spirituels*, Paris, Payot & Rivages, 2003.

Chapter 5 Painful feelings and moods

1. The man was called Ötzi because he was found in the valley of the Ötzal, in Austria.

2. Musset, A. de, *Premières poésies: poésies nouvelles*, Paris, Gallimard, 1976.

3. Dalai Lama, *The Four Noble Truths*, New Delhi, HarperCollins, 1997.

4. Droit, R.-P., *Le culte du néant: les philosophes et le Bouddha*, Paris, Seuil, 1997.

5. Montaigne, M., *The Complete Essays of Michel de Montaigne*, Charleston, SC, Forgotten Books, 2008, vol. 2, p. 438.

Chapter 6 Anxieties

1. Shalom, H., Sagiv, L. and Boehnke, K., 'Worries and values', *Journal of Personality*, 2000, 68, pp. 309–46.
2. Nietzsche, F. W., *Twilight of the Idols*, in *Philosophical writings by Friedrich Wilhelm Nietzsche, Reinhold Grimm, Caroline Molina Y Vedia*, New York, Continuum, 1995, p. 192.
3. Cioran, E. M., *Cahiers 1957–1972*, Paris, Gallimard, 1997, p. 602.
4. Pessoa F., *The Book of Disquiet*, London, Penguin, 2002, p. 14.
5. Cioran, *Cahiers 1957–1972*, p. 240.
6. Clarke, P., Macleod, C. and Shirazee, N. R., 'Prepared for the worst: readiness to acquire threat bias and susceptibility to elevate trait anxiety', *Emotion*, 2008, pp. 145–50.
7. Hofmann, S. G., Moscovitch, D. A., Litz, B. T., Kim, H.-J., Davis, L. and Pizzagalli, D. A., 'The worried mind: autonomic and prefrontal activation during worrying', *Emotion*, 2005, 5, pp. 464–75.
8. Davey, G. C. L., Eldridge, F., Drost, J. and Macdonald, B. A., 'What ends a worry bout? An analysis of changes in mood and stop rule use across the catastrophising interview task', *Behaviour Research and Therapy*, 2007, 45, pp. 1231–43.
9. Rosset, C., *Le monde et ses remèdes*, Paris, Presses Universitaires de France, 2000 (2nd edition), p. 47.
10. Startup, H. M. and Davey, G. C. L. 'Inflated responsibility and the use of stop rules for catastrophic worrying', *Behaviour Research and Therapy*, 2003, 41, pp. 495–503.
11. Segiura, Y., 'Responsibility to continue thinking and worrying: evidence for incremental validity', *Behaviour Research and Therapy*, 2007, 45, pp. 1619–28.
12. Twenge, J. M., 'The age of anxiety? Birth cohort change in anxiety and neuroticism, 1952–1993', *Journal of Personality and Social Psychology*, 2000, 79, pp. 1007–21.
13. Hong, R. Y., 'Worry and rumination: differential associations with anxious and depressive symptoms and coping behaviors', *Behaviour Research and Therapy*, 2007, 45, pp. 277–90.
14. Watkins, M., Moulds, M. and Mackintosh, B., 'Comparisons between rumination and worry in a non-clinical population', *Behaviour Research and Therapy*, 2005, 43, pp. 1577–85.
15. Berenbaum, H., Thompson, R. J. and Pomerantz, E. M., 'The relation between worrying and concerns: the importance of perceived probability and cost', *Behaviour Research and Therapy*, 2007, 45, pp. 301–11.
16. Geraerts, E., Merckelbach, H., Jelicic, M. and Smeets, E., 'Long term consequences of suppression of intrusive anxious thoughts and repressive coping', *Behaviour Research and Therapy*, 2006, 44, pp. 1451–60.
17. Allen, W., *The Insanity Defence: The Complete Prose*, London, Random House, 2007.
18. Maner, J. K. and Schmidt, N. B., 'The role of risk avoidance in anxiety', *Behaviour Therapy*, 2006, 37, pp. 181–9.

19. Leahy, R. L., 'Emotional schemas and resistance to change in anxiety disorders', *Cognitive and Behavioral Practice*, 2004, 14, pp. 36–45.

20. Cioran, E. M., *Syllogismes de l'amertume*, Paris, Gallimard, 1980, p. 131.

21. Borkovec, T. D. and Roemer, L., 'Perceived functions of worry among generalized anxiety disorders subjects', *Journal of Behaviour Therapy and Experimental Psychiatry*, 1995, 26, pp. 25–30.

22. Kotov, R., Watson, D., Robles, J. P. and Schmidt, N. B., 'Personality traits and anxiety symptoms: the multilevel trait predictor model', *Behaviour Research and Therapy*, 2007, 45, pp. 1485–1503.

23. Perkins, A. M. and Corr, P. J., 'Can worriers be winners? The association between worrying and job performance', *Personality and Individual Differences*, 2005, 38, pp. 25–31.

24. Stein, M. B. and Heimberg, R. G., 'Well-being and life satisfaction in generalized anxiety disorder: comparison to major depressive disorder in a community sample', *Journal of Affective Disorders*, 2004, 79, pp. 161–6.

25. Mennin, D. S., Heimberg, R. G., Turk, C. L. and Fresco, D. M., 'Preliminary evidence for an emotion dysregulation model of generalized anxiety disorder', *Behaviour Research and Therapy*, 2005, 43, pp. 1281–1310.

26. Parker, G.,Wilhelm, K., Mitchell, P., Austin, M. P., Roussos, J. and Gladstone, G., 'The influence of anxiety as a risk to early onset of major depression', *Journal of Affective Disorders*, 1999, 52, pp. 11–17.

27. Fava, G. A., Ruini, C. and Rafanelli, C., 'Sequential treatments of mood and anxiety disorders', *Journal of Clinical Psychiatry*, 2005, 66, pp. 1392–400.

28. Paquet, Y., 'Relation entre *locus of control*, désir de contrôle et anxiété', *Journal de Thérapie Comportementale et Cognitive*, 2006, 16, pp. 97–102.

29. Koerner, N. and Dugas, M. J., 'An investigation of appraisals in individuals vulnerable to excessive worry: the role of intolerance in uncertainty', *Cognitive Therapy and Research*, 2008, 32, pp. 619–38.

30. There are numerous texts on this theme of allergy to uncertainty: Tiedens, L. Z. and Linton, S., 'Judgment under emotional certainty and uncertainty: the effect of specific emotions on information processing', *Journal of Personality and Social Psychology*, 2001, 81, pp. 973–88; Hsu, M., Bhatt, M., Tranel, D., Adolphs, R. and Camerer, C., 'Neural systems responding to degrees of uncertainty in human decision-making', *Science*, 2005, 310, pp. 1680–3; Carlton, N., Sharpe, D., and Asmundson, G., 'Anxiety sensitivity and intolerance of uncertainty: requisites of the fundamental fears?', *Behaviour Research and Therapy*, 2007, 45, pp. 2307–16.

31. Cervone, D., Kopp, D. A., Schaumann, L. and Scott, W. D., 'Mood, self-efficacy, and performance standards: lower moods induce higher standards for performance', *Journal of Personality and Social Psychology*, 1994, 67, pp. 499–512.

32. Gosselin, P., Dugas, M. J. and Ladouceur, R., 'Inquiétude et résolution de problèmes sociaux: le rôle de l'attitude négative face au problème', *Journal de Thérapie Comportementale et Cognitive*, 2002, 12, pp. 49–58.

33. See, for example, Ladouceur, R., Bélanger, L. and Léger, E., *Arrêtez de vous faire du souci pour tout et pour rien*, Paris, Odile Jacob, 2003. From the start, with Joseph Wolpe and the techniques of 'systematic desensitization', the

behaviouralists have worked on the confrontation with painful images. Wolpe, J., *Psychotherapy by Reciprocal Inhibition*, Stanford, Stanford University Press, 1958. See also Stampfl, T. G. and Lewis, D. J., 'Essentials of implosive therapy: a learning-theory-based psychodynamic behavioral therapy', *Journal of Abnormal Psychology*, 1967, 72, pp. 496–503.

34. Yalom, I., *Existential Therapy*, New York, Basic Books, 1980. See esp. ch. 5, 'Death and psychotherapy'.

35. Borkovec, T. D., Alcaine, O. and Behar, E., 'Avoidance theory of worry and generalized anxiety disorder', in Heimberg R. G., Turk, C. L. and Mennin, D. S. (eds.), *Generalized Anxiety Disorder: Advances in Research and Practice*, New York, Guilford Press, 2004, pp. 77–108.

36. *L'autofictif*, blog by Éric Chevillard, entry dated 15 November 2008, http://l-autofictif.over-blog.com.

Chapter 7 Resentment

1. Bukowski, C., *Ham on Rye*, Edinburgh, Canongate, 2001, p. 271.

2. Bushman, B. J., Baumeister, R. F. and Phillips, C. M., 'Do people aggress to improve their moods? Catharsis beliefs, affect regulation opportunity, and aggressive responding', *Journal of Personality and Social Psychology*, 2001, 18, pp. 17–32.

3. Cioran, E. M., *Cahiers 1957–1972*, Paris, Gallimard, 1997, p. 242.

4. Ellsworth, P. C. and Smith, C. A., 'From appraisal to emotion: differences among unpleasant feelings', *Motivation and Emotion*, 1998, 12, pp. 271–302.

5. In his *Journal*, entry dated 9 April 1894.

6. Cioran, E. M., *Syllogismes de l'amertume*, Paris, Gallimard, 1980, p. 80.

7. Tiedens, L. Z., 'Anger and advancement versus sadness and subjugation: the effect of negative emotion expressions on social status conferral', *Journal of Personality and Social Psychology*, 2001, 80, pp. 86–94.

8. Van Dijk, E., Van Kleef, G. A., Steinel, W. and Van Beest, I., 'A social function approach to emotions in bargaining: when communicating anger pays and when it backfires', *Journal of Personality and Social Psychology*, 2008, 94, pp. 600–14.

9. Verona, E. and Sullivan, E. A., 'Emotional catharsis and aggression revisited: heart rate reduction following aggressive responding', *Emotion*, 2008, 8, pp. 331–40.

10. See Rosenman, R., Brand, R. J., Jenkins, D., Friedman, M., Straus, R. and Wurm, M., 'Coronary heart disease in the Western Collaborative Group Study: final follow-up experience of 8½ years', *Journal of the American Medical Association*, 1975, 233, pp. 872–7; Blumenthal, J., Williams, R. B., Kong, Y., Schanberg, S. and Thompson, L., 'Type A behavior pattern and coronary atherosclerosis', *Circulation*, 1978, 58, pp. 634–9; Zyzanski, S. J., Jenkins, C. D., Ryan, T.J., Flessa, A. and Everist, M., 'Psychological correlates of coronary angiographic findings', *Archives of Internal Medicine*, 1975, 136, pp. 1234–7; Shekelle, R. B., Hulley, S. B., Neaton, J. D., et al., 'The Multiple Risk Factor

Intervention Trial behavioral pattern study: type A behavior pattern and incidence of coronary heart disease', *American Journal of Epidemiology*, 1985, 122, pp. 559–70.

11. See Dembroski, T., et al., 'Antagonistic hostility as a predictor of coronary heart disease in the Multiple Risk Factor Intervention Trial', *Psychosomatic Medicine*, 1989, 51, pp. 514–22; Denollet, J., Sys, S. U., Stroobant, N., Rombouts, H., Gillebert, T. C. and Brutsaert, D. L., 'Personality as independent predictor of long-term mortality in patients with coronary heart disease', *Lancet*, 1996, 347, pp. 417–21.

12. Chödrön, P., *La voie commence là où vous êtes*, Paris, La Table Ronde, 2000.

13. Wimalaweera, S. W. and Moulds, M. L., 'Processing memories of anger-eliciting events: the effect of asking "why" from a distance', *Behaviour Research and Therapy*, 2008, 46, pp. 402–9.

14. Ray, R. D., Wilhelm, F. H. and Gross, J. J, 'All in the mind's eye? Anger rumination and reappraisal', *Journal of Personality and Social Psychology*, 2008, 94, pp. 113–45.

15. Cioran, *Cahiers 1957–1972*, p. 800.

16. Fischer, A. H. and Roseman, I. J., 'Beat them or ban them: the characteristics and social functions of anger and contempt', *Journal of Personality and Social Psychology*, 2007, 93, pp. 103–15.

17. Gagnaire, C., *Versiculets et texticules*, Paris, Laffont, 1999, p. 227.

18. Beck, A. T., *Prisonniers de la haine*, Paris, Masson, 2002.

19. In his subtle and funny blog, *L'autofictif*, entry dated 4 August 2008, http://l-autofictif.over-blog.com.

20. Jacobson, N. S., Christensen, A., Prince, S. E., Cordova, J. and Eldridge, K., 'Integrative behavioral couple therapy: an acceptance-based, promising new treatment for couple discord', *Journal of Consulting and Clinical Psychology*, 2000, 68, pp. 351–5.

21. Rosenberg, M. B., *Les mots sont des fenêtres: introduction à la communication non violente*, Paris, La Découverte, 2002.

22. Averill, J. R., *Anger and Aggression: An Essay on Emotion*, New York, Springer, 1982.

23. Ellsworth, P. C. and Tong, E. M. W., 'What does it mean to be angry at yourself? Categories, appraisals, and the problem of language', *Emotion*, 2006, 6, pp. 572–86.

24. Parkinson, B., 'Relations and dissociations between appraisal and emotion ratings of reasonable and unreasonable anger and guilt', *Cognition and Emotion*, 1999, 13, pp. 347–85.

25. Dante Alighieri, *The Divine Comedy of Dante Alighieri: Inferno*, London, G. Routledge, 1867.

26. Deffenbacher, J. L., Huff, M. E., Lynch, R. S., Oetting, E. R. and Natalie, F., 'Characteristics and treatment of high anger drivers', *Journal of Counseling Psychology*, 2000, 47(1), pp. 5–17.

27. Deffenbacher, J. L., Lynch, R. S., Filetti, L. B., Dahlen, E. R. and Oetting, E. R., 'Anger, aggression, risky behavior, and crash-related outcomes in three groups of drivers', *Behaviour Research and Therapy*, 2003, 41, pp. 333–49.

28. Erwin, B. A., Heimberg, R. G., Schneier, F. R. and Liebowitz, M. R., 'Anger experience and expression in social anxiety disorder', *Behavior Therapy*, 2003, 34, pp. 331–50.

29. Engel, S. G., Boseck, J. J., Crosby, R. D., et al., 'The relationship of momentary anger and impulsivity to bulimic behavior', *Behaviour Research and Therapy*, 2007, 45, pp. 437–47.

30. Weisman, M. M., Klerman, G. L. and Paykel, E. S., 'Clinical evaluation of hostility in depression', *American Journal of Psychiatry*, 1971, 128, pp. 261–6.

31. Quartana, P. J. and Burns, J. W., 'Painful consequences of anger suppression', *Emotion*, 2007, 7, pp. 400–17.

32. *Kirikou et la Sorcière*, film directed by Michel Ocelot, 1998.

33. Quartana and Burns, 'Painful consequences'.

34. Mallick, S. K. and McCandless, B. R., 'A study of catharsis of aggression', *Journal of Personality and Social Psychology*, 1966, 4, pp. 591–6.

35. Wilkowski, B. M. and Robinson, M. D., 'Guarding against hostile thoughts: trait anger and the recruitment of cognitive control', *Journal of Personality and Social Psychology*, 2008, 8, pp. 578–83.

36. See, for example, Baumeister, R. F. and Vohs, K. D. (eds.), *Handbook of Self-Regulation: Research, Theory, and Applications*, New York, Guilford Press, 2004.

37. Amine, P., *Petite éloge de la colère*, Paris, Gallimard, 2008.

38. The best two in French in my view are Van Rillaer, J., *Les colères*, Meschers, Bernet-Danilio, 1999; Pleux, D., *Exprimer sa colère sans perdre le contrôle*, Paris, Odile Jacob, 2006.

39. See, for example, the website www.angerbusters.com.

40. Verona, E. and Kilmer, A., 'Stress exposure and affective modulation of aggressive behavior in men and women', *Journal of Abnormal Psychology*, 2007, 116, pp. 410–21.

41. Fanget, F. and Rouchouse, B., *L'affirmation de soi: une méthode de thérapie*, Paris, Odile Jacob, 2007.

42. Calmes, C. A. and Roberts, J. E., 'Rumination in interpersonal relationships: does co-rumination explain gender differences in emotional distress and relationship satisfaction among college students?', *Cognitive Therapy and Research*, 2008, 32, pp. 577–90.

43. Hayes, S. C., *Get Out of Your Mind and Into Your Life*, Oakland, New Harbinger, 2005.

44. 'La psychologie du pardon', 25th regional scientific workshop of the Association Française de Thérapie Comportementale et Cognitive, Aix-en-Provence, 30 and 31 May 2008.

45. De Waal, F., *De la réconciliation chez les primates*, Paris, Flammarion, 1992.

46. De Sairigné, G., *Mille pardons*, Paris, Robert Laffont, 2006.

47. See Ferro, M., *Le ressentiment dans l'histoire*, Paris, Odile Jacob, 2007; also McMullen, R., *Les émotions dans l'histoire, ancienne et moderne*, Paris, Les Belles Lettres, 2004.

48. Enright, R. D., Mullet, E. and Fitzgibbons, R., 'Le pardon comme mode de régulation émotionnelle', *Journal de Thérapie Comportementale et Cognitive*, 2001, 11, pp. 123–35.

49. Worthington, E. L. (ed.), *Handbook of Forgiveness*, New York, Routledge, 2005.
50. Enright et al., 'Le pardon'.
51. Zechmeister, J. S. and Romero, C., 'Victim and offender accounts of interpersonal conflict', *Journal of Personality and Social Psychology*, 2002, 82, pp. 675–86.
52. Fincham, F. D. and Beach, S. R. H., 'Forgiveness in marriage: implications for psychological aggressions and constructive communication', *Personal Relationships*, 2002, 94, pp. 239–51.
53. Exline, J. J., Baumeister, R. F., Zell, A. L., Kraft, A. and Witvliet, C. V. O., 'Not so innocent: does seeing one's own capability for wrongdoing predict forgiveness?', *Journal of Personality and Social Psychology*, 2008, 94, pp. 495–515.
54. Karremans, J. C., Van Lange, P. A. M., Ouwerkerk, J. W. and Kluwer, E., 'When forgiving enhances psychological well-being: the role of interpersonal commitment', *Journal of Personality and Social Psychology*, 2003, 84, pp. 1011–26.
55. McCullough, M. E., Bono, G. and Root, L. M., 'Rumination, emotion, and forgiveness: three longitudinal studies', *Journal of Personality and Social Psychology*, 2007, 92, pp. 490–505.
56. See Worthington, E. L., O'Connor, L. E., Berry, J. W., Sharp, C., Murray, R. and Yi, E., 'Compassion and forgiveness: implications for psychotherapy', in Gilbert, P. (ed.), *Compassion: Conceptualisations, Research and Use in Psychotherapy*, Hove, Routledge, 2005, pp. 168–92.
57. Berry, J. W., Worthington, E. L., Jr., O'Connor, L., Parrott, L., III, and Wade, N. G., 'Forgiveness, vengeful rumination and affective traits', *Journal of Personality*, 2005, 73(1), pp. 183–225.
58. Chiaramello, S., Munoz Sastre, M. T. and Mullet, E., 'Seeking forgiveness: factor structure, and relationships with personality and forgivingness', *Personality and Individual Differences*, 2008, 45, pp. 383–8.
59. Thibon, G., *L'illusion féconde*, Paris, Fayard, 1995.

Chapter 8 Sadness

1. Cioran, E. M., *Cahiers 1957–1972*, Paris, Gallimard, 1997, p. 682.
2. Ibid., p. 220.
3. Roudaut, J., 'Feuilles séchées d'ancolie', *Le Magazine Littéraire*, 1987, 244, pp. 43–5.
4. Comte-Sponville, A., *Dictionnaire philosophique*, Paris, Presses Universitaires de France, 2001, p. 369.
5. Bobin, C., *L'autre visage*, Paris, Lettres Vives, 1991.
6. Solomon, A., *Le diable intérieur: anatomie de la dépression*, Paris, Albin Michel, 2002, p. 481.
7. Cioran, *Cahiers 1957–1972*, p. 46.
8. Alloy, L. B. and Abramson, L. Y., 'Judgment of contingency in depressed and nondepressed students: sadder but wiser?', *Journal of Experimental Psychology*, 1979, 108, pp. 441–85.
9. Steiner, G., *Dix raisons (possibles) à la tristesse de pensée*, Paris, Albin Michel, 2005, p. 13.

10. Proverbs 25.20, Douay Rheims Bible, 1899 American edition.
11. Comte-Sponville, *Dictionnaire philosophique*.
12. See Spasojevic, J. and Alloy, L. B., 'Rumination as a common mechanism relating depressive risk to depression', *Emotion*, 2001, 1, pp. 25–37; also Nolen-Hoeksema, S., 'The role of rumination in depressive disorders and mixed anxiety/depressive symptoms', *Journal of Abnormal Psychology*, 2000, 109, pp. 504–11.
13. See Evans, J., Heron, J., Lewis, G., Araya, R., Wolke, D. and ALSPAC study team, 'Negative self-schemas and the onset of depression in women: a longitudinal study', *British Journal of Psychiatry*, 2005, 186, pp. 302–7; also Sheppes, G., Meiran, N., Gilboa-Schechtman, E. and Shahar, G., 'Cognitive mechanisms underlying implicit negative self concept in dysphoria', *Emotion*, 2008, 8, pp. 386–94.
14. See notably Rosenbaum, A., *La peur de l'infériorité: aperçu sur le régime moderne de la comparaison sociale*, Paris, L'Harmattan, 2005; and De Botton, A., *Du statut social*, Paris, Mercure de France, 2004.
15. Giordano, C., Wood, J. V. and Michela, J. L., 'Depressive personality styles, dysphoria and social comparisons in everyday life', *Journal of Personality and Social Psychology*, 2000, 79, pp. 438–51.
16. Klein, D. N., Shankman, S. A. and Rose, S., 'Ten-year prospective follow-up study of the naturalistic course of dysthymic disorder and double depression', *American Journal of Psychiatry*, 2006, 163, pp. 872–80.
17. See for review Hammen, C. 'Stress and depression', *Annual Review of Clinical Psychology*, 2005, 1, pp. 293–319.
18. Monroe, S. M., Slavich, G. M., Torres, L. D. and Gotlib, I. H., 'Major life events and major chronic difficulties are differentially associated with history of major depressive episodes', *Journal of Abnormal Psychology*, 2007, 116, pp. 116–24.
19. The World Health Organization considers that at the current rate, in 2020 depression will be the second cause of disability in the world, just behind cardiovascular diseases. See the WHO site, www.who.int/mental_health/managment/depression/definition/en.
20. See Gilbert, P., 'Evolution and depression: issues and implications', *Psychological Medicine*, 2006, 36, pp. 287–97; also Nesse, R. M., 'Is depression an adaptation?', *Archives of General Psychiatry*, 2000, 57, pp. 14–20.
21. Kendler, K. S., Hettema, J. M., Butera, F., Gardner, C. O. and Prescott, C. A., 'Life event dimensions of loss, humiliation, entrapment, and danger in the prediction of onsets of major depression disorder and generalized anxiety', *Archives of General Psychiatry*, 2003, 60, pp. 789–96.
22. Keller, M. C. and Nesse, R. M., 'The evolutionary significance of depressive symptoms: different adverse situations lead to different depressive symptoms patterns', *Journal of Personality and Social Psychology*, 2006, 91, pp. 316–30.
23. France, A., *Le lys rouge*, Paris, 1990, p. 69. (*The Red Lily*, Teddington, Echo Library, 2009, p. 53.)
24. Styron, W., *Darkness Visible*, New York, Random House, 2001, p. 41.
25. Cioran, *Cahiers 1957–1972*, p. 43.

26. Ibid., p. 894.

27. Brochier, J.-L., 'André Gide: la conquête de la liberté', *Le Magazine Littéraire*, 2007, special issue 11, pp. 68–70.

28. Fitzgerald, F. S., 'The Crack-Up', originally published in *Esquire*, February, March and April 1936.

29. See for summary Lôo, H. and Gourion D., *Les nuits de l'âme*, Paris, Odile Jacob, 2008.

30. Gotlib, I. H., Krasnoperova, E., Yue, D. N. and Joormann, J., 'Attentional biases for negative interpersonal stimuli in clinical depression', *Journal of Abnormal Psychology*, 2004, 113, pp. 127–35.

31. Leyman, L., De Raedt, R., Schacht, R. and Koster, E. H. W, 'Attentional biases for angry faces in unipolar depression', *Psychological Medicine*, 2007, 37, pp. 393–402.

32. Joormann, J. and Gotlib I. H., 'Is this happiness I see? Biases in the identification of emotional face expressions in depression and social phobia', *Journal of Abnormal Psychology*, 2003, 115, pp. 705–14.

33. Fu, C. H. Y., Williams, S. C., Brammer, M. J., et al., 'Neural responses to happy facial expressions in major depression following antidepressant treatment', *American Journal of Psychiatry*, 2007, 164, pp. 399–607.

34. Erickson, K., Drevets, W. C., Clark, L., et al., 'Mood-congruant bias in affective go/no go performance of unmedicated patients with major depressive disorder', *American Journal of Psychiatry*, 2005, 162, pp. 2171–3.

35. Kellough, J. L., Beevers, C. G., Ellis, A. J. and Wells, T. T., 'Time course of selective attention in clinically depressed young adults: an eye tracking study', *Behaviour Research and Therapy*, 2008, 46, pp. 1238–43.

36. Donaldson, C., Lam, D. and Mathews, A., 'Rumination and attention in major depression', *Behaviour Research and Therapy*, 2007, 45, pp. 2664–78.

37. Papageorgiou, C. and Wells, A., 'Metacognitive beliefs about rumination in recurrent major depression', *Cognitive and Behavioral Practice*, 2001, 8, pp. 160–4.

38. Jones, N. P., Siegle, G. J. and Thase, M. E., 'Effect of rumination and initial severity on remission to cognitive therapy for depression', *Cognitive Therapy and Research*, 2008, 32, pp. 591–604.

39. Reed, L. I., Sayette, M. A. and Cohn, J. F., 'Impact of depression on response to comedy: a dynamic facial coding analysis', *Journal of Abnormal Psychology*, 2007, 116, pp. 804–9.

40. Rehman, U. S., Boucher, E., Duong, D. and George, N., 'A context-informed approach to the study of negative-feedback seeking in depression', *Behaviour Research and Therapy*, 2008, 46, pp. 239–52.

41. Matt, G. E., Vazquez, C. and Campbell, W. K., 'Mood-congruent recall of affectively toned stimuli: a meta-analytic review', *Clinical Psychology Review*, 1992, 12, pp. 227–55.

42. Lyubomirsky, S., Caldwell, N. D. and Nolen-Hoeksema, S., 'Effects of ruminative and distracting responses to depressed mood on retrieval of auto-biographical memories', *Journal of Personality and Social Psychology*, 1998, 75, pp. 166–77.

43. Lyubomirsky, S. and Nolen-Hoeksema, S., 'Self-perpetuative properties of dysphoric rumination', *Journal of Personality and Social Psychology*, 1993, 65, pp. 339–49.
44. Joormann, J., Hertel, P. T., Borzovich, F. and Gotlib, I. H., 'Remembering the good, forgetting the bad: intentional forgetting of emotional material in depression', *Journal of Abnormal Psychology*, 2005, 114, pp. 640–8.
45. Bergouignan, L., Lemogne, C., Foucher, A., et al., 'Field perspective deficit for positive memories characterizes autobiographical memory in euthymic depressed patients', *Behaviour Research and Therapy*, 2008, 46, pp. 322–33.
46. Sutherland, K. and Bryant, R. A., 'Rumination and overgeneral autobiographical memory', *Behaviour Research and Therapy*, 2007, 45, pp. 2407–16.
47. Patel, T., Brewin, C. R., Wheatley, J., Wells, A., Fisher, P. and Myers, S., 'Intrusive images and memories in major depression', *Behaviour Research and Therapy*, 2007, 45, pp. 2573–80.
48. For a summary of current data on the dream in psychotherapy, see Montangero, J., *Comprendre ses rêves pour mieux se connaître*, Paris, Odile Jacob, 2007.
49. Rosset, C., *Route de nuit*, Paris, Gallimard, 1999.
50. Von Hecker, U. and Meiser, T., 'Focused attention in depressed mood: evidence from source monitoring', *Emotion*, 2005, 5, pp. 456–63.
51. Brinkmann, K. and Gendola, G. H. E., 'Does depression interfere with effort mobilization? Effects of dysphoria and task difficulty on cardiovascular response', *Journal of Personality and Social Psychology*, 2008, 94, pp. 146–57. With a correlation to neuro-imaging, Harvey, P., Fossati, P., Pochon, J. B., et al., 'Cognitive control and brain resources in major depression', *NeuroImage*, 2005, 26, pp. 860–9.
52. Compton, R. J., Lin, M., Vargas, G., Carp, J., Fineman, S. L. and Quandt, L. C., 'Error detection and posterior behavior in depressed undergraduates', *Emotion*, 2008, 8, pp. 58–67.
53. Rottenberg, J., Gross, J. J. and Gotlib, I. H., 'Emotion context insensitivity in major depressive disorder', *Journal of Abnormal Psychology*, 2005, 114, pp. 627–39.
54. Lethbridge, R. and Allen, N. B., 'Mood induced cognitive and emotional reactivity, life stress, and the prediction of depressive relapse', *Behaviour Research and Therapy*, 2008, 46, pp. 1142–50.
55. Guyotat, P. P., *Coma*, Paris, Mercure de France, 2006, p. 229.
56. Solomon, A., *Noonday Demon*, London, Vintage, 2002, p. 443.
57. Dagerman, S., *Le serpent*, Paris, Denoël, 1966 (published in English as *The Snake* in 1945).
58. Styron, *Darkness Visible*, p. 76.
59. Even, C., 'Clinique des troubles dépressifs', in Guelfi, J. D. and Rouillon, F. (eds.), *Manuel de psychiatrie*, Paris, Flammarion, 2007, pp. 257–65.
60. Vos, T., Haby, M. M., Barendregt, J. J., Kruijshaar, M., Corry, J. and Andrews, G., 'The burden of major depression avoidable by longer-term treatment strategies', *American Journal of Psychiatry*, 2004, 61, pp. 1097–103.

61. Fava, G. A., Ruini, C. and Belaise, C., 'The concept of recovery in major depression', *Psychological Medicine*, 2007, 37, pp. 307–17.
62. See notably Dozois, D. J. A. and Dobson, K. S. (eds.), *The Prevention of Anxiety and Depression*, Washington, DC, American Psychological Association, 2004. See also the special edition of *Cognitive and Behavioral Practice*, 2008, 15(1), pp. 1–52, 'Prevention of mental disorders'; and Cuijpers, P., van Straten, A., Smit, F., Mihalopoulos, C. and Beekman, A., 'Preventing the onset of depressive disorders: a meta-analytic review of psychological interventions', *American Journal of Psychiatry*, 2008, 165, pp. 1272–80.
63. Sheline, Y. I., Sanghavi, M., Mintun, M. A. and Gado, M. H., 'Depression duration but not age predicts hippocampal volume loss in medically healthy women with recurrent major depression', *Journal of Neurosciences*, 1999, 19, pp. 5034–43.
64. Watkins, E., Scott, J., Wingrove, J., et al., 'Rumination-focused cognitive behaviour therapy for residual depression: a case series', *Behaviour Research and Therapy*, 2007, 45, pp. 2144–54.
65. Segal, Z. V., Kennedy, S., Gemar, M., Hood, K., Pedersen, R. and Buis, T., 'Cognitive reactivity to sad mood provocation and the prediction of depressive relapse', *Archives of General Psychiatry*, 2006, 63, pp. 749–55.
66. Ramel, W., Goldin, P. R., Eyler, L. T., Brown, G. G., Gotlib, I. H. and McQuaid, J. R., 'Amygdala reactivity and mood-congruent memory in individuals at risk for depressive relapse', *Biological Psychiatry*, 2007, 61, pp. 231–9.
67. Sheppard, L. C. and Teasdale, J. D., 'How does dysfunctional thinking decrease during recovery from major depression?', *Journal of Abnormal Psychology*, 2004, 113, pp. 67–71.
68. Amongst the best guides available in French are Mirabel-Sarron, C., *La dépression: comment s'en sortir*, Paris, Odile Jacob, 2002; Cungi, C. and Note, Y. D., *Faire face à la depression*, Paris, Retz, 2004.
69. Papageorgiou, C. and Wells, A. (eds.), *Depressive Rumination: Nature, Theory and Treatment*, Chichester, Wiley, 2004.
70. Powers, D. V., Thompson, L. W. and Gallagher-Thompson, D., 'The benefits of using psychotherapy skills following treatment for depression: an examination of "afterwork" and a test of the skills hypothesis in older adults', *Cognitive and Behavioral Practice*, 2008, 15, pp. 194–202.
71. See for summary Fanget, F., *Toujours plus: psychologie du perfectionnisme*, Paris, Odile Jacob, 2006.
72. Safran, R. and Mansell, W., 'Perfectionism and psychopathology: a review of research and treatment', *Clinical Psychology Review*, 2001, 21, pp. 879–906.
73. Rosset, *Route de nuit*, p. 15.
74. Spadone, C., 'Rémission cognitive et rémission clinique de la dépression', *L'Encéphale*, 2008, 34, pp. 211–13.
75. Pronin, E. and Wegner, D., 'Manic thinking: independent effects of thought speed and thought content on mood', *Psychological Science*, 2006, 17, pp. 807–13.
76. Cioran, *Cahiers 1957–1972*, p. 219.

Chapter 9 Despair

1. Guillon, C. and Le Bonniec, Y., *Suicide mode d'emploi: histoire, technique, actualité*, Paris, Éditions Alain Moreau, 1982.
2. See the website of Isalou Regen, www.365mornings.com/blog365.
3. Cioran, E. M., *Cahiers 1957–1972*, Paris, Gallimard, 1997, p. 626.
4. Both quotations are from the special edition of *Le Magazine Littéraire* on 'Suicidés de la littérature', 1998, 256, pp. 60–1.
5. Voltaire in a letter to M. Marriott, dated 26 February 1767. Trans. Tallentyre, S. G., in *Voltaire in His Letters*, London, G. P. Putnam's Sons, 1919, p. 208.
6. Paykel, E. S., Myers, J. K., Lindenthal, J. J. and Tanner, J., 'Suicidal feelings in the general population: a prevalence study', *British Journal of Psychiatry*, 1974, 124, pp. 460–9.
7. See Kerr, D., Owen, L. D. and Capaldi, D. M., 'Suicide ideation and its recurrence in boys and men from early adolescence to early adulthood: an event history analysis', *Journal of Abnormal Psychology*, 2008, 117, pp. 625–36; also Marcenko, M. O., Fishman, G. and Friedman, J., 'Re-examining adolescent suicidal ideation: a developmental perspective applied to a diverse population', *Journal of Youth and Adolescence*, 1999, 28, pp. 121–38.
8. Meehan, P. J., Lamb, J. A., Saltzman, L. E. and O'Carroll, P. W., 'Attempted suicide among young adults: progress towards a meaningful estimate of prevalence', *American Journal of Psychiatry*, 1992, 149, pp. 41–4.
9. Bruce, M. L., Ten Have, T. R., Reynolds III, C. F., et al., 'Reducing suicidal ideation and depressive symptoms in depressed older primary care patients: a randomized controlled trial', *Journal of the American Medical Association*, 2004, 291, pp. 1081–91.
10. O'Connor, R. C. and Noyce, R., 'Personality and cognitive processes: self-criticism and different types of rumination as predictors of suicidal ideation', *Behaviour Research and Therapy*, 2008, 46, pp. 392–401.
11. Witte, T. K., Fitzpatrick, K. K., Warren, K. L., et al., 'Naturalistic evaluation of suicidal ideation: variability and relation to attempt status', *Behaviour Research and Therapy*, 2006, 44, pp. 1029–40.
12. Zlotnick, C., Donaldson, D., Spirito, A. and Pearlstein, T., 'Affect regulation and suicide attempts in adolescent inpatients', *Journal of the American Academy of Child and Adolescent Psychiatry*, 1977, 36, pp. 793–7.
13. Miranda, R. and Nolen-Hoeksema, S., 'Brooding and reflection: rumination predicts suicidal ideation at 1 year follow-up in a community sample', *Behaviour Research and Therapy*, 2007, 45, pp. 3088–95.
14. Rudd, M. D., Joiner, T. and Rajad, M. H., 'Relationships among suicide ideators, attempters, and multiple attempters in a young-adult sample', *Journal of Abnormal Psychology*, 1996, 105, pp. 541–50.
15. Chamfort, N., *Maximes et pensées*, Paris, Gallimard, 1982.
16. Thibon, G., *L'illusion féconde*, Paris, Fayard, 1995, p. 17.
17. Styron, W., *Darkness Visible*, New York, Random House, 2001, p. 52.
18. The key article on the feelings of suicidal individuals is Baumeister, R. F., 'Suicide as escape from self', *Psychological Review*, 1990, 97, pp. 90–113.

19. Tolstoy, L., *A Confession*, London, Penguin, 1987.
20. Turvill, J. L., Burroughs, A. K. and Moore, K. P., 'Change in occurrence of paracetamol overdose in UK after introduction of blister packs', *Lancet*, 2000, 355, pp. 2048–9.
21. Bennewith, O., Nowers, M. and Gunnell, D., 'Effects of barriers on the Clifton suspension bridge, England, on local patterns of suicide: implications for prevention', *British Journal of Psychiatry*, 2007, 190, pp. 266–7.
22. Terra, J.-L., 'Prévenir le suicide: repérer et agir', *Actualités et Dossiers en Santé Publique*, 2004, 45, pp. 20–5.
23. A noteworthy investigative article on this subject is Anderson, S., 'The urge to end it', *New York Times*, 6 July 2008.
24. Enns, M. W., Cox, B. J., Afifi, T. O., de Graaf, R., ten Have, M. and Sareen, J., 'Childhood adversities and risk for suicidal ideation and attempts: a longitudinal population-based study', *Psychological Medicine*, 2006, 36, pp. 1769–78.
25. Cheng, A. T. A., Hawton, K., Chen, T. H. H., et al., 'The influence of media reporting of a celebrity suicide on suicidal behavior in patients with a history of depressive disorder', *Journal of Affective Disorders*, 2007, 103, pp. 69–75.
26. Yip, P. S., Fu, K. W., Yang, K. C., et al., 'The effects of a celebrity suicide on suicide rates in Hong Kong', *Journal of Affective Disorders*, 2006, 93, pp. 245–52.
27. Séguin, M., Lesage, A., Turecki, G., et al., 'Life trajectories and burdens of adversity: mapping the developmental profiles of suicide mortality', *Psychological Medicine*, 2007, 37, pp. 1575–83.
28. Sarwer, D. B., Brown, G. K. and Evans, D. L., 'Cosmetic breast augmentation and suicide', *American Journal of Psychiatry*, 2007, 164, pp. 1006–13.
29. Harwood, D. M. J., Hawton, K., Hope, T., Harriss, L. and Jacoby, R., 'Life problems and physical illness as risk factors for suicide in older people: a descriptive and case-control study', *Psychological Medicine*, 2006, 36, pp. 1265–74.
30. 'On the 4th November 1954, Dagerman locked himself in his garage, started his car motor and let himself suffocate. It appears he may have made a final effort to switch off the engine and get out, but it was too late.' See the postscript to Dagerman, S., *Le serpent*, Paris, Gallimard, p. 255.
31. Guelfi, J.-D. and Rouillon, F. (eds.), *Manuel de psychiatrie*, Paris, Flammarion, 2007, pp. 477–80.
32. Sokero, T. P., Melartin, T. K., Rytsälä, H. J., et al., 'Prospective study of risk factors for attempted suicide among patients with DSM-IV major depressive disorder', *British Journal of Psychiatry*, 2005, 186, pp. 314–18.
33. Fairweather, A. K., Anstey, K. J., Rodgers, B. and Butterworth, P., 'Factors distinguishing suicide attempters from suicide ideators in a community sample: social issues and physical heath problems', *Psychological Medicine*, 2006, 36, pp. 1235–45.
34. Jollant, F., Lawrence, N. S., Giampietro, V., et al., 'Orbitofrontal cortex response to angry faces in men with histories of suicide attempts', *American Journal of Psychiatry*, 2008, 165, pp. 740–8.
35. Mann, J. J., 'Neurobiology of suicidal behavior', *Nature Reviews Neuroscience*, 2003, 4, pp. 819–28.

36. See Estryn-Béhar, M., *Risques professionnels et santé des médecins*, Paris, Masson, 2002, esp. 'Taux de suicide', pp. 42–7.

37. Gourdon, G., 'Bernanos: la mort en ce jardin', *Le Magazine Littéraire*, special edition on 'Suicidés de la littérature', 1998, 256, pp. 44–5.

38. Terra, 'Prévenir le suicide'.

39. See Granier, E., *Idées noires et tentatives de suicide*, Paris, Odile Jacob, 2006; also Guillerm, L.-C. and Marc, B., *Le mal de vivre*, Paris, Odile Jacob, 2007.

40. See Goldston, D. B., Reboussin, B. A. and Daniel, S. S., 'Predictors of suicide attempts: state and components', *Journal of Abnormal Psychiatry*, 2006, 115, pp. 842–9; and also Lau, M. A., Segal, Z. and Williams, J. M. G., 'Teasdale's differential activation hypothesis: implications for mechanisms of depressive relapse and suicidal behaviour', *Behaviour Research and Therapy*, 2004, 42, pp. 1001–17.

41. Cioran, *Cahiers 1957–1972*, p. 29.

42. See Williams, J. M. G., Barnhofer, T., Crane, C. and Beck, A. T., 'Problem solving deteriorates following mood challenge in formerly depressed patients with a history of suicide ideation', *Journal of Abnormal Psychiatry*, 2005, 114, pp. 421–31; also Jollant, F., Bellivier, F., Leboyer, M., et al., 'Impaired decision making in suicide attempters', *American Journal of Psychiatry*, 2005, 162, pp. 304–10.

43. Johnson, J., Gooding, P. and Tarrier, N., 'An investigation of aspects of the cry of pain model of suicide risk: the role of defeat in impairing memory', *Behaviour Research and Therapy*, 2008, 46, pp. 968–75.

44. Raust, A., Slama, F., Mathieu, F., et al., 'Prefrontal cortex dysfunction in patients with suicidal behavior', *Psychological Medicine*, 2006, 37, pp. 411–19.

45. Dagerman, *Le serpent*, postscript, p. 276.

46. Blog, *L'autofictif*, entry dated Friday 3 October 2008, http://l-autofictif.over-blog.com.

47. Dervic, K., Oquendo, M. A., Grunebaum, M. F., Ellis, S., Burke, A. K. and Mann, J. J., 'Religious affiliation and suicide attempt', *American Journal of Psychiatry*, 2004, 161, pp. 2303–8.

48. Quoted in *Famille Chrétienne*, 30 September 2006, 1498, pp. 19–28.

49. Midal, F., *ABC du Bouddhisme*, Paris, Grancher, 2008.

50. Cioran, E. M., *De l'inconvénient d'être né*, Paris, Gallimard, 1973.

51. Cioran, E. M., *Syllogismes de l'amertume*, Paris, Gallimard, 1980, p. 74.

52. Beck, A. T., Steer, R. A., Kovacs, M. and Garrison, B., 'Hopelessness and eventual suicide: a 10–year prospective study of patients hospitalized with suicidal ideation', *American Journal of Psychiatry*, 1985, 142, pp. 559–63.

Chapter 10 Fragility

1. According to the expression used by Anna Gavalda in her novel *Ensemble, c'est tout*, Paris, Le Dilettante, 2004. (*Hunting and Gathering*, Riverhead Books, 2007, trans. Alison Anderson.)

2. Lee, W. L., Wadsworth, M. and Hotopf, M., 'The protective role of trait

anxiety: a longitudinal cohort study', *Psychological Medicine*, 2006, 36, pp. 345–51.

3. Feeny, B. C., 'The dependency paradox in close relationships: accepting dependence promotes independence', *Journal of Personality and Social Psychology*, 2007, 92, pp. 268–85.

4. Rosset, C., *Loin de moi*, Paris, Éditions de Minuit, 1999, p. 92.

5. Kagan, J., *La part de l'inné*, Paris, Bayard, 1999; also Aron, E. N., *Ces gens qui ont peur d'avoir peur*, Montréal, Éditions de l'Homme, 1999.

6. Aron, *Ces gens*, pp. 28–9.

7. Brenot, P., *La génie et la folie*, Paris, Odile Jacob, 2007.

8. Kramer, P., *Listening to Prozac*, New York, Viking, 1993.

9. Quoted by Charach, R., in his review of *Poets on Prozac: Mental Illness, Treatment, and the Creative Process* (Baltimore, Johns Hopkins University Press, 2008), *American Journal of Psychiatry*, 2008, 165, p. 1617.

10. Lewis, G., *Sunbathing in the Rain: A Cheerful Book about Depression*, London, Flamingo, 2002.

11. Colman, T., Croudace, T. J., Wadsworth, M. E. J., Kuh, D. and Jones, P. B., 'Psychiatric outcomes 10 years after treatment with antidepressants or anxiolytics', *British Journal of Psychiatry*, 2008, 193, pp. 327–31.

12. Knutson, B., Wolkowitz, O. M., Cole, S. W., et al., 'Selective alteration of personality and social behavior by serotonergic intervention', *American Journal of Psychiatry*, 1998, 155, pp. 373–9.

13. Ekselius, L. and Knorring, L. von, 'Changes in personality traits during treatment with sertraline or citalopram', *British Journal of Psychiatry*, 1999, 147, pp. 444–8.

14. Norbury, R., Mackay, C. E., Cowen, P. J., Goodwin, G. M. and Harmer, C. J., 'Short-term antidepressant treatment and facial processing', *British Journal of Psychiatry*, 2007, 190, pp. 531–2.

15. See Harmer, C. J., Hill, S., Taylor, M. J., Cowen, P. J. and Goodwin, G. M., 'Towards a neuropsychological theory of antidepressant drug action: increase in positive emotional bias after potentiation of norepinephrine activity', *American Journal of Psychiatry*, 2003, 160, pp. 990–2; also Harmer, C. J., Shelley, N. C., Cowen, P. J. and Goodwin, G. M., 'Increased positive versus negative affective perception and memory in healthy volunteers following selective serotonin and norepinephrine reuptake inhibition', *American Journal of Psychiatry*, 2004, 161, pp. 1256–63.

16. Hariri, A. R. and Holmes, A., 'Genetics of emotional regulation: the role of the serotonin transporter in neural function', *Trends in Cognitive Sciences*, 2006, 10, pp. 182–91.

17. Hariri, A. R., Mattay, V. S., Tessitore, A., et al., 'Serotonin transporter genetic variation and the response of the human amygdala', *Science*, 2002, 297, pp. 400–3.

18. Osinsky, R., Reuter, M., Küpper, Y., et al., 'Variations in the serotonin transporter gene modulate selective attention to threat', *Emotion*, 2008, 8, pp. 584–8.

19. See Pezawas, L., Meyer-Lindenberg, A., Drabant, E. M., et al., '5–HTTLPR polymorphism impacts human cingulate–amygdala interactions: a genetic

susceptibility mechanism for depression', *Nature Neuroscience*, 2005, 8, pp. 828–34; also Booij, L. and Van de Does, A. J. W., 'Cognitive and serotonergic vulnerability to depression: convergent findings', *Journal of Abnormal Psychology*, 2007, 116, pp. 86–94.

20. Kilpatrick, D. G., Koenen, K. C., Ruggiero, K. J., et al., 'The serotonin transporter genotype and social support and moderation of posttraumatic stress disorder and depression in hurricane-exposed adults', *American Journal of Psychiatry*, 2007, 164, pp. 1693–9.

21. See Wilhelm, K., Mitchell, P. B., Niven, H., et al., 'Life events, first depression onset and the serotonin transporter gene', *British Journal of Psychiatry*, 2006, 188, pp. 210–15; also Kendler, K. S., Kuhn, J. W., Vittum, J., Prescott, C. A. and Riley, B., 'The interaction of stressful life events and a serotonin transporter polymorphism in the prediction of episodes of major depression: a replication', *Archives of General Psychiatry*, 2005, 62, pp. 529–35; or Zalsman, M. D., Huang, Y. Y., Oquendo, M. A., et al., 'Association of a triallelic serotonin transporter gene promoter region (5–HTTLPR) polymorphism with stressful life events and severity of depression', *American Journal of Psychiatry*, 2006, 163, pp. 1588–93.

22. Seligman, M. E. P., Schulman, P. and Tryon, A., 'Group prevention of depression and anxiety symptoms', *Behaviour Research and Therapy*, 2007, 45, pp. 1111–26.

23. Wichers, M., Myin-Germeys, I., Jacobs, N., et al., 'Genetic risk of depression and stress-induced negative affects in daily life', *British Journal of Psychiatry*, 2007, 191, pp. 218–23.

24. Fitzgerald, F. S., *The Crack-Up*, Harmondsworth, Penguin, 1965, p. 46.

25. Roffman, J. L., Marci, C. D., Glick, D. M., Dougherty, D. D. and Rauch, S. L., 'Neuroimaging and the functional neuroantomy of psychotherapy', *Psychological Medicine*, 2005, 35, pp. 1385–98.

26. Johnson, W. and Krueger, R. F., 'Higher perceived life control decreases genetic variants in physical health: evidence from a national twin study', *Journal of Personality and Social Psychology*, 2005, 88, pp. 165–73; also Taylor, S. E., Lerner, J. S., Sherman, D. K., Sage, R. M. and McDowell, N. K., 'Are self-enhancing cognitions associated with healthy or unhealthy biological profiles?', *Journal of Personality and Social Psychology*, 2003, 85, pp. 605–15.

27. Quoted by Pigeaud, J., in *Melancholia*, Paris, Payot, 2008, p. 11.

28. Sémelin, J., *J'arrive où je suis étranger*, Paris, Seuil, 2007.

29. Rilke, R. M., *Les cahiers de Malte Laurids Brigge*, Paris, Gallimard, 1991.

Chapter 11 Calm and energy

1. Traditionally attributed to the French doctor René Leriche, 1936.

2. See for summary Thayer, R. E., *The Origin of Everyday Moods: Managing Energy, Tension and Stress*, Oxford, Oxford University Press, 1996.

3. Entry for 30 January 1889.

4. Thayer, R. E., 'Problem perception, optimism, and related states as a function

of time of day (diurnal rhythm) and moderate exercise: two arousal systems in interaction', *Motivation and Emotion*, 1978, 11, pp. 19–36.

5. I found this message on a packet of children's biscuits, encouraging an active lifestyle in order to use up calories absorbed by eating too many of these over-sweetened products.

6. See, for example, the journal entirely devoted to these links between physical and mental health: Taylor, A. and Faulkner, G., 'Inaugural editorial', *Mental Health and Physical Activity*, 2008, 1, pp. 1–8.

7. See, for example, Thayer, R. E., et al., 'The influence of walking on mood, diet and sleep', paper presented at the annual Congress for the Association of Psychological Science, New York, 2006; or Thayer, R. E., et al., 'Amount of daily walking predicts energy, mood, personality and health', paper presented at the annual Congress of the American Psychological Association, Washington, DC, 2005.

8. Watson, D., *Mood and Temperament*, New York, Guilford Press, 2000, p. 87.

9. Otto, M. W., Church, T. S., Craft, L. L., Smits, J. A. J., Trivedi, M. H. and Greer, T. L., 'Exercise for mood and anxiety disorders', *Journal of Clinical Psychiatry*, 2007, 68, pp. 669–76.

10. Blumenthal, J. A., Babyak, M. A., Moore, K. A., et al., 'Effects of exercise training on older patients with major depressions', *Archives of Internal Medicine*, 1999, 159, pp. 2349–56.

11. Mather, A. S., Rodriguez, C., Guthrie, M. F., McHarg, A. M., Reid, I. C. and McMurdo, M. E. T., 'Effects of exercise on depressive symptoms in older adults with poorly responsive depressive disorder', *British Journal of Psychiatry*, 2002, 180, pp. 411–15.

12. Broman-Fulks, J. J., Berman, M. E., Rabian, B. and Webster, M. J., 'Effects of aerobic exercise on anxiety sensitivity', *Behaviour Research and Therapy*, 2004, 42, pp. 125–36.

13. Kubesch, S., Bretschneider, V., Freudenmann, R., et al., 'Aerobic endurance exercise improves executive functions in depressed patients', *Journal of Clinical Psychiatry*, 2003, 64, pp. 1005–12.

14. De Moor, M. H. M., Boomsma, D. I., Stubbe, J. H., Willemsen, G. and de Geus, E. J., 'Testing causality in the association between regular exercise and symptoms of anxiety and depression', *Archives of General Psychiatry*, 2008, 65, pp. 897–905.

15. McCrone, P., Darbishire, L., Ridsdale, L. and Seed, P. T., 'Cost-effectiveness of cognitive behavioural therapy, graded exercise and usual care for patients with chronic fatigue in primary care', *Psychological Medicine*, 2004, 34, pp. 991–9.

16. Novotney, A., 'Get your clients moving', *Monitor on Psychology*, 2008, 39(7), pp. 68–9.

17. Inserm (Institut National de Prévention et d'Éducation pour la Santé), *Activités physiques: contextes et effets sur la santé*, Paris, Éditions Inserm, 2008. Abstract available online, http://ist.inserm.fr/basisrapports/activite-physique/activite-physique_synthese.pdf.

18. Cascua, S., *Le sport est-il bon pour la santé?*, Paris, Odile Jacob, 2002.

19. Manzoni, G. M., Pagnini, F., Castelnuovo, G. and Molinari, E., 'Relaxation training for anxiety: a ten-years systematic review with meta-analysis', *BMC Psychiatry*, 2008, 8, p. 41, available at www.biomedcentral.com/1471-244X/8/41.

20. Jorm, A. F., Morgan, A. J. and Hetrick, S. E., 'Relaxation for depression', *Cochrane Database of Systematic Reviews*, 2008, 4, CD007142.

21. Del Vecchio, T. and O'Leary, K. D., 'Effectiveness of anger treatments for specific anger problems: a meta-analytic review', *Clinical Psychology Review*, 2004, 24, pp. 15–34.

22. See, for example, Servant, D., *Relaxation et meditation: retrouver son équilibre émotionnel*, Paris, Odile Jacob, 2007; or Cungi, C. and Limousin, S., *Savoir se relaxer*, Paris, Retz, 2003.

23. Gailliot, M. T., Baumeister, R. F., DeWall, C. N., et al., 'Self-control relies on glucose as a limited energy source: willpower is more than a metaphor', *Journal of Personality and Social Psychology*, 2007, 92(2), pp. 325–36.

24. Thayer, *Origin of Everyday Moods*, p. 28.

25. Ibid., p. 242.

26. Omvik, S., Pallesen, S., Bjorvatn, B., Thayer, J. F. and Nordhus, I. H., 'Night-time thoughts in high and low worriers: reaction to caffeine-induced sleeplessness', *Behaviour Research and Therapy*, 2007, 45, pp. 715–27.

27. See, for example, Servan-Schreiber, D., *Guérir*, Paris, Robert Laffont, 2003; also Presles, P. and Solano, C., *Prévenir: cancer, Alzheimer, infarctus, et vivre en forme plus longtemps*, Paris, Robert Laffont, 2006.

28. Schwarzer, R., Luszczynska, A., Ziegelmann, J. P., Scholz, U. and Lippke, S., 'Social-cognitive predictors of physical exercise adherence: three longitudinal studies in rehabilitation', *Health Psychology*, 2008, 27(1), suppl., pp. S54–S63.

29. Desharnais, R., Jobin, J., Côté, C., Lévesque, L. and Godin, G., 'Aerobic exercise and the placebo effect: a controlled study', *Psychosomatic Medicine*, 1993, 55, pp. 149–54.

30. Crum, A. J. and Langer, E. J., 'Mind-set matters: exercise and the placebo effect', *Psychological Science*, 2007, 18(2), pp. 165–71.

31. Quoted in Lake, J. H. and Spiegel, D., *Complementary and Alternative Treatments in Mental Health Care*, Arlington, American Psychiatric Publishing, 2007.

Chapter 12 Regulating feelings and moods

1. Casagrande, C., 'Quand la mélancolie était un péché', *L'Histoire*, 2004, 290a, pp. 10–12.

2. Carver, C. S. and Scheier, M. F., 'Origins and functions of positive and negative affects: a control-process view', *Psychological Bulletin*, 1990, 97, pp. 19–35.

3. Schwarz, R. M. and Garamoni, G. L., 'Cognitive balance and psychopathology: evaluation of an information processing model of positive and negative states of mind', *Clinical Psychology Review*, 1989, 9, pp. 271–4.

4. Schwarz, N. and Strack, F., 'Evaluating one's life: a judgment model of

subjective well-being', in Strack, F., Argyle, M. and Schwarz, N. (eds.), *The Science of Well-Being*, Oxford, Pergamon Press, 1991, pp. 27–47.

5. Kuppens, P., Realo, A. and Diener, E., 'The role of positive and negative emotions in life satisfaction judgment across nations', *Journal of Personality and Social Psychology*, 2008, 95, pp. 66–75.

6. Shiota, M. N., 'Silver linings and candles in the dark: differences among positive coping strategies in predicting subjective well-being', *Emotion*, 2006, 6, pp. 335–9.

7. Gross, J. J. (ed.), *Handbook of Emotion Regulation*, New York, Guilford Press, 2007.

8. See reference article: Larsen, R. J., 'Towards a science of mood regulation', *Psychological Inquiry*, 2000, 11, pp. 129–41.

9. Hemenover, S. H., Augustine, A. A., Shulman, T., Tran, T. Q. and Barlett, C. P., 'Individual differences in negative affects repair', *Emotion*, 2008, 8, pp. 468–78.

10. Tamir, M., John, O. P., Srivastava, S. and Gross, J. J., 'Implicit theories of emotion: affective and social outcomes across a major life transition', *Journal of Personality and Social Psychology*, 2007, 92, pp. 731–44.

11. Van Rillaer, J., *La gestion de soi*, Liège, Mardaga, 1992, p. 186.

12. Larsen, 'Towards a science of mood regulation'.

13. Koster, E. H. W., Rassin, E., Crombez, G. and Naring, G. W., 'The paradoxical effect of suppressing anxious thoughts during imminent threat', *Behaviour Research and Therapy*, 2003, 41, pp. 1113–20.

14. Pessoa, F., *The Book of Disquiet*, London, Penguin, 2002, pp. 296–7.

15. See for summary Sher, K. J. and Grekin, E. R., 'Alcohol and affect regulation', in Gross, *Handbook of Emotion Regulation*, pp. 560–80.

16. Steel, C. M. and Josephs, R. A., 'Alcohol myopia: its prized and dangerous effects', *American Psychologist*, 1990, 45, pp. 921–33.

17. Hull, J. G., 'A self-awareness model of the causes and effects of alcohol consumption', *Journal of Abnormal Psychology*, 1981, 90, pp. 586–600.

18. Cooper, M. L., Frone, M. R., Russell, M. and Mudar, P., 'Drinking to regulate positive and negative emotions: a motivational model of alcohol use', *Journal of Personality and Social Psychology*, 1995, 69, pp. 990–1005.

19. See for summary of this research Hull, J. G. and Slone, L. B., 'Alcohol and self-regulation', in Baumeister, R. F. and Vohs, K. D. (eds.), *Handbook of Self-Regulation: Research, Theory and Applications*, New York, Guilford Press, 2004, pp. 466–91.

20. See for summary of this research Sayette, M. A., 'Self-regulatory failure and addiction', in Baumeister and Vohs, *Handbook of Self-Regulation*, pp. 447–65.

21. Thayer, *Origins of Everyday Moods*, p. 68.

22. Carter, B. L., Lam, C. Y., Robinson, J. D., et al., 'Real-time craving and mood assessments before and after smoking', *Nicotine and Tobacco Research*, 2008, 10, pp. 1165–9.

23. Vann Dillen, L. F. and Koole, S. L., 'Clearing the mind: a working memory model of distraction from negative mood', *Emotion*, 2007, 7(4), pp. 715–23.

24. Lejoyeux, M., *Overdose d'infos: guérir des névroses médiatiques*, Paris, Seuil, 2006.

25. Coifman, K. G., Bonanno, G. A., Ray, R. D. and Gross, J. J., 'Does repressive coping promote resilience? Affective-autonomic response during bereavement', *Journal of Personality and Social Psychology*, 2007, 92, pp. 745–58.

26. Campbell-Sills, L., Barlow, D. H., Brown, T. A. and Hofmann, S. G., 'Acceptability and suppression of negative emotion in anxiety and mood disorders', *Emotion*, 2006, 6, pp. 587–95; also Kashdan, T. B., Barrios, V., Forsyth, J. P. and Steger, M. F., 'Experiential avoidance as a generalized psychological vulnerability: comparisons with coping and emotion regulation strategies', *Behaviour Research and Therapy*, 2006, 44, pp. 1301–20.

27. Cioffi, D. and Holloway, J., 'Delayed costs of suppressed pain', *Journal of Personality and Social Psychology*, 1993, 64, pp. 274–82.

28. Koster et al., 'Paradoxical effects of suppressing anxious thoughts'.

29. Liverant, G., Brown, T. A., Barlow, D. H. and Roemer, L., 'Emotion regulation in unipolar depression: the effects of acceptance and suppression of subjective emotional experiences on the intensity and duration of sadness and negative affect', *Behaviour Research and Therapy*, 2008, 46, pp. 1201–9.

30. Gross, J. J. and John, O. P., 'Individual differences in two emotion regulation processes: implication for affects, relationships and well-being', *Journal of Personality and Social Psychology*, 2003, 85, pp. 348–62.

31. Kashdan et al., 'Experiential avoidance'.

32. Wegener, D., *White Bears and Other Unwanted Thoughts: Suppression, Obsession and the Psychopathology of Mental Control*, New York, Viking, 1989.

33. Gratz, K. L., Bornovalova, M. A., Delany-Brumsey, A., Nick, B. and Lejuez, C. W., 'A laboratory-based study of the relationship between childhood abuse and experiential avoidance among inner-city substance users: the role of emotional non-acceptance', *Behavior Therapy*, 2007, 38, pp. 256–8.

34. Berking, M., Margraf, M., Ebert, D., et al., 'Emotion regulation skills as a treatment target in psychotherapy', *Behaviour Research and Therapy*, 2008, 46, pp. 1230–7.

35. See in particular Hayes, S.C., Strosahl, K. and Wilson, K. G., *Acceptance and Commitment Therapy: An Experiential Approach to Behavior Change*, New York, Guilford Press, 1999.

36. 'Accept' comes from the Latin *accipere*, 'receive, let in, admit'. See Hayes, S., 'Comment l'acceptation et l'engagement deviennent thérapeutiques', in Meyer, C. (ed.), *Les nouveaux psys: ce que l'on sait aujourd'hui de l'esprit humain*, Paris, Les Arènes, 2008, p. 778.

37. Masedo, A. L. and Esteve, M. R., 'Effects of suppression, acceptance and spontaneous coping on pain tolerance, pain intensity and distress', *Behaviour Research and Therapy*, 2007, 45, pp. 199–209.

38. Low, C. A., Stanton, A. L. and Bower, J. E., 'Effects of acceptance-orientated versus evaluative emotional processing on heart rate recovery and habituation', *Emotion*, 2008, 8, pp. 419–24.

39. Marcks, B. A. and Woods, D. W., 'A comparison of thought suppression to an acceptance-based technique in the management of personal intrusive thought: a controlled evaluation', *Behaviour Research and Therapy*, 2005, 43, pp. 433–45.

40. Watkins, E., Moberly, N. J. and Moulds, M. L., 'Processing mode causally influences emotional reactivity: distinct effects of abstract versus concrete construal on emotional response', *Emotion*, 2008, 8, pp. 364–78.

41. Campbell-Sills, L., Barlow, D. H., Brown, T. A. and Hofmann, S. G., 'Effects of suppression and acceptance on emotional responses of individuals with anxiety and mood disorders', *Behaviour Research and Therapy*, 2006, 44, pp. 1251–63.

42. Forman, E. M., Hoffman, K. L. and McGrath, K. B., 'A comparison of acceptance and control-based strategies for coping with food-craving: an analog study', *Behaviour Research and Therapy*, 2007, 45, pp. 2372–86.

43. Twohig, M. P., Hayes, S. C. and Masuda, A., 'Increasing willingness to experience obsessions: acceptance and commitment therapy as treatment for obsessive-compulsive disorder', *Behavior Therapy*, 2006, 37, pp. 3–13.

44. Vowles, K. E., McNeil, D. W., Gross, R. T., et al., 'Effects of pain acceptance and pain control strategies on physical impairment in individuals with chronic low back pain', *Behavior Therapy*, 2007, 38, pp. 412–25.

45. McMullen, J., Barnes-Holmes, D., Barnes-Holmes, Y., Stewart, I. and Cochrane, A., 'Acceptance versus distraction: brief instructions, metaphors and exercises in increasing tolerance for self-delivered electric shocks', *Behaviour Research and Therapy*, 2008, 46, pp. 122–9.

46. 'Clément Rosset dans l'œil du cyclone', as reported by Didier Raymond, interview in *Le Magazine Littéraire*, 2002, 411, pp. 18–22.

47. Cioran, E. M., *Cahiers 1957–1972*, Paris, Gallimard, 1997, p. 433.

48. Lopes, P. N., Salovey, P., Côté, S. and Beers, M., 'Emotion regulation abilities and the quality of social interaction', *Emotion*, 2005, 5, pp. 113–18.

49. Rimé, B., *Le partage social des émotions*, Paris, Presses Universitaires de France, 2005.

50. Pasquier, A., Bonnet, A. and Pedinielli, J.-L., 'Anxiété, dépression et partage social des émotions: des stratégies de régulation émotionnelle interpersonnelles spécifiques', *Journal de Thérapie Comportementale et Cognitive*, 2008, 18, pp. 2–7.

51. Langston, C. A., 'Capitalizing on and coping with daily-life events: expressive responses to positive events', *Journal of Personality and Social Psychology*, 1994, 67, pp. 1112–25.

52. Dunn, E. W., Biesanz, J. C., Human, L. J. and Finn, S., 'Misunderstanding the affective consequence of everyday social interactions: the hidden benefits of putting one's best face forward', *Journal of Personality and Social Psychology*, 2007, 92, pp. 990–1005.

53. Wilson, T. D., Wheatley, T., Kurtz, J., Dunn, E. and Gilbert, D. T., 'When to fire: anticipatory versus post-event reconstrual of uncontrollable events', *Personality and Social Psychology Bulletin*, 2004, 30, pp. 340–51.

54. Winkielman, P. and Cacioppo, J. T., 'Mind at ease puts a smile on the face: psychophysiological evidence that processing facilitation elicits positive affects', *Journal of Personality and Social Psychology*, 2001, 81, pp. 989–1000.

55. Joormann, J., Siemer, M. and Gotlib, I., 'Mood regulation in depression:

differential effects of distraction and recall of happy memories on sad mood', *Journal of Abnormal Psychology*, 2007, 116, pp. 484–90.

Chapter 13 Curing ourselves of the disease of materialism

1. See the excellent official site, www.cdc.gov/nccdphp/dnpa/obesity/trend/maps.
2. This is what is known as the 'cafeteria rats' experiment recorded by Gérard Apfeldorfer in his book *Vivre mince* (Paris, Robert Laffont, 1983, p. 12): 'Rats which have constant access to a limited range of rich and enjoyable foods do not become obese. They only succumb to obesity if they are offered several different dishes each day. When this happens they become obese within six weeks. As long as they continue to have access to a large quantity of varied foodstuffs nothing changes . . . This explains why obesity is rare in countries where food although abundant in quantity is of limited variety. This is certainly not the case for us, the inhabitants of the privileged Western countries, who have access to all the foodstuffs our globe is capable of producing.'
3. Adès, J. and Lejoyeux, M., *La fièvre des achats*, Paris, Les Empêcheurs de Penser en Rond, 2002.
4. See summary in Faber, R. J. and Vohs, K. D., 'To buy or not to buy? Self-control and self-regulatory failure in purchase behavior', in Baumeister, R. F. and Vohs, K. D. (eds.), *Handbook of Self-Regulation: Research, Theory and Applications*, New York, Guilford Press, 2004, pp. 509–24.
5. Rook, D. W. and Gardner, M. P., 'In the mood: impulse buying's affective antecedents', *Research in Consumer Behaviour*, 1993, 6, pp. 1–28.
6. Christenson, G. A., Faber, R., deZwaan, M., et al., 'Compulsive buying: descriptive characteristics and psychiatric comorbidity', *Journal of Clinical Psychiatry*, 1994, 55, pp. 5–11.
7. See Kasser, T., *The High Price of Materialism*, Cambridge, MA, MIT Press, 2002; also Bauman, Z., *S'acheter une vie*, Paris, Jacqueline Chambon, 2008.
8. Lipovetsky, G., *Le bonheur paradoxal: essai sur la société d'hyperconsommation*, Paris, Gallimard, 2006.
9. Rosenbaum, A., *La peur de l'infériorité: aperçu sur le régime moderne de la comparaison sociale*, Paris, L'Harmattan, 2005.
10. Vohs, K. D., Baumeister, R. F., Schmeichel, B. J., Twenge, J. M., Nelson, N. M. and Tice, D. M., 'Making choices impairs subsequent self-control: a limited-resource account of decision making, self-regulation and active initiative', *Journal of Personality and Social Psychology*, 2008, 94, pp. 883–98.
11. Girard, C., 'Pour une télé-vision de la télévision', *Le Monde*, 24 October 2008, p. 12.
12. Cohen, P. and Cohen, J., *Life Values and Adolescent Mental Health*, Mahwah, NJ, Erlbaum, 1996.
13. Kasser, T. and Ahuvia, A. C., 'Materialistic values and well-being in business students', *European Journal of Social Psychology*, 2002, 32, pp. 137–46.
14. Nickerson, C., Schwarz, N., Diener, E. and Kahneman, D., 'Zeroing in on the

dark side of the American dream: a closer look at the negative consequences of the goal for financial success', *Psychological Science*, 2003, 14, pp. 531–6.

15. Sheldon, K. M., Elliot, A. J., Kim, Y. and Kasser, T., 'What is satisfying about satisfying events? Testing 10 candidate psychological needs', *Journal of Personality and Social Psychology*, 2001, 80, pp. 325–39.

16. See review in DeAngelis, T., 'Consumerism and its discontents', *Monitor on Psychology*, June 2004, pp. 25–54.

17. Kasser, T. and Sheldon, K. M., 'Of wealth and death: materialism, mortality salience, and consumption behavior', *Psychological Science*, 2000, 11(4), pp. 267–351.

18. See review in DeAngelis T., 'Too many choices?', *Monitor on Psychology*, June 2004, pp. 56–7.

19. Schwartz, B., *The Paradox of Choice: Why More Is Less*, London, HarperCollins, 2005.

20. Schwartz, B., Ward, A., Monterosso, J., Lyubomirsky, S., White, K. and Lehman, D. R., 'Maximizing versus satisfying: happiness is a matter of choice', *Journal of Personality and Social Psychology*, 2002, 83, pp. 1178–97.

21. Iyengar, S. S. and Lepper, M. R., 'When choice is demotivating: can one desire too much of a good thing?', *Journal of Personality and Social Psychology*, 2000, 79, pp. 995–1006.

22. Sagi, A. and Friedland, N., 'The cost of richness: the effect of the size and diversity of decision sets on post-decision regrets', *Journal of Personality and Social Psychology*, 2007, 93, pp. 515–24.

23. Kabat-Zinn, J., *Où tu vas, tu es*, Paris, J'ai Lu, 2004, p. 69.

24. Cryder, C. E., Lerner, J. S., Gross, J. J. and Dahl, R. E., 'Misery is not miserly: sad and self-focused individuals spend more', *Psychological Science*, 2008, 19(6), pp. 525–30.

25. Zweig, S., *The World of Yesterday: An Autobiography*, Lincoln, University of Nebraska Press, 1964, p. 140.

26. Thoreau, H. D., *Life without Principles*, Charleston, SC, Forgotten Books, 1936, p. 18.

27. Thoreau, H. D., *Walden. Vol. 1*, Boston, Houghton Mifflin, 1854, p. 27.

28. Nietzsche, F., *Untimely Meditations, 3, 4: Schopenhauer as Educator, 3, 4. Vol. 1* (translation quoted in Hadot, P., *Philosophy as a Way of Life: Spiritual Exercises from Socrates to Foucault*, Oxford, Blackwell, 1995, p. 253).

29. Lawrence, D. H., *The Plumed Serpent. Vol. 2*, Sydney, ReadHowYouWant, p. 12.

30. Cioran, E. M., *Cahiers 1957–1972*, Paris, Gallimard, 1997, p. 628.

31. Folope, V., Coëffier, M. and Déchelotte, P., 'Carences nutritionnelles liées à la chirurgie de l'obésité', *Gastroentérologie Clinique et Biologique*, 2007, 31, pp. 369–77.

32. *Thibon 95* by B. Charbonneau. Bernard Charbonneau is a largely forgotten philosopher, a pioneer of political ecology.

33. De Botton, A., *The Consolations of Philosophy*, London, Penguin, 2001, p. 5.

34. Kasser, *High Price of Materialism*, p. 10.

35. Vohs, K. D., Mead, N. L. and Goode, M. R., 'The psychological consequences of money', *Science*, 2006, 314, pp. 1154–6.

36. Singer, P., 'The root of all evil', guardian.co.uk, 17 August 2008, www.guard ian.co.uk/commentisfree/2008/aug/17/psychology.

37. Van Boven, L., Dunning, D. and Loewenstein, G., 'Egocentric empathy gaps between owners and buyers: misperception on the endowment effect', *Journal of Personality and Social Psychology*, 2000, 79, pp. 66–76.

38. Kasser, *High Price of Materialism*, p. 61.

39. Ibid., p. 43.

40. Ibid., p. 73.

41. Rosenbaum, *La peur de l'infériorité*, p. 86.

42. DeAngelis T., 'America: a toxic lifestyle?', *Monitor on Psychology*, April 2007, pp. 50–2.

43. Thoreau, *Life without Principles*, p. 3.

44. Sheldon, K. M. and McGregor, H., 'Extrinsic values orientation and the "tragedy of the commons"', *Journal of Personality*, 2000, 68, pp. 383–411.

45. Richins, M. L. and Dawson, S. A., 'Consumer values orientation for materialism and its measurement: scale development and validation', *Journal of Consumer Research*, 1992, 19, pp. 303–16.

46. *L'autofictif*, blog by Éric Chevillard, entry dated 11 October 2008, http://l-autofictif.over-blog.com.

47. Rinpoché, Y. M., *Bonheur de la méditation*, Paris, Fayard, 2007, p. 143.

48. Ruys, K. and Stapel, D. A., 'How to heat up from the cold: examining the preconditions for (unconscious) mood effects', *Journal of Personality and Social Psychology*, 2008, 94, pp. 777–91.

49. In Guéguen, N., *Cent petites expériences de psychologie du consommateur: pour mieux comprendre comment on vous influence*, Paris, Dunod, 2005, p. 36.

50. Swami, V. and Tovée, M. J., 'Does hunger influence judgments of female physical attractiveness?', *British Journal of Psychology*, 2006, 97, pp. 353–63.

51. Nordgren, L. F., van der Pligt, J. and van Harreveld, F., 'Evaluating Eve: visceral states influence the evaluation of impulsive behavior', *Journal of Personality and Social Psychology*, 2007, 93, pp. 75–84.

52. See Guégen, *Cent petites expériences*.

53. Novotney, A., 'What's behind American consumerism?', *Monitor on Psychology*, 2008, 39(7), pp. 40–2.

54. Bateson, M., Nettle, D. and Roberts, G., 'Cues of being watched enhance cooperation in a real world setting', *Biology Letters*, 2006, 2, pp. 412–14.

55. Joule, R.-V. and Beauvois, J.-L, *La soumission librement consentie*, Paris, Presses Universitaires de France, 1998.

56. Elster, J., *Agir contre soi: la faiblesse de volonté*, Paris, Odile Jacob, 2007, p. 35.

57. Ben Shahar, T., *L'apprentissage du bonheur*, Paris, Belfond, 2007.

58. Van Boven, L. and Gilovitch, T., 'To do or to have? That is the question', *Journal of Personality and Social Psychology*, 2003, 85, pp. 1193–202.

59. Amongst the many books on exercises in simplifying our lives are Loreau, D., *L'art de la simplicité*, Paris, Marabout, 2005; also Maeda, J., *De la simplicité*, Paris, Payot, 2007.

60. La Boétie, E., *The Politics of Obedience: The Discourse of Voluntary Servitude*, Whitefish, MT, Kessinger, 2004.

61. Kahneman, D., 'New challenges to the rationality assumption', *Journal of Institutional and Theoretical Economics*, 1994, 150, pp. 18–36.

62. See, for example, 'Les Bhoutanais heureux comme des démocrates', *Courrier International*, 2007, suppl. 'Alors, heureux?', 874–5–6, p. 21.

63. See 'De quoi avons-nous (vraiment) besoin? Bonheur, consommation, capitalisme', *Mouvements des Idées et des Luttes*, 2008/2, 54.

64. Layard, R., *Happiness: Lessons from a New Science*, New York, Penguin, 2005.

65. Diener, E. and Suh, E. M. (eds.), *Culture and Subjective Well-Being*, Cambridge, MA, MIT Press, 2000.

66. Delteil, J., *La cuisine paléolithique*, Paris, Éditions de Paris, 2007.

67. Des Forêts, L.-R., *Pas à pas jusqu'au dernier*, Paris, Mercure de France, 2001.

Chapter 14 Living mindfully

1. Monestès, J.-L., *Faire la paix avec son passé*, Paris, Odile Jacob, 2009.

2. Lucretius, *On the Nature of Things*, London, Penguin, 2007, p. 103.

3. *L'autofictif*, blog by Éric Chevillard, http://l-autofictif.over-blog.com.

4. Yalom, I., *Existential Therapy*, New York, Basic Books, 1980, p. 162.

5. See, for example, the autobiographical account of Fritz Zorn, *Mars*, Paris, Gallimard, 1979, or the books of Thierry Janssen, *La solution intérieure*, Paris, Fayard, 2006.

6. Ariès, P., *L'homme devant la mort*, Paris, Seuil, 1985.

7. Donne, J., *Devotions upon Emergent Occasions*, 1624.

8. Interview with Christine Ferniot, 'Christian Bobin, à la pointe du vivant', *Lire*, December 2007, 361, pp. 28–9.

9. Celli, N., *Le Bouddhisme*, Paris, Hazan, 2007, p. 234.

10. Comte-Sponville, A., *Dictionnaire philosophique*, Paris, Presses Universitaires de France, 2001, p. 395.

11. Quoted by Assouline, P., in his blog *La république des livres*, entry dated 10 September 2008, 'Le jour où Boutès sauta'.

12. Todorov, T., *Face à l'extrême*, Paris, Seuil, 1994, p. 99.

13. Quoted by Jean Vanier, founder of the Arche community, in an interview with Lena, M. and Adrian, L., *Famille Chrétienne*, special edition, 'N'ayez pas peur', 2009.

14. Darnall, K. T., 'Contemplative psychotherapy: integrating Western psychology and Eastern philosophy', *Behaviour Therapist*, 2007, 30, pp. 156–9.

15. Germer, C. K., Siegel, R. D. and Fulton, P. R. (eds.), *Mindfulness and Psychotherapy*, New York, Guilford Press, 2005.

16. Kabat-Zinn, J., *Full Catastrophe Living*, New York, Delta, 1990.

17. Linehan, M., *Traitement cognitivo-comportemental du trouble de personnalité état-limite*, Geneva, Médicine et Hygiène, 2000.

18. Notably Kabat-Zinn, J., *Où tu vas, tu es*, Paris, J'ai Lu, 2004; also Williams, M.,

Teasdale, J., Segal, Z. and Kabat-Zinn, J., *Méditer pour ne plus déprimer*, Paris, Odile Jacob, 2009.

19. 'Démystifier la méditation', interview with Florence Evin, *Le Monde*, 22 October 2008, p. 26.

20. Comte-Sponville, A., *The Book of Atheist Spirituality*, London, Random House, 2009, p. 136.

21. Lucretius, *On the Nature of Things*, p. 186.

22. Frewen, P. A., Evans, E. M., Maraj, N., Dozois, D. J. A. and Partridge, K., 'Letting go: mindfulness and negative automatic thinking', *Cognitive Therapy and Research*, 2008, pp. 758–74.

23. Nielsen, L. and Kasniak, A. W., 'Awareness of subtle emotional feelings: a comparison of long term meditators and non-meditators', *Emotion*, 2006, 6, pp. 392–405.

24. Lutz, A., Greischar, L. L., Rawlings, N. B., Ricard, M. and Davidson, R. J., 'Long-term meditators self-induce high-amplitude gamma synchrony during mental practice', *Proceedings of the National Academy of Sciences*, 2004, 101, pp. 16369–73.

25. Brown, K. W. and Ryan, R. M., 'The benefits of being present: mindfulness and its role in psychological well-being', *Journal of Personality and Social Psychology*, 2003, 84, pp. 822–48.

26. Masuda, A., Hayes, S. C., Fletcher, L. B., et al., 'Impact of acceptance and commitment therapy versus education on stigma toward people with psychological disorders', *Behaviour Research and Therapy*, 2007, 45, pp. 2764–72.

27. LeBel, J. L. and Dubé, L., 'The impact of sensory knowledge and attentional focus on pleasure and on behavioral responses to hedonic stimuli', presented at the 13th Annual Convention of the American Psychological Society, Toronto, 2007.

28. Rosenfeld, F., *Méditer c'est se soigner*, Paris, Les Arènes, 2007.

29. Berghmans, C., Strub, L. and Tarquinio, C., 'Méditation de pleine conscience et psychothérapie: état des lieux théorique, mesure et pistes de recherche', *Journal de Thérapie Comportementale et Cognitive*, 2008, 18, pp. 62–71.

30. Kenny, M. A. and Williams, J. M. G., 'Treatment-resistant depressed patients show a good response to mindfulness-based cognitive therapy', *Behaviour Research and Therapy*, 2007, 45, pp. 617–25.

31. Ostafin, B. D., Chawla, H., Bowen, S., Dillworth, T., Witkiewitz, K. and Marlatt, G., 'Intensive mindfulness training and the reduction of psychological distress: a preliminary study', *Cognitive and Behavioral Practice*, 2006, 13, pp. 191–7; also Twohig, M. P., Hayes, S. C. and Masuda, A., 'Increasing willingness to experience obsessions: acceptance and commitment therapy as a treatment for obsessive-compulsive disorder', *Behaviour Therapy*, 2006, 37, pp. 3–13.

32. Comments made by an internet user on the subject of Vipassana meditation, on the website www.psychologies.com.

33. Hadot, P., *N'oublie pas de vivre: Goethe et la tradition des exercices spirituels*, Paris, Albin Michel, 2008.

34. Williams, J. M. G., 'Mindfulness and modes of mind', *Cognitive Therapy and Research*, 2008, 32, pp. 721–33.
35. Pessoa, F., *The Book of Disquiet*, London, Penguin, 2002, p. 115.
36. According to a meta-analysis by Glenn Wilson, professor of Kings College London: www.newscientist.com/article/mg18624973.400-infooverload-harms-concentration-more-than-marijuana.html.
37. Thoreau, H. D., *Life without Principles*, Charleston, SC, Forgotten Books, 2008, p. 16.
38. Kabat-Zinn, J., *Coming to Our Senses*, New York, Hyperion, 2005.
39. Camus, A., *The Myth of Sisyphus*, London, Penguin, 2005.
40. Cioran, E. M., *Cahiers 1957–1972*, Paris, Gallimard, 1997, p. 642.
41. Maître Eckhart, *Conseils spirituels*, Paris, Payot & Rivages, 2003.

Chapter 15 Compassion, self-compassion and the power of gentleness

1. Comte-Sponville, A., *Dictionnaire philosophique*, Paris, Presses Universitaires de France, 2001.
2. Depraz, N., 'Empathie et compassion: analyse phénoménologique et enseignements bouddhistes', in Berthoz, A. and Jorland, G. (eds.), *L'empathie*, Paris, Odile Jacob, 2004, pp. 183–99.
3. Gilbert, P. (ed.), *Compassion: Conceptualisations, Research and Use in Psychotherapy*, Hove, Routledge, 2003, pp. 280–3.
4. Gilbert, P. and Proctor, S., 'Compassionate mind training for people with high shame and self-criticism: overview and pilot study of a group therapy approach', *Clinical Psychology and Psychotherapy*, 2006, 13, pp. 353–79.
5. Verplanken, B., Friborg, O., Wang, C. E., Trafimow, D. and Woolf, K., 'Mental habits: metacognitive reflection on negative self-thinking', *Journal of Personality and Social Psychology*, 2007, 92, pp. 526–41.
6. Glassman, L. H., Weierich, M., Hooley, J., Deliberto, T. and Nock, M., 'Child maltreatment, non-suicidal self-injury, and the mediating role of self-criticism', *Behaviour Research and Therapy*, 2007, pp. 2483–90.
7. Park, R. J., Goodyer, I. M. and Teasdale, J. D., 'Self-devaluative dysphoric experience and the prediction of persistent first-episode major depressive disorder in adolescents', *Psychological Medicine*, 2005, 35, pp. 539–48.
8. Teasdale, J. D. and Cox, S. G., 'Dysphoria: self-devaluative and effective components in recovered depression patients and never depressed controls', *Psychological Medicine*, 2001, 31, pp. 1311–16.
9. Neff, K. D., Rude, S. S. and Kirkpatrick, K., 'An examination of self-compassion in relation to positive psychological functioning and personality traits', *Journal of Research in Personality*, 2007, 41, pp. 908–16.
10. Leary, M. R., Tate, E. B., Adams, C. E., Allen, A. B. and Hancock, J., 'Self-compassion and reactions to unpleasant self-relevant events: the implications of treating oneself kindly', *Journal of Personality and Social Psychology*, 2007, 5, pp. 887–904.

11. Kelly, M. A. R., Robert, J. E. and Bottonari, K. A., 'Non-treatment-related sudden gains in depression: the role of self-evaluation', *Behaviour Research and Therapy*, 2007, 45, pp. 737–47.
12. Neff, K. D., Kirkpatrick, K. and Rude, S. S., 'Self-compassion and adaptive psychological functioning', *Journal of Research in Personality*, 2007, 41, pp. 139–54.
13. Leary et al., 'Self-compassion and reactions', p. 901.
14. Neff, K. D., 'Self-compassion: moving beyond the pitfalls of a separate self-concept', in Wayment, H. A. and Bauer, J. J. (eds.), *Transcending Self-Interest: Psychological Explorations of the Quiet Ego*, Washington, DC, American Psychological Association, 2008, pp. 95–105.
15. Gilbert, *Compassion*, p. 293.
16. Leary et al., 'Self-compassion and reactions'.
17. Franck, E. and De Raedt, R., 'Self-esteem reconsidered: unstable self-esteem outperforms level of self-esteem as vulnerability marker for depression', *Behaviour Research and Therapy*, 2007, 45, pp. 1531–41.
18. Schimel, J., Arndt, J., Pyszczynski, T. and Greenberg, J., 'Being accepted for who we are: evidence that social validation of the intrinsic self reduces general defensiveness', *Journal of Personality and Social Psychology*, 2001, 80, pp. 35–52.
19. Hillesum, E., *An Interrupted Life: The Diaries 1941–1943 and Letters from Westerbork*, New York, 1996, p. 339.
20. Keltner, D., Ellsworth, P. C. and Edwards, K., 'Beyond simple pessimism: effects of sadness and danger on social perception', *Journal of Personality and Social Psychology*, 1993, 64, pp. 740–52.
21. Gilbert, *Compassion*, pp. 250 and 258.
22. Luther King, M., speech made at Mason Temple, Memphis, Tennessee, 3 April 1968.
23. www.thauma.fr/index.html.
24. Mairowitz, D. Z. and Crumb, R., *Kafka*, Arles, Actes Sud, 1996.
25. Rabagliati, M., *Paul a un travail d'été*, Montréal, Éditions de la Pastèque, 2002. p. 109.
26. See, for example, André, C., *Imparfaits, libres et heureux*, Paris, Odile Jacob, 2006.
27. Leary et al., 'Self-compassion and reactions'.
28. Ricard, M., *Why Meditate: Working with Thoughts and Emotions*, New York, Hay House, 2010, p. 82.
29. Davidson, R. J., 'Towards a biology of positive affect and compassion', in Davidson, R. J. and Harrington, A. (eds.), *Visions of Compassion*, Oxford, Oxford University Press, 2002, pp. 107–30.
30. Gilbert, P. and Irons, C., 'Focused therapies and compassionate mind training for shame and self-attacking', in Gilbert, *Compassion*, pp. 263–325.
31. Marcus Aurelius, *The Communings with Himself of Marcus Aurelius Antoninus, Emperor of Rome*, London, Heinemann, 1970, p. 337.
32. See, for example, Einhorn, S., *L'art d'être bon*, Paris, Belfond, 2008; also Ferrucci, P., *L'art de la gentillesse*, Paris, Robert Laffont, 2007.
33. Leary et al., 'Self-compassion and reactions'.

Chapter 16 Happiness

1. Lucretius, *On the Nature of Things*, London, Penguin, 2007, p. 99.
2. Diener, E., et al., 'Happiness is the frequency, not intensity, of positive versus negative affect', in Strack, F., Argyle, M. and Schwarz, N. (eds.), *The Social Psychology of Subjective Well-Being*, Elmsford, NY, Pergamon Press, 1990, pp. 119–39.
3. Chateaubriand, F.-R., *Vie de Rancé*, Paris, Gallimard, 1986.
4. Gasper, K. and Clore, G. L., 'Attending to the big picture: mood and global versus local processing of visual information', *Psychological Science*, 2002, 13, pp. 34–40.
5. King, L. A., Hicks, J. A., Krull, J. and Del Gaiso, A. K., 'Positive affect and the experience of meaning in life', *Journal of Personality and Social Psychology*, 2006, 90, pp. 179–96.
6. Ibid.
7. Davis, C. G., Wortman, C. B., Lehman, D. R. and Silver, R. C., 'Searching for meaning in loss: are clinical assumptions correct?', *Death Studies*, 2000, 24, pp. 497–540.
8. Harker, L. A. and Keltner, D., 'Expressions of positive emotion in women's college yearbook pictures and life outcomes across adulthood', *Journal of Personality and Social Psychology*, 2001, 80, pp. 112–24.
9. Mueller, U. and Mazue, A., 'Facial dominance in *Homo sapiens* as honest signaling of male quality', *Behavioral Ecology*, 1996, 8, pp. 569–79.
10. Strack, F., Martin, L. and Stepper, S., 'Inhibiting and facilitating conditions of the human smile: a nonobtrusive test of the facial feedback hypothesis', *Journal of Personality and Social Psychology*, 1988, 54, pp. 768–77.
11. Stepper, S. and Strack, F., 'Proprioceptive determinants of affective and non-affective feelings', *Journal of Personality and Social Psychology*, 1993, 64, pp. 211–20.
12. Philippot, P., Chapelle, C. and Blairy, S., 'Respiratory feedback in the generation of emotion', *Cognition and Emotion*, 2002, 16, pp. 605–27.
13. Papa, A. and Bonnano, G. A., 'Smiling in the face of adversity: the interpersonal and intrapersonal functions of smiling', *Emotion*, 2008, 8, pp. 1–12.
14. Ekman, P. and Davidson, R. J., 'Voluntary smiling changes regional brain activity', *Psychological Science*, 1993, 4(5), pp. 342–5.
15. Quoted by Comte-Sponville, A., *Impromptus*, Paris, Presses Universitaires de France, 1996.
16. Bonnanno, G. A. and Keltner, D., 'Facial expressions of emotion and the course of conjugal bereavement', *Journal of Abnormal Psychology*, 1997, 106, pp. 126–37.
17. Keltner, D. and Bonnanno, G. A., 'A study of laughter and dissociation: distinct correlates of laughter and smiling during bereavement', *Journal of Personality and Social Psychology*, 1997, 73, pp. 687–702.
18. See Ong, A. D., Bergeman, C. S., Bisconti, T. L. and Wallace,.K. A., 'Psychological resilience, positive emotions and successful adaptation to stress in later life', *Journal of Personality and Social Psychology*, 2006, 91, pp.

730–49; also Filkman, S. and Moskowitz, J., 'Positive affect and the other side of coping', *American Psychologist*, 2000, 55, pp. 647–54.

19. Fredrickson, B. L. and Levenson, R. W., 'Positive emotions speed recovery from the cardiovascular sequelae of negative emotions', *Cognition and Emotion*, 1982, 12, pp. 191–220.

20. See Tugade, M. M. and Fredrickson, B. L., 'Regulation of positive emotions: emotion regulation strategies that promote resilience', *Journal of Happiness Studies*, 2007, 8, pp. 311–33; also Tugade, M. M. and Fredrickson, B. L., 'Resilient individuals use positive emotions to bounce back from negative emotional experiences', *Journal of Personality and Social Psychology*, 2004, 86, pp. 320–33.

21. Thich Nhat Hanh, *Soyez libres là où vous êtes*, Saint-Jean-de-Braye, Dangles, 2003.

22. Thich Nhat Hanh, *Le cœur des enseignements du Bouddha*, Paris, La Table Ronde, 2003, p. 221.

23. Paukert, A. L., Pettit, J. W. and Amacker, A., 'The role of interdependence and perceived similarity in depressed affect contagion', *Behaviour Therapy*, 2008, 39, pp. 277–85.

24. Oishi, S., Diener, E., Choi, D. W., Kim-Prieto, C. and Choi, I., 'The dynamics of daily events and well-being across cultures: when less is more', *Journal of Personality and Social Psychology*, 2007, 93, pp. 685–98.

25. Damasio, A., *Looking for Spinoza: Joy, Sorrow and the Feeling Brain*, New York, Harcourt, 2003, p. 275.

26. Quoted by Steiner, G., in *Maîtres et disciples*, Paris, Gallimard, 2003, p. 186.

27. Comte-Sponville, A., *Dictionnaire philosophique*, Paris, Presses Universitaires de France, 2001, p. 590.

28. Interview in *Philosophies Magazine*, November 2007, 14, pp. 52–5.

29. Rosset, C., *Le monde et ses remèdes*, Paris, Presses Universitaires de France, 1964.

30. Thich Nhat Hanh, *Le cœur des enseignements du Bouddha*, p. 31.

31. Ersner-Hershfield, H., Mikels, J. A., Sullivan, S. and Carstensen, L. L., 'Poignancy: mixed emotional experience in the face of meaningful endings', *Journal of Personality and Social Psychology*, 2008, 94, pp. 158–67.

32. Fung, H., Carstensen, L. L. and Lutz, A. M., 'The influences of time on social preferences: implication for life-span development', *Psychology and Aging*, 1999, 14, pp. 595–604; also Carstensen, L. L., Isaacowitz, D. M. and Charles, S. T., 'Taking time seriously: a theory of socioemotional selectivity', *American Psychologist*, 1999, 54, pp. 165–81.

33. In the series *France, portrait social: édition 2008*, Paris, Insee, 2008. See also on their website, www.insee.fr/fr/themes/document.asp?reg_id=O&ref_id=FPORSOCO8n.

34. Carstensen, L. L., Pasupathi, M., Mayr, U. and Nesselroade, J., 'Emotional experience in everyday life across the adult life span', *Journal of Personality and Social Psychology*, 2000, 79, pp. 644–55; also Charles, S. T., Reynolds, C. A. and Gatz, M., 'Age-related differences and change in positive and negative affect over 23 years', *Journal of Personality and Social Psychology*, 2001, 80, pp. 136–51.

35. Bauer, J. J., McAdams, D. P. and Sakaeda, A. R., 'Interpreting the good life: growth memories in the lives of mature, happy people', *Journal of Personality and Social Psychology*, 2005, 88, pp. 203–17.

36. Pennebaker, J. W. and Stone, L. D., 'Words of wisdom: language use over the life span', *Journal of Personality and Social Psychology*, 2003, 85, pp. 291–301.

37. Carstensen, L. L., lecture at the National Academy of Sciences, 14 November 2007, Washington, DC. See paper published in *Issues in Science and Technology*, winter 2007, www.issues.org/23.2/carstensen.html.

38. Ong, A. D. and Bergeman, C. S., 'The complexity of emotions in later life', *Journal of Gerontology: Psychological Sciences*, 2004, 59B, pp. 117–22.

39. Larsen, J. T., Hemenover, S. H., Norris, C. J. and Cacioppo, J. T., 'Turning adversity to advantage: on the virtues of the coactivation of positive and negative emotions', in Aspinwall, L. G. and Staudinger, M. (eds.), *A Psychology of Human Strengths: Perspective on an Emerging Field*, Washington, DC, American Psychological Association, 2003, pp. 211–16.

40. Davidson, R. J., 'Well-being and affective style: neural substrates and bio-behavioural correlates', *Philosophical Transactions of the Royal Society*, 2004, 359, pp. 1395–411.

41. See Lyubormirsky, S., Sheldon, K. M. and Schkade, D., 'Pursuing happiness: the architecture of sustainable change', *Review of General Psychology*, 2005, 9, pp. 111–31; also Lyubomirsky, S., 'Why are some people happier than others?', *American Psychologist*, 2001, 56, pp. 239–49.

42. Nes, R. B., Røysamb, E., Tambs, K., Harris, J. R. and Reichborn-Kjennerud, T., 'Subjective well-being: genetic and environmental contributions to stability and change', *Psychological Medicine*, 2006, 36, pp. 1033–42; also Vaillant, G. E., DiRago, A. C. and Mukamal, K., 'Natural history of male psychological health, XV: retirement satisfaction', *American Journal of Psychiatry*, 2006, 163, pp. 682–8.

43. Ben Shahar, T., *L'apprentissage du bonheur*, Paris, Belfond, 2007.

44. Damasio, *Looking for Spinoza*.

45. Roberts, B. W. and Mroczek, D. K., 'Personality trait change in adulthood', *Current Directions in Psychological Science*, 2008, 17, pp. 31–5.

46. Mroczek, D. K. and Spiro, A., 'Personality change influences mortality in older men', *Psychological Science*, 2007, 18, pp. 371–6.

47. Kahneman, D., Diener, E. and Schwarz, N. (eds.), *Well-Being: The Foundations of Hedonic Psychology*, New York, Russell Sage, 1999.

48. Bergsma, A., 'The advice of the wise: introduction to the special issue on advice for a happy life', *Journal of Happiness Studies*, 2008, 9, pp. 331–40.

49. Seligman, M., Steen, T., Park, N. and Peterson, C., 'Positive psychology progress: empirical validation of interventions', *American Psychologist*, 2005, 60, pp. 410–21; also Snyder, C. R. and Lopez, S. J., *Handbook of Positive Psychology*, Oxford, Oxford University Press, 2002.

50. Gable, S. L., Gonzaga, G. and Strachman, A., 'Will you be there for me when things go right? Supportive responses for positive events disclosure', *Journal of Personality and Social Psychology*, 2006, 91, pp. 904–17.

51. Rimé, B., *Le partage social des émotions*, Paris, Presses Universitaires de France, 2005.

52. Saxbe, D. E., Repetti, R. L. and Nishina, A., 'Marital satisfaction, recovery from work, and diurnal cortisol among men and women', *Health Psychology*, 2008, 27(1), pp. 15–25.

53. Cioran, E. M., *De l'inconvénient d'être né*, Paris, Gallimard, 1973.

54. In the words of André Comte-Sponville.

55. Oishi, S., Schimmack, U., Diener, E., Kim-Prieto, C., Scollon, C. N. and Choi, D. W., 'The value-congruence model of memory for emotional experiences: an explanation for cultural differences in emotional self-reports', *Journal of Personality and Social Psychology*, 2007, 93, pp. 897–905.

56. Fowler, J. H. and Christakis, N. A., 'Dynamic spread of happiness in a large social network: longitudinal analysis over 20 years in the Framingham Heart Study', *British Journal of Medicine*, 2008, http://bmj.com/cgi/content/full/337/dec04_2/a2338.

57. Christakis, N. A. and Fowler, J. H., 'The spread of obesity in a large social network over 32 years', *New England Journal of Medicine*, 2007, 357, pp. 370–9.

58. Christakis, N. A. and Fowler, J. H., 'The collective dynamics of smoking in a large social network over 32 years', *New England Journal of Medicine*, 2008, 358, pp. 2249–58.

59. Howes, M. J., Hokanson, J. E. and Loewenstein, D. A., 'Induction of depressive affect after a prolonged exposure to a mildly depressed individual', *Personality and Social Psychology*, 1985, 49, pp. 110–13.

60. Bahrick, H. P., Hall, L. K. and Da Costa, L. A., 'Fifty years of memory of college grades: accuracy and distortions', *Emotion*, 2008, 8, pp. 13–22.

61. Wilson, T. D., Centerbar, D. B., Kermer, D. A. and Gilbert, D. T., 'The pleasures of uncertainty: prolonging positive moods in ways people do not anticipate', *Journal of Personality and Social Psychology*, 2005, 88, pp. 5–21.

62. See the Random Acts of Kindness Foundation, www.actsofkindness.org.

63. Schooler, J., Ariely, D. and Loewenstein, G., 'The pursuit and assessment of happiness can be self-defeating', in Carillo, J. and Brocas, I. (eds.), *The Psychology of Economic Decisions*, Oxford, Oxford University Press, 2003, pp. 41–70.

64. Montesquieu, M., *Mes pensées*, in *Œuvres complètes. Vol. 1*, Paris, Gallimard, p. 975.

Chapter 17 Wisdom

1. See, for example, the special edition of the *Nouvel Observateur*, 'La sagesse aujourd'hui', April–May 2002, 47.

2. Comte-Sponville, A., *Dictionnaire philosophique*, Paris, Presses Universitaires de France, 2001.

3. Quoted by Castermane, J., *La sagesse exercée*, Paris, La Table Ronde, 2005, p. 22.

4. *The New Yorker: l'intégrale des dessins*, Paris, Les Arènes, 2005.

5. Comte-Sponville, A., *La philosophie*, Paris, Presses Universitaires de France, 2005, p. 121.

6. Ibid., p. 123.

7. Hadot, P., *Exercises spirituels et philosophie antique*, Paris, Albine Michel, 2002, pp. 303 and 325.

8. Ibid., p. 300.

9. Reiss, S., 'Epicurus: the first rational-emotive therapist', *Behavior Therapist*, winter 2003, pp. 405–6.

10. Kunzmann, U. and Baltes, P., 'The psychology of wisdom: theoretical and empirical challenges', in Sternberg, R .J. and Jordan, J. (eds.), *Handbook of Wisdom*, Cambridge, Cambridge University Press, 2005, pp. 110–35.

11. Baltes, P. B., Glück, J. and Kunzmann, U., 'Wisdom: its structure and function in regulating successful life span development', in Snyder, C. R. and Lopez, C. J. (eds.), *Handbook of Positive Psychology*, Oxford, Oxford University Press, 2002, pp. 327–47.

12. Damasio, A., *Descartes' Error: Emotion, Reason and the Human Brain*, London, Random House, 2008.

13. See for summary Csikszentmihalyi, L. and Nakamura, J., 'The role of emotions in the development of wisdom', in Sternberg and Jordan, *Handbook of Wisdom*, pp. 220–42; also Keltner, D. and Gross, J. J., 'Functional accounts of emotions', *Cognition and Emotion*, 1999, 13, pp. 467–80.

14. Cocteau, J., *Le grand écart*, Paris, Stock, 1991.

15. Droit, R.-P. and De Tonnac, J. P., *Fous comme des sages*, Paris, Seuil, 2002.

16. Bluck, S. and Glück, J., 'From the inside out: people's implicit theories of wisdom', in Sternberg and Jordan, *Handbook of Wisdom*, pp. 84–109.

17. Paulhus, D. L., Wehr, P., Harms, P. D. and Strasser, D. I., 'Use of exemplar surveys to reveal implicit types of intelligence', *Personality and Social Bulletin*, 2002, 28, pp. 1051–62.

18. Baltes, P. B. and Staudinger, U. M., 'The search for a psychology of wisdom', *Current Directions in Psychological Science*, 1993, 2, pp. 75–80.

19. Le, T. N. and Levenson, M. R., 'Wisdom as self-transcendence: what's love (and individualism) got to do with it?', *Journal of Research in Personality*, 2005, 39, pp. 443–57.

20. Pierre Lory, in the special edition of the *Nouvel Observateur*, 'La sagesse aujourd'hui', pp. 58–9.

21. 'Leçons de vie des philosophes grecs', *Le Nouvel Observateur*, 15–21 July 2004, p. 13.

22. Steiner, G., *Lessons of the Masters*, London, Harvard University Press, 2003, pp. 4 and 105.

23. Quoted by Arpi, C., 'Un moine dans le monde', *Le Nouvel Observateur*, April–June 2003, special edition 50, 'Le Bouddhisme', pp. 10–11.

24. Special edition of the *Nouvel Observateur*, 'La sagesse aujourd'hui', pp. 96–7.

25. Interview with Rémi Brague, *Le Point*, 2 August 2002, 1559, p. 73.

26. Sternberg and Jordan, *Handbook of Wisdom*.

27. Nielsen, L., Knutson, B. and Carstensen, L. L., 'Affect dynamics, affective forecasting and aging', *Emotion*, 2008, 8, pp. 318–30.

28. Ecclesiastes 1: 18.
29. Kinsman, U. and Bruhn, D., 'Age differences in emotional reactivity: the simple case of sadness', *Psychology and Aging*, 2005, 20, pp. 47–59.
30. Interview with Jean-Michel Apathie in *Télérama*, 10 September 2008, 3061, p. 157.
31. Bailly, S., *Le meilleur de l'absurde*, Paris, Mille et Une Nuits, 2007, p. 80.
32. Special edition of the *Nouvel Observateur*, 'La sagesse aujourd'hui', pp. 96–7.
33. Feeney, B. C., 'The dependency paradox in close relationships: accepting dependence promotes independence', *Journal of Personality and Social Psychology*, 2007, 92, pp. 268–85.
34. Lacouture, J., *Album Montaigne*, Paris, Gallimard, 2007.
35. Kramer, D. A., 'Wisdom as a classical source of human strength: conceptualization and empirical inquiry', *Journal of Social and Clinical Psychology*, 2000, 19, pp. 83–101.
36. Interviewed in *Psychologies Magazine*, May 2007, pp. 22–8.
37. Reus, V. I., 'An argument for mind', *American Journal of Psychiatry*, 2008, 165, pp. 922–3.
38. See as an introduction Comte-Sponville, A., *De l'autre côté du désespoir: introduction à la pensée de Svāmi Prajndnânpad*, Paris, L'Originel, 1997; also Prakash, S., *L'expérience de l'unité: dialogues avec Svāmi Prajndnânpad*, Paris, L'Originel, 1986.
39. Droit and De Tonnac, *Fous comme des sages*.
40. Comte-Sponville, *Dictionnaire philosophique*, p. 280.
41. Todorov, T., *Devoirs et délices: une vie de passeur*, Paris, Le Seuil, 2002, p. 228.
42. Todorov, T., *Face à l'extrême*, Paris, Seuil, 1994, p. 233.
43. Interviewed in *Psychologies Magazine*, 2006, 256, pp. 20–8.

Conclusion: see you tomorrow, life

1. Comte-Sponville, A., *Le miel et l'absinthe*, Paris, Hermann, 2008, p. 12.
2. Enthoven, J.-P., *Ce que nous avons eu de meilleur*, Paris, Grasset, 2008.
3. You need to see the whole film. In the meantime, if you are in a hurry, www.youtube.com/watch?v=cXNApZ2ALiQ.
4. Pessoa, F., *The Book of Disquiet*, London, Penguin, 2002, p. 381.
5. Hadot, P., *N'oublie pas de vivre: Goethe et la tradition des exercices spirituels*, Paris, Albin Michel, 2008, p. 36.

Index